Rescue Archaeology
Foundations for the future

Rescue Archaeology
Foundations for the future

Editors
Paul Everill and Pamela Irving

with
Joe Flatman, Tony Howe, and Reuben Thorpe

Other contributors
Paul Blinkhorn, Chris Clarke, Hannah Cobb, Malcolm Cooper, Hester Cooper-Reade, Chris Cumberpatch, George Dennis, Robin Densem, Neil Holbrook, Diana Friendship-Taylor, Mike Pitts, Dominic Powlesland, Ginny Pringle, Ian Ralston, Anthony Sinclair, Harvey Sheldon, John Shepherd, Kathryn Stubbs, John Walker, Pete Wilson

Published by RESCUE the British Archaeological Trust
15a Bull Plain, Herefordshire, SG14 1DX
Registered Charity no 1064836
website: www.rescue-archaeology.org.uk

British Library Cataloguing in Publication Data. A catalogue record for this book is
available from the British Library

Published with a grant from the John and Ruth Howard Charitable Trust

Contributors have waived royalty rights in favour of RESCUE: the British
Archaeological Trust

ISBN no 978-0-903789-20-2

Design: Peter Powell, Maidstone
Cover design: Reuben Thorpe with Paul Everill and Tony Howe
Typeset in Times New Roman
Printed in Great Britain by Alphaprint Ltd, Colchester

Contents

SECTION FOUR: Rescuing the future

List of figures

SECTION ONE

Chapter 2

Chapter 4

SECTION TWO

SECTION THREE

SECTION FOUR

List of tables

Editorial foreword

Paul Everill

This book was conceived in the run-up to the 40th anniversary of the founding of RESCUE, when the discussion among council members was focused on the best way to commemorate this landmark while also emphasising the continued relevance of the organisation. It seemed to me then, and remains the case, that a successor to the RESCUE volume of 1974, edited by Philip Rahtz, was the perfect way to do both.

The 1974 book was as much a summary of the current state of the discipline as it was a statement of intent, and a banner that drew in a whole generation of professionals, practitioners and talented amateurs to the cause of protection for the historic environment. Appearing three years after RESCUE was formed, the energy of the founding members had already transformed the government approach to archaeology (particularly in terms of funding) and the book was able to trumpet their collaborative achievements, while identifying the on-going causes of concern. In some respects the book was published at a high point for RESCUE, and the years that followed saw the emergence of new professional standards and the management of archaeology as the principal tool by which the historic environment could be protected. The 1970s and early 1980s also witnessed the developing schism between academic and developer-led archaeologists; between unit managers and diggers; and between advocates of the new single context recording system and the more traditional approaches. The disciplinary shift towards focusing on the management of the archaeological process, supported ultimately by the embedding of the discipline within the planning system after 1990, could be interpreted as a victory for the profession and the fulfilment of its original 1970s manifesto, indeed many archaeologists might have begun to wonder if there was still a need for an organisation like RESCUE. However, bodies such as the Chartered Institute for Archaeology (CIfA), Council for British Archaeology (CBA), and Association of Local Government Archaeological Officers (ALGAO) and even Historic England, Cadw and Historic Scotland to some extent have had to be reactive organisations for the most part, finding ways of implementing policy through standards and guidance documents, rather than campaigning for wholesale changes to approach and policy in order to better protect the historic environment. The need for a body like RESCUE has never, in reality, waned. Today the need is perhaps greater than it has been since the late-1970s, as the governmental response to economic crises has been to make swingeing harvests of the low-hanging fruit of heritage protection at local and national level, while shifting the 24 year old emphasis in planning advice from the preservation of the historic environment, towards an emphasis on removing obstacles to (re)development. Viewed in conjunction with age-old issues like pay and conditions of employment within professional archaeology, which in part result from the poorly conceived competitive marketplace into which archaeology was thrust; the sea-change in the way that Higher Education is funded (and with it the threats to Departments of Archaeology and consequently the training of future professionals) there is currently a perfect storm that threatens to leave the discipline in tatters.

Even ten years ago, an anniversary publication of this kind would have been a far more straightforward affair, but in proposing it towards the beginning of 2010 no-one but the prescient could have foreseen the full impact of the coalition Government's austerity drive on all aspects of our lives, not just the historic environment. In producing this book, we have seen chapters overtaken by events and revised on more than one occasion as we worked hard to produce something that was as up-to-date as possible. This would not have been possible without the hard work and commitment of all involved. This foreword would be incomplete without thanking Pam Irving, my co-editor, who has managed the production of this RESCUE publication with great skill, and the Section Editors Joe Flatman; Tony Howe; and Reuben Thorpe who have all devoted their valuable time, energy and expertise to this endeavour. I must also thank RESCUE council for their continued faith in us and the John and Ruth Howard Charitable Trust for their funding. However, particular thanks also go to our authors. Their chapters represent a snapshot of British archaeology as it is now. Many were inspired by the sight of the 1974 book on their shelves, and the prospect of contributing to something that might still inspire others in 40 years' time. Their patience, as we negotiated the rapid and unpredictable changes affecting the discipline, has been key to bringing this project to fruition.

The original Rahtz volume was conceived and produced at a time of great concern, a low point for the discipline, but perhaps also present in those pages was great optimism as things were, tangibly, just starting to improve. This current volume may have started life as a 40th anniversary project, but since its conception the rapidly shifting sands on which the discipline is built have affected all of us. However, these moving targets have also dramatically underscored the need for a successor to the Rahtz volume. A clarion call and banner to which all those who seek to preserve our historic environment can rally as the discipline faces a return to the darkest days we have seen since the 1970s.

RESCUE: historical background and founding principles

Harvey Sheldon, with George Dennis and Robin Densem

Introduction

If, by the early 1960s, it was obvious that much of the built historic environment in the cities and towns of modern Britain was at risk from increasingly ambitious redevelopment schemes, it was abundantly clear by the end of the decade that the buried historic environment was also in danger of disappearing; vanishing without the opportunity to record and therefore understand it. The threat to its survival came not just from urban redevelopment, or the building of new towns and housing estates in the countryside; or through the increased extraction of minerals and the construction of transport routes that these activities made necessary. Newer agricultural methods, including deep ploughing, were putting at risk buried rural landscapes, not just the settlement sites that had existed within them. Surveys also revealed that many of the upstanding, visible, field monuments in the countryside, including those supposedly protected by the government for the nation through inclusion on its Schedule of Ancient Monuments, had either disappeared or become seriously damaged (Barker 1974a, 29).

Although alarm bells had been sounded by the Royal Commission on the Historical Monuments of England at the beginning of the decade (RCHME 1960) there was little sign that the increasing scale of the problem, or its potentially disastrous consequences, was being recognised, acknowledged and addressed at local or national level. That perhaps was an indication that despite the presence of archaeologists in universities, museums and government services, and despite the co-ordinating activities of the Council for British Archaeology, which brought together amateur and professional bodies at regional level, there was little in place to protect Britain's buried historic environment from the forces of economic change that had then been unleashed.

A Catalogue of Unrecorded Destruction: The Bristol Conference, May 1969

In May 1969 a conference of extra-mural university tutors in Bristol focused on this as a national issue which required resolution. They heard delegate Philip Barker, of

Birmingham University, describe:

> *'a catalogue of unrecorded destruction covering all of Britain from city centres to remote highland afforestation schemes'*. (Barker 1974b, 280)

As a group, these university tutors, with their local expertise, were in a good position to know the extent of the problem, as were the many students who passed through their hands. One of the positive outcomes of the expansion of Adult Education provision by universities since 1945 had been the growth of archaeology as a subject area. It has been calculated that the number of courses grew from 195 in 1961 to 538 in 1971 and they continued to increase in the following decade (Speight 2002, 79). The courses, often in part focusing on the archaeology and history of Britain, including predominantly residential training excavations had risen from 7 in 1953 to 45 in 1966 (Speight 2002, 75). Many of the adult students, now informed, knowledgeable and experienced in the field, were engaged in local research and serving on archaeology committees, and were as well aware as their tutors of the threats to the archaeological resource within their own environs.

Philip Barker was to become one of the key figures in establishing RESCUE. Following the Bristol meeting, in what he described as a *'state of fermenting gloom'*, Barker produced a discussion paper entitled *'Not Waving Just Drowning'* (Barker 1974b, 280). It was an apt way to describe the situation in 1969, even if not quite corresponding to the title of Stevie Smith's poem as he later realised (Barker 1987, 7)! Barker's paper was circulated to about half a dozen colleagues, not only his fellow extra-mural lecturers, John Alexander at Cambridge and Peter Fowler at Bristol, but also to other prominent archaeologists, including Martin Biddle who had undertaken large-scale urban excavations in Winchester. Barker and his colleagues were to become convenors of two further residential sessions, at Barford, Warwickshire and Newcastle in 1970. The proceedings there led to the decision to convene the public meeting in London early in 1971, at which RESCUE was born.

The Past *'Fed Into The Fire'*: Professor Cunliffe's Inaugural Address December 1969

Barry Cunliffe, Professor of Archaeology at Southampton, was also one of the recipients of Barker's 1969 discussion paper. Cunliffe, well known for his excavation of the palatial Roman building at Fishbourne, used his inaugural address, which was delivered in December 1969, to highlight the scale of the crisis, asserting that archaeology in Britain was:

> *'in a state of turmoil'* because *'a large proportion of our primary data is being, and is about to be, totally destroyed by developments of various kinds'* (Cunliffe 1970, 5).

The potential information necessary for studying Britain's past, now buried in the ground, was *'being fed into the fire'* (Cunliffe 1970, 11). He concluded that *'no other discipline ... has ever been faced with such a rate of data destruction'* (Cunliffe 1970, 12). He gave two specific examples: Gloucester, a city originating as a Roman Colonia, where almost a fifth of the town's nucleus had been destroyed, and the Downlands of southern Britain, where the continued practice of modern farming methodologies would succeed in obliterating '*most of the visual evidence for settlement patterns within a decade*' (Cunliffe 1970, 7,10).

Any solution to the crisis, Cunliffe argued, would require making the public aware of the situation in order to help exert pressure on government to provide more supportive legislation, increase funding and establish a new organisational structure, a State Antiquities Service. This he envisaged would include a central policy-making body which would co-ordinate the work of Regional Antiquities Centres. At a regional level the centres would have the responsibility for providing, or commissioning, all stages of 'rescue' archaeological work within their areas, from examining planning applications through to excavation, finds analysis, publication and archiving (Cunliffe 1970, 16–17).

Sites, monuments, landscapes and townscapes: quantifying the Evidence

By 1970 considerable evidence quantifying the threat to Britain's archaeology, such as that discussed in May 1969 by the extra-mural tutors in Bristol, and publicly voiced in December by Cunliffe, was either available, or would soon emerge through new studies. This compendium included a 1964 survey undertaken in Wiltshire, which revealed that out of the 640 Scheduled Ancient Monuments that had existed 10 years previously, 250 had either been completely destroyed or were now badly damaged. By definition, these were, or had been, monuments of the highest quality, representative of those theoretically protected for the nation by the government. Similarly, in South Dorset, of 871 recorded Bronze Age barrows, more than 90% had been damaged by 1963. Also, according to Barker, a national survey of deserted medieval villages had revealed that about 300 had been destroyed between 1950 and 1970 (Barker 1974b, 28–9).

An indication of the problem in urban centres came from a CBA study of historic towns in Britain (Heighway 1972). This enquiry concluded that 583 of them were threatened by development schemes. Of these only 21, less than 5%, were judged to have adequate archaeological provision. It was also estimated that, without better provision, 159 of these historic towns, about 25%, would be lost to archaeology within the next 20 years.

It was not just archaeological studies that indicated the gravity of the situation. Statistics compiled for official purposes revealed the increasing scale of land disturbance, often through the removal of geological deposits attractive to earlier settlement. Sand and gravel extraction had risen by 50% between 1960 and 1970 and in the same period, other forms of stone quarrying had increased, sometimes by more 100%. Additional to mineral quarrying, peat in lowland areas was being extracted and new forests, requiring preparatory deep ploughing, planted (Barker 1974a, 31–3). The fast moving, heavy machinery utilised in all these activities could rapidly destroy not just sites, but whole ancient landscapes.

Heavy machinery was also used in motorway construction. These routes, entailing linear cuts through the countryside, had commenced in Britain during the late 1950s with the construction of the M1. About 1000 miles of motorway had been constructed by the beginning of the 1970s, much without archaeological surveillance. Efforts to ensure that investigations did take place on the M5 and other routes, from 1969 onwards were successful and revealed a surprising density of sites: it was found that an average of two sites per mile were likely to be encountered (Fowler 1974, 128) which suggested that potentially about 1100 or more sites had been lost during the earlier phase of motorway building.

The move towards founding RESCUE:
Barford, February 1970; Newcastle, November 1970; and London, January 1971

At the May 1969 Bristol conference one observer present characterised professional archaeologists, at a time of crisis, as collectively '*diffuse, woolly, disunited and unaggressive*' (Barker 1987, 7). The meeting had clearly stimulated a search for remedies. Momentum built up at a second gathering, in Barford, Warwickshire in February 1970. Though some 30 archaeologists attended, the need to involve colleagues from further north, led to a 3rd meeting in Newcastle held in November with around 50 participants. Despite the criticism of archaeologists as a group, quoted above, it seems clear that what had emerged from this series of discussions was a unity of resolve to tackle the situation head-on and to create new bodies to deal with it even though that involved making a radical break with existing arrangements.

To enable change, following significant ground work to put a new organisation in place, a public meeting was convened in London where the situation could be brought before the public and discussed openly. This meeting took place at Senate House on January 23rd, 1971. It was attended by more than 700 people with the proceedings covered by a largely sympathetic news media. The meeting agreed two major proposals:

Firstly a new and independent organisation, to be named RESCUE, should be established to increase public awareness of the destruction of archaeological sites. RESCUE should make the public aware of what was happening and lead a campaign for better legislation and increased funding. To further the cause, RESCUE should contribute to the provision of training, recording and preservation; and publish a quarterly newsletter and handbooks.

Secondly; presumably resulting from such campaigning, a State Archaeological Service with 20 Regional Centres, should be established. Essentially this proposal, to establish an organisational provision capable of responding to the threat to Britain's archaeological resource, was the remedy that had first publicly surfaced in Cunliffe's 1969 lecture. It was to feature in RESCUE's discussions with government in the years that followed.

RESCUE: The title and the role

The name RESCUE, though not universally approved at the London meeting, did seem fitting: it clearly conveyed the immediate sense of urgency and was not unfamiliar to archaeologists. Some 20 years previously the Ministry of Works had described excavations it had carried out during the construction of airfields and on other WW2 related sites as '*in the nature of rescue work*'. (HMSO 1949). After the war ended, on bomb damaged city sites awaiting inevitable redevelopment, a programme of excavations could sometimes precede the inevitable destruction of any archaeological deposits that survived, during the building work to follow. From the 1950s onwards, as post-war reconstruction accelerated, the term 'rescue', seemed applicable to the programmes of site-watching and sometimes frantic digging on urban sites shared with demolition teams or builders. So too on rural sites, where archaeologists tried to record archaeological deposits as machines rapidly moved earth and extracted gravel. (When RESCUE was set up in 1971 its logo, an earth-moving machine carrying off Stonehenge, although intended to represent the unthinkable, didn't seem entirely unimaginable! (see Figure 1)

RESCUE was established at the Senate House meeting amid a great deal of media and public interest. It counted Yehudi Menuhin, Henry Moore and John Piper amongst its patrons; eminent archaeologists, such as Mortimer Wheeler and Christopher Hawkes served on its advisory Council, and its Executive Committee included Martin Biddle, Barry Cunliffe and other leading figures of the then younger generation. As a result it is perhaps not surprising that the Government did indeed sit up and take notice of the threats to the historic environment being highlighted by the new organisation.

RESCUE: What the new organisation stood for

RESCUE was created primarily as an independent organisation that would, in the context of the immediate crisis, publicly and forcibly campaign for change. It was to be a body that could bring together professional archaeologists, irrespective of what institutions employed them, amateur archaeologists and everyone else who was sympathetic to the fate of the nation's archaeological sites. RESCUE would also stand for the protection and, where necessary, investigation of archaeological sites against all who might destroy them.

It was recognised that at the very least achieving change would have to involve new government funding, if only to ensure that rescue archaeological work could be carried out. There is no doubt that after RESCUE was set-up funding did increase. Government spending on rescue archaeology, largely in the form of grants, rose from less than £0.5m in 1972–3 to nearly £5m in 1982–3 (Wainwright 1982). British Museum Director David Wilson suggested that the additional money was largely '*a result of the crusading zeal of the founders of the Rescue Movement*' (Wilson 1986, 7). Philip Barker, looking back on the early years of RESCUE from a mid-1980s vantage point, seems to suggest that the increase in funding had been RESCUE's greatest achievement (Barker 1987, 8). Much of this funding went to archaeological units that were established during the 1970s, usually on a county-wide, or metropolitan borough basis. By about the mid-1980s there appear to have been 70 or 80 active archaeological rescue teams in Great Britain. These were museum, local authority or independently based, with perhaps about 600 permanent staff (Sheldon 1987, 124). It is hard to imagine how this local institutional growth could have occurred without the increase in central government funding during the 1970s and 1980s and perhaps Barker might have judged that organisational outcome an achievement too.

Figure 1 1970's RESCUE poster of an earth-moving machine carrying off Stonehenge

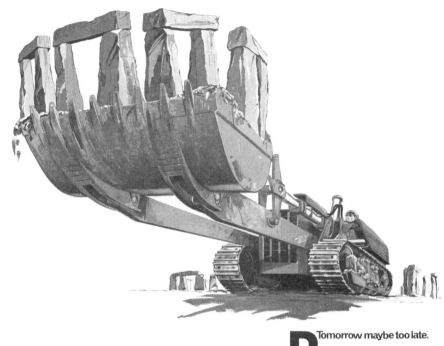

Tomorrow may be too late.

Rescue

The Trust for British Archaeology. Central Office, 25 The Tything, Worcester, Worcs. Tel: Worcester 20651

Retrospectively, Barker was less sanguine about other outcomes. RESCUE, which had been set up with offices first in Worcester and later in Hertford had ambitious plans beyond campaigning. These included raising funds for archaeology through membership, donations and bequests, to be used to help record, provide training, undertake surveys and publish books.

The heady optimism that accompanied the founding of RESCUE seemed to suggest that large numbers would subscribe, thus giving the organisation financial strength and weight of support in dealing with government. Neither mass-membership nor substantial funds materialised. Barker also suggested that the *'failure of many academic archaeologists to take up the cause of recue archaeology'* (Barker 1987, 8) was a reason for RESCUE not being able to keep up the pressure for increased resources.

A State Archaeological Service, the institutional solution for dealing with the problem proposed both by Cunliffe in 1969 and at the Senate House meeting where RESCUE was established, also failed to materialise. Setting up such an organisation clearly figured in discussions and communications between RESCUE and government in the early

1970's. It also featured in a joint RESCUE and Council for British Archaeology (CBA) statement, '*Archaeology and Government: A Plan for Archaeology in Britain*', published in response to a government statement in May 1974 on its proposed regional policy for seeking archaeological advice, which was clearly considered unsatisfactory. Here RESCUE and the CBA called for the establishment of what they now termed a National Archaeological Service, operating through regional offices, within which the emerging County and District archaeological structures would continue to exist (RESCUE and CBA 1974).

The lack of government interest in this proposal probably had less to do with any perceived RESCUE weakness and more to do with the presence of archaeological units with coverage which clearly related to County and District authority planning areas, rather than geographical regions. Their establishment, ironically, was partly a result of the success of RESCUE's campaign to raise more government funds. Is it also not too difficult to envisage reluctance, at both central and local government level, to create a new national archaeological authority with regional constituents, particularly if this might imply a weakening of their existing control over planning decisions.

More than 40 years have elapsed since RESCUE began campaigning, but today it is still needed to ensure that Britain's historic environment resources are properly considered, protected and investigated when under threat. Much has changed in the intervening years: there was some optimism in 1990 when it was finally accepted by government that archaeological considerations were central to the planning process (PPG 16, Nov 1990), but even now after a further 25 years of apparent progress, there are still archaeological issues beyond the bounds of planning control, both on land and water, demanding action. Recent aspects of 'Austerity Britain' give further cause for concern. Nearly a fifth of the 400 or so local authority archaeologists who advise planners and monitor developments have lost their jobs since 2008 and the downward rate is apparently accelerating (Heyworth 2014). That's especially worrying in the context of the latest series of light touch regulatory approaches to development proposals, exemplified in 2012's *National Planning Policy Framework* (DCLG 2012), with the promise of more deregulation to come. Current plans to separate English Heritage from the Historic Buildings and Monuments Commission, handing its statutory duties and responsibilities to a new, but as yet unformed body, to be called Historic England might also raise fears as to whether this successor organisation will have the power and authority of its predecessor.

Three London case studies

In conclusion it is worth considering three post-war archaeological episodes from the City of London and its immediate environs, each separated by about a decade. All three portray aspects of the problems that led to the formation of RESCUE, but only the last, early in 1972, occurred after its birth. The media and, following news coverage, the public, took an interest in all three, perhaps at least partly because each portrayed aspects of the long-standing uneven struggle between archaeologists, attempting to retrieve archaeological evidence on sites and the alliance of much more powerful interests undertaking City developments. Without RESCUE'S very public intervention in the latter, which galvanised moves to create a permanent investigatory team within the Guildhall Museum, is it probable that the eventual outcome for archaeology in the City of London would have been far less satisfactory.

Mithras 1954

On Sunday September 26th 1954, at the height of public interest in the Temple of Mithras, discovered in London's Walbrook and following much concerned debate about whether the ancient structure would survive, a cartoon (see Figure 2) appeared in the

Figure 2 Cartoon in the *'Sunday Dispatch'* of September 26th 1954 *'Rebuilding London – If They Have To Preserve These Roman Discoveries'*

Sunday Dispatch entitled '*Rebuilding London – If They Have To Preserve These Roman Discoveries*'. It portrays a detailed but dystopian near-future London townscape, in which archaeologists had clearly run riot! Because of vast numbers of 'Roman Ruins', now guarded by policemen, streets were blocked, cars and buses had tumbled into holes and the only way that office workers could gain access to newly built tower blocks was by clambering up to entrances 30ft above the ground!

It is undoubted that the discovery of the Temple along with associated statues was popular, at least with the public. On the day the cartoon appeared, 35,000 people '*formed a long queue*' in the hope of visiting the site of the Mithraeum, or so the *News Chronicle* reported on September 27th. Not all of them were successful, the last group dispersing at about 7.30pm, following the arrival of the police in a Black Maria (*Daily Sketch, September 27th*)!

Perhaps the cartoon did reflect genuine fear that archaeological discoveries would disrupt the post-war reconstruction of Britain's major financial centre, even if, as in this case:

'*the public imagination was fired... by an astonishing structure of "major importance which had made an impression on learned and unlearned alike.*' (*The Times*, Oct 2nd, 1954).

In the same article *The Times* optimistically reported that the '*actual remains would be happily catered for*', but, apart from the finds and records from the excavation, all that did survive was an unsatisfactory, re-sited, reconstruction of the base of the Mithraeum, set on a raised podium outside one of the new office blocks of Temple Court. Much of the rest of this extensive site was re-developed and the deposits removed without an archaeological presence. As in earlier times, concerns about recording and preserving the City's past were easily brushed aside by those with political and financial clout.

What happened here in the Walbrook Valley was to be repeated on many subsequent city redevelopments. Peter Marsden, an active field worker of this time, and the City's Guildhall Museum Field assistant from the late 1950's onwards, described the years up to 1972 as '*a bad dream with missed opportunities and the ruthless destruction of large parts of Roman London*'.

Anne Mowbray 1964–5

In December 1964 contractors working on a building site just east of the City dug up a coffin containing the remains of Anne Mowbray, Duchess of York, child bride of one of the Princes in the Tower. The coffin was recovered from Leman Street police station by Dr Francis Celoria, Peter Marsden's counterpart at the London Museum in Kensington Palace. When the news of the discovery was released a month later *The Sunday Times* of January 17th, 1965 carried a story linking it to the unsatisfactory state of archaeology in London and attempts being made to ameliorate the situation. Although the builders who found Anne Mowbray's remains were praised for being '*more public spirited than many contractors (who) kick aside the odd skull rather than risk an expensive break in work*', the *Sunday Times* article reported that '*twenty sites a week are lost in central London alone*'. On one of them, '*ten thousand square feet of a Roman site (had been) abandoned because of lack of funds to work it*'. The report noted that '*though some counties appoint an archaeological officer the wealthy City of London does nothing.*'

The report also focused on Celoria's assistants, described as '*buccaneer archaeological teams*' formed within the last 10 years by '*wildly enthusiastic amateurs appalled by the inadequacies of London archaeology brought about by lack of funds*' now being organised into local societies and site watching groups. Many of them in London had been '*recruited at evening classes at Morley College*' where the lecturers included Celoria. That the problems experienced on London's archaeological sites were now being recognised as an aspect of a national problem was demonstrated by an article by Jacquetta Hawkes in the *Sunday Times* Magazine of the same date.

Baynards Castle and RESCUE 1972–3

In February 1972 Peter Marsden, aided by volunteers, began excavation on the site of the medieval Baynard's Castle, close to the river in the southwest of the city. It then emerged that a planned a six month excavation now had to be completed by early April when the land would be handed over to contractors to commence a road widening scheme. While it was hoped still to record the medieval fortification, the time available was far too short. The archaeological efforts culminated during the Easter weekend with '*large numbers of volunteers working desperately ... before everything was destroyed on April 5th.*' (Sheppard 1991, 156). At the entrance a hand written sign written in true Blitz spirit read: '*Baynards Castle, Built 1281 Disappears Next Wednesday*'!

The importance and impending fate of the site, situated conveniently close to Fleet Street, attracted much media attention, most of it hostile to the Corporation of London. It included TV coverage of a visit to the site by RESCUE's first chair Martin Biddle on March 21st. RESCUE then initiated much debate, highlighting what had happened here as an example of the inadequacy of provision for archaeology within the City. As at the time of the Mithras discovery, questions were asked in the House of Commons. RESCUE wrote a critical letter to the Corporation of London in June 1972 whilst preparing '*The Future of London's Past*', an examination of the scale of the problem in the City and the remedies required (Biddle *et al* 1973). The prospect of the study's publication, was apparently so dreaded, (Sheppard 1991, 158), that the Corporation agreed to accept proposals made by its own Guildhall Museum to establish a Department of Urban Archaeology there. This organisation, at last providing '*a properly funded professional archaeological unit for the City*' (Sheppard 1991, 156), began work in December 1973, becoming part of the new Museum of London, when the Guildhall and London Museum's merged in June 1975.

It could be argued that as a result of RESCUE's intervention, the Corporation bowed in the face of public pressure. If so, it was the first time since 1843, when Charles Roach Smith, with parliamentary assistance, successfully opposed the demolition of the City Wall at Tower Hill. What happened following the Baynards Castle excavation in 1972–3 surely provides a good example of how necessary establishing RESCUE as a campaigning body in 1971 had been. The chapters that follow unfortunately demonstrate a continuing need for an independent, vigorous campaigning body over 40 years later.

References

Barker, P, 1974a, *The scale of the problem*, in Rahtz 1974, 28–34

Barker, P, 1974b, *The origins and development of RESCUE*, in Rahtz 1974, 280–85

Barker, P, 1987, *RESCUE: antenatal, birth and early years*, in Mytum and Waugh 1987, 7–9

Biddle M, Hudson D M, Heighway C, 1973, *The future of London's past: a survey of the archaeological implications of planning and development in the nation's capital*, RESCUE publication **4**, Worcester

Cunliffe, B W, 1970, *The past tomorrow: an inaugural lecture*, Southampton 1970

Department for Communities and Local Government (DCLG), 2012, *National Planning Policy Framework*, The Stationery Office, London

Department of the Environment (DoE), 1990, *Planning Policy Guidance 16: Archaeology and Planning (PPG 16)*, HMSO, London

Fowler, P, 1974, Motorways and archaeology, in Rahtz 1974, 113–29

Heighway, C M, (ed), 1972, *The erosion of history: archaeology and planning in towns*, Council for British Archaeology, London

Heyworth, M, 2014, *Digging in the right direction*, at http://www.adjacentgovernment.co.uk/pbc-edition-002/feature-digging-in-the-right-direction/ (accessed 23 Jan, 2015)

Her Majesty's Stationery Office (HMSO), 1949, *War and archaeology in Britain*, London

Longworth, I, and Cherry, J, (eds), 1986, *Archaeology in Britain since 1945*, British Museum, London

Mytum, H, and Waugh, K, (eds) *Rescue Archaeology, what's next? Proceedings of a RESCUE conference at the University of York, Dec 1986*, Dept of Archaeol, University of York Mono **6**, York and Hertford

Rahtz, P A, (ed), 1974, *Rescue Archaeology*, Pelican, Harmondsworth

Royal Commission on the Historical Monuments of England (RCHME), 1960, *a matter of time: an archaeological survey of the river gravels of England*, HMSO, London

RESCUE and the Council for British Archaeology (CBA), 1974, '*Archaeology and Government: A plan for archaeology in Britain*, Hertford and London

Sheldon, H, 1987, *RESCUE: a near death; towards a renaissance*, in Mytum and Waugh, 123–28

Sheppard, F, 1991, *The Treasury of London's Past*, Museum of London, London

Speight, S, 2002, *Digging for history: archaeological fieldwork and the adult student 1943–75*, Studies in the Education of Adults **30.2**, Spring 2002, 68–85

Wainwright, G J, 1982, An analysis of central government (DAMHB) support in 1982–3 for the recording of archaeological sites and landscapes in advance of their destruction' April 1982. (Revised text of a lecture to the Prehistoric Society in January 1982

Wilson, D M, 1986, Foreword, in Longworth and Cherry, 1986, 7–8

SECTION ONE: Current framework

Introduction

Tony Howe

In his Foreword to the forerunner of this volume, Martin Biddle (1974) noted that in the three years following the creation of RESCUE much had been achieved, but yet more required attention. Whilst public and Government attitudes towards archaeology had shifted, Biddle was clear that archaeological legislation was inadequate, that state and regional archaeological services were non-existent, and that there were insufficient arrangements for technical and professional training. Only in the field of financial assistance did he perceive the situation to have improved, and be improving still with increasing levels of Government funding.

Curiously, this opening section to RESCUE's 40th anniversary sequel to that volume might arguably concede much of this position to have been switched. Malcolm Cooper and Ian Ralston detail the principle elements of 40 years of legislative provision in their assessment of policy frameworks, demonstrating that Biddle's concerns regarding legislature have been examined at high levels, whilst Kathryn Stubbs' exposition of the role of the Local Authority in the archaeological development control process articulates modern provisions for covering at least partially the dearth of official regional archaeological expertise that Biddle highlighted. In the past 40 years state-funded regional excavation units of a type that Biddle might have envisaged have been, and subsequently largely gone, through the creation and loss of the County Units, to be replaced by the commercial organisations of a type described in Hester Cooper-Reade's investigation of the process of commercial archaeology. With training programmes and a framework of professionalism also having been provided for in the last 40 years (*see* Sinclair, Chapter 17), for better or for worse it could be concluded that Biddle's 1974 concerns have largely been addressed. Why then, have we arrived at a need for this volume at all?

The answer, is that this conclusion would deny the piecemeal and *ad-hoc* development of the legislation, the profession and the discipline of archaeology in the intervening period, and the new problems and issues that have been created as a result. My own final piece for this introductory section details some of what we might have missed, and to which we might aspire, as a lead to the subsequent sections of this volume. Looking at the four papers together, perhaps what has been missing ultimately has been the overview and

1

control **of** the professional heritage sector, **by** the professional heritage sector, that would have meant that we as heritage experts had controlled both the pace and nature of change, and the development of our profession overall. Yes, we have the legislative documents that Biddle called for, but are they those that we would have devised ourselves? Similarly, are the arrangements for national, regional and local archaeological regulators, and for commercial archaeological practitioner bodies, those we would create as best suiting the needs of the archaeological resource? And where are the stability and the statutory instruments to ensure the survival of these elements? Only in the sphere of training do we have significant control of our own direction, but even this is dictated by the nature of the professional discipline and legislative landscape to which we are subject and it is one that we have not been fully involved in or proactive in creating.

Funding too has not continued along the optimistic route outlined by Biddle. Current funding levels for the historic environment clearly exceed those set out in the opening to the 1974 volume, but as this volume goes to press levels of funding are falling annually and markedly. Back then, through the lobbying of groups like RESCUE, the value to the nation of archaeology had been acknowledged by the Government, and resourcing for its investigation, albeit small, had been provided. These days, that national value requires additional articulation and returns need to be 'value added': a sometimes difficult concept within culture and heritage disciplines. Despite clear evidence having been presented of the importance of the historic environment to the economy through tourism (for example), no conclusive financial link has been established to demonstrate this in a form that adequately and accurately depicts the commercial value and return of investment in heritage to the national economic statistics. A report for *VisitBritain*[1] (2014) estimated that the value of tourism to the UK economy in 2013 amounted to £127 billion or 9% of the overall GDP, yet how much would this figure fall if our historic environment were denuded and heritage tourism was discounted? It is impossible to say. Similarly, it is impossible to argue for any percentage rise in these figures being linked to a percentage rise in heritage-related Government spending. Consequently, the financial importance of what we do and the resource we serve and protect is often buried and inaccessible within a mass of other data. The Government now requires all of us to be increasingly financially innovative and creative under threat of withdrawal of the little support that remains. This alone is a situation that threatens our professional survival and represents a reversal of the 1974 situation.

We must first examine the existing heritage framework before drilling into some of the core issues in the rest of this volume. This framework forms the foundation above which the rest of the structure of our profession is built, but as for for any structure, if the foundation is ultimately found to be wanting, where does that leave the stability of the structure itself? What we do have, is a framework that displays a polished appearance of stability, professionalism, accountability, efficiency, and value for money. But how far does this appearance extend, and is it only a veneer that masks fundamental structural flaws?

---

[1] VisitBritain is the national tourism agency, a non-departmental public body, funded by the Department for Culture, Media and Sport, responsible for promoting Britain worldwide and developing its visitor economy.

References

Biddle, M, 1974, Foreword, in Rahtz, P A, *Rescue Archaeology*, Pelican, Harmondsworth, ix–x

VisitBritain, 2014, *Visitor Economy Facts – updated May 2014*, at http://www.visitbritain.org/insightsandstatistics/visitoreconomyfacts/ (accessed Dec 2014)

Chapter 1

National legislation, policy and government agencies in Britain

Malcolm A Cooper and Ian Ralston

Introduction

'A great many people today think, if they happen to think at all about the remains of the past in Britain, that in some way it is up to our Government to intervene.' (Thomas 1974, 3)

So wrote Charles Thomas in the opening chapter of *Rescue Archaeology* in 1974. For an effective rescue archaeology system to function a number of things were needed:

- Databases identifying the location of archaeological sites and deposits
- A framework of legislation, policy and guidance to allow assessments of the significance of, and to provide the basis for subsequently managing, archaeological remains in the face of development
- An organisational infrastructure throughout Britain capable of undertaking various roles from training, survey and advice-giving through to excavation, post-excavation, archiving and publication
- Experts to define and carry out these various roles
- Political and public support, and
- Appropriate levels of funding

However, in 1973 despite the efforts of professional and amateur archaeologists alike, available resources of all kinds were simply inadequate for the task. The Historic Buildings and Ancient Monuments Act of 1953 had introduced a management framework for those ancient monuments designated under the Act, but this legislation and its predecessors had been designed with nationally important *monuments* in mind, that is, discrete structural remains and upstanding earthworks. The work of RESCUE, the Council for British Archaeology, local societies, and other organisations and individuals was beginning to reveal the hitherto unsuspected, vast extent and significance of remains in urban areas, in river valleys and arable land, in the rural uplands and on the coastal margins.

Urban surveys such as the Council for British Archaeology's *The Erosion of History* (Heighway 1972) and rural surveys such as that in the Upper Thames Valley (Benson and Miles 1974), together with the long-term archaeological excavations in urban areas such as at Winchester, indicated clearly the potential of urban and rural archaeological deposits, but these received little or no protection in law at that time. Even where archaeological information about particular sites was held on existing databases, the formal mechanisms in place to ensure that significant remains were either avoided or excavated in advance of their destruction were highly limited. Neither the 1953 Act, nor town planning or rural legislation provided adequate support for rescue archaeology, with the majority of town centre developments, gravel quarries, road schemes, agricultural improvements, forestry plantations and the like, going ahead without consideration of their impact on archaeological remains. Even where access conditions for archaeological investigation were placed on development (*see, for example*, Baker 1975; Hedges 1977), there was also a limited capacity and a lack of funding to undertake rescue excavation; a shortcoming which was seen as increasingly out-of-step with the needs of the time. For many years museums, local societies and universities had been running rescue and research excavations and training archaeologists, drawing on their own resources to do so, but these were frequently undertaken as summer activities. However, the recognition both of the relative ubiquity of archaeological remains and the speed of destruction from development suggested the need for a far greater number of archaeologists who were highly trained, flexible, and above all who were available to undertake fieldwork all-year-round! In short the profession, if one could call it that, needed to be expanded rapidly both geographically and numerically. Faced with the increasing evidence of destruction, bodies such as RESCUE and the CBA called urgently for new legislation, the employment of an archaeologist by all major planning and related authorities, the creation of a national network of excavation committees (to agree local priorities and allocate resources), and for government funding to be substantially increased.

Government steps in to create a professional infrastructure

There was, of course, some capacity in place by the early 1970s to deal with rescue archaeology. As already noted, scheduled monuments were protected through the provisions of the 1953 Act, administered in England by the Directorate of Ancient Monuments and Historic Buildings within the Department of the Environment (DoE) and by their counterparts in due course in the Welsh and Scottish Offices. Inspectors of Ancient Monuments, working with administrative teams and under the guidance of national Ancient Monuments Boards, were not only responsible for scheduling, guardianship and casework on scheduled sites, but they also gave out grants for rescue archaeology (in England in the early 1970s this amounted to some £800k per annum). This grant-aid frequently went to locally-based rescue archaeology committees, at least in England, which might bring together an archaeological society, local authority museum service and university. Elsewhere, provision was generally even more *ad hoc*. There was also some capacity for Government to undertake major rescue excavation directly through in-house field units in England and latterly in Scotland.

However the campaign by RESCUE, the CBA and others was having an effect. The key characteristic through the 1970s and 1980s was increased state intervention in order to create what was intended in due course to be a robust organisational infrastructure for rescue archaeology across Britain (detailed information on the state of archaeology and organisational arrangements in the early 1970s can be found in Rowley and Breakell 1975, 1977). Meanwhile the arrangements for archaeology in Wales were well in advance of England and Scotland. The *Rescue Archaeology Group* had been created in 1970, staffed by a small number of professional archaeologists, to provide a response for the country as a whole. By 1975 this was replaced by four regional Trusts with core-funding from the DoE's Welsh Inspectorate. These multi-purpose Trusts developed sites and monuments records as well as undertaking rescue archaeology and educational work and thus provided a robust and effective model (Owen-John 1986).

In England however, while the DoE continued to pursue the creation of a network of regional archaeological units, matters proved less straightforward. Differences of view had emerged over the correct geographical range for individual field-units and in governance terms whether they should be independent organisations or based within local authorities. There were also the vested interests of the existing archaeological bodies, and the likely provision of funding for the new model to be taken into account. The overarching vision in England was for a state-funded service with financial support from both national and local government, but therein lay the difficulty. While national government did not intend to pick up the unpredictable and potentially very large costs of rescue archaeology, local authorities similarly struggled, with the additional difficulty of potentially funding organisations which were envisaged to operate regionally rather than within specific local authority areas. Progress in developing this system was therefore slow and more fragmentary than had been intended. Archaeologists were in the meantime creative in seeking funding, with developers beginning to provide some funding for rescue excavation on a voluntary basis in, for example, London. In the 1970s archaeologists also began to take advantage of various job-creation schemes (whereby government made grants available to organisations via the Manpower Services Commission to provide training for the long-term unemployed). Many excavations were funded in part or in full by these schemes, which both provided a platform for training a new generation of excavators, whilst also supporting existing professional archaeologists who were paid as supervisors. Running rescue archaeological projects through job-creation schemes raised a number of problems however. Translating the fieldwork into final reports, for example, proved difficult under this regime as there were significant obstacles to the extension of job-creation funding into the post-excavation phase (ie the analysis, conservation of objects, publication of reports and preparation of the excavation archive). This needed a far smaller number of staff but these frequently needed to be highly experienced archaeologists rather than trainees. This led to more problems of 'archaeological backlogs', with important excavations remaining unpublished and un-archived and with, in some cases, the material lying scattered in garages and stores long after the death of the excavation director. Diverting state funding to this post-excavation backlog however meant that less funding was available for new rescue archaeology projects.

In England a far more complex organisational structure was developing than in Wales, and later in the decade the DoE took explicit steps to rationalise the number of archaeological field units. It also began to pursue the idea of a separation of what we would now recognise as the curatorial advisory function (envisaged as being supported at a local level) from the rescue fieldwork function (supported by Government grant-aid). There was also a policy shift for government grant-aid to be allocated on the basis of 'project-funding' rather than to provide 'core-funding' for archaeological units. This was to cause significant difficulties for the managers of the emerging field units who were trying to establish and, importantly, to retain core teams of experienced archaeologists. Rather than employment being underwritten by a predictable annual core-grant from the Government's national heritage agencies, continuity of employment would now depend on the field units managing to secure end-to-end projects and grants (while also achieving savings which could be drawn on to pay staff wages and overheads when gaps between projects opened-up or to tackle post-excavation backlogs). This was extremely difficult to achieve and led to insecurity of employment for many staff and to particular difficulties for the retention of experienced staff in the post-excavation stages (as individuals were tempted to move at an early stage to new long-term projects as they saw their current contracts running out). Meanwhile the Scottish Development Department put funds into rescue archaeology north of the border and created its own central excavation unit. However an infrastructure of locally-based units developed far more slowly in Scotland and was only ever very patchy. A small number of local authorities began to employ archaeological advisors from the mid-1970s, but a nationwide network was achieved only in the 1990s.

New archaeological legislation

The 1970s closed with the introduction of new legislation for the protection of ancient monuments and archaeological remains. The Ancient Monuments and Archaeological Areas Act 1979 consolidated and clarified the earlier ancient monument legislation (*see,* Champion 1996) and still provides, albeit in an amended form, much of the underlying legislative framework for ancient monument protection and management across Britain. This legislation contained a requirement to compile the schedule of nationally important monuments, set out a process for controlling works to monuments, and gave various powers to take archaeological sites into state guardianship and for their subsequent management. A novel component of the 1979 Act came in Part II, the creation of *Archaeological Areas.* This was an attempt to introduce a protective framework for urban archaeological deposits by giving local authorities the powers to designate specific urban areas and to identify an archaeological *investigating authority* which would have certain powers to undertake any archaeological work deemed necessary. Once an urban area was designated, a 6-week notice-period was given to the investigating authority before any development-related operations could be carried out on the land; rights of entry also existed for inspection. This process in turn could lead to the investigating authority serving a notice of intention to excavate (this was however limited by the legislation to a maximum period of 4 months and 2 weeks). A number of problems with the provisions of Part II were immediately apparent, there was no mechanism for funding the archaeological interventions and the 4½-month maximum timescale for excavation was entirely inconsistent with the recognised nature and complexity of urban deposits. As a result, by 1984 only five archaeological areas had been designated; Canterbury, Chester, Exeter, Hereford and York, and this remains the present case (also the UK Government has signalled its intention to remove this part of the legislation in due course). Although used in England, Part II of the Act was never employed in the other constituent parts of the UK.

While the effectiveness of the Areas of Archaeological Importance was limited in practice therefore, an alternative approach was adopted elsewhere. A number of urban areas in England, such as in Worcester, were scheduled as ancient monuments under Part I of the Act. This was done, not with the intention of preserving all urban archaeological deposits *in situ*, but to act as leverage to ensure mitigation strategies were devised (such as the reduction or removal of proposed below-ground disturbance in archaeologically sensitive areas) or to ensure the provision of significant levels of financial support and longer timescales for rescue excavation. In such cases, mitigation strategies and funding for rescue excavation were made a requirement of scheduled monument consent.

The new national bodies

If the 1970s were characterised by increasing Government support and funding for archaeological remains threatened by development; by attempts to create curatorial functions within local authority planning and other bodies, and by the core-funding regional networks of 'territorial' field units, the focus changed significantly in the 1980s. This reorientation was related to the nature of the state bodies which undertook the Government's responsibilities with regard to archaeology and the broader historic environment. As we have seen, in Scotland, Wales and England, and indeed in Northern Ireland, these responsibilities were met by government departments, which increasingly tailored their outlooks to local circumstances. Furthermore, from the late 1970s onwards the political philosophy of the various administrations was to reduce the cost of central and local government and where possible to introduce market economics, avowedly to help drive efficiencies and improvement (*see* Cooper 2010). Heritage activities seemed particularly appropriate to this model, not least because of the potential for the government's own historic property portfolio to be operated on a far stronger commercial basis. It was envisaged also that additional income would be generated to reduce the overall cost to the public purse of dealing with heritage issues.

In 1983 the National Heritage Act led to the creation of a new Non-Departmental Public Body (NDPB) referred to as the Historic Building and Monuments Commission for England, its popular name was English Heritage (*see* Thurley 2013, 250–1). The intention here, although only for England, was to bring together all elements of the Government's responsibilities relating to the historic environment within one organisation, which was to operate at *arm's length* from government. Its stated aims were to secure the preservation of ancient monuments and historic buildings, to promote the preservation and enhancement of the character and appearance of conservation areas in England, and to encourage the public's enjoyment and advance their knowledge of the historic environment and its preservation. The appointment of Lord Montagu of Beaulieu as its first Chairman signalled the intention that the new organisation should adopt a strongly commercial focus as he was well-known for having developed a commercially successful visitor attraction at his own stately home. Similar changes followed in Wales in 1984 with the creation of CADW, whose staff included a number drawn from the Wales Tourist Board. Later in the decade Historic Scotland was created but its constitution as an Agency rather than a NDPB meant that it always remained much closer to Government control (as its staff represent the Government, they could not for example publicly criticise Government policy or practice). Historic Scotland would therefore develop rather differently from its English and Welsh counterparts. In 1984 the UK government also ratified UNESCO's 1972 *World Heritage Convention*, opening the way for certain major archaeological sites to be designated by UNESCO as of 'outstanding universal value.'

In the 1980s the clearer recognition of the need to have accurate information on the location of archaeological sites to feed into the land-use planning system and for broader research and rescue activities led to a strong move to establish, or to make more comprehensive, the sites and monuments records (SMRs) across the country, particularly in England and Wales, but also in Scotland (this function remained with central government in Northern Ireland). This complemented and further developed the work that the Royal Commissions on Ancient and Historical Monuments had been undertaking since early in the 20th century. Early SMRs (with advisory staff) already existed in some local authority areas and in some historic towns, often developed initially from the index cards prepared by the Ordnance Survey mapping teams (*see*, Harley 1975). English Heritage pursued the development of county council-based SMRs as a priority, in a number of cases providing funding to develop the records and for the staff to manage them. This was a trend that continued into the following decade, albeit with a shift in emphasis. As we have already seen, in Wales a similar approach of funding was adopted but focused on the four regional trusts. The development of SMRs led to a broader tension across Britain which was to be a characteristic for much of the remaining period, should there be a monuments-record maintained and developed by the Royal Commission(s) on a national basis or should monument records be housed in local authorities, given their role as advisors in the land-use planning process and, in either case, who should be responsible for setting data standards? In practice both developed in parallel, but at times unhelpful rivalries between local authority archaeologists and the Royal Commissions became only too apparent. In Scotland a system of locally-based sites and monuments records was developed, with the first being integrated into planning authorities in the second half of the 1970s; at that time in-house archaeological expertise was located in the upper of the two-tier local authority system produced by local government reorganisation. Support was provided from the Royal Commission on the Ancient and Historical Monuments of Scotland. A variety of mechanisms was devised to implant and sustain these records, including, on the Northern Isles for example, the use of heritage trusts independent from the planning authorities to house the records. The massive size of certain council areas, notably the old Highland Region which covered an area the size of Wales, caused significant operational and logistical issues for the small number of professional staff they employed.

However, despite improvements in the records of sites and increases in capacity, there was still a need to find an effective mechanism for managing non-scheduled archaeological sites in the face of development proposals. Some further steps in this direction were taken with the release of DoE Circular 8/87 which, although entitled *Historic Buildings and Conservation Areas – Policy and Procedures*, made archaeological remains a material consideration in the planning process for the first time. Arguably, though, it was not until 1990 that the use of the land-use planning system for managing non-scheduled archaeological remains came of age.

Archaeology and land-use planning

For all those working in field archaeology in England, the 1990s saw a significant breakthrough in the effective management of archaeological remains in relation to development, with the formal recognition by government that the land-use planning process should be used to this end and that this could only be achieved if a new approach and method of funding were adopted. The introduction of *Planning Policy Guidance Note 16: Archaeology and Planning* (PPG 16, DoE 1990) in November 1990 represented a sea-change for both Government and the profession. Under this guidance mechanisms were strengthened, via the land-use planning system, for local authorities to manage their archaeological heritage in relation to proposed development. Key to the approach was a presumption in favour of the preservation of nationally important archaeological remains (whether scheduled or unscheduled) together with the need to take informed planning decisions drawing on information provided by site-reconnaissance techniques such as pre-determination archaeological evaluation. The guidance strongly encouraged planning authorities to include relevant policies in their development plans, to seek pre-determination archaeological-evaluation in the form of ground-invasive fieldwork to allow them to assess potential impacts, and to ensure appropriate mitigation measures were included within development proposals. Wales followed suit in 1991, introducing their own version of PPG 16 (Wales), subsequently replacing this with *Planning and the Historic Environment: Archaeology* (Welsh Office Circular 60/96) and in 1994 *National Planning Policy Guideline 5: Archaeology and Planning* together with *Planning Advice Note 42: Archaeology – the Planning Process and Scheduled Monument Consent* appeared in Scotland. At last there were unequivocal statements from Government in the form of published planning guidance as to why non-scheduled archaeological remains were important.

Underlying this new system, which followed the wider environmental philosophy advocated by the United Nations, was the 'polluter-pays principle.' Principle 16 of the *Rio Declaration* (United Nations 1992) introduced the requirement that developers were expected to meet the environmental costs of development. In Britain this principle was applied to ensure effective mitigation of the archaeological consequences of development.

Under the land-use planning system, developers were now expected to meet all legitimate archaeological costs such as the funding of pre-determination survey and archaeological evaluation, rescue excavation, conservation of finds, publication and archiving. While there was some variability in the way in which local authorities used these powers, overall, the new arrangements led to a very significant and positive growth in available funding for rescue archaeology, now seen as a legitimate cost of development, and this in turn enabled the further strengthening of the archaeological profession. The success of the Rio Summit also encouraged archaeologists to develop stronger links with the developing environmental or 'Green' movement (Swain 1993).

The introduction of PPG 16 was also to have broad-ranging ramifications in terms of the structure of the profession. Developers, now effectively forced to pay for archaeological services, increasingly sought to select their own archaeological contractors (as they already did with other specialist services, with archaeological works commissioned through a competitive tendering process. This was to put the final nail in the coffin of territorial units as acknowledged experts established within particular geographical areas, and with near-monopoly status. It also meant continued pressure to separate the curatorial advice-giving function from contracting activities (where previously locally-based archaeological organisations had frequently conducted both activities) and it also necessitated the development of mechanisms to enable and to manage the resulting competitive process. These included, for example, the development of archaeological briefs by which archaeological works were defined by the planning authority, together with the introduction of monitoring processes by which the quality and scope of resulting work was then evaluated against the brief's requirements. This also gave a strong boost to the Institute of Field Archaeologists (as it was then called) to monitor and ensure effective governance, and that appropriate standards of professional behaviour were adopted by archaeologists and their employing bodies. Worryingly, the problem of post-excavation backlogs continued, however, due to the reluctance of developers to pay for, in some cases many years of, post-excavation analysis, with problems arising because of poorly-costed and managed excavation and post-excavation projects, or from the unanticipated complexity and/or importance of the archaeological remains. Discussions about the nature of archaeological management and the difficult issue of value-for-money and quality standards also began to surface both within and outside the profession (*see, for example*, Hunter and Ralston 1993, *and in particular* Cooper *et al* 1995).

In England, as we have seen, the government focus had been to create expertise and capacity at local-authority level. However this aspiration was significantly impacted on, not only by the separation of curatorial and contracting functions, but also by a series of broader changes affecting local government including cost-cutting, competitive tendering, privatisation, and local government reorganisation. These changes led, for example, to the privatisation of many local authority or museum-based field-units and to the creation of shared curatorial services (ie a single service providing advice to a number of local authorities) also appeared in response to the dissolution of the metropolitan county councils in England (as had occurred in Scotland when the upper-tier regional authorities created in 1974 were abandoned in the mid-1990s. The process of developing SMRs nonetheless continued, with in England for example, government-funding being made available for the preparation of detailed urban archaeological databases for historic towns and to undertake detailed rural surveys.

A major development late in the 1980s was the arrival of Environmental Impact Assessment (EIA) legislation. It was first introduced by a European Community Directive in 1985 in order to improve environmental protection and standardise best practice (subsequent amendments were introduced in 1997 and 2003). EIA was incorporated into UK legislation in 1988, with the current regulations adopted in 1999 (again with subsequent amendments). It was also linked to the process of Strategic Environmental Assessment, designed to evaluate the environmental effects of the strategic plans and programmes developed by public and other bodies, as opposed to those of individual projects. The Directive refers to the need to include material assets and cultural heritage in impact assessments and this has provided a reasonably robust mechanism for ensuring that the impact of major infrastructure and other developments with regard to archaeological remains is both assessed and adverse impacts mitigated. A major outcome of this process was to encourage developers to recognise the potential benefits offered by the early involvement of archaeological advisors in project design, since significant archaeological deposits could be avoided by redesign at that stage thereby eliminating later, and often costly, mitigation measures. The assessments have become increasingly sophisticated and now often include *Landscape and Visual Impact Assessment (LVIA),* which has provided significant levels of activity and stimulated much debate and methodological development *(for a broader discussion, see* Carroll and Turpin 2009 and Landscape Institute 2002). However, both EIA and SEA have been seen as expensive, highly bureaucratic and time-consuming, and therefore have been perceived as anti-development, and this has added weight to the broader move to streamline the land-use development process in Britain.

The eventual ratification of the *European Convention on the Protection of the Archaeological Heritage,* known as the Valetta (or Valletta) Convention (Council of Europe 1992), by the UK government in 2000 bound constituent parts of this country more formally into making adequate provision for the conduct of rescue or developer-funded archaeology than had previously been the case. The Convention aimed to provide a succinct statement of best practice, on the one hand defining the archaeological heritage holistically and on the other adopting best practices in dealing with archaeological resources in regard to planning and development processes. Potentially deleterious side-effects of the Convention, such as a worsening split between professional and amateur field-projects (or the demise of amateur field archaeology entirely) which some had feared might result from the requirement in Article 3 (that fieldwork should be conducted by 'qualified, specially authorised persons') have proved to be unfounded.

Streamlining of legislation

Given the increasing levels of protection for the historic environment across Britain, it was perhaps inevitable that there would be an adverse response from some sectors concerned with promoting development and economic improvement. The complexity of the multiple regulatory systems applying to the historic environment (comprising buildings, monuments, wreck sites, and historic areas, including battlefields, historic parks and gardens, and historic landscapes) and broader concerns about the constraining nature of the land-use planning system, have led successive governments to commit to 'reduce the burden of regulation' and to streamline land-use planning and related processes. In terms of broader political philosophy, a growing emphasis on localism has also led to pressure to move a range of activities from central government to either local government or third-sector organisations. In England and Wales the general move towards streamlining led to a major initiative termed *Heritage Protection Reform* (HPR), developed by English Heritage and taken forward by Central Government. Its origins can be traced back to the early part of the decade with a Department of Culture, Media and Sport consultation entitled *Protecting our Historic Environment: Making the System Work Better* in 2003 and *Review of Heritage Protection: The Way Forward* in 2004. The latter identified both short-term and longer-term changes of emphasis and practice which would necessitate primary legislation. In 2007 the Government published a White Paper, *Heritage Protection for the 21st Century*, followed in 2008 by a draft Heritage Bill. The key intentions of the proposed changes were to create a single *Register of Heritage Assets* (termed 'unified designation'). As with the existing system, consent would need to be granted for works affecting a designated heritage asset, but the intended streamlining of the system envisaged a single consent process, with the primary recipient and determining body being the local planning authority for all heritage assets, with the national heritage bodies only being consulted in certain circumstances (but holding the power to direct that certain major applications be referred to them rather than being determined at a local level). Another proposed innovation was the creation of *heritage partnership agreements*. This was intended to streamline processes by allowing planning authorities either to grant a single consent for certain types of repetitive work (thereby avoiding having to make identical applications repeatedly) or by waiving the need for consent to be granted at all in certain circumstances. As with the previous regime, ecclesiastical exemption (whereby certain properties designated as places of worship are exempt from certain listed-building requirements through the operation of its own internal consents system) was proposed for retention. However, despite raised expectations and to the disappointment of many both within and outside the profession, the proposed Bill was not included in the 2009 legislative programme and while it is not clear if such regulation will appear in the future, some elements of the earlier Bill intended to streamline the consents process were incorporated into the 2013 *Enterprise and Regulatory Reform Act*.

In Scotland, where the management of culture and heritage has been devolved to the Scottish Executive (now referred to as the Scottish Government), a different approach was adopted. Commencing in 2006, heritage policy was reviewed leading to the publication of a series of Scottish Historic Environment Policy (SHEP) documents which were subsequently consolidated into the single *Scottish Historic Environment Policy*. This was followed by the

Historic Environment Amendment (Scotland) Act 2010 which, while less ambitious than the intended Heritage Protection Reform Programme being pursued in England, resolved a series of known problem-areas relating to the existing heritage legislation (whilst avoiding the major expense and long time-period envisaged to achieve the HPR in England). In addition, Scotland took the decision to break away from the rest of Britain in terms of its marine policy, with the opportunity taken to include the management of marine heritage assets within the 2010 *Marine Scotland Act* (thereby aligning the management process for these with that of other natural and cultural marine features).

It is important to stress that the introduction of planning reform across the constituent parts of the UK has led to large amounts of planning guidance being deleted and replaced by more streamlined (and far shorter) documents. This move has also been accompanied by a shift of emphasis in the policy toward 'sustainable economic development'. The worry here is that important elements of heritage policy have been lost and that the 'sustainable' part of the 'sustainable development' philosophy will, in practice, be downplayed or ignored. This would once again lead to archaeological remains being vulnerable to development on the basis of broader economic arguments alone. As part of a programme of planning reform underway in Scotland, separate planning guidance for heritage was subsumed within a single planning guidance note, *Scottish Planning Policy*, published in 2010. In England a similar process of consolidation saw *Planning Policy Guidance Notes 15 and 16* replaced by the single *Planning Policy Statement 5: Planning and the Historic Environment*, with this in turn being subsumed within the *National Planning Policy Framework* (Department of Communities and Local Government 2012). Against the broader backdrop of a continual streamlining of the land-use planning system as a whole, with Government restricting itself to producing high-level strategic planning guidance and placing more emphasis on local decision-making, the intention has been to simplify the framework for managing heritage. As the broad streamlining and anti-regulatory philosophy continues to find favour across Britain, there would seem to be a significant danger of a reduction in the level of protection for archaeological remains within the land-use planning system and heritage management legislation, accompanied by an increasing variability of approach at a local level.

Conclusions

RESCUE's great achievement was to create a highly visible campaign for archaeological remains across these islands, one that forced Government to act. As a consequence, the subsequent period has witnessed the creation of relatively effective heritage management systems across the UK. For much of the past 40 years, the pattern has been one of increasing levels of understanding about the nature, distribution and value of archaeological remains, together with strengthening legislative protection and a better management infrastructure. Protection has been based to a very great extent on two main pillars, historic environment legislation and land-use planning legislation (together with supporting policy and guidance), both of which have become both stronger and more effective over time. The management system was also enhanced by the introduction of environmental assessment legislation and the adoption of various European heritage conventions. The developing organisational model saw curatorial roles for archaeologists working at both local and national levels, with national bodies providing strategic guidance, grant aid, undertaking designation and determining consent applications for certain types of nationally important archaeological remains. Archaeological databases were created both nationally and at a regional or local level, and the consents and planning regimes increasingly provided a framework for assessing the impact of development proposals and securing mitigation measures. The importance of the land-use planning process for protecting and managing archaeological remains meant that curatorial archaeological expertise was necessary either within local planning-authorities or in the organisations providing curatorial advice to these authorities. There was recognition also of the need for professional archaeological units to provide a range of activities including survey, excavation, post-excavation and advisory services (as part of broader mitigation strategies) and these gradually developed, although different models were followed in England, Wales and Scotland. The arrival of developer-funding and its expansion, however, led to varied arrangements for field units as competition and market economics took effect. Indeed, contracting archaeological units now vary in scale from major organisation operating nationally and internationally, to individual practitioners, a reflection of the increasing diversity of the market for archaeological services. Such units are now the major employers of professional archaeologists in Britain, despite the downturn represented by the mid-2000s economic crash.

In 1974 Charles Thomas speculated that there were perhaps '*as few as a couple of hundred real, fully trained and properly qualified professional archaeologists in the British Isles.*' (Thomas 1974)

Now we have over 3000 members of the Institute for Archaeologists and at its peak, before the current recession took effect, those in archaeological employment were considerably over twice that number (*see* Aitchison 2012). However the increasing reliance on government-based systems has come at a cost. It has meant that the emergence and consolidation of the profession have been influenced not only by advances driven from within the discipline, but also by broader changes in political philosophy in relation to the nature and role of government itself (Cooper 2010). We have seen significant shifts in the way in which government services are procured and delivered, the nature and use of public funds, and perhaps most importantly of all, the nature and role of regulation as an acceptable mechanism in relation to the historic environment. There has also emerged a strong focus on localism and communities, and on inclusivity. Each of these currents has had a direct impact on organisational infrastructure, on the changing roles of national and local government, on the role of the private sector, on the uses of legislation and regulation, and on funding and its sources. The sense is that these changes will continue to have a direct impact on applied archaeology in the different constituent parts of Britain and on the broader historic environment, and there have been worrying developments which suggest that we may be seeing significant changes and weakening of the archaeological management systems currently in place.

In an increasingly devolved Britain, particularly in terms of governmental provision for culture and heritage, greater diversity is to be anticipated, as relevant matters are perceived differently in Belfast, Cardiff, Edinburgh and London. While it is not clear how the ongoing modification of heritage legislation will continue in England, the granting of powers for the Welsh Government to create primary legislation will allow it to design and implement its own heritage reform, and discussions are already underway to this end. In the lead up to the referendum on Scottish independence in September 2014, the Scottish Government sought to drawn its agencies very close to the centre, and a new historic environment policy aligned closely with Scottish identity and the Scottish Government's overarching objective of sustainable economic development was published (Scottish Government 2014). It is perhaps inevitable that the current economic difficulties have given more power to those seeking to reduce regulation whilst also placing significant downward pressures on the amount of funding available for bodies such as English Heritage, CADW and Historic Scotland, as well as for local government. Following earlier reorganisations in England, consideration of the independent status of the Royal Commissions on Ancient and Historical Monuments in Scotland and in Wales seemed to have gained significant momentum. However, while the Scotland Government continues to progress a merger between RCAHMS and Historic Scotland, the Welsh Assembly has decided not to follow a similar route for RCAHMW and CADW, at least for the time being. Meanwhile English Heritage seems set to be split into two separate bodies, one managing the historic properties portfolio and the other responsible for policy, statutory designation, advice, and provision of grant-aid (*see* also Howe, Chapter 4 and *for details* Walker, Chapter 17, footnote 2).

Well-publicised concerns over the potential weakening of heritage protection as part of planning reform in England, led by the National Trust, have emphasised the increasing need once again for strong independent voices in the heritage sector. The changes at a national level and the fact that many of the arms-length or nominally-independent archaeological organisations are being drawn very closely into government or are increasingly reliant on central-government grants (thereby potentially weakening their independence) gives cause for concern at a time when the emphasis appears once again to be the pursuit of economic development *simpliciter* (rather than *sustainable* economic development). The majority of Britain's archaeological remains have relied for their protection not on ancient monument legislation, but on land-use planning framework. Such regulation is, however, becoming increasingly out-of-favour, with the world's financial crises of the past decade and Britain's perceived economic performance giving strength to those arguing for a reduction in State interference and in 'bureaucratic red tape'. There is a danger therefore that the levels of protection will be reduced and there is an additional concern that the historic environment sector is not well-positioned in terms of the sustainability agenda. Well-preserved historic and archaeological landscapes, for example, have tended to survive in rural areas with low population density. However these areas have become increasingly attractive for Britain's woefully unmanaged wind-farm strategies, with the physical and visual impact of wind-farms on Britain's historic landscapes and archaeological sites becoming an increasing concern. Similarly, historic buildings are frequently seen as exhibiting problems of energy-efficiency, but rather than exempting them from energy-efficiency measures, they appear increasingly vulnerable to a range of invasive activities and unproven technologies. Meanwhile the continued levying of VAT on repairs to the majority of historic buildings, but not on their demolition and rebuilding, remains a national embarrassment.

The past 40 years has undoubtedly been a success story and archaeologists across the UK have worked in a generally improving environment. They have witnessed the establishment of a new profession, seen significant advances in data-sets and the underpinning frameworks of knowledge, and been able to draw on levels of funding undreamt of in the early 1970s. Since the commencement of this journey, which began with the RESCUE conference of 1973, the direction of travel has been exceptionally positive and the story is one of great achievements. There are though worrying signs that the management structures, and the processes for protecting the historic environment, are coming under increasing pressure and that the story of continuing improvement might be about to falter. Continued vigilance in the face of emerging challenges would appear to be more necessary than ever.

References

Aitchison, K, 2012, *Breaking new ground: how archaeology works*, Kindle edn, Landward Research Ltd, Sheffield

Baker, D, 1975, Planning and archaeology: problems of mutual understanding, in Rowley, T, and Breakall, M, (eds), *Planning and the historic environment,* 53–60, Oxford

Benson, D, and Miles, D, 1974, *The Upper Thames Valley: an archaeological survey of the river gravels,* Oxford

Carroll, B, and Turpin, T, 2009, *Environmental Impact Assessment handbook: a practical guide for planners, developers and communities,* 2nd edn, Cambridge, Mass

Champion, T, 1996, Protecting the monuments: archaeological legislation from the 1882 Act to PPG 16, in Hunter, M, (ed), *Preserving the past: the rise of heritage in modern Britain,* 38–56, Stroud

Cooper, M A, 2010, Protecting our past: political philosophy, regulation and heritage management in England and Scotland, *The Historic Environment,* 1, 143–59

Cooper, M A, Firth, A, Carman, J, and. Wheatley, D, (eds), 1995, *Managing archaeology*

Council of Europe, 'Valetta', 1992, *European Convention on the Protection of the Archaeological Heritage (revised 1992),* at http://www.conventions.coe.int/Treaty/en/Treaties/Html/143.htm (accessed 5 June 2014)

Department for Communities and Local Government (DCLG), 2012, *National Planning Policy Framework,* at http://www.gov.uk/government/uploads/system/uploads/attachment_data/file/6077/2116950.pdf, (accessed 6 June 2014)

Department of the Environment (DoE) 1987, Circular 8/87 *Historic Buildings and Conservation Areas: Policy and Procedures,* HMSO, London

Department of the Environment (DoE), 1990, *Planning Policy Guidance 16: Archaeology and Planning (PPG 16),* HMSO, London

Harley, J B, 1975, *Ordnance Survey maps: a descriptive manual*, Southampton

Hedges, J, 1977, Development control and archaeology, in Rowley, T, and Breakall, M, (eds), *Planning and the historic environment,* **II**, 32–64, Oxford

Heighway, C M, (ed), 1972, *The erosion of history: archaeology and planning in towns,* Council for British Archaeology, London

Hunter, J R, and Ralston, I, (eds), 1993, *Archaeological resource management in the UK: an introduction*, Stroud (2nd edn 2006)

Landscape Institute and Institute of Environmental Management and Assessment, 2002, *Guidelines for Landscape and Visual Impact Assessment*, 3rd edn, Abingdon

Owen-John, 1986, *Rescue archaeology in Wales,* Swansea

Rowley, T, and Breakall, M, (eds), 1975, *Planning and the historic environment*, Oxford

Rowley, T, and Breakall, M, (eds), 1977, *Planning and the historic environment* II, Oxford

Scottish Government, 2014, *Our Place in Time: The Historic Environment Strategy for Scotland*, at http://www.scotland.gov.uk/Publications/2014/03/8522, (accessed 6 June 2014)

Swain, H, (ed), 1993, *Rescuing the historic environment: archaeology, the green movement and conservation strategies for the British landscape*, Hertford

Thomas, C, 1974, Archaeology in Britain 1973, in Rahtz, P A, (ed), *Rescue Archaeology*, Pelican, Harmondswort, 3–15

Thurley, S, 2013, *Men from the Ministry: how Britain saved its heritage,* London

UNESCO, 1972, *Convention Concerning the Protection of the World Cultural and Natural Heritage*, at http://whc.unesco.org/en/conventiontext/ (accessed 2 December 2014)

United Nations, (12 August) 1992, *The Rio Declaration on environment and development*, A/CONF.151/26 (vol I), at http://www.un.org/documents/ga/conf151/aconf15126-1annex1.htm, (accessed 5 June 2014)

Chapter 2

Local authorities and archaeology

Kathryn Stubbs

Introduction

Local authorities have a key role in managing change in the historic environment, making decisions on development proposals that affect buildings and areas. As a consequence of past changes and man-made influences the historic environment is a dynamic and changing place. Local authorities protect and enhance the historic environment and are responsible for designated historic assets, listed buildings and conservation areas and the greater number of undesignated historic and archaeological assets, all material considerations in the planning process. Decisions on planning applications, made by elected members advised by specialist officers, are made within a framework of local policy, government legislation and guidance. The historic environment and archaeology are valuable, and central to well-being and a sustainable way of life, particularly at a time of financial uncertainty and constraint.

Local authority archaeological planning officers protect and enhance archaeological remains, giving advice on planning applications, enabling conservation, investigation, and recording. The challenge of the planning process is to gather archaeological evidence, to interpret assessment and evaluation results, to consider archaeological potential, and make recommendations on the impact of a planning application for decision by elected members. The expectations and views of the community, local residents, businesses, workers, and visitors need to be taken into account.

The planning process has competing demands, and decisions have to be made within time constraints set by government. Archaeology will be different on different sites. No two developments or planning applications are the same, and there may be different archaeological outcomes for different developments. Significant archaeological survival can give a unique and added value to a building or development and enhance the character of an area.

Undesignated archaeological assets and monuments are protected in the planning process, and are considered on an assessment of their merit. Designated assets, such as scheduled ancient monuments have statutory protection. A resource of records and archives of recent or past archaeological evidence helps the understanding and interpretation of the historic development of an area and the factors that have shaped it. Through the implementation of a planning application or other work, recording of archaeological remains adds to knowledge, adding to the evidence base in turn benefits prediction of archaeological potential and significance. Development proposals may affect buried archaeological remains, a building incorporating earlier built fabric, or a wider historic landscape, all factors which are considered in policy formulation and development management.

The archaeological importance of an area is set out in policy development and documentation and is applied in the development management process, when advising and negotiating planning applications to seek the right outcome for the archaeology. This includes guiding applicants to provide assessment and evaluation results at the appropriate time in the process. Assessment and evaluation have to be relevant and proportionate to the development, but may only provide partial answers to questions about archaeological survival and character. The reliability and scope of past archaeological records and the accessibility of areas for evaluation have to be considered. An application may raise specific issues in conflict with archaeological priorities; all the relevant policies have to be justified in a proportionate manner and timely decisions made.

Archaeological records are a continually growing resource, as new information is gained; knowledge is increased and new interpretations made. Managing an increasing number of records, and their regional or period research context, is essential to the understanding from which is set the framework and context of new work. Reports on key sites, with significant findings and reliable records, help to place new or more limited data in a wider and meaningful context.

The historic environment and the planning process

Historic buildings, monuments, and buried archaeological remains are a significant part of the environment and an important part of people's lives. They affect where people live, visit and work. In many areas new buildings and developments are part of an evolving city, town or landscape, and may house an historic site, museum or exhibition.

A wealth of information and guidance for evaluating the importance of buildings and the historic environment has been produced nationally and locally, in print and on websites. There are histories of individual buildings, monuments or areas, their management, upkeep and care. There is guidance on making a planning application, undertaking archaeological work and implementing a planning consent affecting archaeology. Reports of archaeological work and building recording can be found in locally-held Historic Environment Records, and national websites such as Heritage Gateway and ADS. A local authority has powers to designate conservation areas, write and adopt character summaries and management strategies, and may identify locally listed buildings. The English Heritage National Heritage List for England includes descriptions and maps of designated assets and they publish Selection Guides and Introductions to Heritage Assets, and since the planning regimes differ, with separate guidance from CADW, Historic Scotland or the Northern Ireland Environment Agency sources.

Where records of past archaeological investigations, maps and written records exist, these are hugely valuable, benefiting assessment of archaeological potential and new investigations. In turn, the results of modern, systematic investigation provide new evidence and dating, helping to reinterpret past work. This can change or reinforce understanding of a monument and the wider landscape. Small or seemingly insignificant areas of archaeological survival often contribute to a wider appreciation of a monument or the historic development of an area. Historic Environment Records, research frameworks, characterisation, archaeological databases and archive guidelines have been developed to manage, analyse and help understand the wealth of available archaeological information.

Planning archaeologists in local authorities deal with a vast range of policy and development proposals including: redevelopment of buildings; detailed design of the basement and foundations; alterations to buildings; to the townscape or landscape proposals. This includes giving advice on pre-planning and planning applications, implementation of a planning consent with conditions covering archaeological investigation and excavation, post excavation assessment and analysis, publication of the results and archiving of the records.

In many cases, the developer or building owner making a planning application will employ an archaeologist as one of a team of professional consultants. Where archaeology is predicted, the developer is required to submit an archaeological or historic environment assessment, in support of a planning application, including the potential archaeological impact of the development. This is the basis for constructive dialogue and negotiation with archaeological planning officers and decision by the elected members. For many complex developments, particularly where archaeological monuments and remains are a significant element, a positive and constructive multi-disciplinary approach with the local authority has evolved, involving the developer, archaeological consultants, planning consultants, engineers and architects. The early consideration of the archaeology can ensure a building design respects archaeological remains; the design of an integrated development programme to take account of the planning decision; an appropriate archaeological investigation, conservation and recording; and whether to achieve preservation *in-situ* or preservation by record. Archaeological work is controlled through conditions imposed as an element of a planning permission, dealing with all on-site excavation and post-excavation work, including archiving and publication of the results of this work, as well as building foundation design. The conditions may be staged to deal with successive phases of work.

Archaeological survival and development

In the City of London, a building's life can be short. The established financial and business role of the City means that there is a high rate of building development. The planning process in the City responds to the many needs of residents, business, community and visitors; it carries out local authority duties, and enhances its history and environment. Archaeological advice is part of an integrated development management service, and has a strong emphasis on pre-application discussion.

Conservation-area legislation, appreciation of individual and group value of buildings, and of townscape and landscape, has also changed building development. The re-use of buildings by re-cladding elevations or rebuilding behind a retained façade has enabled office accommodation to be altered and improved for modern needs, while still retaining a building of character important in the street scene. Approaches to building and engineering designs have changed to enable re-use of parts of a building structure and existing foundations. All these changes can have an archaeological impact, requiring careful consideration to ensure that archaeological remains are protected and recorded whilst retaining the built fabric.

The City is the historic centre of London, and has a long history of commerce and trade with examples of monuments and buildings from every stage of its history. It is rich in buildings, areas, visible and buried archaeological resources, and is a continual source of study and research. It is one of the most investigated urban areas of the country and there is a vast resource of archaeological and historic records, collected over centuries, which complements the built environment and buried remains. Records have been made since the 17th century and nearly 11% of the event records in the Greater London Historic Environment Record are from the City.

The modern townscape has been shaped by extreme events and rebuilding, including after the 1666 Great Fire and World War II. This has influenced building layout, the street plan and construction methods. After the destruction of WWII, in 1945 a large swathe of land was redeveloped; sites were amalgamated, streets realigned and new roads created. Modern buildings were designed to maximise the availability of natural light using rapid building methods and new materials such as reinforced concrete and steel frames. They replaced bomb-damaged buildings, and created new jobs at a time when some materials were in short supply and difficult to obtain. Many offices built in the 1950s and 1960s have since been redeveloped and it is estimated that half the area of office floor space in the City was rebuilt between 1985 and 1993.

The deregulation of the financial market in 1986, and other changes in financial trading led to a demand for a new type of office building, with large open-plan trading floors and higher floor-to-ceiling heights to accommodate services following the increased use of computers. The minimal number of internal columns required to provide flexible and open plan floor areas influenced foundation design and building techniques. New construction methods emphasised early planning of the development programme and integration of all aspects of demolition and construction. This included understanding of building in an historic area, and acknowledging and predicting potential archaeological sites and monuments where investigation was needed. This was especially important where undesignated remains of national importance survived. Archaeological objectives and recording became integrated into the planning and development process.

Where buildings or remains have been lost and not recorded, there are irretrievable gaps. Our knowledge of the historic development is affected by archaeological survival and records and, sadly, such gaps will remain unfilled in many places. The fragmentary nature of archaeological survival, as well as factors that affected the quality and scope of earlier archaeological records is part of the surviving archaeological history. It is therefore important to understand the context of the decision-making current when they were created. Decisions on archaeological potential have to be made on existing information and records of varying reliability.

This resource of archaeological and historic records is however invaluable in assessing the archaeological potential of a development. Evaluation is frequently required to confirm or supplement the findings of archaeological assessment, and to consider the archaeological implications of a planning application. Evaluation can be challenging where the areas under evaluation are inaccessible, but is essential to characterise current knowledge of the archaeological remains and add certainty and understanding of archaeological potential and development impact. In densely built up areas and occupied buildings, evaluation can be difficult. Building occupation and uses, tenancy agreements, potential structural instability of the building, and neighbouring deep reinforced basement-slabs can limit evaluation possibilities and delay obtaining valuable information.

Modern building demolition and construction requires a detailed and precise archaeological response, with an understanding of the archaeological potential and development impact so that an appropriate programme of archaeological work for investigation and recording is designed. The complexity of a demolition and construction programme means that archaeological work may be carried out over an extended period. It may accompany essential structural work for underpinning, façade support, or basement excavation. It can take place within a standing building, or a cleared site, or a combination of both. A development programme involves a complex sequence of activities all with critical stages and timing. The archaeological unit carrying out excavation has to be experienced in a number of areas; understanding the archaeological potential, its context and complexity; working to the approved method statement and sector standards; an understanding of building techniques and truncation; and able to work safely in a building basement or on a site alongside demolition or construction activities.

Post-war recording and the importance of past records

Post-war archaeological recording was planned, during and following devastating war-time bombing, as part of the reconstruction of the City. Historian interest, recording, and artefact collection over many years had confirmed the importance of the City's archaeology and history. The City Wall and Roman Fort Wall was exposed and investigated in several areas and the City took these opportunities to preserve and display them as part of post-war rebuilding, eg in the Barbican. New discoveries and the accuracy of the records made are due to a number of individuals, notably Professor Grimes, Ralph Merrifield, Ivor Noel Hume and Peter Marsden, working with the Roman and Mediaeval London Excavation Council and Guildhall Museum, and many highly motivated staff and volunteers (*see also* Sheldon *et al this volume*).

The pace of post-war change, limited access for archaeological recording and loss of archaeological remains caused great concern. In 1973 the influential RESCUE publication, *The Future of London's Past* (Biddle *et al* 1973*)* concluded that due to building and railway construction, nearly 25% of the City had been archaeologically destroyed by 1970 and the pace of development meant that there was only 15 or 20 years left to discover the early history of the capital. Although the rate of archaeological loss has been high, remains do survive and archaeological potential is assessed and evaluated in the planning process.

The investigation of sites of post-war building developments has led to greater understanding of archaeological survival and the archaeological impact of buildings and foundations of that period. This, in turn, helps prediction of survival on similar sites, all informing the planning process. Knowledge of the extent of destruction by building basements, the impact of constructions such as bank-vaults and lift-cores, and of different piling techniques, has increased and is better understood. A high number of closely-spaced piled foundations, or a deep reinforced-concrete basement floor, can cause total destruction or archaeological evidence, but there are exceptions where there has been astonishing survival in such circumstances. On some sites, where there has been successive post-war rebuilding, archaeological records may have been made on each rebuilding. In these cases the later work can help the reinterpretation of the earlier records. At the Millennium Bridge site, excavation for new foundations revealed medieval structures and buildings, some of which had been archaeologically recorded prior to development 30 years earlier (*see* Figure 1).

Understanding building disturbance, the extent and depth of basements, foundations and methods of construction, is as important as assessing potential archaeological survival and may demonstrate that no archaeology has survived. Contemporary photographs of a building or area, and of war-damage, site-clearance and construction-progress also add valuable information. Ironically post-war road widening has preserved earlier building-lines, sealing archaeological remains below earlier basements. The reinstatement of an earlier building-line for townscape and conservation reasons can here disturb scarce surviving archaeological remains unaffected by post-war building. Evidence of seemingly poor or limited survival still adds to the existing records of an area and can put previous interpretations into context. In many cases excavation on the site of a post-war building has yielded new and significant information, eg on the riverside.

The late 3rd century Roman riverside wall survives in places below a modern road and has been recorded in some areas of previous development. Riverbank House in Upper Thames Street is the 3rd building to be built on this site since the war, and the potential for the Roman wall to survive at the perimeter of the development needed assessment. Digging an evaluation trench would have involved an excavation more than 2 metres deep below 19th century basements and the modern pavement, in an area with multiple modern services including telecommunication cables which could not be moved. A series of boreholes was used to evaluate the area. When the building was demolished, archaeological excavation exposed the riverside wall, it was then recorded, protected and the piled foundations were redesigned to avoid any damage. The post-excavation analysis includes reassessment and enhancement of the previous archaeological records of the site, and includes new dating material.

Figure 1 Excavation prior to the construction of new foundations for the Millennium Bridge, 2007

Photo © Museum of London Archaeology

How to use the archaeological information in planning applications and certainty

Archaeology is often seen as high-risk and high-cost, a cause of delay of a planning application, or of work on site. Developers and building-owners seek certainty in making planning applications and designing new buildings. Early advice and discussion between the archaeological planning-officer and developer, assessment of the archaeological evidence, archaeological potential, and need for planned archaeological investigation and recording, can provide certainty and ensure that archaeology is an integral part of the programme. The City's policies set out the importance of the archaeological resource, and the value of improving understanding and dissemination of new information and new interpretations. With good knowledge of the archaeological potential the chance of unexpected remains is minimal and, where uncertainty may remain, methods to deal with this can be planned into the archaeological and development programme.

Evaluation at an early stage in archaeologically sensitive areas is essential in understanding archaeological survival. Careful planning of this work is needed where areas may be inaccessible due to building occupation or where basement slabs are deep or heavily reinforced. Assessment and evaluation results are part of the local authority's consideration of a planning application, and are used to inform changes to a building design, minimise archaeological impact, and design a programme of archaeological work. Where a development has limited impact, design changes can avoid or reduce archaeological disturbance completely.

The understanding of archaeological potential has to be supported by an archaeological and historical evidence-base, which includes the identification of areas of uncertainty, and the need for additional archive research or evaluation. Analysis of the evidence uses plans, images, and written accounts of existing or past buildings on the site, their foundations and basement design. Many existing buildings were constructed with no consideration of any archaeological potential; material above the natural geology could be recorded by engineers as 'fill', or as obstructions to be removed or worked around. In some cases excavation for basements and foundations may have been very destructive, but in others, only limited areas may have been disturbed. If the latter, it can be astonishing to see how small areas of archaeology survive between large areas of foundation, or see a modern concrete pile has sliced through a robust Roman timber or medieval masonry wall. Continuity of development on a single plot may, in some cases, preserve remains by the re-use of older foundations, or built-over masonry walls survive because it was unnecessary to remove them (*see* Figure 2).

City of London: character and development

The City is a multi-layered environment with buildings of diverse ages and styles. There are many statutory designated assets, including Listed Buildings, Scheduled Monuments, Conservation Areas, Historic Parks and Gardens, as well as undesignated assets including visible and buried archaeological monuments and remains. A rapid rate of re-development has given opportunities to add to knowledge and to enhance this historic environment.

It is one of the most excavated urban areas in the country and the rate of change

Figure 2 Excavations at Basinghall Street showing medieval structures and post-war building foundations, 2005

Photo © Museum of London Archaeology

has given opportunities to add to knowledge and to enhance the historic environment, through conservation, display, and recording.

However where buried remains exist, exposure and display may be avoided where remains are fragile or vulnerable to damage. Marking out features or a building plan in landscaping or within a building, and signage, can successfully reveal the relationship between buried archaeology and the modern townscape. For example the Roman amphitheatre in the Guildhall Art Gallery, in Guildhall Yard (off Gresham Street) London EC2V 5AE, includes masonry and timber remains, in a contemporary display.

Completed in 2000, the modern and historic City can be seen together and the building houses the Art Gallery, City Marketing Suite, City model and offices. Views of the amphitheatre from the Art Gallery and an opening partition between the Marketing Suite and amphitheatre allow the spaces to be used and enjoyed together. Outside, a line of slate paving in Guildhall Yard marks the position of the arena of the amphitheatre; the centre of which is marked by a plaque, drawing attention to the buried archaeology and remains on display. It reflects the historic relationship between the Roman remains and the Guildhall; and the apparent influence of these on the development of the medieval townscape, including the Guildhall, Church of St Lawrence Jewry and surrounding street pattern.

The development of the General Post Office in the early 20th century led to the discovery and preservation of part of the City Wall and a medieval bastion. The re-development of the site as the headquarters of Bank of America 100 years later, gave the opportunity to enhance the display of the monument. The site is in, and borders, three Conservation

Areas, and includes three upstanding and buried Scheduled Monuments, and two Listed Buildings. It also affects the setting of many Listed Buildings within St Paul's Cathedral Protected Views area, as well as non-scheduled archaeological remains. A foundation and basement scheme was designed which avoided the Scheduled archaeological remains and other important remains, but which still provided the office floor-space and large trading-floors required by the bank. The preserved city wall and bastion was given an improved setting, with a dedicated entrance and visible from the courtyard of the new building.

The south-west churchyard of St Paul's Cathedral contains the Grade II listed remains of the pre-1666 Great Fire Cathedral Cloister and Chapter House. The masonry structures were partly buried, and partly visible above ground. The planting and landscaping in this area had grown, obscuring the monument, and its importance and relationship to the Wren Cathedral. Proposals to re-landscape this area and provide level access to the south-transept entrance focussed on the pre-Fire remains, depicting the Cloister and Chapter House in new paving and low stone-walls. A plan of the pre-Fire and Wren Cathedrals, designed by Richard Kindersley in Purbeck marble and Welsh slate, explains in an informative and attractive way the two Cathedrals, their scale, and differences in alignment. It is pleasing to look at and removes the need for an extended amount of information, enhancing the visual amenity of the space and appreciation of the Cathedral and its churchyard.

The building of Bucklersbury House in 1951 on a post-war cleared site, was the cause of a major controversy attracting wide public, media and government attention (*see also* Sheldon *et al this volume*). The discovery of the Temple of Mithras and its sculptures on the site in 1954 by Professor Grimes was one of the most significant discoveries of the 20th century in the City and a rare example of the survival of the plan of a Roman building. It led to a very public debate where strong and conflicting views were expressed; from a wish to preserve the temple in a re-designed building, to objections that preservation would impede essential development and post-war reconstruction of the City. The result was the excavation and subsequent re-building of the temple, some years later, on a different part of the site, divorced from its origins, raised above both the modern street-level and the Roman ground-level. It's incorrect position, orientation, layout, and idealised form were misleading. Although the re-building was controversial and criticised, the reconstructed temple is of national significance and one of the few accessible and visible Roman monuments in the City townscape.

Redevelopment proposals provided the opportunity to relocate the temple to its original position and level. A brief was written and a positive dialogue with the developers and their professional team resulted in a building design incorporating the temple in a two level display space. The site owners, the City of London, and English Heritage entered into a legal agreement to protect the temple. This included its dismantling and storage during re-development, and subsequent reconstruction on the site. The temple is now a Grade II Listed Building. The list description refers to the temple as one of the first examples of development-related archaeological conservation. In the new building, the temple will be restored to its correct level, orientation, and location, accompanied by an exhibition explaining the structure, its history, discovery, and reconstruction.

Figure 3 Design of the display of the Temple of Mithras in its original location in the new building on the site of Bucklersbury House, 2012

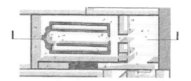

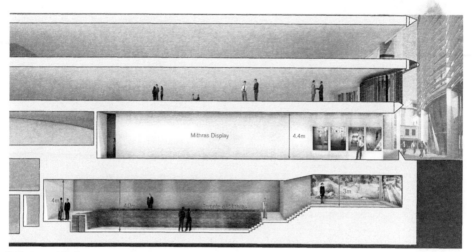

© Foster and Partners

Surviving *in-situ* remains are too fragile to display, and have been protected and preserved, but will be marked out in the floor next to the reconstructed temple.

The redevelopment of the1960s Drapers Gardens tower, designed by Richard Seifert, required a carefully planned programme to allow concurrent archaeological excavation and demolition of the tallest habitable building in the country. The excavation revealed an exceptionally well-preserved Roman landscape. The remains recorded in the waterlogged, but now buried, Upper Walbrook valley included timber-lined channels and drains, fences, a road, buildings and yards, and excellent survival of nationally important finds including timber and metal work. Drapers Gardens was one of the tallest buildings in the City when it was constructed; its demolition required the removal of 3 metre-deep reinforced-concrete raft-foundation with controlled use of explosives. The redevelopment has significantly enhanced understanding of the Roman and later development of this area and the exploitation of the Walbrook River. The replacement of the tower with a lower building has improved skyline and local views of this part of the City, enhancing adjoining conservation areas. The archaeological results will contribute to further study and interpretation of the wider Walbrook valley in and to the north of the City (*see* Figure 4).

Excavation and replacement of statutory services, such as water, gas and electricity supplies, can affect archaeological remains, and the ground below roads and pavements,

Figure 4 Well preserved Roman deposits, surviving between modern pile foundations of the Drapers Gardens, 2007

Photo © Pre-Construct Archaeology Ltd; reproduced by kind permission

where there are no basements, is an important resource. Although the constant digging and replacement of services may have destroyed remains, archaeological recording has, in places, revealed good survival of medieval and earlier structures. The Thames water-main replacement work in the City has been rewarding in uncovering, and preserving, remains of the St Paul's Cathedral precinct wall built by Sir Christopher Wren and remains of the Church of St Bartholomew by the Exchange, demolished in the early 19th century (*see* Figure 5).

This work is permitted under existing planning legislation and does not require planning permission, however it is essential that archaeological monitoring and recording takes place to current standards and guidance so that archaeological information can be recorded and is not lost or destroyed.

Archaeological records and publications increase in number each year and access to them is becoming easier due to the increasing use of websites and 'umbrella' sites such as the Archaeology Data Services and the Heritage Gateway. The digitisation of past publications such as the *London Archaeologist* and *Transactions of the London and Middlesex Archaeology Society* provide a vast and valuable resource for a world-wide audience. There is still a place for printed information, the Museum of London

Figure 5 St Paul's Cathedral precinct wall revealed by Thameswater main replacement work, St Paul's Churchyard, 2009

Photo © Compass Archaeology

Archaeology *Londinium* map (MoLA 2011) updates an earlier Ordnance Survey map and places the Roman city in a (modern) central London context, which includes modern Southwark, and a map and overview of Roman London. In the future, challenges will be to maintain the high publication standards achieved, and to retain their accessibility, specialist reports may be available on the web only. Increasing costs will put pressure on increasing web publication but this may not be accessible for all who would wish to use it. An essential is to provide an increasing amount of data, through websites and other media, to improve accessibility of information and reach differing audiences.

The numbers of developer-funded academic publications increases each year. Extremely well-written and illustrated, and with glowing reviews, they may be supplemented by 'popular' publications and leaflets, at more modest production and sale cost. The major sites merit publication in several forms: a principal academic book, a 'popular' book and perhaps a leaflet, especially where remains and finds from the site are on display.

Publications covering more than one site, a wider area, or a monument may provide a valuable overview, incorporating results of recent and past archaeological work. Questions of building development, street lay-out, topography, and land-uses can be considered in a wider landscape. Research and analysis of both natural and man-made features benefit from this approach, but it can be difficult to finance where publication is developer-funded and site-specific.

Research agendas which set a framework for archaeological work should encourage a closer connection between university-based and developer-funded work, however this can be difficult in practice due to different time constraints. Archaeological work, which is part of a building development and developer-funded, has its own programme including for publication. The published results of the excavation should be linked to the development, to include a description of the new building and the circumstances of its design development, thus placing the new development firmly in its historic context. The donation of the archive of the site to a central repository adds value as this makes it possible for the site to be researched and studied in its wider period or landscape context. The archive has vast potential to increase knowledge and establish links between all archaeological work carried out, whether by amateur, professional, student, research or developer led. The archive and the local authority Historic Environment Record can provide access to the growing amount of 'grey literature', all recording valuable 'unpublished' work. Increasing digitisation and web-based access may help to unlock this potential for a wider use and purpose.

The statutory designation of Scheduling does not recognise all sites or monuments of national importance, and in many cases, only part of a Scheduled Monument may have statutory protection, possibly due to limited knowledge about its survival at the time of Scheduling. Where remains of national importance do survive, sensitive basement and foundation design is needed to respect and ensure preservation; examples in the City include remains of the City Wall, the Roman fort, and the Roman basilica-forum. Such schemes can involve controlled recording of remains to preserve their character and date and to put in place sufficient protection such as covering with Terram (geotextiles used to enhance the performance and design life of granular layers by providing the filtration and separation functions) and sand, prior to reburial. An explanation of the decisions made to preserve and the means of preservation would be contained in the site records.

Conclusions

Great advances have been made in archaeological knowledge and historical developments due to positive engagement within the planning and development process, proportionate and systematic consideration of archaeological potential. Guidance and standards relating to archaeological work of assessment, evaluation, excavation and post excavation method and techniques give consistency. The National Policy Planning Framework (DCLG 2012) provides the current government guidance on the historic environment and the inclusion of all policy guidance in this one document underlines the equal weighting of all policy issues.

Where there may be a chance of unexpected finds, the possibility and implications can be planned in a structured, managed way as an integrated part of development, starting at pre-planning application stage, through to work on-, and subsequently, off-site. In a developed urban area where archaeological knowledge is high, and numerous records exist, this can be easier to understand and achieve, and give confidence in the process. It is to be expected that historical remains survive in an historical area, with a potentially complicated picture of survival below both modern and historic buildings. Good decision-making can achieve the integration of archaeological priorities with development and good design.

The importance of a robust and well-founded evidence-base of archaeological and historic information helps understanding of the resource and is essential to support development-management and ensure that archaeological remains are not removed without recording. The historic environment is valuable in providing a unique identity and sense of place. The balance of maintaining and enhancing high quality services and decision-making which engages with all stakeholders in an uncertain financial climate is essential. This is especially important at a time when localism is becoming established and developments can raise conflicting policy issues. There is a continual need to progress archaeological understanding and techniques, to interpret new and existing records, to add to existing data and to improve access so that existing records in archives and historic environment records are readily available to as wide an audience of potential users as possible.

Acknowledgements
Thanks go to Museum of London Archaeology, Foster and Partners, Pre-Construct Archaeology Ltd . and Compass Archaeology for permission to reproduce their images, and also to Stuart Cakebread, Barnaby Collins, Dr Christopher Constable, Sophie Jackson, Kate Murphy, Geoff Potter, Victoria Ridgeway, Dr Jane Sidell, Adam Single and Kim Stabler.

References
Biddle M, Hudson DM, Heighway C, 1973, *The future of London's past: a survey of the archaeological implications of planning and development in the nation's capital,* RESCUE publication 4, Worcester

Department for Communities and Local Government (DCLG), 2012, *National Planning Policy Framework,* The Stationery Office, London

Museum of London Archaeology (MoLA), 2011, *Londinium: A new map and guide to Roman London,* Museum of London Archaeology, London

Chapter 3

Commercial archaeology:
looking backwards, looking forwards or just going round in circles

Hester Cooper-Reade

Introduction

As archaeologists we have been able to chart the rise of commerce across the centuries. In the modern world, profit, private enterprise and a competitive market are often seen as essential components of any business environment where commerce takes place. This is particularly the case in archaeology where the particular history of the discipline has resulted in the need to stress the commercial as a key differential to the 'un-business-like' and non-commercial, voluntary and local authority-based field archaeology of the decades before PPG16.

However, we should not forget the many other models and economic relationships where commerce also takes place, nor should we forget the fact that the product archaeologists offer is not one that would normally be exchanged in the commercial environment. A number of organisations currently engaged in commercial archaeology such as the archaeological trusts, or the field 'units' based in museums, local authorities and universities, were present before the post-PPG commercial age, and although they have adapted to provide a commercial service, these organisations have often sat uneasily against their private sector counterparts.

This chapter looks back to the position in which archaeology found itself in 1974, the subsequent birth of commercial archaeology, and its development against the changing economic, social, and regulatory framework from the mid-1980s onwards. Although commercial archaeological practice includes a diverse range of activity, the focus here is on the planning-led activity that provides for most of the sector. In keeping with the original RESCUE publication this is a highly personalised account rather than a rigorous academic paper. The intention is rather to provoke thought and discussion around a new 21st century crisis for archaeology and the future that we are trying to create.

A certain amount of navel-gazing in relation to the development of commercial archaeology has perhaps prevented us from understanding the bigger picture. Archaeologists have tended to concentrate on the methods by which academic and research value can be gleaned from rescue archaeology and have as a result failed to understand the market in which we operate. In times of great change it is worrying to report that by all accounts we do not seem to have a robust and sustainable commercial model. Furthermore, although the Southport Report (Southport Group 2011), coming out of the 2010 Institute for Archaeologists annual conference, has helped redress the balance, the preceding decades generally showed a lack of debate on the public value of archaeology and the worth of the asset we were creating.

Commercial exchange requires the goods or services being exchanged to have value. That value might be assigned at several points in the chain; it might even be the case that the person who pays for the goods or services gets less value out of them than the user of the product. Where this is the case and where the use of the product has more value to the end-user than the person who pays for it, problems with the way the market operates will inevitably arise. It is not hard to see why commercial archaeology has proved so problematical both philosophically and practically for those currently involved in that sector.

Commercial archaeological practice: looking back to 1974

If we are to make any sense of the world of commercial archaeology that we find ourselves in today, I believe it is worthwhile re-visiting the context within which the 1974 book, *Rescue Archaeology*, was written. In doing so, it might be useful to reflect on the less than ideal position that the profession currently finds itself in. When *Rescue Archaeology* was published by Pelican Books in 1974, a commercial archaeology of the type we see today would have been entirely inconceivable. As argued by those on the RESCUE committee in the early 1970s, one can only make sense of the present with a proper understanding of the past (*see* Hogarth 1974).

Looking back at the history of the development of commercial archaeology with the luxury of hindsight, it is perhaps not so surprising that we are where we are now. Collectively we have been fairly poor historians; maybe because the present that we do have has been, quite understandably, resisted at every stage from so many quarters and in so many different ways. On the other hand why would an almost entirely voluntary-led profession consider commercialism and a move away from state funding with anything other than hostility and suspicion? Our response to these issues has set the scene for the years to come and, as some would argue, has led to the development of a market that now fails to function at all. The commercial archaeology we have today, with its low wages, poor career-structure and over-flowing stores (all featuring in other chapters in this book), is largely a product of the collective failure of the profession to understand why the market we have persisted in trying to operate in cannot work, and our inability to reconcile the real end-product of archaeology with the process by which it is commissioned and paid for.

If we had embraced the 'commercialism' of archaeology differently, 40 years on, it is difficult to say if we would now be celebrating the development of a mature and respected profession equally at home in the business community as in the academic and voluntary one. How could those writing in 1974 have predicted the impact of Thatcherism and the inevitable rise of the private sector and market place competition? Even a few years ago, who would have predicted the darkening clouds caused by the 'credit crunch' or the new philosophy that champions self-regulation, and a state made smaller? The limitations on what local authorities now consider their core services and the desire to de-regulate and free up the planning process will have an increasing impact on commercial archaeology. I am not sure we can easily predict the nature of the changes, or our response to them, but they will surely engender as radical a change as that of Planning Policy Guideline 16 (PPG 16, DoE 1990).

PPG16 and the 'polluter pays' debate, however, came later and was also unforeseen in 1974. When it did come, the concept of polluter was taken too literally and archaeology became a site-clearance product, divorced from the concept of public benefit. Public benefit has since re-appeared on the agenda, but is only just emerging from a long period during which it was synonymous with open days and popular booklets sold to the buyer of the service. These were seen, at best, as a marketing tool to show the social responsibility of their business, at worst as a planning requirement that must be fulfilled. This is not to take away from some of the often excellent examples of outreach and popular dissemination that have brought archaeology to a much wider audience, but rather to point out that we have lost the 'philosophy' of value, instead replacing it with something that can be measured and priced as part of a project proposal.

From time to time RESCUE have returned to the various iterations of a national structure for archaeology funded by the public purse, or, since the early 1990s and PPG16, a developer tax. However, this model of archaeology has never really found widespread favour amongst archaeological managers and employers, or politicians. At the time of writing commercial archaeology may have developed imperfectly, but the imposition of a tax-led regional structure is still as unthinkable to many as the idea of competition was in the mid-1970s. Imperfect or not, commercial archaeologists currently have to work within a system that requires the 'polluter' to commission and pay for archaeological work directly. How we identify the product or the unit of consumption and what we do with it are entirely different questions. Trying to define these questions, let alone answer them, only tends to highlight the tensions within archaeology and the absence of an over-arching framework within which commercial archaeology sits naturally alongside the other archaeologies; academic, voluntary, museum-based or public.

The publication of *Rescue Archaeology* (Rahtz 1974) coincided with the failure of the Department of the Environment (DoE) initiative to set up a regional structure largely funded by local authorities, and, with it the realisation that the increasing level of development throughout the UK was having an unprecedented impact on the archaeological resource, stretching the existing voluntary system beyond its limits.

In 1974 Robert Kiln and Graham Arnold, both on the RESCUE committee, used their high level business skills to urge a more commercial/business-like approach and the use of modern PR, but this was within the context of fund-raising and ensuring that the local voluntary group had a robust financial and organisational model (Thomas and Arnold 1974, Kiln 1974). Development was hugely destructive and would have a significant impact on the environment, but one gets the impression that it was seen as an inevitable part of 'progress'. There was no argument that those involved in the destruction should be liable for the cost of archaeological excavation. Instead the prevailing view was that it was the Government who oversaw this development and was the responsible party, and therefore funds should rightly come from the public purse. Culture and heritage were too important not to be the responsibility of the state.

Back in 1974, the archaeology described in the Rahtz volume was carried out by 'hobby' or voluntary archaeologists, working on sites often directed and supervised by a small team of professionals paid out of an excavation grant which, in turn, was largely funded out of the public purse. Increasingly the DoE provided a grant on the assumption that the local authority would also contribute. We recognise, in the chapters of the 1974 volume, the beginnings of the Central Unit (founded as such in 1976) and the 'circuit digger' in the small teams of professional archaeologists that travelled far and wide, following DoE funding from dig to dig. We recognise the beginnings of the county archaeologist and archaeological units as the scale of work increased and as local authorities and museums began to employ an archaeological officer to oversee the work that was required in each of their areas. The universities were also much in evidence, although, as the 1974 book points out, the summer excavation was somewhat incompatible with development which was a year round activity. Indeed the idea of digging through the autumn and winter was a relatively novel one at the time the book was written.

We are reminded of the foundations of a number of city-based trusts (Oxford, York, Winchester) formed out of excavation committees and providing the paid, professional back-up for excavations undertaken using volunteers on subsistence payments. More unusually we are reminded of the Kent Rescue Unit, which, along with the new Trusts in Oxford, York and Winchester, perhaps provided the preferred model for the future organisation of archaeology within England. There was no concept that the model would change, how else would those that pursued archaeology for interest without pay remain involved, and who else would provide the labour required to assist with the excavation of sites and any subsequent analysis work. In this world, the ability to negotiate grants or additional funding from the DoE and any other source that could be persuaded to contribute, were the measures of success; although even then the distance that this put between the 'professional' site director and the time 'he' (invariably a 'he' in Rahtz 1974) needed to spend on site thinking about archaeology and supervising relatively unskilled labour was a source of frustration.

Within a few years the 'volunteers' were not hobby archaeologists who earned their income from other sources and spent their holidays digging. Instead, they had become an itinerant group of workers surviving on free accommodation and daily subsistence. Another decade or so on from that, the beginnings of a more commercial archaeology were seen in the drive towards privatisation. From 1980 until 1987, British diggers were predominantly young people on various government-funded community programmes run through the Manpower Services Commission. These schemes, despite the well attested problems they created over publication and backlog, were pivotal in the history of commercial archaeology (Crump 1987; Everill 2012). They perpetuated the idea of a small team of professionals supervising a team of semi- or unskilled excavators, often on low pay; and they cemented the role of the local-authority archaeologists as the key organisational-unit carrying out large-scale archaeological work in the area covered by their authority. Few, if any, of those organisations would qualify as commercial, although much was done to develop the theory of archaeological practice that still defines the way in which commercial archaeology is specified and carried out.

The rise and fall of the Manpower Services Commission coincided with the new philosophies of the Thatcher government. Privatisation was the buzzword of the second term from 1983 onwards and it wasn't long before attention was turned to local government and the health service with the introduction of Compulsory Competitive Tendering. Key to this was the idea that local authorities should be enablers and not providers. CCT as such did not have significant impact on archaeological units until the market testing of the 1990s and Best Value of the early 2000s, but it did start to set the philosophical framework for competition and the idea that other providers could sit alongside, or even replace, the local authority service. During the mid-1980s EU environmental assessment legislation had opened a few people's eyes to the prospect of a role for private-sector consultancy. A very small number of private archaeological practises and consultancies can trace their origins to the period before changes to the planning regulations signalled the slow awakenings of a new commercially-focused archaeology, but these are the exceptions. Add to this the introduction of PPG16 in 1990 and the scene was set for the first growing pains of commercial, competitive archaeology.

When one looks at the organisational history of the commercial archaeologists of today, it is striking that few began as new organisations set up to deliver a different type of commercial archaeology. PCA, Headland and consultancies such as CgMs are unusual and, although the time-line is quite difficult to establish other than from memory and anecdote, the very first privately-formed company that carried out fieldwork was probably Tempus Reparatum (1985/6). That same organisation has the dubious distinction of also being one of the first high-profile business failures.

The theme has been one of adaptation; the Trusts of Wessex and Oxford being amongst the first to embrace competitive tendering and the then radical approach of working outside their traditional geographical area, while AOC, spawned out of the central unit in Scotland, expanded to the whole of the UK. A number of the small and medium-sized privately-owned companies in existence today were set up between 1994 and 1997 (eg, Thames Valley Archaeological Services, AMS (Foundations)). Then as now the rise of private enterprise was often linked to large-scale lay-offs from the more traditional public and third-sector model. All of a sudden the option of setting up on one's own presented itself as a viable course of action. The figures are hard to come by, but the impact of the 2008 Stock Market crash, and the widespread shrinkage in employment opportunities that followed, encouraged many more archaeologists to set up their own commercial practices, often as a sole trader. We have yet to understand whether this was a temporary reaction to the reduction in traditional employment, or an indication of more long-term changes to the commercial landscape.

The slightly mixed heritage of the more long-established organisations has meant that the first decades of commercial archaeology have been characterised by a desire to highlight independence. A quick scan of the websites of most present-day commercial archaeological organisations shows that the word 'independent' is seen as a key selling point. In most cases 'independent' is used to denote 'independently owned' and not constrained by the larger, often publicly-quoted organisation, though in the archaeological sense this is used to denote independent in voice, behind 'Chinese-Wall'. Those with an entirely commercial set-up are keen to stress that they alone can carry out their work for the client without interference from some other stake-holder whose opposing views may hold sway. The charitable trusts were at the forefront of commercialism and through their status they have also retained their commitment to the educational aims of archaeology. The underlying suggestion is that many 'other' organisations operate in an un-business-like manner. Maybe in our desire to be business-led we failed to retain those bits of public-service delivery most helpful in offering a product to an end-user who has no commercial relationship with those paying for and delivering that product. However this alone cannot be the reason for the generally accepted failure of commercial practice to operate with sufficient profit to allow proper investment into their businesses and the wider development of the sector.

At its most basic level commercial archaeology can only succeed if it operates in the context of a mature market and is paid for using a business transaction that gives sufficiently monetary value to sustain the profession required to deliver it, and thus the long-term benefit to the nation. After the first 40 years or so of commercial archaeology we are certainly not operating in a mature market, and few people would claim that the current market-value of archaeology provides for a sustainable profession. If commercial archaeology has until now proved so inadequate in delivering a product universally recognised for its social and community value, what does the future hold? Here in 2014, 40 years on, archaeology is still in the process of change and, as in 1974, the outcomes are not at all clear. There are many more questions than answers.

Where does commercial archaeology sit on a spectrum between those that benefit through the academic and publicly accessible product, and those that pay and have a vested interest in carrying out the work as cheaply, and with as little requirement, as possible? Do we even know who the customers actually are? What is our relationship with those that pay for the work; and does the rest of the sector have any responsibility to take account of their needs even when these conflict with their views on the protection of the heritage? Can commercial archaeology survive as a development of what it currently is, or does it have to look to new models or different ways of working? Does it simply need to become more commercial, find ways of investing for profit, as with any other business, and just get on with it? Does the rest of the sector understand the consequences of a *laissez-faire* approach that, possibly quite rightly, expects commercial organisations to sort out effective competition and working for profit themselves? How is the profession going to deal with the fall-out from the inevitability of failed commercial organisations?

Whether or not the future is bright may well depend on how the archaeological profession answers these questions as it reacts to a new set of challenges that will have just as much impact as the changes that occurred from the mid-1970s onwards. Indeed, it could be argued that these challenges are the result of a continual process of change, the response to which archaeologists have been grappling with since the 1970s.

Commercial archaeological practice: moving forwards from 1974

Despite many imperfections, we have come a long way and at least now have a commercial model which is able to respond to the requirements of the system...just. Economic and social change demands continuous development, whether housing for an ever increasing population, or roads and railways to create a more connected and vibrant economy. The sheer scale of future development and potential destruction of archaeology would have been unimaginable at the time Rescue Archaeology was written in 1974. Though without the intervention of those that made up the RESCUE Committee it is arguable that archaeology would have never been more than a hit-and-miss affair of high profile campaigns and emergency funding for those sites that captured the public imagination. The simple principle that the developer should pay the cost of archaeological work has shaped archaeology in the most recent decades. It is perhaps ironic that the defining concept of the commercial archaeology that we all take for granted is a by-product of Thatcherism, but it has provided the foundation for ensuring that archaeology is afforded some protection within the planning system. Without someone to charge for the product, and without a body of legislation and policy that requires archaeological work, the provision for archaeology would be far weaker than it is.

Archaeologists now have a voice through their own professional body, the Chartered Institute for Archaeologists (CIfA), and, with specific relevance to commercial archaeology, the newly reinvigorated employer's body, The Federation of Archaeological Managers and Employers (FAME). FAME of course began as the Standing Conference of Archaeological Unit Managers (SCAUM), the organisation equivalent to ALGAO for local authority archaeological-unit managers. The Southport Report (Southport Group 2011) and initiatives leading out of it have had some successes in influencing legislation and government policy, and perhaps indicate a developing and more recognised profession. The former IfA has now received its Royal Charter, a huge step on the path to a mature profession. However, with the exception of some of the activities of FAME, none of this seems to have had much impact on the development of commercial archaeological practice or the market within which it operates. Maybe in time the simple economics of supply and demand will allow organisations to operate on a more commercially viable basis; maybe chartership will create barriers to entry. Maybe commercial organisations will find the funds to invest in capacity and training in order to meet an ever-increasing cost of compliance, and an ever-decreasing source of well-qualified archaeologists entering the profession. On the other hand, there are a few warning signs that this will not happen without considerable changes to the environment in which commercial archaeology is delivered, and without a more considered response to the challenges that currently exist. The rescue archaeology of 1974 was perhaps facing a simpler crisis; archaeology was being dug up by development and destroyed without record. The continued rescue of that archaeology is the backdrop to the way in which 21st century commercial archaeology operates and, arguably, colours many of the issues that we now urgently need to solve. We have to be careful that we look forwards, rather than backwards

We need to look forwards in order to deal with a number of pressing issues that will shape the development of commercial practice, not over the next few decades, but over the next few years. The ones that loom largest are dealing with the reduction of state involvement; understanding and engaging all of our customers; considering the impact of decisions within the context of a commercial environment; and facilitating a commercial environment that allows those that employ archaeologists sufficient capacity to invest in training and technological change. These things are the responsibility of the whole profession and are too important to be left to market forces alone.

The single most pressing issue that is likely to have a profound impact on commercial archaeological practice is of course the reduction of state involvement. The current political climate does not provide for the 'polluter pays whatever the cost', and the market in which current commercial practice operates does not allow for the contractor to pass on the cost whatever it is. Government policy is one of freeing-up the planning system and reducing cost in order to kick-start economic development and solve the housing crisis. Deficit-reduction measures can only lead to an accelerating decline in local-government archaeological posts and a weakening of the provision for archaeology in the planning system. Despite its imperfections the current system does at least provide a basic structure for archaeology. However discussions on how the profession will respond to the changing political landscape seemed to have stalled around the idea that we can carry on as normal, better defining the requirements of the system, and allowing the free, largely unregulated and, possibly failed, market to take charge. A decision to assume that a combination of carrot and stick will ensure that commercial practice steps up to the mark to deliver the archaeological vision others have designed is a dangerous strategy, with elements of huge risk and wishful thinking. We probably cannot stop development; equally we cannot excavate, record, and curate all archaeology to the same level of detail. We certainly cannot keep everything we dig up. Possibly we cannot archive everything we decide to keep to the same standard. The discussions on value that have been started need to continue and, furthermore follow through into a more collaborative, development-friendly, and reasoned approach to project design, sampling strategy, and retention.

Often discussed but possibly least understood are the multiple customers of archaeology and the relationships between them. Customers include those that use the product, either through a charge or as a tax-payer, those that pay for it directly, and even the nation-state itself.

In order to survive, a commercial enterprise must have customers; indeed in today's world every service-user is a customer. A planning applicant is as much a customer of the local planning authority as of the commercial archaeological practice; however the contractual relationships which exist between these various service-users are completely different. These rather unsubtle differences are often overlooked and unsurprisingly this has a rather large bearing on the impact of decisions made by the various bodies overseeing archaeological practice. Recognition of the higher-level end-use customer has to sit side-by-side with an understanding of the relationship between the commercial archaeologist, the paying customer and those other stake holders with a commercial interest in the progress of the planning application.

Even RESCUE in 1974 recognised that funding was limited and that this in turn limited the way in which excavation could be approached. Rescuing the archaeology that was being damaged was paramount and this is where quite naturally resources were concentrated; post-excavation was usually dependent on future funding, the nature of which was unknown, uncertain or simply the product of hope. We no longer talk about the pre-PPG16 post-excavation crisis as this has largely been dealt with through public funding for a few lucky projects, archiving of others, the unpaid work of those, often commercial organisations, finding themselves responsible for the legacy, and a capacity to bury the problem out of sight. It is now taken as read that commercial projects need to include post-excavation, and the process leading to publication is well established; rather less so for archiving where, regardless of the introduction of new standards, specifications and requirements, we have a huge and looming crisis for the whole profession (*see also* Shepherd, Chapter 13). We are beginning to understand the real cost of storing in perpetuity, and commercial archaeology is now required to consider how it will meet the increasingly expensive storage solutions and how this cost will be passed on to the client. Unfortunately it is not as simple as it seems. There has been little discussion around the point (if there is one) at which the 'polluter' can discharge responsibility for keeping archive in perpetuity, and one wonders whether the requirements of keeping the resource can be reasonably enforced either through contractual means or through planning legislation.

If there is any failure that needs to be addressed here, it is the result of failing to consider changes within the context of the wider environment, and how to ensure that the archaeology we envisage can successfully work alongside a commercial practice that is operating under increasingly complex procurement processes and contractual relationships. Archive is just one area where, in considering the development of good practice, the profession has given little consideration to the impact on commercial practice. In this case the difficulty of entering into long-term contractual relationships with a client who is often not in fact the owner of the finds, and in a situation where planning enforcement is largely impossible, is rarely considered. Discussions on the topic have to be held by the whole profession and are required with some degree of urgency.

This paper has hardly touched on the need for the commercial sector to engage in technological development and training. Whichever way we look at it, and whoever is considered at fault, investment in these areas is woefully inadequate. Few commercial organisations have been able to address the profound training-needs of the profession: whether basic training in the principles of archaeological excavation or the high-level contract-management required to mitigate commercial risk and ensure payment, or even the training necessary to ensure that employees remain safe and operate in a way that minimises harm to the environment. With a whole raft of infrastructure projects on the verge of happening all at once, and a sudden interest in developing sites that have been mothballed for many years, there is understandable nervousness around the capacity of the commercial sector to deliver the work that will be required. This is alarming on many fronts, and if the fears are realised, are we not in danger of further diluting already frail protection offered to the archaeological resource? Reduction in local authority provision and removal of overly bureaucratic and costly planning-requirements will result in many sites falling through the planning net. Failure of the profession to ensure we have enough trained archaeologists to deal with the planning applications that require some sort of archaeological intervention can only have equally alarming consequences. The CIfA is doing much to educate the profession in the requirements of CPD. What is needed now is a concerted effort to engage with the educational sector to develop a range of vocationally-useful training, which provides us with the tools for working commercially and meeting the demands of our direct clients.

Commercial archaeology sits in an uneasy place: it could be argued that the organisations operating here are the real guardians of heritage protection. After all, commercial organisations are held to account, professionally and financially, if there is a failure to manage the paying customer and achieve the desired outcome. The commercial organisation is expected to ensure that the end-user of the archaeological product (ironically often the paying customer of a local authority through museum, archives or HER use) is satisfied through adherence to a range of requirements and, through their commercial contract with a planning applicant or their agent, are expected to find a way of achieving the funding to do this. There will be arguments on either side as to whether or not this is fair or contractually possible, but suffice to say this is one area that the commercial sector will need to address as it tries to define its product more expertly and as it becomes more and more embedded in a wider, multi-disciplinary sector.

There is a new emphasis on the protection of value and significance, and a slightly more advanced debate on the need for public benefit (Southport Group 2011). Despite this, and the unrecognisable commercial environment in which modern archaeological businesses operate, we are still largely wedded to the old ideas that archaeology should be saved by record, if not by preservation, and that the polluter pays without consultation and regardless of cost. Commercial archaeology means that archaeology has a value, and that value relates to the amount that those who commission it are prepared to pay for it. In deciding how the market operates this value is possibly as relevant, if not more so, than the value that we place on archaeology as a heritage asset. Whilst the capacity of the voluntary sector is huge, the protection of our heritage has a cost, and that requires a commercial response. In 1974 there was still hope that a state-funded structure could intervene. This is no longer the case. We have spent a decade or more trying to ensure that commercial archaeology does not lose sight of its academic roots, and that the work we do contributes to research; we now have a better, if incomplete, understanding that the knowledge we create has to have some wider benefit. Without a better understanding of the commercial impacts of decisions, based on considerations of what is required by way of academic research, best practice, long-term curation of the asset, and public benefit, commercial archaeology has an uncertain future.

We have perhaps now gone full circle and, despite a very different political and social environment, are staring at potentially the same level of destruction as before. In 1974 the archaeological resource was considered valuable because it was an asset for the nation; no other justification was required. Although funding was key, the models by which the asset was saved were not of as much concern as the rescue of that asset from the claws of the bulldozer gracing the front cover of the book.

Where previously it was regarded as axiomatic that archaeology needed to be saved for the nation, we now have to define it in terms of user needs. Where previously the work was undertaken through the voluntary sector employing limited paid-staff, we now have a commercial sector operating in a market that does not value archaeology sufficiently highly to pay well, or to create sufficient surplus for investment. It is difficult to imagine archaeology in another 40 years, but one hopes that barriers to entry through, for example, Chartership of the IfA; a better organised employers' voice through FAME; and a more thoughtful debate on value and public benefit will provide us with some of the tools to meet the challenges of the next 40 years.

References

Crump, T, 1987, The role of MSC funding in British archaeology, in Mytum, H, and Waugh, K, (eds), *Rescue archaeology, what's next? Proceedings of a RESCUE Conference held at the University of York, December 1986*, Dept of Archaeol, University of York Mono **6**, York and Hertford, 41–6

Department of the Environment (DoE), 1990, *Planning Policy Guidance 16: Archaeology and Planning (PPG 16)*, HMSO, London

Everill, P, 2012, *The Invisible Diggers: a study of British commercial archaeology*. 2nd edition. Oxford, Oxbow Books

Hogarth, C, 1974, Survival and archaeology, in Rahtz 1974, 35–50

Kiln, R, Archaeology as a hobby and how to start, in Rahtz 1974, 256–73

Rahtz, P A, (ed), 1974, *Rescue Archaeology*, Pelican, Harmondsworth

Southport Group, 2011, *Realising the benefits of planning-led investigation in the historic environment: a framework for delivery*, at www.archaeologists.net/sites/default/files/node-files/SouthportreportA4.pdf (accessed 28 May, 2012)

Thomas, G, and Arnold, G, 1974, Rescue archaeology and the public, in Rahtz 1974, 241–55

Chapter 4

Building a Heritage Protection regime

Tony Howe

Development should be viewed by all of us as a positive force and is not in itself an objectionable pursuit. It is essential for the economic health and communal wellbeing of the country that development and the cycle of redevelopment occur. Without development, we would have insufficient homes, facilities and infrastructure to accommodate a rising population and allow a balanced society to continue. It must also be remembered that not all development involves structures: National Parks, gardens, farms, Areas of Outstanding Natural Beauty, coastlines, forests, mountains and lakes are all the product of human intervention to some degree; their management and survival also depends upon activities that could be classed as development.

Our environment is a patchwork of modern, historic and prehistoric periods, myriad architectural styles, the religious and the secular, the spectacular and the mundane. These elements have survived for a reason, be it design or mere chance, but all represent an embodiment of the constant process of change. This process is ongoing and it must be recognised that for good reasons it continues, and that we are part of this cycle. Within this patchwork is preserved the very physical essence of our nation state; the tangible fabric that has contributed towards forming what we would consider to be our national identity. It is therefore essential that within the change process, we act with great care and consideration to preserve that which best represents who we are and how we came to be where we are today.

It is a complicated exercise to consider heritage protection, and its operation within the development planning process. Heritage resources (or 'assets' in the current imperfect parlance) and development are not necessarily the happiest of bedfellows, and whilst not entirely mutually exclusive, it is an unavoidable fact that the presence of the former can sometimes considerably disrupt the execution of the latter, and in turn the execution of the latter can sometimes be extremely destructive to the continued existence of the former. Heritage protection also extends beyond the realm of the official 'planning process', with many necessary provisions overlapping and intertwined. A heritage planning protection regime involves a considerable number of interested parties, and a great many rules, regulations and principles. It also requires some compromises be made within in all these areas to work – the trick is to make sure that all sides are making them.

Until recently there was a certain degree of stability. '*Planning Policy Guidance Note 16: Archaeology and Planning*' ('PPG16') was put in place in 1990 and lasted for almost 20 years, being exercised through the efforts of a national network of well-established County Archaeologists. PPG15, dealing with Listed Buildings dated from 1994 and enjoyed similar longevity. Above it all sat English Heritage providing professional support and providing a programme for administering proposed works to Scheduled Monuments and the very best of our Listed Buildings. However the past few years have seen the legislative framework tinkered with to varying degrees of success. Even during the production cycle of this volume, the legislative regime has changed separately within both England and Scotland, whilst Wales and Northern Ireland have conducted reviews of their policies. Slightly further back, radical changes were outlined then largely shelved (at least in legislative terms) during the Heritage Protection Review. Going forward, as this is written there are proposals to split English Heritage into two new organisations (*for details see* Walker, Chapter 17, footnote 2), and further 'streamlining' of the planning system is proposed by both major parties following the 2015 General Election. This constant state of flux renders an in-depth discussion of the validity, value and advantages (or otherwise) of the 'current' system somewhat moot, as there is no guarantees that by the time this volume hits the shelves the current system might not itself be a quaint relic of a previous government's planning vision, along with PPG16 and its short-lived successor PPS5. Setting aside the legislative situation, the current exodus of practitioners from the profession and the tendency of a number of local authorities to conclude that heritage protection is a practice they can no longer afford to support, ensures that even where a national framework exists, there might not be anyone in post to exercise it authoritatively in many areas. How does one properly assess a system of such a potentially transient nature and patchwork implementation effectively?

We must step away from the current system rather than look into it. If we assume that the current system is indeed transient, we are freed from the need to examine it in any detail here and instead are able to investigate what properties a heritage protection system ideally should include.

The starting point is to understand what a planning system is **for**. This might seem obvious, but it helps to articulate it to begin setting out a case for what it should embody. A planning system exists to **allow** development to happen – but in a controlled way. Without a planning system, people would still build, but it would be unregulated. Haphazard development would occur. Poor-quality designs and dangerous structures could be built in inappropriate places. Landscapes and buildings we value as a community could be despoiled if their owners were so minded to build there. Materials could be chosen for cheapness over quality, utilitarianism over aesthetic attractiveness. The construction industry – indeed anyone at all – could operate with unsafe site-practices, and could do to a site or property what they liked, where they liked, when they liked, as long as they owned it and had the money. Clearly this would be unsatisfactory; as a community our natural and built environment is vitally important to us: it can promote a sense of place and belonging, encourage improved community interrelationships, act positively for the reduction of crime and antisocial behaviour, and foster a sense of community wellbeing in ways that though difficult to sometimes identify, are nevertheless tangible in their influence. We also need to consider issues of environmental safety, the use of inappropriate materials and environmental pollutants, as well as looking at creating built environments that are conducive to both community wellbeing and economic growth. It therefore follows that in promoting the health of our community, that community must come together and adopt and maintain a system to regulate the health of our surroundings.

Our heritage is a shared resource; it belongs to everyone – in spirit if not always in law – but within the planning process the interested parties in promoting heritage and community health are: the Government, the Developers, the Heritage Profession and the Public. The principal partner is the Government which has responsibility for creating legislation and driving the economy as well as for the welfare of the nation and upkeep of its resources, but each group in the equation is important to making the system work effectively. Each will have a set of defined absolutes underlying its ideological position – their thin red lines in the sand – but also each must recognise and identify the compromises it will need to address in order to accommodate the other parties' principles. Ultimately few principles on all sides will be totally inviolable, but there will undoubtedly be areas where individual parties believe lines should not be crossed. There will also be flexibility on all sides and even within groups at different times, as to where these lines should occur. This will lead to disagreement, and no system can ever be free of this inevitability; but we can perhaps define a series of idealised principles that should articulate the issues concerning heritage management within the planning process, and if each are addressed within a planning protection system, should also help to minimise conflict.

These principles of development can broadly be broken down into three main areas of concern: '**Protection of Heritage**', which is ultimately the responsibility of the State as it is conducted through the creation and imposition of national legislation and guidance, '**Development of Heritage**', which will be where the construction industry's' interests principally lie, and '**Investigation of Heritage**' which is where the heritage profession should be actively driving the agenda. Clear interrelationships exist between these areas and groups but none of these principles operates in isolation. Dealing with clear areas of responsibility in this way assists in atomising how a conceptual system should be put together.

Protection of Heritage: Principles
1. Legislation is necessary
The vast majority of any national heritage protection regime cannot be voluntary or optional. The UK is bound, through being a signatory to a number of relevant European Conventions, to have in place a legislative framework that protects the built, archaeological and landscape heritage of the UK. The principal Conventions are the 1985 *Convention for the Protection of the Architectural Heritage of Europe* (the *Granada* Convention), The 1992 *European Convention on the Protection of the Archaeological Heritage* (*Valetta* Convention) and the 2000 *European Landscape Convention* (*Florence* Convention).

The *Granada* **Convention** introduces various legal requirements for protecting structural heritage, including statutory measures for the protection of monuments (Article 3(i)), prohibitions on demolition and removal of structures and monuments (Article 4(b) and Article 5), provisions for legal sanctions (Article 9), and for the adoption of a protective framework within town and country planning (Article 10(1)).

The *Valetta* **Convention** requires similar provisions for archaeology – the creation of archaeological reserves (Article 2(ii)), preservation of the archaeological heritage through appropriate and authorised investigation (Article 3) and well-balanced strategies within planning policies for archaeological protection, conservation and management (Article 5(i)).

The *Florence* **Convention** requires recognition of landscapes in law and their integration into town planning policies (Article 5(a) and (d)).

A fourth Convention of relevance exists, but is one that the UK has to date (February 2015) not signed or ratified. The 2005 *Council of Europe Framework Convention on the Value of Cultural Heritage for Society* (*Faro* Convention) requires (again amongst a series of Articles) legislative provisions for exercising the right to cultural heritage (Article 5(c)) and to encourage non-governmental organisations concerned with heritage conservation to act in the public interest. The UK should sign and ratify this convention.

The UK is also a member of UNESCO, the United Nations Educational, Scientific and Cultural Organisation, and as a member is either bound by, or has voluntarily committed to adhere to, a number of additional charters even if it has not explicitly signed them. These include (but are not limited to) the 1954 *Hague Convention* (*Convention for the Protection of Cultural Property in the Event of Armed Conflict*), the 1970 *Convention on the Means of Prohibiting and Preventing the Illicit Import, Export and Transfer of Ownership of Cultural Property*, the 1972 *World Heritage Convention*, and the 2001 *Convention on the Protection of the Underwater Heritage*. There are detailed requirements within all these Conventions and, even if absolutely nothing else is undertaken, each must be carefully examined to ensure that whatever national heritage protection measures are devised within the UK they are fully compliant with the requirements of the European and UNESCO Conventions that the UK has agreed to uphold, or signed and ratified. Where proposed measures fall short of the requirements of the Conventions (for example in the application of voluntary agreements where the convention states that statutory provisions are necessary), clearly augmentation of the proposed measures is necessary.

2. Protection should be equitable
The 'Historic Environment' is an agglomerated resource comprising various elements of past activity. This 'past' need not particularly be of significant antiquity and many elements of what we would call the historic environment were created within living memory. Heritage assets generally (but not exclusively) comprise of habitable and

non-habitable buildings, standing structures, commemorative features, ruins, buried archaeological sites and finds, earthworks, designed landscapes, battlefields, shipwrecks, and inundated and sunken sites at sea. Add to this list sites that are considered of cultural and/or aesthetic importance, and it becomes a group that is of tremendous importance to our surroundings. Protection measures that are devised and utilised to care for this resource should ensure that they provide equal coverage for all parts of the group. Protection measures designed for buildings and structures aren't necessarily suited to addressing the issues that surround archaeological sites and standing ruins. Similarly, measures to protect terrestrial archaeology will not necessarily be suited to protect marine sites of a similar character, and an historic battlefield will require different consideration to an historic garden, even though both are technically landscapes. A regime should ensure that the protection it provides is equitable across the full range of historic environment features, even if the protection measures used within the regime are different for different kinds of heritage.

3. The most important sites must be preserved

Heritage planning must allow for the most important sites to be protected from development harm. Clearly, there are historic sites that exist which should not be lost or excessively altered. This is not to say that development in this context cannot take place – there are clearly occasions when repairs, beneficial restorative works or interpretive facilities are requiring of development practices – but rather that the significance of the site is such that no degradation of the fabric should be allowed. A robust heritage protection regime must have legislative provision for the very best sites to be recognised and categorised as such and preserved in a way that **at the very least** arrests decline in their physical condition.

Figure 1 Preservation: Stonehenge, fenced off and largely inaccessible to the public, some sites are just too important to allow any fabric degradation to take place.

Photo © Tony Howe

4. Heritage requires a grading system

Sites need to be assessed, catalogued and graded according to a series of predetermined criteria, to enable rapid and efficient protection and decision-making. Not all heritage is of equally importance. Some sites are better examples than others of the same type. Some sites have the capacity to contain more archaeological information about a certain period than others. Some sites are unique; others represent a single example of a multitude. Some are exceptionally old, whilst others are relatively modern. Some sites might be significant locally, but have lesser value when viewed in a national context. Heritage grading is required in order to have these concerns examined, articulated, and publically set out so the information is available to all concerned. Blanket and draconian regimes which prohibit change also discourage useful investigation and archaeological recording. A grading system allows for change processes to occur but also empowers better heritage protection through increased understanding and knowledge gained as a consequence of commensurate study.

Ideally, grading should be created through legislation, be prescribed (statutory), robust and nationally consistent, but adaptive enough to be reflective of local characteristics and idiosyncrasies. It should also be flexible and adequately resourced; rapidly allowing for sites to be graded higher should new information arise and similarly reduced in grade should their heritage significance or value be diminished in some way. Furthermore, grading of sites should aim to be all-encompassing of the national heritage resource: the concept of 'undesignated heritage assets' is one that an efficient national heritage protection regime should strive to eliminate for all sites bar those that have only very recently been discovered or recognised. No heritage asset should remain wholly 'undesignated' for any extended period of time, even if the result of an initial grading assessment against the criteria is an indeterminate designation of 'uncertain importance due to insufficient data'. In addition, where heritage assets are under consideration for designation, there should be enforceable and effective interim measures available to the national and local authorities, to ensure prejudicial damage or loss is halted whilst assessment is under way.

5. Heritage requires centralised national support

All heritage is essentially 'local' heritage. Care of heritage has though, to begin at a national level through the legislative process, and then devolve downward and outward to the rest of the community. Central Government requires a dedicated and strong Heritage Department to deal with the specific requirements of the resource, and it requires a highly skilled, specialised and heritage-focussed body to advise it. At this point discussion begins about the role and focus of the advisory body, and to what extent downward and outward devolution of authority is appropriate. Should the body be wholly advisory, or should it have practical functions in determining applications and intervening in local decisions that affect heritage? If so, should there be specific 'Heritage Consents' that are not determined locally at all, but centrally as part of an overall national Heritage Strategy? Should all planning applications involving heritage features require a form of

'Heritage Consent' and be determined by a national centralised body, or should there be a mixture of national and local decision-making powers? If so how to ensure that the other local decision-making bodies have access to the necessary expertise to do so? Should it have a statutory footing? Should it be empowered to purchase and curate sites on behalf of the nation, or should it be policy-focussed only? Should it design and carry out heritage research projects and rescue investigations itself, or just provide expertise advice and guidance to those that do? The possibilities for such a body are myriad, more so than can be listed here, and potentially extremely exciting from the historic environment point of view. Readers will have their own priorities of course, but when the issue is considered what is clear is that such a well-resourced national Government professional heritage advisory and advocacy institution with both a strategic and practical remit is *essential* and should be vigorously supported. No heritage protection, investigation, conservation and enhancement regime could exist without it.

6. Heritage Assets are part of a valuable national shared resource: the default position should be for their continued survival

Where heritage assets exist on a site, the planning system should be weighted in favour of their retention, regeneration and re-use. Heritage assets (ie sites, structures, landscapes and features) enrich our environment, providing, amongst a very long list of benefits, aesthetic pleasure and diversity, educational opportunities, and long-term economic benefits through tourism and town regeneration. The very best examples become icons for a local area or even the country as a whole, but even assets of lesser significance can take on enhanced meaning for communities. It is important not to underestimate the power that sites and structures can exert over a community, and how this power can ultimately work to the detriment of the operation of a planning system. It is also important to understand that 'heritage' is actually being created all the time, and might not necessarily be specifically antique in nature. A proliferation of local and national groups and campaigns aimed at saving specific sites is a strong indicator not just of the need to ensure that heritage concerns are of paramount importance within the planning system, but also of the very real possibility that a planning system might not be adequately considering the cultural heritage and historic environment implications of development, and is therefore inherently flawed. Any planning system that incorporates heritage should recognise this issue, and ensure that if heritage assets are present on a site, the default starting position when it comes to discussions regarding the development of the site is that they be retained and sensitively, and sensibly incorporated fully into the proposals for the future. There should also be an appreciation that modern structures might be of current or future cultural heritage value, and provision for their assessment and possible protection made. Within the operation of this proposed principle, further consideration should be given to introducing financial incentives in the form of tax relief and possibly grant assistance, for projects which involve the sensitive and thoughtful reuse and conservation of heritage assets where there are clear community benefits.

7. The state should intervene as Guardian of Last Resort

The nation state has a responsibility not just to legislate for protecting the very best heritage resources that the country has, but also to curate the heritage assets of the very highest quality on behalf of the people it serves. Consequently, it has to accept a responsibility for guardianship, and to intervene where threats to nationally important assets arise and appear insoluble through conventional means. Compulsory Purchase Orders are already a familiar part of the planning regime and are used by Local Authorities to acquire buildings and other structures for various reasons. However this is generally not for heritage protection-related acquisition and comparable legislation of an altogether more heritage-focussed and *centrally exercised* nature is required where heritage assets are threatened. Where a nationally important artwork or historic object is sold, the Secretary of State regularly imposes export bans, and allows opportunities for relevant institutions or public bodies to acquire items rather than lose them to overseas ownership. This principle: 'saving objects of UK cultural value for the nation' – should be extended to the heritage assets of the country. In the case of an artwork at least losing it overseas doesn't involve its destruction and loss, but losing a site or structure to development often can and does. Effective and comprehensive management of a nation's heritage resources dictates ultimately that where an archaeological site of demonstrable national significance is discovered during development works, or where a nationally important structure is threatened with loss through development, neglect, or wilful and malicious intent, a legislative and financial mechanism should exist for that site or structure to be removed into national guardianship.

Development of Heritage: Principles
8. Heritage features require the development process to take place

Heritage assets cannot survive without a constant process of reassessment, monitoring, repair, and replacement taking place. Heritage practitioners, interested parties, and the wider public must be accepting of change and innovation within heritage conservation regimes, especially where it provides improvement or enhances long-term security. No heritage features (of any great age) currently survive in their original state: all have been conserved, reconstructed, consolidated, repaired, added to or had elements taken away during their use. The concept of preservation in aspic is one that is impossible to achieve today, and in actuality, never existed in the past. Very few sites can be viewed or understood in their original state or context, so once this principle is grasped it is followed by an understanding that the change process is actually essential for the survival of heritage assets.

9. Accept and manage loss where justified or unavoidable

The development change process inevitably requires the damage to and loss of archaeological sites and information, historic structures and landscapes. Managing that loss and reducing it to acceptable and sustainable levels is the key factor, but the first principle – that loss and degradation will happen – must be embraced. Loss of fabric

Figure 2 Justifiable Destruction: Full archaeological investigation of a site will inevitably destroy it. The maximisation of information recovery is vital if such destruction is to be justified, as was the case at this nationally-significant Palaeolithic flint knapping site in Surrey.

Photo © Tony Howe

is an inevitability of many forms of archaeological investigation, so the principle of loss is already enshrined for professionals, but for the public the concept is sometimes harder to grasp, as the benefits of knowledge gained through destructive examination are more difficult to communicate. Development also obviously means that the context for loss or damage is different to that of controlled investigation, and that the damage has a considerably higher chance of being catastrophic and irreversible. From the heritage perspective, total destruction of a site or structure might be justifiable on the grounds of information retrieval, but the case must be carefully made and destruction should usually be carried out only under appropriate archaeological investigation and recording techniques. It is significantly more likely that total destruction will be proposed as a consequence of a development where other factors, such as the intimated public benefit of a new proposal, will outweigh retention. Planners, practitioners and the public will have individual opinions on these instances, which can only really be examined on a case-by-case basis within the wider planning and development framework. Less comprehensive (but still invasive) works to a heritage feature, or piecemeal destruction and damage over a long period are more difficult to manage and require significant forward thinking. Degradation over time can seriously weaken the heritage integrity of a site or structure, so holistic appraisal must be carried out when it is clear that developmental erosion of historic fabric is likely, occurring and/or ongoing. Is there a point in the adaptation, repair, reconstruction and re-use of a structure which means it is no longer of intrinsic or evidential historic interest but merely a relatively modern facsimile in the same location? And for some cases certainly, is the fabric ultimately the most important consideration?

10. Heritage should not be viewed as a resource in isolation.

The historic environment shares many characteristics and has common interests with a number of other disciplines. It is particularly the case, that many natural environment concerns are mirrored by those of the historic environment. Is an Ancient Woodland a heritage asset or an environmental one? The answer of course is that it is both, and is irreplaceable from whichever point of view it is examined. The same is true for other natural environment features such as heritage trees and hedgerows, whilst undisturbed Ancient Woodland can preserve landscape archaeology and environmental data relating to past landscapes. Separating consideration of interrelated disciplines divorces both from their appropriate context and diminishes protection. In the same way, heritage concerns are integral to and should be influencing discussions on town planning, transport, economy, sustainability and design, to name but a few. A lack of integrated planning processes leads to segmented development practices that lack cohesion. When legislation and guidance is devised, heritage should rightly have a suite of policy and practice of its own, but there should be a 'heritage thread' that runs through other documentation – in the same way that environmental concerns are threaded through other legislation – to ensure that protection regimes are fully formed, robust and adequately cross-referenced.

11. Heritage can be threatened by non-planning works

There are a number of activities that fall outside the general orbit of the planning process that can have far-reaching consequences for heritage. Principal amongst these are the works carried out by the Statutory Service Providers (water, gas, electricity and oil companies), whose activities are judged to be in the national interest and therefore conducted to previously-agreed codes of conduct outside the planning system. Obvious threats exist to the setting of valued landscapes and buildings through development of new facilities, but in general these companies tend to be involved in ongoing below-ground operations involving buried pipelines and cables, works which can cause permanent damage to archaeological sites if not properly managed. Similarly, non-planning related rural activities such as forestry operations, ploughing, grazing, animal husbandry, heathland management and even the effects of tourism can cause long-term degradation of heritage features that can be difficult to manage. If a conceptual protection system is to be envisaged, non-developmental works need to be considered and measures devised to ensure that protection is robust and holistic.

12. Not all heritage is physical

For many, the historic environment is a considerably more powerful force than is represented by the presence of structures or places. As outlined previously, our heritage significantly contributes to and legitimises who we believe we are as a nation state. In much the same way that (for example) religion can be the overwhelming factor for some people in constructing their sense of self, so heritage and in particular cultural heritage is the important factor for others. These feelings can also be manifested in the most mundane and inexplicable of places. Whilst a building/institution like Westminster Abbey

Figure 3 Inexplicable Heritage: Nearly 8,000 people signed an online petition to have the '1930s concrete cows' restored to the roof of the Sunbury Dairy Crest building when they were removed by the owner in 2014. The fact that they were a) only fibreglass copies of the 1930s originals and b) actually only placed there in the 1970s, was apparently irrelevant to their community value. The dairy has promised to return them.

Photo © Tony Howe

can be viewed as an icon representing the nation as a whole and is easily quantifiable as a heritage asset, an ordinary house can become equally important to a completely different but potentially wide-ranging community as, say, the final home of singer Ian Curtis. The 2003 UNESCO '*Convention for the Safeguarding of the Intangible Cultural Heritage*' articulates some of these issues, but has not been ratified by the UK and is neither well understood nor widely applied with regard to the historic environment. All planners, practitioners, developers and legislators involved with the management of the historic environment must be fully conscious of the power of the intangible forces that cultural heritage can exercise over the psyche of people, and how that power can polarise opinions and mobilise resistance, if they wish to ensure development takes place without conflict.

Investigation of Heritage: Principles
13. Allow for research to take place within the process
Research is sometimes seen as a luxurious occupation carried out with other people's money for academic gratification. This paper opened with a statement declaring that development is not in itself an objectionable pursuit. A corollary is that within a development context neither is research. It is actually an essential part of both the examination of techniques, and the greater understanding of the historic environment, and is the major contributory factor to the more efficient targeting of resources in the future. Of course by no means should all research projects be carried out within the development and planning process – there is neither sufficient time nor appropriate resources to do so – but research investigation of new processes, sites and methods should not be excluded entirely. Provision for the examination of appropriate research questions should be included within commercial development. In furtherance of this aim it is crucial that the academic sector, particularly the university post-graduate programmes, should actively

participate in the development process to ensure both a more a rounded profession and a greater progression of understanding about how the historic environment should be both investigated, conserved and enhanced. Local Authority archaeologists and the commercial practitioners should create and maintain formal relationships with the academic sector to ensure that proper cooperation and cross-fertilisation of ideas and practice is the norm.

14. Professional and impartial assessment of whether investigation/loss/ destruction is justified

As the development process can be damaging and destructive, it is necessary that somewhere within the planning process there exists a decision-making stage that assesses whether or not damaging proposals are justified from the historic environment viewpoint. This stage should determine (for example) whether heritage losses can be mitigated on grounds of greater levels of understanding or knowledge, whether investigations have been appropriately devised and resourced and whether full consideration has been given to possible alternative proposals that involve less damaging works. It is clear that professional heritage conservation officers with the appropriate skills and qualifications should be fully involved in this assessment process, to ensure planning decisions can be taken on an informed basis. These officers should be impartial, and disconnected from the political and financial issues that inform the wider decision-making process, so they are able to present to planning committees independent assessments of whether or not proposed works to heritage assets are reasonable, have been fully scoped, and have been suitably mitigated. Decisions should be made about the heritage with the interests of the heritage being considered as of equal importance to other factors.

It is also important to remember that there are a number of non-heritage professional groups and individuals that enjoy enhanced relationships with archaeological material, and also have significant personal and professional interactions with the historic environment. Religious organisations, treasure hunters, commercial salvors, hobbyists and others with special interest can all bring considerable popular support to bear when decisions are being taken about heritage assets. However, in the main these groups do not employ or comprise of skilled or qualified heritage practitioners, and very often the care, conservation and enhancement of the heritage, and the furtherance of our knowledge and understanding of the historic environment is not their primary concern. It is appropriate that all are able to participate fully in the planning process, but decision-making should be as factual and balanced a pursuit as is possible and impartial, qualified and fact-based ethical professional argument should carry considerably more weight in the process than impassioned opinion.

15. Requiring of investigation to be carried out by qualified and accredited practitioners

Development rules require that professional, regulated practitioners be involved to ensure quality and safety are maintained. This principle clearly should apply to heritage investigation and mitigation works when conducted within the planning system as well.

Local Authorities and Planners need to be assured that conservation and heritage planning advice is being given impartially and from an informed point of view by qualified individuals and bodies, whilst the Government and the Developers need to be confident that heritage subcontractors can bring a rigorous and safe professional approach to sites in the same way that a subcontracted surveyor or building company will operate. More importantly, the heritage community should insist upon exclusivity of professionalism within all areas of development-related work, to ensure maintenance of standards, consistency of investigative approaches and the quality of results. As heritage practitioners, we owe this much to our primary customer, the heritage resource itself. Professionalism brings with it the opportunity for the whole cycle of evaluation, investigation, recording, assessment, publication and archiving to be addressed properly, whereas in the past and in non-development related projects post-site works have sometimes been difficult to secure. By definition, professionalism also should secure better pay, training and working conditions for practitioners. Formal industry accreditation to regulate professional practice is not a 100% guarantee of either professionalism or quality unless it is prescribed and enforced properly, but it can be a route to assessing and managing individual and organisational qualification and authorisation for working, a principle set out in the Valetta Convention which is required to be addressed.

16. Local expertise and local decision-making

The importance of heritage expertise and advocacy at a national level by a qualified and dedicated department and advisory body has already been outlined in Principle 5. However as previously noted, all heritage is local heritage, and similar dedicated heritage conservation expertise is required at local levels to ensure that the importance of the historic environment to its local area is fully translated into the national protection regime and how it is expressed on a site-by-site, application-by-application basis. No national body could sensibly be expected to fully understand the significance of sites to their local areas and communities, which indicates that even if the most centralised form of planning regime were created that involved Heritage Consents determined by the national heritage body, local expertise must have a formal role in advising and directing the decision-making process. Such local expertise is even more crucial if de-centralised planning and protection systems are the preferred national model. Local heritage advisory capacity should adequately cover the main relevant areas of heritage concern to a locale, be professional, fully informed through access to appropriate information and data, be impartial and almost certainly be a statutory prescription to ensure local compliance with national planning provisions.

17. Require the rapid and constant assimilation of recently acquired knowledge to inform ongoing processes

The pace and nature of development ensures that the assessment, investigation, analysis and ultimate degradation of the heritage resource is a societal constant. With new knowledge comes new understanding, and so it follows that every investigation undertaken has the capacity to better inform, and dictate the approach to, each and every subsequent investigation – both locally and further afield. Backlogs of new information not yet properly entered onto the relevant Historic Environment Records (HERs) not only act to the detriment of the historic environment through pauses and gaps in the advancement of understanding, but also ultimately to the detriment of the developer as potentially useful information – information that might make investigations cheaper, or quicker, or more cost-effective – sits in data-entry backlogs across the country unable to be fully accessed and utilised. It is essential that new information about the historic environment enters the development process as soon as possible, and that the process of maintaining HERs is provided for constantly and consistently.

18. Material and information needs somewhere to go
Excavated material produced as a result of planning and development-related work requires deposition in publically accessible repositories for both its future care as a research archive, and so that it can be examined and re-appraised at later dates and in more favourable circumstances. Furthermore, the physical record and information obtained from the excavations also requires deposition in an accessible location for the same reason. This material and information is created as a direct result of development operations, and is also useful to the future work of the development industry, which surely dictates that the industry should take some responsibility for securing its deposition and long-term care. The state has a role in providing the infrastructure for this arrangement through the creation of the appropriate legislative conditions and the provision of (or at least support for) networks of suitable repositories, but Local Authorities and local groups also have interests in this area and the long-term care of this material should be a collaborative effort. It is difficult to articulate this principle without looking at existing UK measures where these roles are fulfilled by the national and local museums, and by the Local Authority HERs. Developer links with both the knowledge and artefact repositories are largely absent, and both repositories' are unsupported by dedicated national legislation and appropriate finance (*see also* Shepherd, Chapter 13). The heritage profession has long called for Statutory HERs to address the problem of Local Authority indifference to their upkeep, which would be a significant step forward and is highly recommended here, whilst RESCUE has advocated the creation of regional archaeological archives and education facilities – again a recommended undertaking.

19. Funding needs to be provided
The proverbial 'elephant in the room' is the underlying problem regarding financial resourcing for heritage protection. Heritage management requires a significant amount of money to be diverted towards it, and the issue lies in from where to draw this.

If our heritage is indeed a shared resource, it necessarily follows that the upkeep of repositories for excavated material should also be shared. Were burdens to be distributed equally, the development industry, as the principle creator of archive material and principle user of planning heritage management processes, would be the principle contributor to the maintenance of both the heritage assets themselves and also the sector that regulates them. Developer funding of their own archaeological investigations and listed buildings recording works is obvious – the 'polluter pays' principle – but examination of additional or supplementary (or even replacement) funding through measures such as direct development taxation or indirectly through initiatives similar to the Community Infrastructure Levy should be considered as possible methods of sharing the responsibility amongst the development industry more fairly.

Sharing financial burdens also requires other sources of income apart from developers' contributions. There are many possibilities, but to highlight a few: central Government core funding needs to be both guaranteed, and appropriately calculated and distributed, and comparatively small increases in central heritage funding could make considerable improvements. Additional supplementary central funding for heritage could be provided through the diversion of fixed percentages of tax revenues generated for the Government via other cultural revenues (television, tourism or sport), or by ring-fenced minor tax additions to (for example) UK tourist visas. Local authorities should be statutorily required to provide appropriately resourced heritage services, and initiatives such as the Heritage Lottery Fund rightly should exist to enable community funding for heritage projects to be both enshrined within the system and to be resourced appropriately. Both the public and the heritage industry itself should not be exempt from the equation either. The principle of paying for museum entry is contentious and socially undesirable given the educational benefits that they provide, especially for the major national institutions. However, the public must be persuaded that care of the heritage requires some sensible funding and certainly for specified large-scale local restoration or enhancement projects, extraordinary Council Tax levies – similar to that imposed on Londoners to contribute towards the 2012 Olympic games – should be within the power of all local authorities to at least propose and submit to local referenda.

The heritage profession also needs to become considerably better at targeting and marketing its services, and should investigate possibilities for crosscutting service provision into other disciplines (for example commercial site surveying) with more determination. The commercial disposal of cultural and archaeological material to finance the sector is anathema to professional practice and must continue to be so, but it could at least be nationally recognised that artefact conservation is expensive and treasure awards consequently be calculated to include the cost of conserving the objects at hand and rewards to finders reduced accordingly.

Further measures

In addition to these issues, there are additional principles that should be demanded by the end-user of the development process, and the fourth partner in the equation outlined above; the public. Ultimately, all development has an impact on the environment, and as principal users of the environment after development has concluded, and as the 'client' to whom the Government, Developer and Heritage Profession are all eventually answerable, the public has a right to expect certain additional practices to be carried out on its behalf.

In a fully-realised system, these should include:

20. Mandatory reporting of discoveries

The local and national community has a right to be actively informed about work being undertaken, and discoveries being made. Article 2(ii) of the Valetta Convention requires mandatory reporting 'to the competent authorities' of archaeological material discovered by chance. This laudable principle requires proper implementation, but also extension to include mandatory formal reporting of all archaeological material discovered; including that recovered within the planning and development process (ie by design rather than chance). Reporting should be simple and rapid in the first instance but mandated to take place within a defined timescale, and penalties should be in place for deliberate and/or malicious failure to notify the authorities of discoveries within the appropriate period. A comprehensive national annual *Register* of archaeological discoveries should be produced to allow for proper dissemination of information.

21. Only accepting of the highest quality work and principles of best practice

Where work is carried out to heritage assets, it should be carried out to a regime that not only values and espouses high quality and best practice, but one that actively defines, prescribes and enforces it. For developers, this could involve preferences set out within local plans for preservation over demolition, with possible financial incentives for sensitive and innovative schemes that respect, enhance and incorporate heritage features within new developments. For the heritage profession a defined regime of best practice would not only set out and prescribe the standards necessary to achieve high-quality assessment, evaluation and mitigation, but would also secure and enshrine the complete life-cycle of an investigative project including post-excavation assessment, reporting, publication, and archiving. Both the construction industry and the heritage profession should maintain professional standards and guidance which commit both to a series of informed and up-to-date best practice principles.

22. Disseminating knowledge accumulated through investigation

Where information is obtained through (what are essentially) private undertakings, there must be a duty inherent within the process to acknowledge that heritage is a shared resource, and communicate and inform the wider community. Considerable knowledge about the past is accumulated through investigations conducted as part of the planning and development process. The most 'accessible' form of this knowledge tends to be in the summaries of work outlined within Local Authority HERs and in the shape of archaeological reports, so called 'Grey Literature', but it also exists in the vast quantities of archaeological finds that are recovered, the discoveries and conclusions of good desk-top surveys, and in the studies and investigations carried out by amateur colleagues.

Following the conclusion of investigations there should be formal procedures built into the planning and development process for new information to be communicated and utilised for wider public education and edification. Information should not be 'buried'

Figure 4 *'Deathmasking'*: Façade retention has arisen as an architectural sop to historic environment conservation. These recent London examples in Spitalfields and Caledonian Road are particularly disastrous and make no attempt to incorporate the historic environment into the new scheme. Is this 'high quality' heritage preservation?

Photo © Brian Kerr/Tony Howe

within HERs to await possible future use at some unspecified date by some unspecified user. Popular publication, open days, display notices on sites, permanent interpretation boards, heritage-related artwork or community installations on important sites, heritage-themed place-naming, sponsored exhibitions, internships and programmes conducted through schools to inform and educate the younger generation about the discoveries being made in their local area, should all be considered as integral elements of a well-rounded heritage development and planning management process, and included within the scope of activities potentially covered by planning conditions.

23. Enforcement action and penalties for non-compliance are required and need to be exercised
When put together as a collaborative jigsaw, all the principles set out above should provide a relatively efficient framework to conserve and maintain the historic environment. The final piece of this jigsaw needs to set out what happens when the processes go *wrong*. No system such as this is infallible, so provisions are clearly required to address breaches

of conditions and principles in particular, but also deliberate and malicious damage, thoughtless behaviour and criminal acts that affect historic sites. These provisions should be clearly defined, consistent with comparable law relating to similar areas of environmental and planning protection, and take into account both the damage caused to property and physical structures and also the potential loss of heritage knowledge, understanding and value to the wider community. The public should also have confidence that cases will be consistently pursued and prosecuted. Where guilt is proven, penalties should, in addition to the usual suite of conviction; sentence, fines and/or imprisonment *always* involve consideration of the heritage damage or destruction and provide redress through appropriate mitigation or restorative measures. It should be clear that crime against heritage assets adds a secondary layer of concern to civil and criminal offences that will be addressed through further restitution.

A secondary consideration here that also requires addressing is enforcement against bad professional practice. If enforcement regimes *are* to be robust, then the heritage practitioners need to be aware that bad practice can severely damage both the credibility of results to external observers, and create discord internally within the profession. Running in tandem with an effective legal framework for the prosecution of heritage felonies, there needs to be an equally effective professional investigation and chastisement regime to ensure that poor practice be actively policed, pursued, and prosecuted. This process must be equally as transparent as the legal process, if practitioners are to validate and justify the trust that the public has placed in them to curate the heritage resource.

2014

Having set out these principles, existing heritage protection measures can be examined to ascertain effectiveness. As set out at the start, this paper is not intended to be a full critique on the 'current' system, but with a series of principles in place a brief summing up of where we currently stand can be attempted.

The UK is signed up to a number of international obligations with regards to heritage protection, but not all of them. As members of both the European Union and UNESCO, the Government should sign the remaining relevant conventions and ensure their implementation as necessary (**Principle 1**). In particular, elements of the *Valetta* Convention remain inadequately addressed, and the UK remains one of the world's centres for the trade in antiquities, a situation which surely requires investigation at the very least.

Strong domestic legislation (**Principle 1**) with regard to historic buildings within the planning process exists in the form of the 1990 *Planning (Listed Buildings and Conservation Areas) Act,* and for archaeological monuments in the form of the 1979 *Ancient Monuments and Archaeological Areas Act*. These both act to conserve the very best sites (**Principle 3**). The former allows development and manages loss (**Principles 8 and 9**), whilst the latter recognises non-development threats (**Principle 11**), and both prescribe penalties for non-compliance (**Principle 23**). However, problems exist with a lack of a grading system for archaeological sites (**Principle 4**) and a lack of equivalent legislative protection to buildings and structures, for gardens, parks, terrestrial and marine landscapes and archaeology and battlefields (**Principle 2**), all of which are at risk during planning decisions of having their value overruled or outweighed by other concerns. Even UNESCO-designated World Heritage Sites still lack formal national legislative recognition.

Elsewhere in the planning process, the *National Planning Policy Framework* (NPPF) sets out provisions for heritage preservation and recording (**Principles 1 and 3**) and allows for enhancement to sites and change management within what is an integrated and holistic document (**Principles 8, 9 and 10**), but unfortunately specifies that the default position is 'sustainable development' (**Principle 6**) and sets out an inadequate framework for impartial assessment through a failure to include statutory provisions for independent advisory input, and in not ensuring that the appropriate weight be given to informed professional recommendations (**Principle 14**) local expertise (**Principle 16**). No 'heritage thread' exists within accompanying legislation (**Principle 10**) and the imposition of the 20% VAT rate to both repairs and alteration works to Listed Buildings positively acts *against* their best interests and puts their continued survival at a distinct disadvantage (**Principles 2, 3 and 6**). No adequate framework exists for regulating non-development threats (**Principle 11**), which are instead addressed through a series of imperfectly applied and *ad-hoc* voluntary agreements, and there is little appreciation given to public input (**Principle 12**) or communication (**Principle 21**). The 1996 *Treasure Act* sets out a framework for mandatory reporting – but only of artefacts within its strict definition of Treasure, meaning the vast majority of artefacts recovered are not formally required to be registered as the relevant legislation specifies (**Principle 20**).

No national system of archive repositories exists for archaeological material (**Principle 18**), which currently accumulates in the storerooms of private archaeological contractors as museums' stores are full to capacity, and whilst HERs take summary data and are a prescribed service within the NPPF they have no external developer support (**Principle 18**) and do not take primary material or written archives. With Government financial intervention and prescription as Statutory bodies not forthcoming, many HER's have been left in a precarious position with regards to effective function and in some cases actual survival, along with the local advisory services they support (**16**) as their parent bodies downsize and discard non-statutory services.

This lack of resourcing also means that information is slow to be assimilated (**Principle 17**) and even slower to be disseminated (**Principle 22**). The public are largely excluded from development, and only developers have any meaningful input into whether or not heritage is fully incorporated into the process as no provisions exist for Local Authorities to set out and condition either participation or heritage referencing within new developments (**Principle 22**).

Nationally, the Government maintains a Heritage Department of sorts within DCMS and a generally very good, skilled advisory body in the form of the current English Heritage, soon to be Historic England (**Principle 5**). However, DCMS is a small and underpowered department and there are confusing overlaps in responsibilities for heritage with DEFRA and DCLG, whilst English Heritage has historically seen its resourcing cut by successive administrations and now lacks the capacity to operate in a fully effective way, a situation which the forthcoming creation of Historic England does not apparently propose to address. Certain grades of designated sites, for example Grade II Registered Parks and Gardens, are not nationally covered by any advisory services, and only patchy expertise exists locally to address their specific concerns (**Principle 2**), and assessment and designation of new sites has slowed (**Principle 4**). Some core funding for exceptional discoveries is in place and has been provided by English Heritage (**Principle 5 and 19**), but no meaningful mechanism exists for state intervention and rescue of sites as a Guardian of Last Resort (**Principle 7**), and budgets for repairs to existing holdings have been reduced to a point that threatens the survival of some sites (**Principle 6**). Wider distribution of funding and the creation of new income streams is poor and needs exploration, whilst the recent situation whereby the Ministry of Defence and at least two local authorities have shamefully negotiated agreements to sell artefacts for commercial motives shows that appreciation for ethical positions on the sale of artefacts is not universally accepted (**Principle 19**). Research activities have historically not been carried out within the developer-funded system, and the academic sector is virtually invisible within the development process which is a significant waste of resources and expertise (**Principle 13**). Wider advisory functions have been transferred into a series of excellent and very well-informed and cross-referenced written guidance (**Principles 9, 10 and 14**), but the expert voice and personal expertise of specialist advisors has been replaced in many cases with generic and standardised responses of lesser practical value, which carry insufficient authority to protect professionalism (**Principle 14**). Enforcement provisions do exist for non-compliance with certain legislation which is good (**Principle 23**), but these are generally either imperfectly exercised (in the case of Scheduled Monuments) or often inadequately applied and prosecuted by the courts (in the case of Listed Buildings). Scheduled Monument legislation also allows for a defence of 'ignorance' to be valid, the only instance in UK law where this is the case. The Welsh administration is currently investigating removing this provision, but similar moves in England are not proposed to date. 'Heritage Crime' has been recognised as a growing problem and useful and welcome measures are being devised to combat it, but it has not yet been fully incorporated as a distinct offence of its own. Professional enforcement for bad practice provided by practitioners is in place, but is perceived as both inadequate and relatively opaque in nature (**Principle 23**).

Within the profession, there are differing attitudes towards conservation and enhancement exercised by building specialists and archaeologists. This is not necessarily detrimental as both groups can benefit from discussing issues more widely with the other, and do need to work more closely together, but there is a certain amount of disparity between the two groups' ingrained ethos of appearance versus fabric and preservation versus. mitigation which can render approaches confusing and contradictory for clients (**Principle 2**). Archaeologists are considerably better at managing change through mitigation (**Principle 9**) than their conservation colleagues, but conversely are probably worse at managing preservation and ongoing monitoring (**Principle 3**). The heritage sector as a whole lacks cohesion, and the Government in particular clearly finds these vehement differences of perspective difficult to both manage and reconcile. Instead of dictating the national heritage agenda as the Green Lobby dictates the national environmental agenda, the heritage sector has minimal influence and is currently working under the imposition of increasingly generic and bland legislation, probably at least partially as a result of this ingrained ideological fracturing which dilutes the central 'message'. Disagreements also abound within heritage about the role and influence of the developers' own heritage representatives and to what extent these should be relied on within the process as a substitute for independent scrutiny (**Principles 12, 14 and 15**). Many heritage *standards* are framed around set minimum requirements rather than enshrining best practice (**Principle 21**), which encourages mediocrity of service delivery, and accreditation of professionals is not mandatory (**Principle 15**). Recent attempts to develop more holistic heritage services to reflect legislation have not succeeded and although heritage advocacy at higher levels is improving, there are a number of areas where the historic environment is inadequately represented or defended by its professionals (**Principles 5 and 14**). Appreciation of technological innovation, advancement of theoretical disciplines and the practical application of both in day-to-day practice is good (**Principles 12, 13 and 17**). However professionals are not engaged with the Government, the developers or the public as much as they could or should be (**Principles 6, 13, 14, 15 and 22**) and a lot of professionally-produced heritage material is technical and inaccessible.

Looking at it overall, the majority of the outlined principles of concern are covered in some form. Deficiencies abound within the implementation of most but there is much good work going on that we need to recognise, applaud and augment. Perhaps we are half-way towards achieving a fully-satisfactory system and it seems we are broadly heading in the right direction: we just need to go forward and look for opportunities to grasp the remainder.

References
Selected International Policy:

UNESCO, 'Paris, 1970' *Convention on the Means of Prohibiting and Preventing the Illicit Import, Export and Transfer of Ownership of Cultural Property*, at http://portal.unesco.org/en/ev.php-URL_ID=13039&URL_DO=DO_TOPIC&URL_SECTION=201.html

UNESCO, 'Paris, 1972', *Convention Concerning the Protection of the World Cultural and Natural Heritage,* at http://portal.unesco.org/en/ev.php-URL_ID=13055&URL_DO=DO_TOPIC&URL_SECTION=201.html (accessed November 2014)

UNESCO, 'Paris, 2001' *Convention on the Protection of the Underwater Heritage*, at http://portal.unesco.org/en/ev.php-URL_ID=13520&URL_DO=DO_TOPIC&URL_SECTION=201.html *(accessed November 2014)*

UNESCO, 'Paris, 2003' *Convention for the Safeguarding of the Intangible Cultural Heritage,* at http://portal.unesco.org/en/ev.php-URL_ID=17716&URL_DO=DO_TOPIC&URL_SECTION=201.html (accessed November 2014)

Council of Europe 'Grenada, 1985' *European Convention on the Protection of the Architectural Heritage of Europe*, at http://www.conventions.coe.int/Treaty/en/Treaties/Html/121.htm (accessed November 2014)

Council of Europe, 'Valetta 1992', *European Convention on the Protection of Archaeological Heritage* (revised 1992), at http://www.conventions.coe.int/Treaty/en/Treaties/Html/143.htm (accessed October 2014)

Council of Europe, 'Florence 2000', European Landscape Convention, at http://www.conventions. coe.int/Treaty/en/Treaties/Html/176.htm (accessed November 2014)

Council of Europe 'Faro 2005' *European Convention on the Value of Cultural Heritage for Society*, at http://www.conventions.coe.int/Treaty/EN/Treaties/Html/199.htm (accessed November 2014)

Selected National Policy:

Department of the Environment (DoE), 1994, *Planning Policy Guidance 15: Planning and the Historic Environment (PPG15)*, DoE, London

Department of the Environment (DoE), 1990, *Planning Policy Guidance 16: Archaeology and Planning (PPG 16)*, DoE, London

Department for Communities and Local Government (DCLG), 2010, *Planning Policy Statement 5: Planning for the Historic Environment*, HMSO, London

Department for Communities and Local Government(DCLG), 2012, *National Planning Policy Framework (NPPF)*, The Stationery office, London

Additional References:

Concrete cows, at http://www.getsurrey.co.uk/news/surrey-news/sunbury-residents-over-moo-n-return-7797210

Dyer, J, 1983, *Teaching archaeology in schools*, Shire

English Heritage, 2008, *Conservation principles: policies and guidance*, English Heritage, London

Howell, J M P, and Redesdale, Lord R, 2014, *The future of Local Government Archaeology Services*, (unpub rep)

Southport Group, 2011, *Realising the benefits of planning-led investigation in the historic environment: a famework for delivery*, at www.archaeologists.net/sites/default/files/node-files/ SouthportreportA4.pdf (accessed 28 May, 2012)

Swain, H, (ed), 1991, *Competitive tendering in archaeology: Papers presented at a one day conference in June 1990*, RESCUE: The British Archaeological Trust, and Standing Conference of Archaeological Unit Managers, Hertford

SECTION TWO: Experiences of the 21st century archaeologist

Introduction

Paul Everill

This section was conceived, at least in part, as a vehicle for the personal testimonies of a cross-section of those working across the many sectors in which archaeologists find themselves working today. The contributors represent local authority curators (Tony Howe in Chapter 5); directors of commercial organisations (Neil Holbrook in Chapter 6); freelance specialists (Chris Cumberpatch in Chapter 7); commercial site staff (Chris Clarke in Chapter 8); volunteers (Ginny Pringle in Chapter 9) and university lecturers (myself in Chapter 10). These chapters reflect a huge variety of experience and, while the authors cannot be expected to speak on behalf of all their peers, these reflective accounts are indicative of the sacrifices made and challenges/frustrations faced by those pursuing a career in archaeology, or working in the voluntary sector. Perhaps less evident is the passion for the subject that presumably once drove us all on but, like any long-standing relationship, the early joy and thrill becomes tempered with pragmatism and routine. Recently supervising an excavation near Winchester, I was standing on a spoil heap trying to make sense of a series of walls being revealed in a new part of the trench when the penny dropped. That sudden understanding of how they inter-related to form one big structure, after days of looking at them and scratching my head, left me breathlessly excited. It was a great reminder of why I, like many others, was first attracted to archaeology and how it still has the power to excite and inspire. It was also the perfect antidote to the administrative and bureaucratic stresses that now form the bulk of my more usual working day.

Let's be clear, those involved in archaeology still have a lot to complain about: poor pay and conditions of employment; eroding protection for the historic environment; limited communication between professional and amateur groups; bad practice by others that serves to undermine the endeavour of the whole discipline, etc. And yet the criticisms often presented in these chapters are not simply complaints, they are the expression of frustrations encountered over and over again. Had this section been included in the 1974 Rahtz volume shortly after the foundation of RESCUE the chapters would have been very different. The discipline was, after all, far narrower and employed a tiny fraction of the numbers it does today. However, many of the themes would have been familiar to today's archaeologists. Now, as then, many of us soldier on in the face of the challenges we face, remembering the days of breathless excitement, and determined to do and be the best we can in order to protect the historic environment and the unwritten stories it holds. The same is true (or should be) regardless of the sub-discipline or sector that archaeologists now find themselves within, and this 'unity of cause' is our biggest strength.

Fundamentally this section sets the scene for what follows. The personal reflections of a cross-section of archaeologists are followed by consideration of the biggest crisis points facing the discipline in Section Three, at which point many of these themes are considered in sharper focus. But this is also about establishing our own disciplinary historical record. It is about the state of the profession today, and it is vividly depicted by those at the coal face.

Chapter 5

A window on curatorial archaeology

Tony Howe

curator (kjʊəˈreɪtə)
noun
1. the administrative head of a museum, art gallery, or similar institution
2. *law (chiefly Scot.)* a guardian of a minor, mentally ill person, etc.
Derived Forms
    curatorial (ˌkjʊərəˈtɔːrɪəl) adjective
    cuˈrator ship noun
Word Origin
    C14: from Latin: one who cares, from *cūrāre* to care for, from *cūra* care

Collins English Dictionary, 21st Century Edition, 2001

This definition of a Curator as '*one who cares*', would appear in theory to apply to all archaeologists. Certainly anyone within the archaeological profession could claim to 'curate' the archaeological resource in some way or another. However in the last 40 years a branch of archaeology has developed that has claimed, or rather been assigned, the term as its own. This part of the archaeological career landscape did not really exist at the time of the original Rahtz *Rescue Archaeology* volume in 1974 (although the anticipated growth and professionalisation of this sector was seen as a positive [*cf* Musson 1974: 81]), but 'Curator' is now a recognised term for a certain kind of archaeologist, in the same way as 'Digger' or 'Consultant' or 'Specialist'. Working predominantly within Local Authority planning services, Curators provide advice and guidance on those archaeological-related matters that are generated through the operation of the planning and development process. They are also inextricably linked with the management, maintenance and enhancement of the repository indexes of all archaeological information, the Local Authority Historic Environment Records. It would not be unreasonable to argue that in collating all the known archaeological information for the country in these local repositories, and in applying national and local planning legislation and guidance to facilitate development-related archaeological projects, that curatorial archaeologists are the underpinning factor that ensures the rest of the profession, which relies upon the development industry for the overwhelming majority of its projects, has gainful employment to pursue.

Given this central significance to the rest of the archaeology profession, it would be sensible to assume that becoming a curatorial archaeologist should involve specialist application. Dedicated postgraduate study for example, or perhaps the completion of modules within undergraduate courses, or professionally-based career development training which outlined the integral position of national and local legislation, archaeological site management, client and customer liaison, or the understanding and direction of archaeological research from a development control perspective.

Bizarrely there is virtually nothing of the sort, and the career path to becoming a local authority archaeologist is haphazard, idiosyncratic, and dependent almost entirely upon the requirements of each individual Local Authority employer. My own entry to the sector was a culmination of circumstances. I personally found nothing so enjoyable as digging 'stuff' up, surely all archaeologists secretly hanker to do this no matter what position in whatever organisation they occupy? Unfortunately British winters (and schoolboy rugby) took care of my knees, some particularly tenacious (if spectacular) walls on a project in Beirut in the mid 1990s ruined my back, being ambidextrous with a trowel damaged both wrists simultaneously. Continuing in field archaeology was not an option for me, and the curatorial sector beckoned through a handy advert for a job in development-heavy Surrey in the Guardian one Wednesday in 1999. As a busy south-east county with a heavy workload and a savvy and sometimes combative development clientele to contend with, Surrey outlined a role which invited candidates experienced in field practice to apply. I have subsequently found that having a background firmly rooted in fieldwork has been an advantage.

This is by no means universal however and a number of curatorial archaeologists, some very good admittedly, might not have ever wielded a trowel. In addition, many authorities place far less value on the necessity of archaeological experience required to undertake curatorial work, and consequently require less experience and offer inferior remuneration packages, which attracts candidates at an earlier point on their career paths. Anecdotal evidence suggests that there is a disparity and inconsistency of the provision of advice from County to County which probably partly occurs as a consequence of this.

The significance of the Local Authorities, and the power they exert over the practice of modern archaeology, is highly underrated and almost never discussed by archaeologists. The reasons for this lack of discussion are obscure and reflect either entrenched ignorance or ostrich-like denial. It is clear that the archaeological profession is lacking fundamental control of its own destiny in failing to address this. Put bluntly, the health and vitality of professional archaeology currently relies upon having qualified curatorial staff available in the correct numbers and the correct locations, in order to apply the planning conditions that the vast majority of the remaining professional practitioners rely on for their business.

The archaeological profession has no ability to influence whether these staff are in place however, as it is not a national prerequisite. Whether or not archaeological advice and HER provision exists in each authority lies wholly at the whim of Local Authority officers and elected Members to determine individually. Recent initiatives to outline the importance of archaeology within the planning process and Local Authority infrastructure, most notably through English Heritage's 'HELM' initiative, have failed to address the problem that these officers and members often have little empathy with the more esoteric and philosophical concepts associated with the practice of archaeology, and ultimately have scant concern for what they perceive is an area of minority or luxurious interest. For all the profession's protestations regarding its wider value to society, Local Authorities have a very different focus and when they are placed under financial pressure their priorities quickly crystallize. Those services which are neither statutory (ie compulsory), or politically sensitive (ie vote-winning), stand little chance of remaining unscathed when the inevitable 'efficiency review' occurs and the axe begins to hover.

Dealing with formal 'internal reviews' is probably one of the lesser known and more frustrating aspects of working as a Local Authority archaeologist. 'Reviews' are myriad and commonplace, and sometimes run almost consecutively so can be seemingly never-ending. As planning officers, curatorial archaeologists essentially exist within a framework of public financial accountability that other archaeologists do not, and are therefore constantly scrutinised for productivity and performance, outcomes and income, and crucially, persistently and consistently required to justify the benefit to the council tax-paying public of their service provision. Within the role, curators have to regularly deal with a variety of correspondents, not all of whom are friendly or reasonable, but no developer, or consultant, or local resident, is in any way as frustrating as is the behemoth of Local Authority management bureaucracy with a bellicose mantra for 'efficiency' and no appreciation of irony.

The recent recession/depression has provided Local Authorities with the perfect remit for swingeing cuts across the board to services deemed 'additional' to their core responsibilities, but by no means do these strength-sapping exercises cease to exist when the economics are good: the service I work for was opportunistically halved some years ago at the height of the boom, whilst the first County to abolish their service altogether, Northampton, similarly did so at a time of national economic comfort. The common factors are that local conditions (economics, politics and personalities) combine to the detriment of the archaeological provision, which demonstrates the vulnerability of archaeological services when greater umbrella protection through national statutory provision is not in place.

Continually fighting the battles to keep these services surviving on an individual basis is not a strategy likely to succeed in the long run and will eventually incur some significant and costly losses of both services and archaeological sites. As this paper was being drafted York (of all places) has slashed their curatorial protection, so perhaps the first of these costly losses has already occurred. The prospect of a heritage-rich environment such as York being without adequate expertise within the local authority to manage it properly through the transformative development process is frightening and cannot bode well for the future. Statutory Historic Advice services would ensure these losses could at least be minimised, yet the profession's latest attempt at outlining a vision for the future of the sector, the IfA-led *Southport Report* (IfA 2011) failed to address this basic flaw in the supporting framework of our professional organisational structure, stopping short at the lesser recommendation for statutory HER access (a hangover from the discarded draft Heritage Protection Reform Bill of 2008) combined with the production of a new *Standard and Guidance* for Archaeological Advice by Historic Environment Services. Immediately categorised in one Local Authority review that I became aware of recently as 'not compulsory', this voluntary regulatory framework for Local Authority archaeologists will almost certainly perpetuate the lack of authority in the current advisory system that many lament when dealing with planning archaeologists, and will not offer any protection from the attritional process of service reductions. It also leaves the foundations of professional practice so insecure as to render a number of the *Southport* vision's many other laudable recommendations regarding research, public engagement, archiving and adding value to development, potentially unenforceable in practice.

Internal struggles aside; the predominant focus of the busiest curatorial departments remains to recover of as much archaeological information as possible from a site prior to its damage or loss through development. In this respect the role has somewhat disappointingly remained little changed from when County Archaeologists first appeared on the professional landscape in the 1970s and it remains the case that rescue archaeology is alive and well, albeit with a revised, yet still incomplete, supporting legislative structure. On a day-to-day basis, this involves an unending cycle of planning applications to be scrutinised; Desk-top Assessments and Written Schemes of Investigation to be approved; site visits to be conducted; and reports to be read and signed off. Worries about publication proposals, and the perennial problem of where to archive all the excavated material, persist and appear insoluble without central funding. Juggling various different schemes covering different types of site and different periods of archaeology is sometimes an art-form in itself and can be extremely tiring. It's sometimes almost impossible to keep up with, or fully understand, all aspects of projects that are running at any one time, particularly when at any moment the focus can jump between (for example) detailed schemes for the investigation of the Palaeolithic, the protection of Cold War monuments, analyses of soil core-samples or an almost incomprehensible series of piling equations and diagrams. It's a common complaint of field archaeologists (including myself in a former capacity it has to be admitted), that the curator doesn't appear to have as in-depth a knowledge of their particular site as should be expected, but stopping to consider what's being required of a monitor in these cases does provide an appreciation of the almost impossible nature that expectation holds.

In reality, guiding the conduct of archaeological projects through the development process is actually one of the most rewarding parts of curatorial work, and a well-executed project carried out by a competent and efficient organisation is, unbelievably, a joy to be a part of. Improvements in techniques and a significant increase in the professionalism of all archaeologists has also helped to create an enhanced appreciation amongst developers of the value of the archaeology work they are being required to resource, although this appreciation is not universal and justification of the necessity for, and timing of, the various stages of archaeological work to a reluctant developer is a common occurrence still. It is also the case that some of the quality 'compromises' the profession has made in the face of an excessively competitive market-place routinely result in 'disagreements' about projects being adequately-funded or staffed, or specialists not being consulted, or schemes of work not being fully completed on-site, or post-excavation analyses not being undertaken satisfactorily, but this is part and parcel of the monitoring process which vigilance and robust communication skills can address.

If some of this discussion seems somewhat pessimistic, this is because there are (I believe) some wide-ranging problems at the heart of local authority archaeological practice. Appreciation of value, qualifications, provision of training, professional support, and protection of service provision are all uncoordinated, and in a number of areas are extremely poor. However, from the inside looking out, it is clear that Curatorial archaeology is most absolutely one of the most enjoyable disciplines within the wider archaeological profession that I have been involved with, and at the same time, one of the most significant to the continued health and vitality of the archaeological profession and the development of archaeology as a career and a respected vocation.

References

Musson, C, 1974, Rescue digging all the time, in Rahtz, P A, (ed) *Rescue Archaeology*, Pelican, Harmondsworth, 79–89

Southport Group, 2011, *Realising the benefits of planning-led investigation in the historic environment: a famework for delivery,* at www.archaeologists.net/sites/default/files/node-files/SouthportreportA4.pdf (accessed 28 May, 2012)

Chapter 6

Reflections from the head of a commercial fieldwork organisation

Neil Holbrook

I have been the head of Cotswold Archaeology for just over 20 years. When I arrived in Cirencester I still thought of myself as a young man with my life before me; now I try not to think of myself as an old one. Back in 1991 Cotswold Archaeological Trust (as we were originally known) was a fledgling archaeological charity which had been established two years earlier by forward looking members of the Cirencester Excavation Committee who recognised that fundamental changes were about to occur in the way that rescue archaeology was undertaken in England. The first couple of years were a daily struggle as we sought to make our way in the new world of competitive tendering brought about by the introduction of PPG 16 in 1990. Back then no one really knew the rules of this new game, and the UK was also in a tough place economically (plus ça change). In my first year or so in the job I spent most of my time on what would now be described as project management, combined with trying to keep the general show on the road (cash flow was a continual concern). Now my days are mostly filled with more corporate duties commensurate with a company with over 120 staff (we are the fourth largest archaeological contractor, to use this particularly inelegant term, working in the UK). In these crucial first few years our business plan could have been written on a match box and the single word survival would have summed it up. Now the challenges are more multifarious, although finance and quality assurance dominate my time.

I did not start my working life with a conscious plan to become the Chief Executive of an archaeological charity, although from an early stage in my career I enjoyed making things happen and recognised that vigorous administration was the means to achieve this. I don't sneer at pen pushers as long as they deliver something. That said I, like almost everyone else who has ever worked in field archaeology, look back on the digs I participated in (both as digger, supervisor or director) as some of the happiest times in my professional career. For me, however, it was not just the digging as from the very outset I was committed to publishing my excavations. I didn't then, and don't now, believe that it is professionally acceptable to fail to produce a report on the results of a fieldwork project. I am glad that I knew the pre-PPG 16 world because I got the kind of early chances to assume positions of responsibility which are not possible in today's more professionally structured, quality assured and undoubtedly more bureaucratic approach to professional practice. In the 1980s it was frequently sink or swim, and if you sunk as a dig director the archaeology of your site usually went down with you. The converse is now true and it is one of the current challenges in commercial archaeology to enable talented fieldworkers to progress rapidly through the ranks, always assuming of course that we can persuade such individuals to go into fieldwork in the first place. I sense that the young archaeologists of today often perceive desk-based consultancy as a better career path.

Despite the administrative load which goes with the job I still try to find the time to do a bit of archaeology. This is important to me on a number of levels, although principally it is personal choice as I remain deeply interested in the subject and want to make some small contribution to the furtherance of the discipline. I write on the archaeology of the Roman world, my particular area of interest and one which has been with me since I was a school boy. Increasingly this can only be achieved as a spare-time pursuit, but as archaeology is my hobby as well as my job I don't in any way resent this and writing doesn't seem like work. I wouldn't describe myself as obsessional about archaeology, however, and I also pursue a number of other mainstream interests. In the time that I have available I tend to write contextualisations of interesting sites that Cotswold Archaeology has excavated, short papers or reviews. I enjoy it, and it helps to keep me up to date with archaeological thinking and remind me of why I became an archaeologist in the first place. In the day job I am also just starting out on a 3-year project with Professor Michael Fulford at the University of Reading looking at what 20 years of developer archaeology has told us about the countryside of Roman Britain. I am really looking forward to this opportunity to emphasise what most people in field archaeology intuitively know already: that our understanding of Romano-British rural life has changed out of all recognition as a consequence of PPG 16/PPS 5, and that if we can find a way of synthesising the vast quantities of data available there will be a new and fascinating story to tell. On a personal level it will also be an opportunity to stick two (metaphorical) fingers up at an old-school archaeologist with whom I had a memorable (to me at least) exchange early on in my time at Cotswold Archaeology: 'You work in rescue archaeology don't you?' 'Yes'. 'You're wasting your time!' I have never subscribed to the belief that I or my colleagues have been wasting our time. Of course we have all spent time on projects which in retrospect proved to be of pretty low research value, but these are exceptions and we expend the majority of our energies on sites which make a positive contribution to the local and regional scene. And it is this desire to contribute which has guided much of my thinking from an early stage in my career. I will be perfectly content if the reports produced by Cotswold Archaeology are assessed in 50 years time by researchers of the day as 'pretty good by the standards of the time'. By then acronyms such as PPG 16 and NPPF will doubtless (and thankfully) be long forgotten but hopefully our reports will live on as the record of sites long since destroyed.

So much for the retrospective; what of the future? Archaeological fieldwork hasn't been a comfortable place to work in the last couple of years, but we ought to bear in mind that virtually every senior manager of a small to medium-sized enterprise (SME) in virtually every profession in the UK would probably say the same. Archaeology is intimately tied to construction, and as this sector is traditionally first into recession (and, more positively, usually one of the first to recover) it should be no surprise that life has been tough. The biggest challenge that I face is how to plot a strategy that allows us to brave the downturn relatively unscathed, and be in a good place to exploit the opportunities that will come in the recovery. It is hard to escape the conclusion that there is over supply in the current market; more people want to earn a living in commercial archaeology than can be accommodated by current demand. This has led to the inevitable downward pressure on prices, sometimes to almost suicidal levels, and I would venture that there can be hardly any contracting companies which have not sustained a loss over the last couple of years. Archaeology ignores the law of the market because it is a vocation and a way of life (like farming), and people are understandably reluctant to give it up. 'What else could I do?' is a rhetorical question that I often hear, and I would be lying if I denied that these thoughts hadn't crossed my mind. We cannot go on like this for too much longer, although just what the market will look like on the other side of the recession is hard to visualise at present. In the late nineties and up to the banking crash of 2008 it looked like we were moving towards a supermarket scenario with a small number of very large companies slogging it out for high-value contracts (mostly infrastructure, but some urban renewal). The ability to deploy large teams into the field at short notice was paramount. But outside of London and the South East such projects disappeared almost overnight and when they come back we have to question whether there will still be companies with the capability to resource them. Perhaps it will require more flexible collaborations involving a number of different partners. I would maintain that the development of Joint Ventures between otherwise rival companies was one of the more positive and progressive developments of the last couple of decades. We will also need to see how the trend towards fragmentation works out. It does seem that the number of very small operators is multiplying, and as one organisation closes it is replaced by two or three smaller ones offering desk studies, watching briefs and small evaluations at knock down prices. Some of these small companies deliver very good quality work, but there can be problems if they over-stretch themselves onto projects which they are not really geared up to resource. To date we have seen much more evidence of fragmentation than consolidation, although that may yet come. Nor is the future of local authority contracting units clear. Some have gone or are going (Exeter, Gloucestershire); those remaining seem under never-ending review. I imagine that all will be 'externalised' in one form or another over the next few years.

One response to the recession adopted by a number of companies (mine included) has been regionalisation in the hope that if you can get a slice of another geographic market while holding your overheads tight, then this is an effective strategy to counter reduced demand in your home territory. It is too early to tell how many of these regional ventures will succeed. Personally I think that those with real regional presence and expertise, and willingness amongst the staff to become involved with the local professional and general interest community, have the best chance of winning through. I am much less convinced about the '*virtual office*' concept which is often little more than a post box.

I do not believe that everything is dreadful or in crisis in British archaeology, but nor do I hanker for some romantic past where we all dug fascinating archaeological sites without the pressures of competition. In my experience there were a good number of pretty poor archaeological projects in the 1970s and 80s, most of which will never be properly published (a fate sadly shared by some very good projects as well). Of course there are many ways in which the current system of commercial archaeology could be improved. It can be all too easy to fall into a pattern of fieldwork by numbers, with an unquestioning adherence to formulaic, regimented approaches to excavation. The one area where I would really like to see progress is to introduce a greater incentive to be good. There is a huge disparity in the quality and volume of published outputs over the last 20 years amongst different organisations, and this is not always linked to size. How do we recognise and reward those organisations which produce thoughtful, intelligent accounts of their projects, and conversely penalise those that produce very little? The government has developed the Research Excellence Framework for universities as a means of recognising quality, and the score you get really matters as it has considerable funding implications. While it would be possible to devise some form of peer reviewed assessment of the research outputs of commercial archaeological organisations, what would be the reward? While it might be possible to create a system whereby Government contracts were only awarded to organisations who could demonstrate a certain level of achievement, the vast majority of funding derives from commercial developers who will want the freedom to choose whoever they want. It might be thought that an assessment of research quality could be bolted onto the Registered Organisation (RO) scheme administered by the Institute for Archaeologists, but this is unlikely until some form of accreditation to practice is introduced. As long as the present system persists whereby anyone can set themselves up as an archaeological consultant or contractor, those in the RO scheme run the risk of being penalised through additional costs compared to those outside it.

Overall I remain essentially optimistic about the future of commercial archaeology; indeed in my job if you don't think this then it is probably time to call it a day. There is a lot of really good archaeology going on in the UK and fascinating discoveries are being made regularly. While I now only get to bask in the reflected glories of work done by my colleagues, I still ask when they return from site 'What did you find?' with a hopeful inflection. And I try to remember that I am lucky to get paid to do something which many people regard as their hobby.

Chapter 7

'Dark, dark, dark, amid the blaze of noon':
Reflections of a freelance pottery specialist

Chris Cumberpatch

The remit for this contribution specified an '*individual, reflective account*' delivering an '*accurate picture of the challenges faced ... across the profession*'. I have been working in commercial archaeology in Britain since 1991 and, with the exception of a few forays abroad I have been almost continuously engaged in reporting on later prehistoric and post-Roman pottery from commercial excavations throughout this time (Cumberpatch and Roberts 2012). In view of this it will be no surprise that the focus of the article will be on pottery studies although it is hoped that some of the observations will also be relevant to those working in other areas of specialisation.

Addressing the role of specialists in archaeology is no new task and has been the subject of a variety of articles both polemical (Cumberpatch and Blinkhorn 1998; Blinkhorn and Cumberpatch, 2008; Cumberpatch and Roberts 2012) and more reflective (Vince 1987) in recent years. More broadly an awareness of the critical roles played by specialists in the process of archaeological investigation and the creation of the archaeological record has been highlighted by authors commissioned to produce reviews and protocol documents on behalf of English Heritage and various study groups (eg English Heritage 1991; Mellor 1994; Irving 2011).

Ongoing work by study groups has produced numerous examples of what have become known as 'standards documents' (Prehistoric Ceramics Research Group 1991, 1992; Medieval Pottery Research Group 2001; Perrin 2011). General acceptance of these foundational documents has been slow in coming and even today they seem to have had relatively little impact in the remote and exclusive locales where heritage policy is made and the future of our past is decided. It is not even clear that they are regularly cited by archaeological curators when setting the project briefs which structure project designs and they appear to be quite unknown within the museum sector in spite of their significance for archiving. Nor, unfortunately, are they explicitly referred to in the Code of Practice promulgated by the Institute for Archaeologists (IfA 2008).

In Cumberpatch and Roberts 2012 I outlined, from a personal perspective, the challenges faced by pottery specialists in working within a structure of practice created using a model partially and inexactly derived from one based on civil engineering and its various ancillary services and it would be otiose to repeat the substance of that article here (*see also* Chadwick 2000). Instead I shall discuss some of the broader areas in which the relationship between specialist studies of a specific artefact category articulates more or less imperfectly with other fields within archaeology and the wider historic environment. My intention is to highlight some of the broader issues which threaten to undermine the appearance of a mature, self-confident and self-reflective archaeology which fulfils its potential in producing consistent and coherent but also contentious, disruptive and socially and politically inconvenient accounts of the past.

The integration of the various branches of archaeological specialisation was strongly advocated in MAP II (English Heritage 1991), a document which although sometimes criticised for its rigidity and over-prescriptive nature seems in retrospect to have had much to recommend it; a clear case of not valuing what we had until it was gone. With its focus on the notion of a 'project team' (1991; Appendix 1) and on horizontal rather than vertical integration within that team, it offered a model of practice far superior to the atomised, vertically-orientated structures that exist today and within which most artefact specialists are employed.

It is rightly said that context lies at the heart of archaeology and this applies whether the word is used to refer to the stratigraphic context of a find or feature or more broadly to the institutional or sub-disciplinary context within which aspects of the past are investigated and through which the past is written and the archaeological record comes into being. The widely accepted (but contested) current model of practice sees the task of the archaeologist as removing impediments to wealth accumulation from sites identified as suitable for development in the fastest time and at the lowest cost possible (Chadwick, 2000; Cumberpatch and Blinkhorn 2001; Thorpe, this volume). In this model, the role of the specialist is to apply his or her skills and experience to a body of data with the aim of producing a report that will accord with the constraints and parameters set out in the project brief and/or the written scheme of investigation. The basic scope of such reports has been established by practice and, while different contractors and curators may have different requirements, few seem to acknowledge the essentially research-driven nature of pottery and other specialist studies. In the vernacular the requirement is to 'do the pottery' (Blinkhorn and Cumberpatch 2008) and this is generally understood to involve a primary focus on a single assemblage with such broader comment as can be inserted at the whim of the analyst, but without any requirement to systematically review comparable assemblages or to undertake investigative activity that might be classed as 'research'. The assumption, sometimes made explicit in conversation is that '*others will have the opportunity to do the research in the future*' although, for reasons that I shall describe below, this is far from being a certainty or, increasingly, even a possibility.

No two pottery assemblages are ever the same and all are the result of a wide variety of formation processes (or impacts) which act together to produce a unique profile for every site. Added to this there are fundamental issues which can only be tackled at a higher level than the individual site. In medieval pottery studies for example we have achieved a high degree of precision in identifying the origin of specific sherds or vessels, of dating the lifespan of individual potteries and of documenting the distribution of specific ware types. Broader issues remain poorly investigated; regional and comparative studies for example are severely underdeveloped as are the phenomenological aspects of pottery production and use. At one time it was possible to look to central government funding via English Heritage to support such essential work but cross-party hostility towards English Heritage has effectively precluded it from carrying out this vital role through a succession of punitive budget cuts and externally-imposed priorities that have left it virtually powerless to conduct or support modern archaeology on a realistic scale. Nor does it seem possible to look to universities for a consistent and coherent commitment to working in tandem with the commercial archaeological sector. The highly idiosyncratic rules and often pernicious employment conditions drawn up by university administrators seem explicitly designed to crush effective and significant research beneath a landslide of petty rules, restrictions, targets and methods of assessment that are crippling a once vibrant higher education sector. The rise and fall of commercial units attached to university archaeology departments was, in most cases, too rapid for them to have had any significant impact on broader research themes or to allow the development of a symbiotic relationship between research and commercial excavation. The existence of these units should have offered an unprecedented opportunity to revitalise the commercial sector and to introduce to the academic sector huge bodies of largely untapped artefactual and ecofactual data through which significant areas of the past could have been investigated. In the author's experience (and with a few honourable exceptions) this was not done and the closure of several university-based units (in at least one case leaving important excavation reports incomplete) seems to mark the end of an experiment that failed in many of its aspects. As a direct result, the distance between the academic and commercial sectors has continued to grow and as it has done so the opportunities for new and innovative work on finds assemblages has dwindled, to the detriment of archaeology as a whole.

A side issue here, although perhaps one with long term implications for archaeology, is the extent to which artefact specialists are institutionally separated from mainstream academic discourse and from teaching. There are no effective mechanisms through which specialists working primarily in the commercial sector (most of whom are self-employed) can become engaged in university teaching unless they are prepared to accept conditions of pay and employment that are, for all practical purposes, unsustainable. This means that there are no effective mechanisms for the skills and knowledge of one generation of artefact specialists to be passed on to the next. Thus one of our foremost experts on medieval pottery (and the author of an earlier review of pottery studies for RESCUE; Vince 1987) was never able to assemble a body of students who could learn directly from him and his experience or take his work forward. More generally it means that there are few new entrants into areas of specialisation other than osteology and palaeopathology which seem to flout the more general trend. This must be accounted a failure for both commercial archaeology and the academic system. Every generation must learn anew and this is self-evidently both absurd and inefficient.

Artefact specialists are dependent upon the work of their predecessors and contemporaries in order to develop new and innovative interpretations of archaeological data. Such work is collaborative and accumulative even where disputes about theory and methodology may be vibrant and dynamic. Nowhere else is the sheer asininity of Tessa Jowell's statement *'the field of academic research is competitive, and that is as it ought to be'* (Dept of Culture, Media and Sport 2005; RESCUE 2005) so clearly demonstrated. Knowledge of the past is constructed through a hermeneutic process involving a continual interplay between theory and data with contingent interpretation the intermediate outcome of this process. While some of the necessary work can be done using published data, archaeology is at base a materialistic discipline which requires the analyst to engage *mano a mano* with the subject of his or her study. This raises the issue of archaeological archives, something that RESCUE has been involved in for many years (eg RESCUE 2004, 2005, http://rescue-archaeology.org.uk/cuts). Archaeological investigation creates the past through its engagement with the materiality of that past and the most significant and important results of any archaeological excavation are the archive and the final report (whether the latter is a traditional monograph or a digital publication). For serious scholars it is the archive that is the primary source of information and the essential resource for reinterpretation. Given this, the greatest threat to archaeological knowledge is the destruction of those very archives which constitute it.

In recent years the world has watched in horror as religious zealots have destroyed buildings, archaeological artefacts, libraries and archives in pursuit of their apocalyptic goals and the triumph of an androcentric world order in which a vicious authoritarianism replaces the liberal values of contingency and curiosity and tolerance. What has passed almost without comment is that archaeology in Britain faces a similar apocalypse, but one driven by consistent and long-term under-funding and the imperatives of professional bureaucrats rather than religious fanatics.

The impulse to destroy archives (often under the guise of such bland terms as 'dispersal' or 'de-accessioning') is one which remains controversial within the museum world (Museums Association 2012a, b and c) but seems to be much less so amongst politicians and bureaucrats even though the practice not only undermines the future of museums as places of learning and teaching but will also ultimately, by removing the very raw material upon which we depend for our interpretations, preclude us from writing adequate accounts of the past. Without the artefactual archives to interrogate and re-interrogate we shall be reduced to a futile logo-centric process of textual commentary without the opportunity to return to the material basis of our discipline in order to apply new techniques and new approaches to our data. The danger for museums is that they will become venues for the presentation of bland and uncontentious accounts of the past which offer nothing to the critical audience and are, in effect, little more than extensions of the schoolroom or the face-painting workshop. It is not only through the active destruction of existing archives that this will take place. The imposition of absurdly high charges for archive deposition (several hundred pounds per box in some places) will inevitably incline some of the less reputable contractors and consultants to advise their clients on 'sampling' strategies which owe nothing to statistical principles and everything to a desire to reduce project budgets to a minimum. Government inaction over many years (and particularly in relation to the spending of national lottery money within the museums sector) has ensured that our archival infrastructure is wholly inadequate to the task of ensuring that our archives are preserved and, once assured of preservation, are available for analysis and reanalysis. It is of particular concern that there has been little or no dialogue between archaeologists (and particularly artefact specialists) and museum curators in this matter and that the principles set out in documents such as the MPRG's minimum standards document seem to have been entirely ignored within the world of museum administration. RESCUE has, on a number of occasions, tried to draw attention to this situation but the response has been negligible and with the most recent round of cuts to local authority budgets it appears that the active destruction of archives to save space and money will soon become a reality.

This brief and polemical review has painted the current situation in apocalyptic terms and some may consider it to be an exaggeration. It builds however on a body of evidence familiar to the author and to many other artefact specialists. This evidence indicates that while we have the methodological potential to undertake ever more innovative forms of analysis and to construct increasingly subtle and sophisticated interpretations of past lives (and thus to engage the interest and commitment of the wider community), the opportunity is being squandered as a result of poorly conceived spending decisions, short sighted administrative and bureaucratic priorities and a philistine notion of value that prefers the meretricious and superficial over the profound and thought-provoking.

References

Blinkhorn, P W, and Cumberpatch, C G, 2008, *Unbolting the potshed door: The future of the role of the ceramic analyst in the archaeological process*, at http://independent.academia.edu/CCumberpatch/Talks/14923/Unbolting_the_potshed_door

Chadwick, A M, 2000, Taking English archaeology into the next millennium: a personal view of the state of the art, in *Assemblage* 5, at http://www.assemblage.group.shef.ac.uk/5/tableofc.html

Cumberpatch, C G, and Blinkhorn, P, 1998, The analysis of artefacts and the tyranny of the field archaeologist, in *Assemblage* 4, at http://www.shef.ac.uk/~assem/4/tableofc.html Dept of Archaeol and Prehist, Sheffield University

Cumberpatch, C G, and Blinkhorn, P, 2001, Clients, contractors, curators and archaeology: who owns the past? in Pluciennik, M, (ed), *The responsibilities of archaeologists: archaeology and ethics*, British Archaeol Rep Internat Ser **981,** Oxford, 39–46

Cumberpatch, C G, and Roberts, H M, 2012, Life in the archaeological marketplace, in Rockman, M, and Flatman, J, (eds), *Archaeology in society: Its relevance in the modern world*, Springer, New York, 23–43

Department of Culture, Media and Sport, 2005, *Understanding the future: Museums and 21st century life*, DCMS Consultation Document

English Heritage, 1991, *Management of archaeological projects*, English Heritage, London

Institute for Archaeologists (IfA), 2008, *Standard and guidance for the collection, documentation, conservation and research of archaeological materials*, at http://www.archaeologists.net/sites/default/files/node-files/ifa_standards_materials.pdf

Irving, A, 2011, *A research framework for post-Roman ceramic studies in Britain*, Med Pottery Res Group occ pap **6**

Mellor, M, 1994, *Medieval ceramic studies in England*, Med Pot Res Group/English Heritage

Medieval Pottery Research Group 200, *Minimum standards for the processing, recording, analysis and publication of post-Roman ceramics*, Med Pottery Res Group Occ pap **2**

Museums Association, 2012a, at http://www.museumsassociation.org/ethics/ethics-of-disposal)

Museums Association, 2012b, at http://www.museumsassociation.org/ethics/12538

Museums Association, 2012c, at http://www.museumsassociation.org/ethics/11947

Perrin, R, 2011, *A research strategy and updated agenda for the study of Roman pottery in Britain*, Study Group for Roman Pot Occ pap **1**

Prehistoric Ceramics Res Group, 1991, *The study of later prehistoric pottery: general guidelines*, Prehistoric Ceramics Res Group Occ pap **1**

Prehistoric Ceramics Res Group, 1992, *The study of later prehistoric pottery: guidelines for analysis and publication*, Prehistoric Ceramics Res Group Occ Pap **2**

RESCUE: The British Archaeological Trust, 2004, *Museums in crisis: an outline of the RESCUE position*, at http://rescue-archaeology.org.uk/2004/06/16/museums-in-crisis/

RESCUE: The British Archaeological Trust, 2005, *Understanding the future: museums and 21st century life; A response by RESCUE: The British Archaeological Trust*, at http://rescue-archaeology.org.uk/2005/06/28/understanding-the-future-museums-and-21-st-century-life/

Vince, A, 1987, Pottery studies: stamp collecting for the enthusiast? in Mytum, H, and Waugh, K, (eds) *Rescue Archaeology, what's next? Proceedings of a RESCUE conference at the University of York, Dec 1986*, Dept of Archaeol, University of York Mono **6**, York and Hertford, 17–22

Chapter 8

14 Years in...and still digging

Chris Clarke

Beginnings

In reviewing my career to date I thought it would be a simple case of detailing the key events that had marked my progress in the job. What I did not anticipate was the emotive exercise it would become. Before now I have reflected regularly on 14 years of being a professional archaeologist, in the form of fleeting recollections, or remembering funny moments over a pint with colleagues, but never before had I consciously sat down and reviewed the whole landscape of memories. The result of this process was the realisation of how strongly these events have shaped who I am today; my motivations and ambitions. In many ways you can say archaeology is more than a job, potentially more than a vocation as well. I believe that this can be held true for many archaeologists and I hope that this chapter provides not only an insight into life as a professional archaeologist in the first decades of the 21st century, but also an insight into archaeology as a defining passion.

As my title suggests, I am now in my 14th year as a professional archaeologist, having achieved the position of supervisor in a medium-sized archaeological unit with national coverage. In this role my time is split fairly evenly between the field and the office so, while I still get to enjoy a hands-on role on site in all weathers, I also spend time in the office writing up projects, and bringing them to conclusion. Psychologically, I still very much enjoy what I do and consider my career to be going strong and, ultimately, I hold the view that archaeology will be my career for life.

Like the majority of 'diggers' of my generation, I come from a middle-class background and received a fairly standard state education. Thanks to several motivated and influential teachers, history soon became a favourite subject at school, supported by regular days out exploring numerous castles, stately homes and watching episodes of '*Time Team*'. By the age of 17 I had my sights firmly set on taking archaeology as an undergraduate. With two weeks of voluntary digging on a Roman villa site prior to the start of my degree, I knew I was sold on the subject.

The majority of my three years at Bournemouth University is a blur of drinking, partying, studying and cramming, and by the end of it I came out of it with a 2:1 and an even greater passion for archaeology. Despite the vocational nature of the course and the inclusion of 'professional studies', I found, like many diggers, that the course prepared me poorly for the industry I was about to be launched into. However, it did provide me with an advantage over those graduating from other universities as I entered the professional arena with six months experience of drawing plans and sections, writing context sheets, taking levels, and getting a grasp of stratigraphy. Many of my fellow job hunting graduates often had less than half of that experience, and frequently struggled with even the most basic tasks on site.

Getting established

The industry I encountered on graduation was reasonably unforgiving; with new diggers facing a steep learning curve and having to immediately get to grips with tight deadlines, poor conditions, low pay and a lack of training. I quickly learnt that what you put in, you got out. If you put the energy and effort into what you did, you were soon rewarded with good archaeology, the respect of your peers, and recognition by your superiors.

Graduating in the summer of 2000 I was fortunate that the industry was still riding the upward curve of the late 1990s' building boom, with big excavations aplenty and units hiring any graduate that could hold a trowel. Even so, to get a job close to home in London I still had to volunteer for a two-week period, during which I proved my worth.

Getting to know the team on site was not difficult. Accommodation was provided so we both worked and lived together, enjoying a vibrant social scene, and occasionally popping home with a rucksack full of dirty washing. The social experience was made all the easier by the inclusive attitude of most archaeologists. If you worked hard and played hard it didn't matter who you were or where you came from, as long as you could hold your drink and keep up with the banter. Many of the people I met on my first professional dig I still count as some of my closest friends to this day.

When the rookie sheen began to wear off I started to really notice the negative aspects of what I was getting myself into. Low pay, short-term contracts, basic working conditions, minimal career structure, and a lack of training were all issues that we had to come to terms with. The issue of low pay was the most significant of these factors, starting on an annual salary of approximately £13,500 (higher than average due to being based in London) and ultimately working up to £21,000 as a Supervisor over the course of my career. Such poor levels of graduate pay affected all those I worked with, and the situation did not improve over the course of the next decade, as even by 2007/8 the average digger's wage was just under £14,500 (Aitchison and Edwards 2008, Table 72). Living on such a low wage had a significant impact on people's lives. In the short term this meant living in shared rental accommodation with the majority of your wages covering transport, food and clothing. The concept of actually being able to save any money was wishful thinking. This resulted in many of my friends leaving archaeology within five years of graduating, completely disenchanted with the lack of prospect of having any sort of future within the industry, a common experience documented by the Invisible Diggers survey (Everill 2009). Even now diggers are struggling to earn a living wage as the rising cost of living is drastically stripping away any money they earn (Rocks-Macqueen 2012).

The longer you work as a digger, the more the realities of your chosen career path hit home. For me it was realising (within the first two years of professional employment) that many of my university contemporaries were earning up to double my wage and had, in some cases, already been promoted. They were employed on secure, permanent contracts, and had employers that were actually investing in them. They were becoming financially secure, renting their own places, buying cars, paying off student loans, and able to think realistically about starting a family. I was rapidly realising that my choice of job was highly unlikely to provide this stability. My choice of job was not only a career-choice; it was becoming a lifestyle choice as well.

Yet, fresh out of university and in our early twenties, most diggers feel invincible and often these difficulties are ignored while they enjoy the social aspect of the job. On top of this, most diggers have to cope with a transient lifestyle working the 'circuit', moving from site to site, unit to unit, county to county, all the time chasing the next three month contract for the next big job. Some units provide accommodation, the quality of which ranges from self-catering apartments with pool tables and Jacuzzis, through to poorly-maintained houses where mice live in the toaster. If you find a long enough contract then it might be possible to find your own place to rent, but frequently the only solution is taking a room in a shared house.

Limited horizons

Within my first two years on the job, despite the limited opportunities for career advancement, I enjoyed the work. I had been given a permanent contract, and had worked on some fantastic archaeology. My skills and experience developed quickly as I worked on a range of projects.

Those friends who did not leave the industry, but still yearned for a more stable career path, would regularly voice their frustrations with the job over a pint, asking why no-one seemed to be doing anything to change the situation. My philosophy has always been that there is no point in moaning about something if you are not prepared to try to change it yourself. I started to investigate two organisations that seemed to be trying to improve things, yet were often criticised for not doing enough. These were the Trades Union, Prospect, and the Institute of Field Archaeologists (now, of course, the Institute for Archaeologists). In 2003, convinced that the situation was not as futile as it appeared, I not only became a member of the IFA council, but began to sit in on Prospect's 'Archaeologists Branch' Committee. At that time Prospect was working to improve the situation by directly negotiating with employers on pay and conditions, as well as pushing on issues such as training and health and safety. Despite setting minimum pay levels within the industry, much of the work the IFA did went unobserved by the digger on the ground as its implementation of standards and guidance impacted at a higher level within the industry, only influencing those on the ground in more indirect ways. This dual Prospect/IFA experience taught me that one person could make a difference, but also that, unless there was a sea change in peoples' attitudes, the road to real improvement would be long and frustratingly slow.

In archaeology, it seems, promotion primarily comes down to being in the right place at the right time, as well as knowing the right people, or even being in a relationship with the boss. For me, attempting to attain the role of supervisor was never simple. Despite working for the same company for three years and increasing my skills and experience at every turn, no formal promotion was forthcoming. At first I was asked to take on more responsibility in an ad-hoc fashion whenever the workload picked up, without any additional training or pay. This continued until I had clearly proven my ability in the role, and repeatedly badgered the unit managers, at which point I was paid to 'act up' when required, although there was no change in title or contract. Ultimately, after over a year of constantly 'acting up', my work was finally reflected in a promotion in 2006.

On reflection, the greatest frustration in regards to trying to develop my career as an archaeologist was the lack of a defined career structure. I know this is something that many diggers suffer from, since the majority of commercial field units do not operate any formal training schemes or structure staff experience in a direction suited to greater responsibility and promotion. Where staff appraisal systems are in place they are often not worth the paper they are written on. This leaves the initiative primarily on the shoulders of the individual employee, and when you are in your early twenties with only limited experience, this can be very daunting. Without visible opportunities available, most diggers are left fumbling around in the dark, stumbling from one short-term contract to another, just hoping for a lucky break instead of making informed choices regards their career.

As a digger, one of the biggest challenges is getting a unit to invest in you. With digging contracts often short, most units have a very disposable attitude towards their staff, particularly the more junior diggers. *'Why'* they say *'should I invest in my staff when they'll only leave soon to join one of our competitors?'* However, it is more often the other way round. The very fact that units do not invest in them, whether it be financially, contractually, or via skills development, means that they will be forced to seek other opportunities in order to develop their career.

As for my own career, my opportunities have continued to grow since 2006, including greater responsibility in regards to the size of sites directed, and the managing of budgets and resources. On the back of this there has been an increase in my post-excavation responsibilities; processing large volumes of site data leading to publication. As a result, despite what could still be termed a relatively junior position, I have amassed a respectable publication record. Most of these skills were developed by being thrown in at the deep end, a common experience among most at this grade. Training often consists of being given an example of a previous report or publication and being told to write the new document in the same format, to the same time frame as an experienced member of staff would. It certainly ensures that skills are acquired and honed very quickly, but often limits the understanding of the processes involved or the rationale behind them.

Since the credit crunch of 2008 every unit has been slashing costs in order to survive and remain competitive. Of course, one of the easiest targets in the cost-cutting process has been training budgets, with some companies reducing them to near non-existent levels. This removal of even the most basic training provision has hit junior staff members the hardest, denying them access to skills those higher up the company structure take for granted. This results in a situation in which greater reliance is placed on staff members with existing skills. When they move on, units have to bring in new staff members with similar skills and experience, rather than promoting junior staff into more responsible positions having developed their skillset.

As a digger's career develops, it is hard to avoid the disillusionment that often accompanies it. As much as I have consciously tried to avoid this, I often find myself taking a negative perspective and questioning whether we are achieving anything at all in the work that we do. We all have our down days, especially when we are standing in mud to our knees, getting drenched by persistent downpours on a negative watching brief, and of course friends and colleagues have left the industry when these bad days outnumber the good. People can, and do, lose sight of why we do the job in the first place, and the reality of the situation starts to outweigh the passion for it. Digging for fun allows me to focus on the pleasure of it, and remind myself why I got into the job in the first place. We have all got to find our own survival mechanisms, but it would be very sad to see the growing professionalisation of the industry come at the price of archaeologists' passion. We all have a duty to make sure that archaeology can remain a 'live to work' environment rather than a 'work to live' type of job.

The future

What about the future? No archaeologist could doubt that the current economic situation has cast a very long shadow over us all, with some smaller archaeological units closing, and even the largest continuing to make redundancies. Nothing is certain at the moment. As for me, this uncertainty has made me even more aware of my strengths and weaknesses as an archaeologist. This self-analysis comes from a need to understand and evaluate the skills required to strengthen my employment position, while demonstrating the value of existing skills to ensure that they are not being taken for granted by those around you. Ultimately, it is about valuing your own skills and experience, and making sure that you are not selling yourself short. Archaeologists in general can be very bad at this, with many employers taking advantage of highly experienced staff for their own commercial gain. The only thing you can do in uncertain times is keep your options open. Seek to gain the maximum benefit from the situation you are in, but at the same time always keeping an eye open for new opportunities and greater rewards. This may mean taking risks, but the hope is that it will lead to a working environment which both respects your passion and recognises your true value. In the short term I plan to ride out the hard times in the best way I can, ready to take maximum advantage of more positive times ahead. As for the longer term, well, I'm still here after 14 years, I hope I'm still getting dirty in another 14 years' time.

References

Aitchison, K, and Edwards, R, 2008, *Archaeology labour market Intelligence: Profiling the profession 2007–08,* Institute of Field Archaeologists, Reading

Everill, P, 2009, *The Invisible Diggers: A study of British commercial archaeology*, Heritage Research Ser **1**, Oxbow Books, Oxford

Rocks-Macqueen, D, 2012, Is it getting better? Pay and inflation, *The Archaeologist* **86**, 18–21

Chapter 9

A valued partnership: volunteers and archaeology

Ginny Pringle

Volunteers possess a passion and whole-hearted commitment to archaeology that can never be doubted. We may be amateurs with an interest in archaeology or we may be professional archaeologists who volunteer in our spare time, but we all have one thing in common; enthusiasm beyond reason! Why else would we choose to spend our time in rain and mud for no pay? Why else do we absorb high fuel-costs to travel far and wide to help with curatorial tasks or to seek out fieldwork? Why else do we spend much of our spare time supporting local archaeological societies and planning events? I have enjoyed volunteering for many years, serving both the *Basingstoke Archaeological and Historical Society* and *CBA Wessex*. I am also aware of the opportunities and challenges that the voluntary sector now faces.

Writing in *Rescue Archaeology* shortly after the formation of RESCUE 40 or so years ago, Philip Rahtz found it difficult to define volunteers. He noted they were often a substantial part of the labour force on rescue digs, on occasions up to 40 or 50 strong. They were composed of a huge variety of people, from school-children to the elderly, from housewives to professionals and they possessed a similarly broad range of experience from the novice to experience of extra-mural lectures in archaeology (Rahtz 1974). In other words just about everyone and anyone could volunteer.

We still come from a variety of backgrounds, but times have moved on and today many volunteers possess an even broader range of experience, often supported by intensive study courses or even PhDs in archaeology. A proportion of volunteers may well have higher academic qualifications than some professional colleagues. More significantly many of us are likely to be retired or generally mature in years. Given an ageing population; the fact that younger people with aspirations often have to work demanding hours; an increased cost of living; and many women choosing to juggle work with bringing up families; this is not surprising. Whether our numbers have actually increased or decreased since the 1970s is open to question and would make for interesting research, but the type of work we do is certainly much more varied; it needs to be.

From post-WWII times through to the 1980s the name of the game was rescue archaeology and, following the large-scale urban development during this period, there were plenty of opportunities to volunteer. Sadly, for those volunteers participating in rescue digs, the implementation of PPG 16 in 1990 saw much of archaeological practice become developer-led and dominated by commercial units. Volunteers have had to adapt and find alternative fieldwork, often based on research-led projects, as well as a multitude of other tasks. Many of us who volunteer belong to one or more local societies and it is through these organisations that opportunities for volunteering are often channelled. Volunteers from my local society enjoy a huge variety of work including desk-based research, sorting out museum archives, arranging training excavations, organising outreach events and much more. We work both independently and alongside professional archaeologists, according to the task undertaken.

My local society is typical of most with a significant proportion of members being fairly mature in years. Whilst many are content to attend talks and do the odd day trip, an enthusiastic proportion actively engages with fieldwork. Fieldwork, when it can be found, is like gold dust. It might be field walking (*see* Figure 1) or woodland survey, and we have even been known to do the odd bit of dowsing; a bizarre sight when 20 or so people plod in formation across the local common with dowsers at the ready! Above all, excavation remains our most popular form of fieldwork (who can resist the temptation of the trowel?) and we are fortunate in having strong ties with our county museum service which has allowed us to excavate for a couple of weeks each year under professional guidance at the county council owned site of Basing House in Hampshire (*see* Figure 2).

For those who are more mature in age physical limitations need to be considered; often despite protests to the contrary. One of our members, a retired builder with two replacement hips, insists on putting more energy into his digging than many an 18-year-old student. I just wish I had known about his artificial hips before he spent a whole day helping me with a magnetometry survey. Other than this we just need to watch the general pace, allow plenty of rest breaks and attempt to avoid back injuries. Accordingly for some who volunteer, survey work or finds processing may be more appropriate than heavy digging.

Figure 1 Members from the Basingstoke Archaeological and Historical Society take a break during field walking

Photo: © G Pringle

Figure 2 Volunteers from BAHS excavating at The Grange, Basing under direction of staff from Hampshire County Museums Service

Photo: © D Allen

Despite a few age-related hiccups, a cohort of mature volunteers definitely has advantages. A wide variety of experience and skills acquired over a lifetime together with reliability and a (sometimes!) sensible outlook, bring a valuable contribution to any society or project. This sector is also more likely to have the time, a degree of reasonable income and access to private transport; all of which facilitate volunteering. There is however the very real possibility of a significant decline in numbers of future volunteers when the current generation is replaced by those who face shrinking pensions and the necessity to remain in work for longer. So a major concern of mine is not only how to attract a younger membership but a membership that has plenty of time!

Local universities offering degree courses in archaeology might provide a ready supply. My local society offers well publicised events with keynote speakers such as Professor Sir Barry Cunliffe, but attending visitors are from much the same age-group as the general membership, a pattern I often see repeated across other archaeological societies. On the other hand the Young Archaeologists Clubs, originating with RESCUE: The British Archaeological Trust but now organised through the Council for British Archaeology (CBA), are extremely successful in engaging the interest of the very young who, like most people keen on archaeology, love doing fieldwork (*see* Figure 3). Unfortunately local-society membership, including my own, is underwhelmed by the younger generation where conversely the generation gap must be somewhat overwhelming.

Figure 3 Volunteers of the future? YAC members seeking excavation skills

Photo: © D Allen

If local societies are undermined by a perception of being the terrain of the grey-haired, then unless we innovate, we will continue to struggle to attract numbers of younger people. I strongly believe that local societies must be prepared to provide activities which offer engagement at family level. Ideally our societies and committees would have a proportion of younger members generating a fresh input of ideas and willingness to implement them. All very easy to state, but in order to achieve this forward-thinking strategies must be developed by existing members.

Economic austerity has created substantial opportunities for volunteers, particularly within the public sector; although not without challenge. Volunteers from my local society often work alongside public-sector professionals assisting with the care of archaeological collections and finds processing. Public-sector services have suffered severe expenditure cuts over the past couple of years, meaning that in many places professional leadership has been reduced and volunteers are coming to be regarded as a substitute. The accompanying redundancies of professionals can undermine not only the co-operation and trust between the two groups, but also between volunteers. Such events are divisive and unpleasant and my local society has not been alone in dealing with them.

Sadly, the excavations we enjoyed at Basing House are now restricted due to cuts in public expenditure and reductions in the professional staff that previously directed the work. At the same time voluntary-sector opportunities at Basing House have arisen for front-of-house duties where professional curatorial staff have been made redundant!

We now attempt to draw a line between those tasks we have traditionally volunteered for and newer tasks created by redundancies. The latter we treat with caution for fear of alienation from both redundant professionals and fellow volunteers, but with continued tight public expenditure, opportunities for the voluntary sector will no doubt continue to increase.

The voluntary sector faces more challenges than seeking out opportunities for fieldwork, ageing demographics and political issues. It also faces an explosion of archaeology into multi-disciplinary approaches with individual disciplines becoming increasingly specialist. The modern volunteer should ideally possess a good set of basic archaeological skills and considerable background knowledge, not to mention good IT skills which are essential for communication. My local society and regional CBA group are very proactive and organise low-cost study days for traditional skills such as site-recording or pottery and worked flint identification. We also make available specialist study-days on topics such as animal bones, human bones, and environmental archaeology. These study days, usually led by specialists from local universities or commercial units (*see* Figure 4) have proved very popular and participants are able to practise their new-found skills by volunteering for various tasks including post-excavation work and curatorial tasks.

Figure 4 Volunteers from the Hampshire Field Club attending a pottery study day run by staff at Wessex Archaeology

Photo: © M Peryer

Some specialist skills are far more difficult to acquire. Geophysical survey for example, requires technical equipment and skills which make it difficult for volunteers to undertake these non-intrusive surveys, now seen as a prerequisite before, or indeed as an alternative to, excavation. I can think of a good number of potential research sites in my local area but specialist equipment for survey and geophysics is expensive, difficult to obtain, and requires training to use. Those who have the equipment are understandably reluctant to loan it out. In addition the resultant data requires specialist software and knowledge to interpret the results. Hiring in commercial units to do the work can be prohibitively expensive and somewhat defeats the object of volunteering. Results from the CBA's survey of community archaeology in the UK (Thomas 2010), indicate that my local society is not alone; but we do at least own a Total Station theodolite!

It would certainly be of great help if specialist equipment could be made more accessible, the software easy to use, and appropriate training made available for volunteers. I have known professional archaeologists quake in their shoes at the thought of amateurs doing geophysics, but there is no reason why not as long as a rigorous project-design has been formulated and volunteers properly trained. The *Jigsaw Cambridgeshire* community archaeology project, assisted by the Heritage Lottery Fund, promises just this (Jigsaw Cambridgeshire 2012), and may be a model upon which other archaeological groups can draw. Another project, still in its infancy, is the *Wessex Academy for Field Archaeology*; an initiative of my CBA regional group where geophysics courses will be offered alongside other field-based training (Wessex Academy for Field Archaeology 2014).

Despite the environment of austerity, grants for archaeological projects are available but usually offered with conditions for community involvement, as demonstrated by the *Jigsaw Cambridgeshire* project (Jigsaw Cambridgeshire 2012). Consequently the concept of community archaeology is currently riding on a wave of social inclusion, aspiring to involve non-professionals and local communities and to engage them with their local heritage. However, whilst engaging with the community at large, professional practitioners of community archaeology should also recognise those existing volunteers quietly working in the background and offer them targeted training and support. Rather than being seen as amateurs pursuing a hobby we might be more usefully viewed as unpaid skilled practitioners making a valued contribution.

I argue that community archaeology projects led by volunteers have the potential to create more opportunities to develop a wider set of skills, for example project management, than if led by professionals where the level of engagement for volunteers might be restricted to more basic tasks. An associated problem is that setting up community projects requires orchestrated effort and a great deal of time; something which those volunteers yet to retire can find difficult to deliver due to other more pressing commitments. Despite this, community archaeology can provide a way forward for engaging and developing volunteers for the future. It demonstrates a wider audience can be reached and that the potential exists for a younger and more diverse audience (Thomas 2010). My local society has plans for a community project in a local village where participating residents and the local primary school will dig test pits in their own back yards. I am confident this will prove popular, but we will need to consider post-excavation strategies if we are to continue to engage with the local community and to attract wider audiences to our membership once the initial phase is complete.

Friends of Ancient Monuments (FOAM) engages volunteers to relieve selected ancient monuments of unwanted scrub, giving these sites the care and attention they deserve (CBA Wessex 2014). The beauty of *FOAM*, an initiative of popular archaeologist Julian Richards, is that it does not require specialist knowledge and so is ideal for community involvement. Through *FOAM* the site at Odiham Castle in Hampshire has benefitted not only from local society volunteers but also from enthusiasm and energy provided by local scout-groups who love the outdoors. *FOAM* also helps identify volunteers who want to learn more specialist archaeological skills. However this is not an excuse for using unpaid gardeners and morale can quickly wane if sites are subsequently not maintained by the relevant authorities; promises of sheep grazing do need to be implemented! WARNING: volunteers are completely free to switch projects at short notice!

The voluntary sector faces at least one more challenge; that of increasing professionalism. Methodologies and standards have steadily improved over the years and quite rightly so. Networking between local societies, museum services, county archaeologists and commercial units can provide a solution where professionals might volunteer to assist with amateur-led projects. Alternatively volunteers might consider seeking their own accreditation such as through the Institute for Archaeologists (IfA). Although 'Affiliate' membership is suggested for those who are generally interested in heritage, for example volunteers, it lacks an associated accreditation programme. To gain professional accreditation 'Corporate' membership needs to be purchased and the programme for this demands both an on-going personal development plan and a 'Continuing Professional Development' log (IfA 2009a). Such requirements favour the employed rather than those who volunteer and although there are some concessions (IfA 2013), the fee structure is hardly geared towards the unwaged or unpaid.

As far as the voluntary sector is concerned, the current IfA requirements for accreditation could be considered rather overwhelming. In addition many volunteers give the IfA little attention since the general perception is that the organisation represents those in the paid sector. To counter this I suggest the IfA should consider a scheme specifically geared towards volunteers whereby we are able to seek accreditation for specific specialist skills. This would not only qualify us to undertake particular tasks with confidence, but ensure that the quality of our work meets professional standards. An alternative for volunteers is to gain an NVQ in Archaeological Practice but with this costing upwards of £2000 (IfA 2009b), it is unlikely to be popular.

To be fair, both the CBA and to a certain extent the IfA with its fairly new Voluntary and Community Special Interest Group are developing an improved awareness of the voluntary sector. According to the IfA, the CBA has worked closely alongside the IfA to develop a set of guidance material for the voluntary sector (IfA 2012). This is a worthy start but volunteers need to know that this material exists and how to access it.

Funding awarded by the Heritage Lottery Fund to the CBA in 2012 in order to extend the number of CBA community archaeology bursaries by twenty-four places is of merit (CBA 2012). I hope that through this scheme there will be proactive engagement with local archaeological societies and CBA regional groups in order to reach our existing cohort of volunteers. The CBA must continue to develop strategies that link community archaeology, local societies and existing volunteers.

In conclusion, I suggest the CBA and the IfA could work together with local and county societies and CBA regional groups to tease out a continuum of activities that can capture the imagination of the local community; progress willing volunteers into low-skill activities that support local sites or services; and identify and train specialist volunteers into more skilful support-roles. Local societies and community archaeology projects will then attract new and hopefully younger blood. Otherwise it is entirely possible that the numbers of existing volunteers will fall and dwindle due to an ageing demographic, and because specialism and professionalism do increasingly dominate the sector. If volunteers are to successfully bridge gaps in the public sector and also conduct or participate in fieldwork and research using best practice, then we must be given targeted support and training, together with optional accreditations that can be economically completed in a relatively straightforward manner.

Returning to the inimitable Philip Rahtz, over a generation ago he described a golden era where volunteers of all ages and backgrounds and levels of experience were in ample supply, and participating in rescue digs was a rather novel activity (Rahtz 1974). Times have moved on and many volunteers are now likely to be more mature of age and keen to develop a variety of skills. Others may be professionals passionate about volunteering in their spare time. Either way, a wide range of skills and experience is essential since although fieldwork and particularly excavation remains popular, we are now likely to be engaged in a huge variety of archaeological tasks. Above all, we need to be excellent networkers and highly focussed in order to continue to successfully expand our engagement with archaeology.

Despite the challenges, all the volunteers I work with continue to thoroughly enjoy and remain fully committed to archaeology. Opportunities for engagement, particularly in community archaeology, are steadily increasing after the long vacuum created by commercial archaeology. With cuts in public expenditure the voluntary sector has now entered a pivotal period where in the 'Big Society' we are a powerful resource. Together, volunteers and professionals will contribute to a valued partnership that should not be under-estimated but first, such partnership must be firmly secured.

References

Council for British Archaeology, 2012, *CBA awarded major new HLF funding for community archaeology,* at http://www.britarch.ac.uk/news/120528-hlfnews (accessed 30 May 2012)

Council for British Archaeology Wessex Region, 2014, *FOAM: Friends of Ancient Monuments,* at http://www.cba-wessex.org.uk/foam.html (accessed 13 May 2014)

Institute of Field Archaeologists 2009a, *Individual Membership,* at http://www.archaeologists.net/ join/individual (accessed 17 May 2012)

Institute of Field Archaeologists (IfA) 2009b, *The Qualification in Archaeological Practice, NVQ Levels 3 and 4,* at http://www.archaeologists.net/sites/default/files/node-files/IfA_nvq_info.pdf (accessed 15 May 2012)

Institute for Archaeologists (IfA), 2012, *Voluntary and Community Special Interest Group, Newsletter 01, Spring 2012,* at http://www.archaeologists.net/sites/default/files/node-files/ Newsletter1.pdf (accessed 17 May 2012)

Institute for Archaeologists (IfA), 2013, *Subscriptions,* at http://www.archaeologists.net/ membership (accessed 20 May 2013)

Jigsaw Cambridgeshire, 2012. *Jigsaw Cambridgeshire,* available at http://www.jigsawcambs.org (accessed 17 May 2012)

Rahtz, PA, 1974, Volunteers, in Rahtz, P A, (ed), *Rescue Archaeology,* Pelican, Harmondsworth, 274–9

Thomas, S, 2010, *Community Archaeology in the UK: Recent Findings, Council for British Archaeology, York,* at http://www.britarch.ac.uk/sites/www.britarch.ac.uk/files/node-files/ CBA%20Community%20Report%202010.pdf (accessed 17 May 2012)

Wessex Academy for Field Archaeology Ltd, 2014, *Courses Available 2014,* at http://www.wafa. org.uk/courses-available/ (accessed 13 May 2014)

Chapter 10

Archaeology in Higher Education

Paul Everill

Introduction

In writing this I have tried to strike a balance between an overview of the current situation faced by academics, and personal reflection. Needless to say my views are coloured by my experiences and so I do not claim this represents the universal experience of those working in Higher Education (HE). Like the other chapters in this section it is simply an exemplar from which the reader might draw indicative conclusions. Many academics might disagree vehemently with my views on the role of HE in preparing students for professional practice and that is their prerogative. However, I firmly believe that anyone graduating with a degree in archaeology, and consequently anyone calling themselves an archaeologist, should have a sound knowledge of the principles and processes of excavation, recording and interpretation. That process is the defining core of our discipline, even if one then specialises in one of the many other allied disciplines that contribute greatly to or support archaeological research. Excavation (and recording) is an important specialisation in itself. However, it is one that has been treated as the poor relation for some time and suffered at the hands of those that seem to believe that anyone can dig, but not everyone can interpret. The critical role of the primary site archive suggests that the two cannot be disentangled. I make no apologies for this view of archaeology, and the importance of Higher Education in preparing the next generation of archaeologists.

Higher Education

There is a perception, though it is not clear how widespread or, indeed, accurate it is, that academics predominantly follow a narrow professional path from Bachelor's degree to Doctorate, and onto a lectureship via one or more post-doctoral research/teaching positions. This was certainly often the case historically, but perhaps fewer new lecturers are lucky enough to travel such a direct route to academic employment. That said, I feel very strongly that students are luckier to find themselves taught by academics with a greater breadth of professional experience and, come to that, life experience. Put crudely, my background in commercial archaeology means I have far more experience in the field, spent with some inspirational and innovative excavators (and exposure to modern, professional project management) than I could have achieved in a whole career spent purely on summer research excavations.

There is also a greater variety in the nature of institutions, and the character of archaeology degree programmes, than was ever the case in the past. The Conservative Government's Further and Higher Education Act 1992 created a number of so-called 'Post-92' universities from the existing polytechnics and colleges of higher education. This has led to what some characterise as a division between the research-intensive, traditional universities and the more teaching-led 'new' universities. This, perhaps overly simplistic, division looks likely to be reinforced by current Government policy, under which the financial rewards for research 'excellence' seem certain to favour those institutions already able to support staff research to a significant level, with rewards for aspiring, but lower scoring, institutions reduced or cut altogether. While some might imagine that archaeology is found predominantly within the older universities, my recent survey of all archaeology degree programmes (Everill and Nicholls 2011) demonstrated that only 56.8% of the 44 universities then offering degree programmes belonged to the research-intensive Russell Group and 1994 Group universities. Eleven (25%) of the universities were independent, and the rest belonged to smaller groupings such as the University Alliance, which emphasises innovation, enterprise, and strong links with community and industry.

The long-term effects of the increase in tuition fees to a maximum of £9,000 (implemented in December 2010 following the Browne Report) are also still unclear, but many universities are reporting a drop in applications. Here at Winchester; where tuition fees were initially set below the maximum, applications for our archaeology and related programmes seem to be holding relatively steady, but it is not clear how far this reflects the experience across the teaching-led HE sector or, indeed, how long that might last. Research-intensive universities seem to be adversely affected by the curious Government policy of removing the recruitment cap on students achieving AAB or higher at A-Level, making it one of the few ways that universities could expand student numbers. Needless to say that pool is finite, yet some Russell Group universities made it their primary target. This policy seems likely to produce some big losers, and already the University of Birmingham has closed its Institute of Archaeology and Antiquity citing reduced applications, with 2012 seeing the last intake to their undergraduate Single Honours programme in archaeology. The recruitment cap is now set to be removed altogether for the 2015 intake, and this seems likely to result in fierce competition for students, and potentially the demise of those archaeology departments who fail to retain their share.

Reflections

Returning to my own experiences, it is probably only fair to start by discussing the ways in which my career to date does not reflect that of a typical academic (however Cobb, Section 4 this volume, contains a number of parallels). In doing so I am conscious that I might be about to unmask myself as someone who does not fit the standard academic label, however it seems to me that many colleagues, perhaps particularly those in the first few years of a lectureship, live with a near constant fear of being 'found out'. This is perhaps because of the constant use of metrics to measure our performance as teachers, researchers, writers and ultimately as deliverers of education to students who are increasingly perceived as consumers. However, we were also once undergraduates and we cannot help but compare ourselves to the academics that shaped our career and our interests; perhaps remembering their apparent excellence and infallibility when viewed from that perspective.

Despite an unpromising performance as an undergraduate at Saint David's University College, Lampeter, and subsequent failure to find work in developer-led archaeology, my passion for archaeology was only slightly dented. After spells of factory work and data entry, I got back in contact with a lecturer who had, in the meantime, moved from Lampeter to Southampton. I had presumably performed rather better in the field than in the lecture theatre as an undergraduate because he offered me my first paid archaeological work, as site-assistant on his new project. At the conclusion of that excavation I decided to apply for a part-time MA at Southampton, armed with a reference and the offer of a spare room in an undergraduate house. Recognising that this might be my only chance to pursue a career in archaeology, I applied myself to my studies rather better than before, and set about accruing more field experience. Within days of submitting my dissertation I was offered a digging job by a developer-led company in Ireland.

A number of years spent dodging redundancy in Ireland and then Britain perhaps do not equate to a career in commercial archaeology, but all of my discipline-specific skills were learnt or honed in that sector. It was a steep learning-curve, which started from day one on a chaotic road project in County Clare and included the exhilarating transition from a quiet field in County Tipperary to the stunning, deeply stratified archaeology of the City of London. It was a priceless education and one that, as I have subsequently found, makes me something of a rarity in academia. My decision to leave commercial archaeology was ultimately borne out of frustration. Not necessarily with the money, though I would be lying if I said that was not a factor, but mostly with the slow pace of career advancement and scarce opportunities to take on greater responsibility. Like many others I opted to leave the commercial sector and retrain, however I was fortunate to be able to change direction without leaving archaeology.

My PhD, back at Southampton, looked at the broader issues of British commercial archaeology. I continued to work for local units for 1, 2 or 3 month spells during my research, and following my viva in 2006 I returned to full-time commercial work with the Southampton Council unit; when, in 2008, a post was advertised here at Winchester it was initially a non-academic position (Demonstrator in Applied Techniques) and very part-time. I was advised that it was worth a gamble, despite the fact that, at the time, it actually represented a pay-cut. I had also seen many talented PhD graduates leave Higher Education and even archaeology altogether after failing to find employment, and felt that this might be my only opportunity. When my application was successful I gave myself a few months to see if it was financially viable, but before long I had picked up an additional part-time post within the Faculty, which finally brought my earnings up to the level I had been on before.

Increasingly the non-academic nature of the post became a source of frustration as, in reality, the only differences between the Demonstrators and academic staff were that we were not expected to have personal tutees, or contribute to the Research Excellence Framework (REF: the metric assessment of a department's research output and successor to the Research Assessment Exercise). In 2010, following the arrival of a new Dean in the Faculty, we were re-graded as 'Lecturers in Applied Archaeological Techniques'.

The current state of archaeology in HE

It is now over six years since I left commercial archaeology (for the second time) and the gamble has, in part, paid off. I have recently been made Senior Lecturer, and Programme Leader for our undergraduate degree programmes. I remain part-time, like a significant number of those in Higher Education, but I have found an academic position in a department that is serious about the teaching of archaeological skills. In comparison, a lot of teaching at Higher Education seems irrelevant to the commercial sector, which, let's not forget, provides the bulk of archaeological jobs for our graduates. I personally do not feel that it is adequate to cite 'theoretical frameworks' and 'transferable skills' as being of primary importance in terms of our delivery of an **archaeological** education, though interpretative skills and report writing, for example, are important elements of an archaeologist's tool-kit. The fact is that undergraduate programmes are now the pre-requisite for employment in commercial archaeology. Even if only 10–15% of graduates (which, in 2011, would have been 159 to 239 UK graduates annually (Everill and Nicholls 2011)) pursue a career in that sector, we are surely letting them down by allowing the remaining 85–90% of students (who might have no interest in archaeology beyond providing 'bums on seats' for universities) to determine course content and delivery. That is not to say, of course, that transferable skills and discipline-specific skills are mutually exclusive, and skills such as writing, presenting and teamwork will be valuable regardless of the graduate's destination. However, it seems that many archaeology degrees simply do not provide enough key disciplinary-skills to properly equip graduates for professional practice.

The reasons behind this are manifold. The first, and perhaps most paralysing, seems to be a fundamental lack of will amongst some senior academics to develop curricula that give equal weight to theoretical and practical skills and recognise that interpretation of the archaeological record might be underpinned by the former, but is utterly dependant on the adequate execution of the latter. Of course, practical skills are not limited to excavation and some, such as pottery analysis, tend to be developed through postgraduate study. However, it is hard to get beyond the fact that those graduating with a degree in archaeology should have a sound understanding of the fundamental, and defining, process of archaeological data collection: excavation. The cost implications of increasing fieldwork experience are nothing new of course. Despite the media portrayal of universities awash with money under the new tuition fees regime this is simply not the case. The reality is that the current Conservative-led Coalition Government is simply transferring the full cost of Higher Education onto students. It is nothing more than political spin to suggest that universities will be better funded as a result. This is particularly true if one factors in cuts to many of the previously publically-funded grants that supported Higher Education Institutions, especially across the humanities sector within which archaeology most commonly resides; and the loss of additional 'B and C' funding that supported subjects like psychology and archaeology, which have higher running costs because of their laboratory and fieldwork requirements.

Add to this the cost in terms of staff-time of increasing fieldwork against a backdrop of an increasingly bureaucratic workload. The fascination with metrics (producing league tables that are supposedly designed to enable 'consumer choice') has generated an abundance of overly bureaucratic and time-consuming procedures that actually undermine the ability of academics to contribute fully to the discipline. This would be less damaging if the metrics were genuinely useful. Instead, academics faced with producing four highly-rated, peer-reviewed publications for the Research Excellence Framework (REF), might overlook the many excellent journals produced by local societies through which their work might have a genuine impact. Instead they might focus on publishing in a journal of one of the international schools/institutes, which may actually have a smaller circulation, but is deemed to have a greater impact. In REF terms, international importance is often all that matters and a British focus is sometimes deemed to be parochial and less significant.

In other senses the measures of performance and productivity (and activity) have been beneficial. The days of Professor Embolism[1] (the blockage in the system: slowing career advancement and recruitment on the rungs below; failing to write up excavations older than some lecturers; and giving the same lectures, in the same style, as they gave 10 or even 20 years ago) are now thankfully numbered, though they do still exist. There is a welcome focus on improving the delivery of teaching, and maximising the opportunities to embrace new technologies and innovative assessment practice. The downside, once again, is the bureaucratic burden of demonstrating to university managers that one is fully engaged with these practices. Meanwhile, the workload of a junior lecturer has not diminished and, on taking up a new post, the production of teaching material for a range of new modules (some of which might just be the modules that no-one else wants to teach and are off-loaded onto the newcomer) can be crippling until one is more established. Of course the teaching load varies greatly between institutions for reasons outlined above.

In terms of students, every intake is different. However, I frequently find when talking to colleagues at other institutions that good and bad year-groups at Winchester correspond surprisingly well to intakes elsewhere. Quite why, and how, this is the case is unclear, but often good year-groups are characterised by motivated mature students who serve to enthuse those around them, so there are perhaps wider socio-economic agents at work. I am constantly surprised, and disappointed, by the reduced ability of school leavers to write well, or indeed something approximating English. Furthermore, the emergence of the internet as a vast repository of information (and misinformation) sometimes creates a sense that students no longer read for a degree, they surf for it.

---

[1] I have a feeling that this joke first appeared in the 'Bluffers Guide to Archaeology'

Wikipedia is the best known of the various online sources, and many smaller information-sites base their own content on it. Undoubtedly these sites represent a useful starting point for research, however they are fundamentally unreliable as sources of 'facts', often with no sources cited and having very light editorial control over changes made to the content. Even entries compiled on the basis of rigorous research can be subjected to change. I have lost count of the number of times that students have confidently made erroneous statements based on internet sources that they have not verified. For example, Winchester was apparently chosen as the capital of the kingdom of Wessex in 1519, if you believe the many websites that have repeated a typographic error that may first have appeared on ask.com - and at least one student essay that used it for 'research'.

Conclusion

While recognising that not everyone will share my views on the role of HE, I believe that a significant number of staff involved in teaching come to the sector via a much more circuitous route than was ever the case in the past. Bureaucracy across the sector seems to have ballooned in recent years. At the same time there is an increasing need for academics to focus on improving a student's basic writing skills, which used to be the responsibility of schools (and, as anyone who has struggled to interpret illegible scrawl on a context sheet would recognise, perhaps handwriting should also be included!). I regularly come across students who are academically average, but who excel in the field and feel a degree of sympathy for them. The question, perhaps, is not whether HE is the right training ground for future archaeologists, but whether it can adapt to the current situation. With an increased financial burden on students, and commercial archaeological wages moving forward at glacial pace, I strongly suspect that the teaching of archaeology will increasingly focus in non-research intensive institutions as traditional universities focus on other, more lucrative, areas. Academic archaeology has exploded since the original RESCUE volume was published in 1974. It is now, perhaps, starting to contract, and who knows where it will be in 40 more years time, but one thing is certain and that is that it needs to adapt in order to better reflect demand.

References

Everill, P, and Nicholls, R, 2011, *Archaeological Fieldwork Training: Provision and Assessment in Higher Education*, University of Winchester and the Higher Education Academy

SECTION THREE: Crisis points

Introduction

Joe Flatman

Section three of this book is entitled 'crisis points', and considers five key areas of concern in British archaeology. These concerns are as follows:

- Chapter 11: professional practice (Dominic Powlesland)
- Chapter 12: careers, pay and conditions (Paul Everill)
- Chapter 13: museums, archives and storage (John Shepherd)
- Chapter 14: maritime heritage (Joe Flatman)
- Chapter 15: metal detecting (Pete Wilson)

All of these crisis points were in place in 1974 when Rahtz's *Rescue Archaeology* was published; the question that these chapters ask is: what, if anything, has changed? Reviewing each of these chapters in turn, it becomes clear that the past 40 years has been a case of 'two steps forward, one step back', with marked improvements in most cases in terms of the identification, prioritisation, protection and promotion of the historic environment, but serious ongoing problems that remain (especially funding/ resource problems) as well as new fields of concern such as new threats like renewable energy developments. Writing in 2014, at the tail-end of a recession involving significant government cutbacks at both the local and national levels, there is also a marked sense of *déjà vu*, with some of the crises in rescue archaeology last experienced in the 1970s resurgent once again after decades of dormancy.

In particular, like a disease that we had hoped was long eradicated, the spectre of uncontrolled development without proper, or indeed any, monitoring by local government or intervention by professional archaeologists once again raises its head at this time, due to a combination of local government cutbacks and central government deregulation. Within this, a particular thread that can be identified in all of the chapters in this section is that of public understanding of the significance and thus 'value' of archaeology. For all of the hard work undertaken over the past 40 years, there remains a worrying lack of public understanding of the social, cultural, environmental, and crucially the *economic* value of the historic environment.

This lack of popular understanding translates into a lack of political understanding and thus strategic influence that the historic environment lobby can wield upon politicians at every level, from parish councillors to privy councillors. The historic environment continues to punch below its weight in this respect when compared to similar lobby groups, such as the diverse array of natural-environment special-interests who see much greater popular understanding of and support for their cause, and thus much enlarged political engagement. Such a failure to first gain, and second to maintain, sustained popular support has direct negative impacts on individual historic sites. One of the most obvious of these impacts is the continued threat to many such sites by vandalism and looting (Chapter 15 on metal detecting); another is the ostensibly benign but in fact extremely destructive impact of many modern farming practices on plough-zone archaeology (Chapter 11 on professional practice).

A different set of problems remain within the heritage community, but again, the overarching problem seems to be one of *perception* more than action. As Shepherd outlines in Chapter 13 one of the biggest problems among heritage professionals is the continued perception of archaeological archives as a burden rather than a blessing. Everill identifies essentially the same problem in Chapter 12 which discusses how the lack of internal understanding of the nature of 'professional' archaeological practice has led to what amounts to a crisis of training provision of future archaeologists within the university sector. Powlesland highlights similar concerns in Chapter 11, reflecting on the pressures currently placed on professional practice and training alike. If the heritage community cannot manage to communicate key messages within its own small confines, then no wonder that the 'public' continue to maintain a mixed message about the importance of our sector.

For all of the doom and gloom, the five chapters of this section do have some good news. Just as was visible in 1974, these chapters show a strong sense of 'duty' is maintained in the heritage community in the face of adversity; of championing a series of corners despite the many problems that beset us, with generation after generation of archaeologists picking up the same mantle and continuing the fight. Such a sense of duty is heartening indeed, and if nothing else, this book serves as a record of that struggle. But returning to an earlier point, the key question is, how do we expand that sense of duty beyond our immediate community and out into the wider world? Until the heritage community achieves strategic 'break out' in this crucial respect, then the crisis points of archaeology discussed in this section are likely to remain for another 40 years and more.

Chapter 11

Crisis in the countryside

Dominic Powlesland

In 1971 at the inaugural public meeting of RESCUE, at Senate House, University of London, there was a tremendous buzz in the air, a charged atmosphere that was driven by the desire to address both the challenge arising from the increasing threat to an undiscovered or inadequately understood archaeological resource in the face of a national development boom, and the challenge to do 'better archaeology'. There was an understandable focus upon the threats to the archaeology of urban areas and of the expanding network of motorways which carved swathes through poorly understood archaeological landscapes. It is very unlikely that a single person in that crowded meeting had any comprehension at the time of the true scale and complexity of the archaeological record as a whole, and particularly that of the rural countryside. Urban excavations, particularly those being conducted on a massive scale by Martin Biddle in Winchester, had exposed both the seriousness of the threat to archaeology posed by urban regeneration, and also the scale of response required if the unique and fragile evidence of our urban past were not to be lost forever. This paper takes a reflexive view based primarily upon anecdotes, remembered observations and discussions from the past 40 years and a personal view of some areas of crisis within field archaeology today.

A period of transition

The 1970s was a period of tremendous change in the scale and volume of work undertaken as much as in the approaches both to excavation and recording. The pressures of urban regeneration let to the creation of urban archaeological units in many towns in England at the same time as archaeological units developed in many local authority planning departments. The organic and reactive way in which many of these archaeological organisations emerged, in response to threats invariably in progress, was made possible through an expanding budget made available from the Department of the Environment's Ancient Monuments Branch (the forerunner of English Heritage). Whilst the national budget expanded during the 1970s and 1980s, faced with the increasing scale of work needed, the available funds were still very limited; the concept of archaeology as a profession was hardly established, and the majority of archaeological projects undertaken were only made possible through the deployment of vast numbers of volunteer excavators and excavation supervisors paid only a subsistence allowance. Large excavations were manned by teams gathered from willing archaeology students and other volunteers from around the world, camping or staying in basic hostel accommodation. They were for the most part characterised by hard work, lots of fun and intense debates held in the evenings in pubs or around camp-fires about almost every aspect of how fieldwork was conducted and documented. These excavations also provided the training ground for the generation of archaeologists who would later form the commercial archaeology units that dominate the archaeological profession of today.

Increases in government allocations during the 1970s and 1980s funded rescue-excavations and underpinned the ad-hoc formation of archaeological units in Urban and Local Authority contexts. In addition funding was directed towards air photography and the creation of Sites and Monuments Records (SMRs) at national and county level, the forerunners of today's Heritage Environment Records (HERs). The increase in the scale of archaeological air-photography not only greatly expanded the database of known 'sites' but also led to widespread scheduling of crop-mark sites to afford them some degree of statutory protection. We have since learned that many of these remarkable crop-mark sites may have been less deserving of preservation than we thought; the clear crop-marks being an indication that the archaeological evidence in the ground has been truncated, thereby giving the greatest contrast between the undisturbed natural and features cut into it, thus producing unusually clear crop-marks. The increase in airborne remote-sensing and the development of paper and then computerised SMRs reflected a need to quantify the scale of the archaeological resource in the face of increasing threats both from development and the impacts of modern agriculture.

Prior to the emergence of archaeological field units the majority of excavations were small scale, conducted within the context of academic enquiry, and directed by either university based academics or archaeologists based in museums (Jones 1984, 5–9).

The 1980s and early 1990s was also a time when major changes were taking place in universities, the subject was expanding and saw the beginnings of a polarisation between the many engaged in full-time field-archaeology and those with posts in universities. With few exceptions, those employed in universities increasingly had neither the freedom, facilities or, in some cases, the experience to engage in large-scale excavations. Those running large field-projects did not have the time or opportunity to contribute towards the academic programmes within the universities (Roskams 2001, 23–5). The debates that dominated the late-night sessions in pubs and on excavation camp-sites frequently revolved around attitudes to 'archaeological theory' which had emerged as a subject in its own right, frequently employed self-consciously complex language and often seemed, to those in the field, to exclusively overlook the role of primary data (Binford 2001; Chadwick 2003, 97–9; Lucas 2012). There was ongoing and enthusiastic debate about how to record on site (Barker 1969; Biddle and Kjolbye-Biddle 1969; Boddington 1978; Harris and Ottaway 1976; Hirst 1976; Jefferies 1977) and about where rescue excavation sat within the concept and practice of archaeological research (Hawkes 1954; Lucas 2001; Lucas 2006; Roskams 2001, 32, fig 1; Sullivan 1978). It should be of interest to us today that the intensity and scope of these (on-going) debates were not fully reflected in widespread publication at the time and are remembered within archaeological folklore rather than celebrated through definitive contemporary publication.

In a valiant campaign to raise the profile of research within rescue funded excavations English Heritage introduced the concept of project-funding of excavation[1], including rescue excavation, framed within a detailed research design with explicit and cogently argued research objectives linked to the requested budget (Wainwright 2000, 918).

This was closely followed by the publication of *Management of Archaeology Projects* (English Heritage 1989) which was then expanded and revised to become *Management of* Archaeological *Projects* (English Heritage 1991a), popularly known as MAP 2. These initiatives defined a structural framework within which fieldwork, post-excavation analysis, and publication should be approached, but even when carefully followed, did not necessarily secure the full budgets requested, and thus of necessity aspects of the research ambitions set out in project designs often had to be trimmed to match the available funds.

Archaeology as a subject was also being transformed at the same time. New methods of excavation and recording and the increasing role of scientific approaches to analysis, the increasing role of environmental archaeology, and changes in scientific dating were revolutionising the subject and transforming the returns from excavation (Collis 2001, 11–19).

Crisis, what crisis?

Things were however, far from perfect, although the levels of funding for rescue archaeology steadily increased during the 1970s and 1980s (*see* Everill, Chapter 14, and Thorpe, Chapter 16, *this volume*) the total budget was hopelessly inadequate relative to the levels of archaeological threat (English Heritage 1991b). The government had observed the increasing spend on excavation, in particular through the rescue-archaeology budget, and the principle of 'the polluter pays' began emerging as an alternative to government funding of the environmental impacts of development (English Heritage 1986; Wainwright 1991).

The publication of *Planning Policy Guidance Note 16* (PPG 16) (Department of the Environment 1990) can be seen as a reflection of the formal transfer of responsibility for archaeological investigation associated with development in the UK from the state to the private sector. PPG16 advocated the preservation of important archaeological sites and their settings *in situ*. Where this was not possible, or the archaeology was not considered sufficiently important to support refusal of planning permission, then excavation prior to development could be required (at the expense of the developer) as a planning condition. The significance of this transfer of financial responsibility from the state to the developer should not be underestimated, and although no one could argue that this did not lead to a huge increase in the amount of archaeological investigation being

---

[1] This was also to provide a framework in which to review applications in order to prioritise, and to be able to demonstrate that the allocation of a reducing pool of funds had a fair and logical basis

conducted; it completely changed the nature of rescue excavation and the archaeological process. With the advent of PPG16 the available funds from central government rapidly diminished (Wainwright 1991) but were importantly targeted towards emergency assistance for projects producing exceptional but unexpected results, and research-driven projects.

In a perfect world the replacement of publicly funded rescue archaeology with work funded by the developer could be seen as a simple change in accounting, however the world is not perfect and after 20 years of developer funding it is clear that there are significant problems in archaeological practice (Chadwick 2010; Cumberpatch and Roberts 2012; Everill 2012; Harward 2012). These have been amplified and exacerbated by the economic collapse resulting from the global banking crisis exposed in 2008. It would be easy to argue that the crisis in archaeology today is simply down to a lack of funds, but it is not that simple; the overall expenditure on archaeology today is vastly greater than it was 20 years ago (Aitchison 2012; Wainwright 2000) even allowing for the catastrophic effect the recent collapse in the building industry has had on the profession as a whole. The position we are in today owes much to the way that PPG 16 has been applied and the way that the relationships between the developers, curators, and practitioners have developed over the last 20 years. PPG16 was replaced by Planning Policy Statement 5: *Planning for the Historic Environment* (PPS5) in 2010 (Department for Communities and Local Government 2010) which has itself since been superseded by the *National Planning Policy Framework* (NPPF) (Department for Communities and Local Government 2012). We have yet to see how these current planning policies will change our subject, but it is difficult to take a positive view of planning policies that diminish the statutory provision for professional guidance with reference to archaeology in the planning process. There is clear evidence of a very-real risk that budget-cuts might result in archaeological planning decisions being made by people with no archaeological qualifications at all, and with minimal access to HERs or other crucial resources.

Managing the resource ('How much archaeology is out there?')

The whole process of developer-funding and managing the resource is predicated upon assumptions that may not be correct. Most significant is the fact that those managing development controls can only manage the identified resource; this may seem obvious but the HERs that underpin heritage planning advice are far less comprehensive than we tend to realise, and directly reflect the nature of past archaeological discovery rather than the true distribution of past human activity. If we examine the process of archaeological discovery at a landscape level we quickly realise that the majority of the information contained in the various HERs has been accumulated from chance discoveries. As such the HERs are a product of reactive rather than pro-active research. 'Sites' are known and recorded on the basis of many factors, including the survival of earthworks or upstanding structural evidence, chance discovery of material culture at ground level, the discovery of archaeological evidence during development, or the observation and recording of crop-marks from the air. The immense contribution of air-photographic survey is appreciated by all, but we need to remain aware that even when the same landscape is repeatedly flown at appropriate times over more than three decades, as has been the case in the Vale of Pickering, previously unobserved crop marks are still discovered almost every year (Powlesland 2006, also for similar observations elsewhere *see* Riley 1980, 1–4).

These 'new' discoveries seem more and more to result from increasing plough-damage rather than simply from poor coverage and failed observation in previous years. During the last 15 years geophysical survey has also become increasingly important in giving an alternative, and often more consistent, view of landscape-scale features; enhancing and expanding upon what has been observed from the air. But we cannot simply rely on such remote sensing data: for example, excavations being conducted ahead of sand-extraction at Cook's Quarry, West Heslerton in the Vale of Pickering, continue to reveal dense domestic and other activity from the late-neolithic to early-medieval periods in an environment where, with the exception of a massive pit-alignment, geophysical surveys showed nothing (Powlesland 2006, 2009, 2011).

It is difficult to see how we can develop a rigorous archaeological management strategy focussed upon 'heritage assets', to use current terminology, if we do not know where they all are. Sophisticated computer mapping and GIS applications may give the impression through distribution maps that we have a good understanding of the scale and distribution of the archaeological resource. However, zoom in on these maps and we find that the picture is far from complete. The concept of 'site'; a fundamental one in archaeological terminology, is clearly inappropriate when applied at the landscape level, and emphasises the disconnected dots in our distribution maps to the detriment of the white space in-between. In very real terms the absence of evidence cannot be seen as a true indicator of evidence of absence. The concept of 'site' owes most to identifications and attitudes established in the 19th century and earlier. It is a concept associated with public access and the associated fenced boundaries, and is enshrined in the way that so many English Heritage guardianship or World Heritage sites are presented to the public.

This is in no way a criticism of the local authorities' HERs, or English Heritage and the National Record of the Historic Environment. It is simply a fact that after the great advances made in the two decades prior to 2000, no SMR or HER has had the necessary financial support to contemplate pro-actively expanding the record through research. Amongst the most significant contributions of the last 25 years, the English Heritage National Mapping Programme has transformed our awareness of the crop-mark record, but the results still only reflect the distribution of known evidence (English Heritage 2013a). This is all the more important given the emphasis and terminology used in the NPPF, which is concerned with loosely defined 'Heritage Assets' and subjective issues such as the 'Setting' of those Assets, or aspects of significance within what are so often very seriously depleted archaeological landscapes. To argue, for instance, that the installation of wind turbines compromises the archaeological integrity of the landscape (where almost all the known archaeological evidence has been plough damaged to a point of invisibility) is unsupportable.

A moment of change

The Aggregates Levy Sustainability Fund (ALSF) introduced in 2002 effectively doubled the English Heritage archaeology budget by introducing, initially, up to £5 million pounds per year into the budget. It included specific objectives with regard to identifying both the scale and sustainability of the archaeological resource in aggregates landscapes. The introduction of the ALSF funds made it effectively possible, for the first time, to investigate large areas of those landscapes most suited to prehistoric and later settlement in a pro-active fashion rather than in response to an immediate threat. Between 2002 and 2011, when the ALSF contribution was withdrawn, the ALSF funding distributed by English Heritage supported many nationally important, innovative and subject-changing research projects (Flatman *et al* 2008). The extraordinary research on Doggerland, undertaken by Vince Gaffney and a team from Birmingham University, and the Landscape Research Centre's (LRC) work in the Vale of Pickering, have transformed our understanding of the archaeology both beneath the North Sea and on land (Gaffney, Fitch and Smith 2009; Powlesland *et al* 2006; Powlesland 2009, 2010, 2011). In both cases the ALSF budget made it possible to undertake fundamental research at a scale that would otherwise have been impossible, the results of which have completely changed our comprehension of the nature and extent of the archaeological resource. The returns from these two projects alone have exposed, on the one hand, hundreds of square kilometres of late-palaeolithic to neolithic landscape beneath the sea and, on the other, tens of thousands of features in a landscape once considered to have limited archaeological interest.

The work in the Vale of Pickering indicates that we have underestimated the sheer quantity of archaeology that lies beneath the fields of our valley landscapes by a factor of ten or more. Sadly without other similar, large-scale survey projects elsewhere, the evidence exposed will be seen as anomalous, when it is more likely to be a true reflection of what we might expect in similar environments throughout eastern England. The contribution of the ALSF supported a range of research and community projects that, for nearly a decade, transformed our understanding of aggregate landscapes in general, but also exposed how poor is the evidence base for the majority of aggregate landscapes. The withdrawal of the annual ALSF contribution which, in the case of archaeology in 2010/11, represented a little less than 1% of the tax levied, was a hopelessly short-sighted move to save public funds. It had a catastrophic effect on our ability to carry out pro-active research targeted at identifying the scale of the archaeological resource. Although the ALSF levy is still raised, the decision to cancel the application of a tiny percentage of it to research into sustainability makes it effectively impossible for us to undertake comprehensive landscape research. Such research is needed if we are to interpret past landscapes, or develop long-term and appropriate management strategies for the archaeological resource.

Plough-damage is not simply a threat

It is difficult for the heritage managers and curators within the planning system to make cases based on 'likely levels of activity' when gaps in the HERs can be shown to reflect gaps in the available information base rather than in the incidence of archaeological evidence. It is yet more difficult to determine the significance and quality of the resource as identified in the available record. If we are to make planning decisions based on archaeological significance or value, then we need to consider aspects of preservation that are not conventionally encompassed within the structure of HERs. In the Vale of Pickering for instance, and arguably in many other locations, linear trackside 'ladder settlements' are found running for many kilometres along the valley margins. Research over the last 30 years has shown that in some areas intact floor-deposits survived where the buried archaeology had been protected by deposits of blown-sands (Powlesland et al 2006; Powlesland 2009, 2011). The exceptional conditions that had contributed to the preservation of the sort of deposits only rarely seen in arable landscapes are far from static. It is increasingly clear that industrialised agriculture, employing ever larger tractors pulling bigger ploughs, is truncating buried archaeology at accelerating rates. Plough damage remains the single most destructive agent of archaeological evidence in Britain, and continues to occur on an annual basis effectively unnoticed and un-monitored at a national scale.

Undocumented casual observation across the area being studied by the LRC around West Heslerton indicates the extent of plough damage over 30 or more years. In this time ploughing has probably removed considerably more than 50% of the intact stratified deposits that still survived beneath blown sands when the research began in the late 1970s. This statistic is an estimate which is retrospectively un-confirmable in a landscape that has been a continuous focus for research. However, the failure to instigate or even consider the need for a fact-based study of plough damage over the last three decades may in the future be put down to irresponsibility. If nothing is done to manage the ongoing impact of agricultural damage it is likely that within the next 30 years we will see the majority of the rural archaeology of Britain hopelessly compromised. This is not intended to be alarmist and nor is it intended to imply that we should restrict farming practices at a large scale. However if we do continue to look the other way as agricultural plant gets larger and the industrial production of root-crops, for instance, increases, we will only have ourselves to blame for the devastation of the buried record of the human past that even now barely survives in the ground.

It is essential that we increase public-awareness of the fragility of the buried and invisible archaeological resource if it is to be afforded the same degree of protection that is applied to aspects of the living natural environment. There is clearly a need to engage in proactive research to identify well-preserved components within the archaeological landscape, and to develop novel approaches to secure the future of landscape samples, at least, which could be sustained through long-term management arrangements. The publication of '*Archaeology under the Plough*' by English Heritage in 2003, and the incorporation of 'Ploughzone Archaeology' as a priority under the National Heritage Protection Plan, reflects an awareness of the problem. However, a nationwide awareness campaign targeted towards farmers, initiated in July 2012, is focussed upon the tiny number of scheduled monuments, which are already provided some degree of protection, rather than at the landscape in general where the problem really lies (English Heritage 2003; 2011, 29; 2013b).

Developer *under*-funding?

The serendipitous nature of chance discovery and reporting have resulted in limitations within the HERs as reflecting only evidence which has been encountered or is known, rather than undiscovered or unsuspected evidence has been described above. Conceptual changes to our subject and newly introduced paradigms regarding aspects such as the quality, value and significance of the resource, also pose a huge challenge for curators and heritage managers at a time when much of the physical resource is being invisibly eroded at alarming rates.

Even after more than 20-years of developer-funded archaeology we still encounter, with alarming regularity, developers who have difficulty engaging with the concept that they should fund archaeological work prior to or during development, or that the analysis and publication of the results of such work is in any way their responsibility.

This situation can, in part, arise from the sometimes ambiguous legal interpretation of the various planning guidance notes, but more often than not is simply a reflection of a lack of understanding, and/or a desire to spend as little as possible on something they deem to have little or no value. The unpredictable nature of archaeology in the ground, combined with a culture of competitive-tendering, a hallmark of contemporary capitalism, is particularly problematic within developer-led archaeology. In an environment where unknown quantities far outweigh the known, the concept of competitive tendering is probably flawed. The result all too often is that 'doing the archaeology' is assigned to those offering the cheapest rather than the most appropriate response. One has the impression that we archaeologists, whether consultants or practitioners, have gone out of our way to make things as affordable as possible for the developer and have forgotten the responsibility we have to the unique resource that we are engaged to document and investigate. In the case of large projects where multi-stage works include pre-development evaluation, designed to reduce the uncertainty of the archaeological record, excavation sampling strategies have been applied which are frequently driven by dogma and are minimalist and presented as somehow 'scientific'. Sampling theory gains its scientific validity from the fact that sampling is applied to known entities. This is not the same as cutting trenches to cover, for instance, a 2% random sample of a field within which nothing is known; this might realistically be called sampling by chance. It would be difficult to argue that, in the case of rural environments, the distribution and nature of human activity in the landscape was not substantially driven by environmental factors and availability and proximity of resources. If sampling strategies are to be in any way useful they must be designed with this in mind. Sampling strategies must take on board the physical landscape-context in terms of topography, soils, and environmental potential, as well as the scale of the potential archaeological resource.

Sampling experiments applied to the dataset from the large excavated areas of the early to middle-saxon settlement at West Heslerton indicated the limitations of random sampling. Applying hypothetical 2m square trenches to the dataset, it was not until considerably more than 25% of the whole area was exposed that the limits of the settlement could be identified. Although the southern portion of this settlement was ultimately mapped using geophysical survey prior to excavation, the location of the settlement was first discovered using a series of 2m wide trenches located using the 'this seems like a good place to site a building' approach. Using this strategy eight out of 12 trenches exposed post-holes or parts of Anglo-Saxon *Grubenhäuser* (Lyall and Powlesland 1996; Powlesland *forthcoming*).

Where mineral extraction or large-scale housing developments are contemplated one is tempted to question why evaluation through sample trenches is required at all. This contributor is not aware of any examples where planning permission has been refused following such an evaluation exercise, although there have been cases where parts of a proposed development have subsequently been omitted from the development. A full 'strip, map and record' strategy in the case of such projects would often be a far more efficient and ultimately cost-effective approach. Sampling policies based on simple percentages of features examined during excavation can also seem inflexible and inappropriate, following a pre-determined set of rules rather than responding to the evidence as it emerges. Surely it would be better to apply flexible excavation strategies, which target the recovery of the most informative dataset, rather than a fixed percentage of features identified? The whole process of building an evidence-base with which to interpret the results of any excavation cannot be pre-determined and must respond to the evidence as recovered. Over-reliance on inflexible procedures fails to engage those conducting fieldwork, and can diminish the results of fieldwork through the recovery of, for example, purposeless soil-samples or uncontrolled assemblages, which can have an adverse influence on the post-excavation process.

Training, what training?

If inflexible and predetermined or rote evaluation, excavation and sampling strategies reflect a crisis in the approach to developer-led fieldwork, then it is tempting to see this as a consequence of the pressure to cut costs, but also of changes in the nature of archaeological training and the role played by universities. The massive changes that have taken place in Higher Education in the last 30 years can be characterised in university archaeology departments by changes in the level of engagement in field-archaeology in an almost inverse relation to the increasing size of the departments.

The large volunteer-based excavations of the 1970s and 80s provided an opportunity for thousands of aspiring archaeologists every year to gain fieldwork training through active participation in fieldwork. Volunteer excavations, advertised internationally in the Council for British Archaeology (CBA) Calendar of Excavations, were coded to indicate the availability of hostel or camp-site accommodation, and provision of food and subsistence payments. Undergraduates were encouraged to go digging during the summer before starting their degrees, and were actively encouraged to spend as much of the vacations as possible doing fieldwork or working in museums. University training-excavations were often optional, particularly if experience could be demonstrated with alternative excavations. The combination of free food, accommodation and subsistence payments meant that one could spend several months doing fieldwork at little or no personal financial cost. The social aspect of excavations with hostels or camp-sites not only provided the perfect environment for, but also encouraged, lively debate about all aspects of the excavation process. The training offered on these large volunteer excavations was progressive and revolved around volunteers engaging in different parts of the process as they demonstrated proficiency in each area of work. More often than not those supervising on long-term projects had many months' experience in those projects over a number of seasons. There was nothing proscriptive in this approach which was driven by the research objectives of the excavation in progress, rather than a requirement to teach everybody about every aspect of field archaeology.

The situation is very different today. Changes in employment and health and safety legislation, even the definition of volunteer, make it much harder for excavations to be run on the same basis. At the same time the nature of university education, modular degrees, the lack of grant-funding for undergraduate degrees, and the fee structure, have resulted in a reduction of the required level of fieldwork needed to fulfil the degree requirements. The profession as a whole should be concerned that it is possible in some institutions to get a degree in archaeology with a very limited fieldwork component.

As commercially-funded excavations replaced volunteer-supported fieldwork apprenticeship-style training was no longer supported. The hierarchical structure with directors, supervisors, site-assistants and volunteers was considered by some to be un-democratic and a new emphasis was placed upon each excavator doing their own recording rather than this being handled by the supervisory staff. This approach is still the subject of heated debate especially in the light of what might be considered a box-ticking approach to fieldwork training in some institutions (Harward 2012). The process of excavation and interpretation is complex and interactive and requires that those creating the records have sufficient experience to ask appropriate questions during the recording process; it might for instance only take a day to learn how to create a scale-drawing using a planning-frame and drafting film but it takes months of digging experience to be able to interpret what is being drawn.

The increase in the number of undergraduate places to study archaeology bears no relation to the number of jobs available and there is clearly no longer a vocational link between the degrees being awarded and the practical side of the subject. The diversity of interests reflected in the staff of our university departments is greater than it has ever been, and the academic emphasis upon archaeological theory as a stand-alone subject, and an avalanche of publication with which it has been associated, has arguably made the least impact upon the practical aspects of our work, and been the least influenced by the changing results of that work. The apparent disconnect between the academic interpreters and the data generators is now greater than it has ever been, a situation made worse by the fact that within commercially-driven archaeology the difficulty in securing full-funding for post-excavation analysis and publication means that the majority of the fieldwork undertaken is only reported within 'grey literature'. One does not wish in any way to belittle the contribution made by the large number of interventions which only make it into 'grey literature' in reports held within the county HERs or archived through the

Archaeological Data Service (ADS), but the lack of peer review or an editing process means that the quality of these reports can be highly variable. Elements that may seem insignificant to one excavator could be considered critically important by others. Making these reports accessible through digital on-line delivery systems like the ADS is critically important for the future of archaeological research, however the value of this material will ultimately revolve around the degree to which the content can be searched, particularly for data that may not have been explicitly identified. In an example recently observed, a feature identified in an excavation report as a working hollow was in fact far more likely to have been an Anglo-Saxon *Grubenhaus* according to the documented evidence presented in the report.

Conclusions

While this discussion demonstrates the author's strongly held views, it is not intended to be entirely negative or to apportion blame. The present state of field-archaeology in Britain can be said to be in crisis but this has probably always been the case. It would be easy to say that what is needed is greater funding, but money alone would not resolve the issues raised here. What is blatantly clear as that all these issues are interrelated. A massive injection of funds might make it possible to increase the scale of fieldwork or primary research needed to underpin the planning-process but without the availability of a highly-trained human-resource this would still be impossible. It is easy also to raise questions or argue about the quality and relevance of training, sampling, excavation techniques, recording or the need for a more comprehensive record of the scale of the resource in isolation, but the condition of the subject as a whole is most heavily influenced by the degree to which it is valued by developers who fund so much of the work and by the public, the rightful beneficiaries of the work we do. If our subject is poorly understood and undervalued then it will be exceptionally difficult to change, particularly at a time when the prevailing economic conditions are appalling and almost any excuse can be used to cut funds or diminish planning-control under the banner of austerity.

One area of crisis is however both very real and understated, plough-damage is catastrophically diminishing the potential to understand the rural archaeology that encompasses most of our past; it occurs almost invisibly and on such a scale that it would be impossible to control even if we wished to. Perhaps we should be thinking about the creation of archaeological reserves, small portions of landscapes managed and farmed in a sustainable way that will secure the future of samples of our buried landscapes for the long-term benefit of society at large. To face this challenge we have to identify those areas most worthy of preservation, emphasise and make more implicit the link between the human past and the natural world, a world in which the status of archaeology matches that of the living natural world, a world in which humanity is not only contributing to the destruction of the natural environment but is also a key component of that environment. To achieve these aims we will have to adopt novel new approaches and work in new partnerships with farmers, communities and government institutions absorbing rather than rejecting change. All is not necessarily lost. Confirmation arrived during the writing of this paper that on two farms, the subject of detailed survey and research by the

Landscape Research Centre in the Vale of Pickering, large arable-areas with identified and significant archaeological components, are to be put down to grass and managed within a High Level Stewardship schemes supported by Natural England. This land will not be ploughed for ten years at least, time to reflect and consider plans for a more permanent approach to sustaining and researching our past.

References

Aitchison, K, 2012, *Breaking new ground: how professional archaeology works,* Kindle edn, Landward Research Ltd, Sheffield

Barker, P, 1969, Some aspects of the excavation of timber buildings, *World Archaeology* **1.2**, 220–35

Biddle, M, and Kjolbye-Biddle, B, 1969, Metres, areas and robbing, *World Archaeology* **1.2**, 208–19

Binford, L, 2001, Where do research problems come from? *American Antiquity* **66.4**, 669–78

Boddington, A, 1978, *The excavation record: Part 1 stratification.* Northampton: Northamptonshire County Council

Chadwick, A, 2003, Post-processualism, professionalisation and archaeological methodologies. Towards reflective and radical practice. *Archaeological Dialogues* **10.1**, 97–117

Chadwick, A, 2010, *What have the post-processualists ever done for us? Towards an integration of theory and practice; and radical field archaeologies,* at http://www.academia.edu/239345/ Chadwick_A.M._2001-2003_2010 (accessed 23 Sept 2014)

Collis, J, 2001, *Digging up the past,* Sutton Publishing, Stroud

Cumberpatch, C G, and Roberts, H, 2012, The relevance of commercial archaeology in England: a dialogue, in Cumberpatch, C G, and Roberts, H M, 2012, Life in the archaeological marketplace, in Rockman, M, and Flatman, J, (eds), *Archaeology in society: Its relevance in the modern world,* Springer, New York, 23–43

Department for Communities and Local Government (DCLG), 2010, *Planning Policy Statement 5: Planning for the Historic Environment,* The Stationery Office, London

Department for Communities and Local Government(DCLG), 2012, *National Planning Policy Framework,* The Stationery Office, London

Department of the Environment (DoE), 1990, *Planning Policy Guidance 16: Archaeology and Planning (PPG 16),* HMSO, London

English Heritage, 1986, *Rescue archaeology funding: a policy statement,* English Heritage, London

English Heritage, 1989, *The management of archaeology projects,* English Heritage, London

English Heritage, 1991a, *Management of archaeological projects,* English Heritage, London

English Heritage, 1991b, *Rescue archaeology funding: a policy statement, English Heritage Conservation Bulletin* **14**, 7–9

English Heritage, 2003, Archaeology under the Plough, English Heritage, London

English Heritage, 2011, National Heritage Protection Plan, English Heritage, London

English Heritage, 2013a, National Mapping Programme, at http://www.english-heritage.org.uk/ professional/research/landscapes-and-areas/national-mapping-programme/ (accessed Feb 2013)

English Heritage, 2013b, Nationwide survey of farmers to find answers for archaeology at risk, at http://www.english-heritage.org.uk/about/news/nationwide-survey-farmers/ (accessed Feb 2013)

Everill, P, 2012, *The Invisible Diggers: A study of British commercial archaeology,* (2nd edn ebook), Oxbow books, Oxford

Flatman, J, Short, J, Doeser, J, and Lee, E (eds), 2008, *Aggregates Levy Sustainability Fund Dissemination Project 2002–07 Benchmark Report: Sustainable heritage: Aggregates extraction and the historic environment,* London, UCL Centre for Applied Archaeology, on behalf of English Heritage

Gaffney, V, Fitch, S, and Smith, D, 2009, *Europe's lost world, the rediscovery of Doggerland,* Council of British Archaeology, York

Harris, E C, and Ottaway, P J, 1976, A recording experiment on a rescue site, *Rescue Archaeology* **12**, 6–7

Harward, C, 2012, Reskilling the diggers: handing over the means of interpretation, *The Archaeologist* **83**, 26–29

Hawkes, C F C, 1954, Archaeological theory and method: some suggestions from the Old World, *American Anthropologist* **56.2.1**, 155–68

Hirst, S, 1976, *Recording on excavations I: The written record,* RESCUE: The British Archaeological Trust, Hertford

Jefferies, J E, 1977, *Excavation records. Techniques in use by the Central Excavation Unit,* Directorate of Ancient Monuments and Historic Buildings Occasional Papers, Department of the Environment, London

Jones, B, 1984, *Past imperfect: the story of rescue archaeology,* Heinemann, London

Lucas, G, 2001, Destruction and the rhetoric of excavation, *Norwegian Archaeol Review* **34.1**, 35–46

Lucas, G, 2006, Changing configurations: the relationships between theory and practice, in Hunter J, and Ralston, I, (eds), *Archaeological resource management in the UK: an introduction,* 15–22, Sutton, Stroud

Lucas, G, 2012, *Understanding the archaeological record,* Cambridge University Press, Cambridge

Lyall, J, and Powlesland, D J, 1996, The application of high resolution fluxgate gradiometery as an aid to excavation planning and strategy formulation, *Internet Archaeology* **1**, at http://intarch. ac.uk/journal/issue1/index.html (accessed August 2014)

Powlesland, D, 2006, Redefining past landscapes: 30 years of remote sensing in the Vale of Pickering, in Campana S, and Forte M (eds), *From Space to Place, 2nd International Conference on remote Sensing in Archaeology,* December 4–7, 2006, Rome, Italy, British Archaeol Rep Internat Ser **1568**, 197–202, BAR, Oxford,

Powlesland, D, Lyall, J, Hopkinson J, Donoghue G, Beck, D, Harte, M, and Stott, D, 2006, Beneath the sand: Remote sensing, archaeology, aggregates and sustainability. A case study from Heslerton, the Vale of Pickering, North Yorkshire, England, *Archaeological Prospection,* **13–4**, 291–99

Powlesland, D, 2009, Why bother? Large scale geomagnetic survey and the quest for real archaeology, in Campana S, and Piro S, (eds) *Seeing the unseen, geophysics and Landscape Archaeology,* 167–82, Taylor and Francis, London

Powlesland, D, 2010, Identifying, mapping and managing the unmanageable: the implications of long term multi-sensor research into the archaeology of the Vale of Pickering, Yorkshire, England, in, Campana, S, Forte, M, and Liuzza, C (eds), *Space, Time, Place Third International Conference on Remote Sensing in Archaeology, 17th–21st August 2009, Tiruchirappalli, Tamil Nadu, India,* British Archaeol Rep Internat Ser **2118**, 9–16, BAR, Oxford

Powlesland, D, 2011, Identifying the unimaginable; managing the unmanageable, in Cowley, D, (ed), *Remote sensing for archaeological heritage management in the 21st century,* European Archaeol Council Occ Pap **5**, 17–32, Budapest

Powlesland D, forthcoming, *West Heslerton: The excavation of the Anglian Settlement,* Landscape Research Centre

Riley, D N, 1980, *Early landscape from the air: studies of crop marks in South Yorkshire and North Nottighamshire,* Dept of Prehistory and Archaeology, Sheffield University, Sheffield

Roskams, S, 2001, *Excavation,* Cambridge University Press, Cambridge

Sullivan, A P, 1978, Inference and evidence in archaeology: a discussion of the conceptual problems, *Advances in archaeological method and theory* **1**, 183–222

Wainwright, G, 1991, Competitive tendering for archaeology projects: a statement by English Heritage, in Swain, H, (ed), *Competitive tendering in archaeology: Papers presented at a one day conference in June 1990*RESCUE: The British Archaeological Trust, and Standing Conference of Archaeological Unit Managers, Hertford, 51–3

Wainwright, G, 2000, Time Please, *Antiquity* **74.4**, 909–43

Chapter 12

Fifteen Windows:
Pay and conditions in British commercial archaeology

Paul Everill

In 2014 there is a very real sense that a chapter has closed, one that will be looked back at with some fondness as the 'golden age' of British archaeology. That label is beginning to be used retrospectively with regard to the structure and funding of Higher Education that has seen significant changes under the current Coalition Government (Sinclair 2010, 31), but also the era of PPG16, the planning policy guidance which enshrined British developer-led archaeology from 1990 to 2010 (DoE 1990). Those two decades saw greater numbers of archaeology students at British universities than ever before, who provided the new entrants to the sector, and an increase in the workforce supported by a period of stability and growth in professional practice. Of course that period was not without its problems. The recession of the early 1990s impacted on development and slowed that growth and, more recently, the global financial crisis has seen significant job losses in commercial archaeology. However, even at the height of the 'golden age', archaeological employment was characterised by low wages and short, fixed-term contracts. The title of this chapter is a reference to a large archaeological project in the heart of London near the start of the millennium which, despite employing a total of 60 or so field archaeologists and post-excavation specialists over a period of several years, reportedly only cost the same as 15 of the windows in the Norman Foster designed building that was planned for the site. These issues are a continuing legacy of the profession's historic development in the second half of the 20th century.

Rescue archaeology
Before the Second World War archaeological fieldwork was almost invariably an academic exercise. So-called 'Rescue' archaeology in this period was often just a matter of recovering finds from the contractors' spoil heaps. As Rahtz (1974b) recalled:

> *'the research worker or the good amateur archaeologist was usually too engrossed in his particular problems to watch building sites or to undertake an excavation of a site for no better reason than that it was going to be destroyed'.*

The war saw important changes within archaeological practice. Principally the widespread construction of large defence installations, such as airfields and other bases, brought the destruction of archaeology by development firmly under the remit of the government, which was required to act under Ancient Monument legislation. The pace of development in the 1940s and 1950s was, to some extent, reflected in the increase of state funding for archaeology through the Ministry of Works. This funding was still, however, woefully inadequate. By the 1960s the widespread destruction of archaeological sites by developers was a cause of great concern amongst archaeologists (Addyman 1974; Barker 1974a; Thomas 1974). However, with full-time professional archaeologists thin on the ground (Wainwright 2000), most rescue excavations were staffed by volunteers or undertaken by local amateur-groups that had been able to negotiate some time before development. Only a small number of these were lucky enough to receive funding. Even in the case of Scheduled Ancient Monuments, government agencies struggled to organise adequate excavation prior to development. Desperate projects such as those at Faversham Royal Abbey in 1964 (Philp 2002) and York Minster from 1969 (Morris 1999) were the rule rather than sad exceptions and it was this situation that forced archaeologists to come together. Like-minded fieldworkers, John Alexander, Philip Barker, Martin Biddle, Barry Cunliffe, Peter Fowler and Charles Thomas, called a meeting at Barford, Warwickshire in February 1970 that led ultimately to the foundation of RESCUE in 1971 (Barker 1974b, 281).

The early years of RESCUE are discussed at the beginning of this volume, but its initial impact was heartening. The level of Government funding for rescue archaeology rose dramatically from £133,000 in 1970 (Barker 1987) to £450,000 in 1972 and £800,000 in 1973 (Barker 1974b). However, despite the efforts of RESCUE and increased media and public interest in archaeology, this level of funding increase could not be maintained by central Government. By 1986 it had more or less plateaued at £5,000,000 (Barker 1987). The early success of RESCUE was able only to slow the crisis and from the early 1970s it was clear that rescue archaeology needed some degree of financial independence from the Department of the Environment if it was to survive in any meaningful way.

The Manpower Services Commission 1974–87

Shortly after the creation of RESCUE and the associated increase of government subsidies to archaeology, the Manpower Services Commission was created. It was a response to the economic troubles of the early 1970s and from 1974 it provided jobs and training for the long-term unemployed. Archaeology, with its high labour-requirements, was ideally suited to this and featured heavily in the Community Programmes run through the MSC after 1980:

> ...the Community Programme (CP) is designed for adults of 25 and over who have been unemployed for 12 of the preceding 15 months, (and have been unemployed in the 2 months preceding the start of the project), and for people aged 24 and over, who have been unemployed for 6 months previously. (Green 1987)

By 1986 the MSC provided funding of £4.8 million for archaeology, compared to £5.9 million from the Historic Buildings and Monuments Commission (Crump 1987), and in

September 1986 there were 1,790 places on archaeological projects through the CPs. On top of the dependence archaeology developed on MSC funding there were a number of side effects to this relationship:

> ...*ironically, one positive 'spin-off' from MSC involvement in archaeology is that volunteer rates may have gone up in some areas to bring them into line with CP wages. Also, as site safety is one of the areas monitored by MSC, standards have to be rigorously maintained. The provision of safety clothing and foul weather gear by MSC also marks an improvement except where unscrupulous sponsors spend this part of the 'capitation grant' on machine-time and volunteers.* (Crump 1987)

There were also some criticisms of the effect that the MSC was having, both on archaeologists and the unemployed that it was designed to help. The old 'circuit' had been replaced by CP projects and there were concerns that recent graduates were finding it harder to find work in archaeology. There were also concerns that the average CP wage of £67 a week meant that the CP workforce was not encouraged to have a commitment to the project and supervisors spent as much time policing the site as excavating it (Crump 1987). However, despite this there is no doubt that MSC funding was vital to archaeology and when the commission was scrapped in 1987 it left a huge hole. During the 1980s the relationship between archaeological units and developers had started to solidify and the void left by the MSC was to become increasingly filled by funding from developers.

Developer-led archaeology

The trend towards developer funding and competitive tendering within archaeology had begun to emerge during the 1980s, but was to become an integral part of the future of the profession after the launch of Planning Policy Guidance Note 16 in November 1990. Overnight the 'polluter pays' principle was enshrined in planning policy (Graves-Brown 1997) and a largely academic discipline was transformed into a commercial enterprise. PPG16's biggest success, though not uncontroversial, was to embed archaeology firmly within the planning process. For the first time local authorities had a responsibility to ensure that fragile, and potentially important archaeological remains were protected. Furthermore, although PPG16 was only guidance and was not statutory, it allowed local authorities to place an archaeological condition on planning permission.

There can be no doubt that archaeological jobs became more numerous and marginally better-paid and more stable as a result of PPG16, although perhaps not to the extent that was hoped by those within the profession. It was a turning point for the discipline that has ensured that hundreds of important sites have been preserved either by record, following excavation, or by being left *in situ* by developers who have been made aware of the significance of the archaeological remains on their land. PPG16 represented a vast improvement in the protection afforded to archaeological remains, with even the language of government bureaucrats reflecting their importance *'as a finite and non-renewable resource'*(DoE 1990). Richard Morris, in a brief review of the effects of PPG16 four years on, wrote that it:

...has brought undoubted benefits to archaeology. It has provided a framework for locating development away from archaeologically sensitive areas; and it (quite reasonably) requires developers to pay for any reconnaissance needed. (Morris 1994)

He also noted, however, that it generated a new set of problems for the profession, principally that the system of competitive tendering does not always deliver the highest quality archaeological work; that local authority Sites and Monuments Records (now known as Historic Environment Records), which support the system, are not statutory and are often under-funded; and crucially that units keep running costs down by largely employing young archaeologists on short-term contracts. In hindsight it seems likely that an historic dependency on unpaid/low-paid volunteers or MSC trainees to fill a significant proportion of the labour requirements; and a lack of commercial expertise on the part of many senior archaeologists at the time, were contributory factors in the emergence of the poor business model in 1990 which relied on a continuing acceptance of low wages among the new private sector 'professionals'.

Professionalisation

The boom in professional practice post 1990 had, however, been foreshadowed by increasing numbers of local authority units and trusts established from the mid-1970s. Formed in 1982, the Institute of Field Archaeologists (initially the IFA, but since 2008 renamed the Institute for Archaeologists [IfA]) was established to define the standards required of professional archaeologists. RESCUE and others had, since 1971, been successful in raising the profile of archaeological work, and in pushing for greater financial assistance from the State. However, by the mid 1970s there was a feeling amongst many senior British archaeologists that a body needed to be established that would support and encourage the growing professionalism within the 'rescue' sector. In 1974 an early attempt by the Council for British Archaeology to create such a body was brought to a grinding halt by the negative reaction of academic and amateur archaeologists, who '*saw, or thought they saw, a threat to their own interests in the introduction of a national lobby of full-time professionals*' (Hobley 1987, 41). However, in 1978 Philip Barker, one of the driving forces behind the creation of RESCUE, enlisted the support of a 'Management Studies' expert who observed that field archaeology was poorly managed and in need of modernisation:

> *'Philip Barker, with Trevor Rowley, immediately 'grasped the nettle' and in early 1979 put field archaeology on the road to professionalism by establishing the Association for the Promotion of an Institute of Field Archaeology, or APIFA. Thus the recognition of the need for modern management skills in archaeology made this initial and important contribution to the establishment of an Institute'* (Hobley 1987, 41).

Barker asked 36 archaeologists to each submit 20 names and this approach produced 400 invited members of the newly established APIFA (Hobley 1987). In total over 500 archaeologists were to join the APIFA and from these a committee was set up which was to determine the form of the proposed body. Philip Barker and Brian Davidson, amongst others, wanted to see the new Institute lead the way in raising standards in the field in order to protect archaeological remains from bad practice:

'but for others it was the archaeologists that needed protecting. For them, IFA was to be a trade union, guarding the livelihood of the workforce, the circuit diggers who had come in from the cold and were anxious not to return there. For others again it was to be the voice of authority; a new platform from which to direct British archaeology. The new field professionals felt they were represented neither by the CBA ... nor the Society of Antiquaries of London ... The IFA was to become the right hand of the profession, like the RIBA for architects' (Carver 2006, 8).

Ultimately, the debate was won by those archaeologists who, like Philip Barker, wanted an organisation that would set standards for all areas of archaeological practice and the IfA was born. Its focus, therefore, was on improving standards in the management of archaeological work; establishing a working party on archaeological standards in 1990 (Hinton 1996); and the agenda was set by those already involved in management. However, in recent years the IfA has turned its attention to the central issue of poor pay in archaeology. It first established an advisory pay minima for jobs advertised at the membership grades of 'Practitioner' (PIfA), 'Associate' (AIfA), and 'Member' (MIfA) in 1996, linked to Local Government pay scales. These grades relate broadly to the level of experience and responsibilities required of Site Assistants (PIfA), Supervisors (AIfA), and Project Officers (MIfA), but have been extended to incorporate the increasing diversity of specialist roles undertaken by archaeologists beyond excavation.

Recognising that commercial archaeological salaries did not compare well with similar professions, the IfA established a 'Benchmarking Archaeological Salaries' project in 2007. Advised by representatives of the IfA's Committee for Working Practices in Archaeology, Diggers' Forum (this author), Prospect, Unison and the Standing Conference of Archaeological Unit Managers (now the Federation of Archaeological Managers and Employers) the resulting report unsurprisingly identified the commercial marketplace as responsible for keeping wages low over the previous two decades:

'the acceptance of job-by-job tendering also had an impact, and in terms of pay and conditions, seriously affected how pay rates and employment conditions were established. The advent of job-by job tendering also saw a change in the main mechanism effecting terms and wages of the majority. Around 60–70% of staff are now employed by organisations whose level of wages tends to be dictated not by reference to wider external norms, but by the need to ensure the survival of the organisation in an archaeological market' (Price and Geary 2008).

The project utilised the 'Job Evaluation and Grading Support System' (JEGS), which had been widely used in the public sector, to provide a score range for each of the IfA membership grades. The score was derived from the weighting of a number of factors, namely 'knowledge and skills' (20%); 'contacts and communications' (10%); 'problem solving' (20%); 'decision making' (15%); 'autonomy' (10%); 'management of resources' (20%); and 'impact' (5%) (Price and Geary 2008). The project identified a significant gap between IfA salary minima and external comparators that ranged from 13–53% (Table 1) and concluded that:

> *...in order to raise IFA minimum salaries to a level more appropriate to the work complexity and the qualifications, skills and experience required by professional archaeologists, an increase of at least 13% would be required.* (Price and Geary 2008).

Table 1 Data derived from the Benchmarking Archaeological Salaries report

IfA Grade	Example posts	JEGS SCORE	IfA pay minimum in 2007	Median from comparable professions
PIfA	Site Assistant/Technician/HER Assistant	330 - 469	£14,197	£18,431
AIfA	Supervisor/Finds Officer/ Archives Officer/Project Officer	470 - 499	£16,536	£22,396
MIfA	Project Officer/Project Manager/ Planning Archaeologist	500 +	£21,412	£28,992

Source: Price and Geary 2008

IfA council voted to implement this recommendation in 2008, deciding to increase minimum salaries by 13% over inflation over a 5-year period. However, within a few months the deteriorating global economic situation started to seriously impact the commercial sector, which saw widespread redundancies, and instead IfA pay minima were frozen. By the time that they were 'thawed', in Spring 2012, the numbers employed in commercial archaeology were down by 15.78%, and curatorial archaeologists by 13.67%, on their August 2007 levels (Aitchison 2011).

In early 2013 the IfA removed its own requirement that Registered Organisations should abide by IfA pay minima, while simultaneously raising the recommended starting salaries by a significant amount. This move, presumably intended to ensure that IfA ROs were not uncompetitive, while still encouraging higher salaries, has led to accusations that the IfA have abandoned serious efforts to raise salaries and created a greater sense of disenfranchisement amongst site staff. Salaries have, of course, increased significantly since PPG16, but the data compiled by the Institute (Table 2; Figure 1) from jobs they have advertised since 1995, clearly shows that even the significant increase in salary for a 'Site Assistant'/PIfA level post is not keeping pace with the increase in the UK National Average Salary, which one might use for comparative purposes. Between 1997 and 2007 this was 153% for the former; and 157% for the latter.

The Effect

It is perhaps unsurprising to see the gap between most commercial archaeological salaries and the UK average resulting in significant levels of dissatisfaction in staff and a high rate of 'turnover'. A proportion of this might be ascribed to the large number

Table 2 Average archaeological earnings

	Excavator (PIFA)	Supervisor (AIFA)	Project Officer (MIFA)	Project Manager	National Average Salary
1995	£8597	£11911	£13616	£18094	–
1996	£9281	£12011	£13644	£16942	–
1997	£9880	£12029	£13484	£16606	£19167
1998	£10314	£12732	£14274	£18268	–
1999	£11311	£12700	£13788	£18671	–
2000	£12024	£12868	£15518	£19447	–
2001	£12378	£12741	£15572	£20881	–
2002	£13232	£14806	£18489	£21536	£24498
2003	£12903	£14765	£16592	£19701	–
2004	£13710	---------	£16563	£20957	–
2005	£14179	£15900	£17598	£22259	–
2006	£14294	£15879	£18593	£23350	–
2007	£15078	£17037	£19928	£25535	£29999
2008	£15299	£18715	£21200	£28532	–
2009	£16032	£18926	£22548	£30585	–
2010	£16744	£19016	£22160	£30262	–

Source: Data compiled from Turner 1997; Aitchison 1999; Malcolm 2000; Aitchison and Edwards 2003; Drummond-Murray2007; Aitchison and Edwards 2008; Rocks-Macqueen 2011

Figure 1 Average archaeological earnings from Table 2

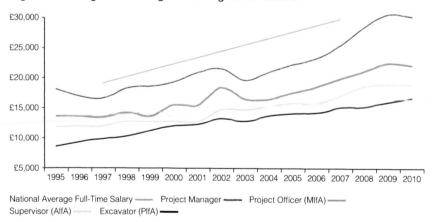

National Average Full-Time Salary —— Project Manager —— Project Officer (MIfA) ——
Supervisor (AIfA) —— Excavator (PIfA) ——

of staff employed in 'Site Assistant', or 'Excavator' roles and equivalent, versus the small number of supervisory posts, and the consequent difficulties many find for career advancement. Given that even the lowest rung of the ladder has required a degree for many years, it is unsurprising that many seek appropriate levels of remuneration and responsibility in other sectors, when their preferred option offers no viable opportunities. And the response of many in senior positions, who cut their teeth in a very different climate, that if an excavator is good enough and prepared to make sacrifices 'like they did' they'll make it, is also unhelpful.

The reality is that many good and talented excavators are being lost to the profession simply because they are not being appropriately rewarded, or given opportunities to utilise their skills, or progress along a career path.

Recent surveys by the author (Everill 2012) and the Diggers' Forum (Harward *et al* 2012) have considered the effects of low pay on the profession. The Diggers' Forum survey established that 64% of staff were expected to undertake so-called 'away' work (ie work that takes staff away from their main residence for a night or more), receiving a subsistence payment which was most commonly £15 per night: a figure that has now not seen any increase for a number of years. A significant number of site-staff stated that prolonged periods of 'away' work made a real difference to their pay packets, with some stating that it was only this subsistence payment and overtime that brought their salary up to a reasonable level. However, 'away' work was also clearly a source of some discontent for a number of archaeologists who were expected to spend significant spells away from their home, often at short notice.

Clearly for many this is an unwelcome aspect of the job, but one that they might not be able to afford to do without (Harward *et al* 2012, 26–43). In summarising the results of the survey the report's authors make a strong and heartfelt plea for transparency in the advertising of archaeological jobs. In order to protect best-practice employers, and enable prospective employees to make informed decisions this should include an increased clarity about what is, and is not, included in the employment package.

'at present many employers are attempting to pay their staff properly for the long hours spent travelling on work business, or living away from home and family; these employers are losing contracts to those companies that choose to not pay any travel time, but demand the same long hours. The Diggers' Forum believes that the employees, already suffering on low wages, should not be the ones to suffer further financial distress for the benefit of their employers. We as Diggers need to stand up to bad employers, not be grateful for any work at all. There is a price to poor wages and conditions, and it is paid for in our colleague's abandoned careers. By making this issue public, and by continuing to shine a light on poor employers we will strive to level the field so that contracts can be won on standards and quality of work, not who is prepared to rip off their employees the most' (Harward *et al* 2012, Summary).

The Invisible Diggers surveys of 2005 and 2012 (Everill 2009, 2012) have demonstrated the impact of the huge numbers of staff choosing to leave the profession after only a few years. An interesting, and perhaps unexpected, result of the recent recessions appears to be a lengthening of the time younger diggers stay in the job. The 2005 survey suggested that they were choosing to leave after 3–5 years, but the recent survey shows the profile of staff being typically several years older, with the big drop in numbers now being after 6–10 years' experience (Figure 2). It is possible to relate this peak to an increased intake of staff during the boom, as with other economic events (Figure 3); or perhaps the relative absence of alternative opportunities; or the apparent absence of a significant intake of new diggers forcing more experience Site Assistants to reassess their lack of career advancement. The reality may well be a combination of all these factors.

Figure 2 Fieldwork experience by gender (percentage of all responses)

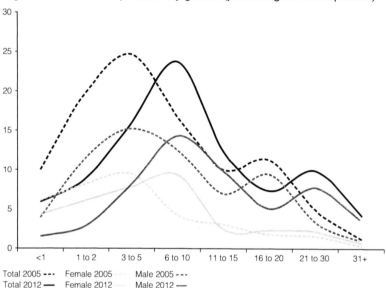

Total 2005 ---   Female 2005   Male 2005 ---
Total 2012 —   Female 2012   Male 2012 —

Conclusion

It is tempting to use the language of commercial 'apologisers', and state that the current situation is a *fait accompli*; that it is far from ideal, but it is the best that we have had; that archaeology has high labour requirements, and consequently low wages are the only way of making commercial archaeology acceptable to developers. However, the fact is that archaeology has moved on considerably since the 1970s and 80s. Site-staff in particular are no longer the itinerant 'circuit' diggers who were simply grateful for a paid professional post. Current Site Assistants, Supervisors and Project Officers, as well as many more senior post holders, hold undergraduate, or increasingly postgraduate, qualifications. Greater numbers now have a level of experience and expertise in full-time archaeology that was hard to envisage 20 years ago. In fact, Higher Education is now looking out of date and out of touch as the principal provider of training prior to initial employment. For HE to maintain its connection to commercial practice, academics need to emerge from the bunker of research excellence and recognise that they are in real danger of becoming an irrelevance to the majority of archaeologists working in the UK.

For now it must be hoped that employers are able to raise pay minima by 13% over inflation when the economy emerges from the current recession, but with the IfA

Figure 3 Fieldwork experience by gender (percentage of all responses) mapped against UK economic events

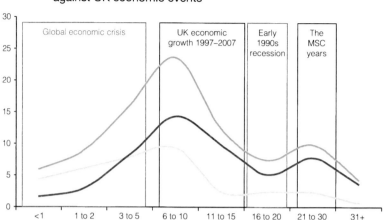

abdicating its lead role in this it seems unlikely. And yet, for commercial practice to move forward as a viable and truly professional employer of skilled practitioners, it needs to break the shackles of pay levels that date to a period when we undervalued our own expertise.

References

Addyman, P, 1974, York: The anatomy of a crisis in urban archaeology, in Rahtz 1974a, 153–6

Aitchison, K, 1999, *Profiling the profession: a survey of archaeological jobs in the UK*, Council for British Archaeology, English Heritage and Institute of Field Archaeologists, York, London and Reading

Aitchison, K, 2011, *State of the archaeological market: October 2011*, Report for the Institute of Field Archaeologists and Federation of Archaeological Managers and Employers, Landward Research Ltd, Sheffield, at http://www.archaeologists.net/sites/default/files/node-files/JoblossesOctober2011.pdf (accessed November 2014)

Aitchison, K, and Edwards, R, 2003, *Archaeology labour market intelligence: profiling the profession 2002–03,* Cultural Heritage National Training Organisation, Bradford

Aitchison, K, and Edwards, R, 2008, *Archaeology labour market intelligence: profiling the profession 2007–08,* Institute of Field Archaeologists, Reading

Barker, P, 1974a, The scale of the problem, in Rahtz 1974a, 28–34

Barker, P, 1974b, The origins and development of RESCUE, in Rahtz 1974a, 280–85

Barker, P, 1987, RESCUE: antenatal, birth and early years, in Mytum, H, and Waugh, K (eds), 7–9

Carver, M, 2006, Thinking allowed, *Rescue News* **100**, 6-8

Crump, T, 1987, The role of MSC funding in British archaeology, in Mytum, H, and Waugh, K (eds), 41–46

Department of the Environment, 1990, Planning Policy Guidance Note 16: Archaeology and Planning, HMSO, London

Drummond-Murray, J, 2007, Jobs in British Archaeology 2006, The Archaeologist **66**, 13

Everill, P, 2009, The Invisible Diggers: A study of British commercial archaeology, Heritage Research Ser **1**, Oxbow Books, Oxford

Everill, P, 2012, The Invisible Diggers: A study of British commercial archaeology (2nd edn eBook) Oxbow Books, Oxford

Graves-Brown, P, 1997, S/he who pays the piper... archaeology and the polluter pays principle, Assemblage **2**, at http://www.shef.ac.uk/assem/2/2gb2.html (accessed November 2014)

Green, F, 1987, MSC: Their involvement in archaeology, in Joyce et al 1987, 28–34

Harward, C, Neale, M, and Watson, S, 2012, Diggers Forum report on away work and travel in UK commercial archaeology, 2011, Institute for Archaeologists, Reading

Hinton, P, 1996, Good archaeology guaranteed: standards in British Archaeology, Field Archaeologist **26**, 7–11

Hobley, B, 1987, The need for professionalism and modern management in Archaeology, in Joyce et al 1987, 41–46

Joyce, S, Newbury, M, and Stone, P (eds), 1987, Degree, digging, dole: Our future? Papers Presented at Young Archaeologists Conference '85 Southampton, YAC'85 Organising Committee for Southampton University Archaeology Society, Southampton

Malcolm, G, 2000, Jobs in British archaeology 1999, The Archaeologist **37**, 11–12

Morris, R, 1994, Taking archaeology into a new era, British Archaeology News **18**, 9

Morris, R, 1999, An abiding faith in archaeology's worth, British Archaeology **45**, 15

Mytum, H, and Waugh, K (eds), 1987, Rescue archaeology, what's next? Proceedings of a RESCUE conference held at the University of York, December 1986, Dept of Archaeol, University of York Monograph **6**, York and Hertford

Philp, B, 2002, Archaeology in the front line: 50 years of Kent rescue 1952–200, Kent Archaeol Trust and Kent Archaeol Rescue Unit, Dover

Price, F, and Geary, K, 2008, Benchmarking archaeological salaries, Institute of Field Archaeologists, Reading

Rahtz, P A, (ed) 1974a, Rescue Archaeology, Pelican, Harmondsworth

Rahtz, P A, 1974b, Rescue digging past and present, in Rahtz 1974a, 53–72

Rocks-Macqueen, D, 2011, Jobs in British archaeology, The Archaeologist **82**, 12–13

Sinclair, A, 2010, The end of a golden age? The impending effects of the economic collapse on archaeology in higher education in the United Kingdom, in Schlanger, N, and Aitchison, K, (eds), Archaeology and the global economic crisis: multiple impacts, possible solutions, Culture Lab Éditions, Tervuren, 31–44

Thomas, C, 1974, Archaeology in Britain 1973, in Rahtz 1974a, 3–15

Turner, R, 1997, Jobs in British archaeology 1996, The Archaeologist **29**, 6–7

Wainwright, G, 2000, Time please, Antiquity **74.4**, 909–43

Chapter 13

Museums, archaeologists and archaeological archives

John Shepherd

'*Plus ça change, plus c'est la même chose*' Alphonse Karr, *Les Guêpes* (1849)

Like many scientific disciplines, British archaeology is a house of many chambers each with its own variety of host, clientele and priorities. There is the Higher Education sector with the learning needs of its students, increasingly driven by value for their money, at the fore. There is the commercial sector, with a client base that largely begrudgingly contracts their services for motives related to the pursuit of planning consent rather than the intrinsic and collective worth of the archaeology on their development sites. There is the voluntary sector (comprised largely of local societies and special interest groups), formerly at the vanguard in archaeological work of all kinds in their respective communities, and attracting a younger audience. Now these groups are relegated to a role in 'community archaeology' and the recipients of infrequent trickle-down initiatives from professionals. Then there is the heritage-management sector, co-ordinating activities especially between the commercial sector and their clients, but also working with their colleagues at national and local government level to ensure the protection of known and potential heritage-resources. Finally there is the largely public-funded museum sector, a body with close historical links to the voluntary sector that has been charged, over the last century at least, with the curation, care and dissemination of historical and archaeological knowledge at a community level, but that has increasingly over the last few decades had to justify its long-term existence when short-term financial ideologies have been imposed.

In the main, the numerous successes over the last 40 years have occurred when each of these sectors has pursued its own unilateral agenda. There are times when permutations of sectors might come together; the Higher Education sector with the Museum sector through individual AHRC collaborative funded projects for example, or the Commercial with the Voluntary sector for client-funded outreach projects. While the concept might be repeatable, attempts to put in place long-term and sustainable cross-sector initiatives are difficult to achieve because of the variations in client bases, funding and general sector priorities and objectives. Nothing illustrates better the failure of all the sectors to work together and promote a sustainable and effective response to a core archaeological phenomenon, common to all the sectors, than the long-term curation and care of and access to the primary records and finds created in the course of archaeological interventions. The 'archaeological archive', which each and every archaeologist knows, teaches and professes to be the most important element of any work that has resulted in the conversion of the *in situ* resource into an *ex situ* record, is still a major and embarrassing issue for our discipline. Furthermore, it is generally accepted that the resulting archive, as both a physical collection and a physical space, can become the venue and centre for the interaction of all archaeological sectors. The resulting interactions would generate partnerships and new opportunities in addition to one most important corollary, the intellectual development of the contents of each archive.

So why is it the case that, after 40 years, we still do not have an integrated, national network of archaeological archives in the same way as, for example, there are local history centres and archives across the country? Is there any kind of solution that can be applied nationally, some kind of generic formula to solve this crisis? Or do we need a dramatic change, a paradigm shift even, in the way we think about how we are to ensure the long-term survival and safety of each case of 'preservation of archaeological remains by record'?

Some of the trends and common denominators related to attempts to preserve this record, this 'archaeological archive' and their impact upon museums are examined. I will also make some observations, born from experience setting up and running the London Archaeological Archive and Research Centre (LAARC) in the Museum of London, which are sure to be interpreted as too idealistic or altruistic. The truth is, however, that while each sector in our house of many chambers might see from their own point of view the merits of any proposal to create new depositories for the preservation of the *ex situ* resource, new funding to achieve these aims does not exist within the profession at large and is likely to never exist. The funding must come from elsewhere; and there's the rub, or at least one of them!

Where did it start to go wrong?

As a teenager, together with members of the Springhead Excavation Group, a sub-committee of the Gravesend Historical Society, I attended the second meeting of RESCUE held in London on the afternoon of 15 January 1972 at the Beveridge Hall, Senate House. I recall that, during the afternoon open-meeting, there was some confusion as to what RESCUE's purpose should be. Some believed that it ought to be a central excavation unit with the resources to descend upon threatened sites and save them from destruction. Two additional points emphasised RESCUE's aim to support archaeological work in the country, and also to act as an important direct-link between the archaeologist in the field and the then Department of the Environment at ministerial level. The emphasis at that time was of course upon the ever-growing threat to the nation's *in situ* archaeological resource, itself a response to severe damage inflicted in the previous two decades of development. Matters related to the management of the nation's heritage were of great significance of course, as too were issues concerned with the publication of the results of fieldwork, but even at that time, when there was a great collective demand for some sort of coordinated response to the threat to the *in situ* resource, *ex situ* resource (the excavated finds of various sorts and the documentation and records that accompanied them) was not given major consideration. It was generally accepted that museums across the country were dealing with the influx of finds from fieldwork and long may this continue.

The emphasis on publication became more apparent three years later, with the publication of the seminal Frere Report (Frere 1975). This responded to the newly identified crisis in the physical publication of the results of archaeological work. As more fieldwork was being done in an ever more scientific fashion with associated detail in, for example, specialist contributions, and with ever-growing costs in printing, there was the real potential that vitally important archaeological data would not be available for study. The report famously defined four levels of records.

- Level I: the site itself and the excavated finds
- Level II: records produced on site
- Level III: full illustration and description of structural, stratigraphic and artifactual/ environmental data
- Level IV: a synthetic description with supporting illustrations

While Level IV was regarded as the ultimate goal *'for all rescue excavations and, indeed, for archaeological excavations in general'*, two key conditions for the entire publication and dissemination process were identified as essential, that:

'(i) ... all the original records of the excavations, properly organised and curated, are housed in readily accessible form in a permanent archive' and that *'(ii) ... data at what we have described as Level III are readily available on request'* (Frere 1975, section 2.6)

The priority given here is to the records generated by the archaeologist mindful that, paraphrasing Curwen, excavation can equate to destruction if no proper record is created and preserved of that archaeological work (Curwen 1937, 6). However, the 1975 report was not unaware of the significance of the finds archive. The working party considered it:

'essential that all Level III material should be lodged in an archive, together with all the relevant Level I and Level II original records, and, most importantly, that Level III material that has not already been published should be available ad hoc at the cost price of reproducing it' (Frere 1975, section 3.6).

The report continues that:

'it is desirable that excavation archives should be housed with the finds. Some museums already undertake the custody of both with success. We recommend that all museums should be encouraged to do so as a necessary condition of obtaining custody of the finds, and that it should also be a condition that custody of excavation records should involve a duty to make available unpublished Level

III data on request, by either photographic copy, xerox, microfilm or, where appropriate, computer print-out, at cost price.' (Frere 1975, section 3.7).

There is the root, then, of what followed over the next four decades. There is an implicit expectation that museums will automatically be the final depository and that they should insist, as a condition of obtaining the finds, that all other records should be deposited in perpetuity with them also. The report notes that where conditions for the custody of records cannot be fulfilled by museums then they should be housed in the National Monuments Record. The corollary of this is that, even though the finds are regarded as important, the excavation records themselves appear to take dominance in the process towards study and publication. The fact that the sheer volume of excavated material and records would grow, year on year, while museum storage resources are always, at any given moment, finite was not taken into account at these early, formative stages.

A year later another DoE working party, in association with the Greater London Council (GLC) and the newly formed Museum of London (MoL) to consider the archaeology of Greater London, published *Time On Our Side? A Survey of Archaeological Needs in Greater London* (Bird and Kington 1976). Though confined, according to its brief, to Greater London alone, some of the observations about the long-term curation of *ex situ* archaeological resources were, and remain, appropriate to the country at large. In 1976 there were 22 museums in Greater London that included in their policy the collection of local archaeological material, only one of which (the new MoL) had a Greater London remit. The report commented, in words applicable to the country as a whole, that:

> *'[these museums] do not have the staff to keep abreast of the conservation of their collection, they are constantly in search of additional storage space, and are more often than not cramped for exhibition space. It is hardly surprising if in such circumstances new finds from archaeological excavations are sometimes accepted with misgiving.'* (Bird and Kington 1976, 12).

For London, even in 1976 the skills and storage crisis was looming large. Only 15 of the 22 museums had qualified archaeologists on their payrolls. Many of those conducted fieldwork, but there was insufficient staffing-capacity to do everything the museum was supposed to do. Furthermore only 13 museums thought they had space to accept new depositions; six were trying to find new storage space at the time of publication of the report. Lack of space aside, the real crisis was that:

> *'even when space can be found, however, material brought into the museum from the field has frequently to be left in its temporary packing through lack of staff to catalogue it. Four museums estimate that they could cope with an increased rate of accession of objects recovered from sites excavated in advance of destruction. Three more would require extra staff and storage space before accepting any new major intake of material. Fifteen see no prospect of being able to deal with such an intake.'* (*ibid*, 13).

The report concludes that:

> '*if a greater amount of useful information about the historical development of what is now Greater London is to be rescued from oblivion, some more constructive thought must urgently be given to the storage of this information and to its dissemination. Some of the basic source material will be in the form of site-records, drawings and photographs. Some of it will be in the form of artifacts - fragments of pottery, metal and bone, and occasionally large items of stone and timber. All of it must be stored and conserved*' (*ibid*, 14).

By the mid-1970s, therefore, the scene was already set. There was a clear awareness that museums would not be able to cope with the anticipated increase of material being generated by rescue excavations but there was no urgent and constructive thought about how museums were to proactively manage the reception and storage, in perpetuity, of this material.

The growth of the crisis and some solutions

Irrespective of the amazing new discoveries that were being made and could be used to furnish new displays, it was known that each and every excavation carried with it a nasty sting in its tail. It has to be said, although this is likely to be vigorously denied by the excavators, that after the hot flush of discovery and understanding of what they had found has subsided, this same material transubstantiates from exciting-insights-into-the-past (published with respect and reverence and presented to clients as justification for them funding excavations in the first place) into a space-consuming-annoyance. Attention turns very quickly, for obvious reasons, to incoming material related to live projects. The *ex situ* resource has, then, near Gothic novel-like qualities, like some archaeological version of *The Picture of Dorian Gray*. A glowing narrative of discovery with fine objects and stories on public display, and well-appreciated by them, in galleries and presented in highly professional and articulate form in publications, while hidden away in the darkest recesses of unit and museum stores resides the site's alter ego; an encumbrance growing ever more corrupt, unrecognisable and unapproachable with age.

There have, though, been some notable exceptions that have helped to alleviate or arrest this issue. To name just a few (with apologies for omissions) the Archaeological Resource Centre at York, Hampshire County Council's storage and access facilities at Chilcomb House, Winchester, the Museums Resource Centre at Standlake, in Oxfordshire and, more recently (it is the most recent of these initiatives although it has already celebrated its 10th anniversary since opening in 2002), the London Archaeological Archive and Research Centre or LAARC). Each of these initiatives, and others, was created in order to address the issues that each parent-body had to contend with. Decisions were taken, plans put in place, funding sought and secured and the resulting access and storage facilities successfully put in place. The solution was a large store that would gather the archives from a large district or region and, as a result of economy of scale, curate and care for the collection as a 'regional' centre. Outreach and research projects could then be engineered with each archive at its core.

The common denominator for each of these projects, however, is that there was only one parent-body taking the lead. Whether it be a single Trust (York), County Council (Oxfordshire and Hampshire) or Museum (London), a single executive was responsible for initiating the project and guiding it through to its completion. Successful multiple-partner initiatives are rare. This does not mean that there is not an initial will to make something happen. There have been many steering committees made up of Museum professionals and their colleagues from their Borough or County Council Town Halls and these have embarked upon successful exercises to identify and, in some cases, accurately quantify the scale of the problem they are collectively facing, but few advance beyond this stage. The reasons rest with the diversity of localised requirements and expectations. These partisan responses come in the form of, for example:

- Difficulty or unwillingness, due to other priorities, for Local Authority heritage managers to persuade their own managers and the respective authority's elected members of the merits of funding long-term storage projects;

- Difficulty also in persuading elected members to support the funding of projects that are likely not to be completed until after the next round of local elections;

- Title to the collections would rest with more than one party. Proportional funding would resolve this but would need to be accurately calculated from the start and revised as and when major redevelopment took place. The variation in proportional responsibility can be seen in Table 1 for Northamptonshire. This varies from 1.37% (Corby) to 38.62% (East Northamptonshire);

- Museums are concerned that access to collections on the community 'doorstep' will not be conducive to the realisation of their own access policies;

- Many museums fear loss of control of their archaeological archive to a central store, negating their own tenuous involvement in the planning process which, for many, is an important selling point to justify the Local Authority funding of both the museum and its staff.

Table 1 Northamptonshire: proportion of archive in Northamptonshire by Borough

	2004 volume	% of total
East Northants	92.57 cu m	38.62%
South Northants	31.15 cu m	13%
Wellingborough	18.17 cu m	7.58%
Corby	3.28 cu m	1.37%
Northampton + colls	66.76 cu m	27.84%
Daventry	18.62 cu m	7.77%
Kettering	9.16 cu m	3.82%
	239.71 cu m	

While any of these concerns remain in place, the creation of the much-vaunted regional stores in the future will be either impossible to design, due to complex over-arching management and cross local-authority funding arrangements, or difficult to keep in place and make sustainable for the same reasons. While there is no alternative at the single store or single parent-body level, the situation gets progressively worse.

Over the last 40 years, this total of material, whether it be paper, photographic, digital or physical finds, has continued to increase. Figure 1, shows the accurate quantifications, in terms of number of modular 1m shelves, of just bulk finds (pottery, animal bone, and building material) deposited in the LAARC for the period from 1972 to 2001. The bulk has increased from *c* 400 cu m to *c* 1600 cu m. This, it should be remembered, includes material deposited since 1990 that has been sampled to a greater level of detail than previously. Building materials especially are well-sampled now in London, with detailed quantification replacing bulk deposition. The graph, however, is self-explanatory. The total volume of the archive continues to grow at a rate estimated at approximately 175m of shelving per annum (*pers com* Steve Tucker, LAARC Collections Manager). The total of bulk material that had been excavated at the time of the publication of the *Time on Our Side* report is now less than 25% of the total. On a smaller scale, over the four year-period from 2000 to 2004 the Northamptonshire archive increased by a total of 7.5% (Table 2).

Figure 1 Cumulative totals from London from 1972 to 2001

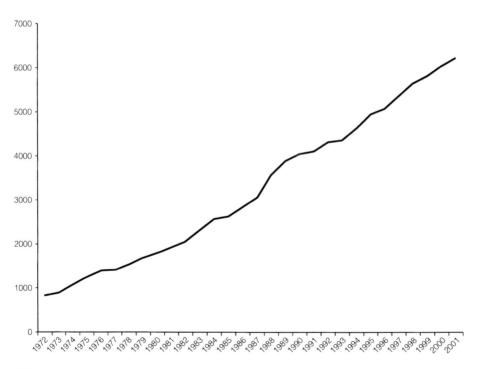

Table 2 Northamptonshire: increases in archive volume from 2000 to 2004

	Volume in 2000	Volume in 2004	Increase in 4 years
East Northant	89.71 cu m	92.57 cu m	2.86 (3.18%)
South Northants	26.49 cu m	31.15 cu m	4.66 (17.60%)
Wellingborough	14.69 cu m	18.17 cu m	3.48 (23.67%)
Corby	2.47 cu m	3.28 cu m	0.81 (32.98%)
Northampton	56.58 cu m	60.04 cu m	3.46 (6.11%)
Daventry	17.28 cu m	18.62 cu m	1.34 (7.76%)
Kettering	5.01 cu m	5.23 cu m	0.22 (4.42%)
Northants colls	3.93 cu m	3.93 cu m	0
Kettering Colls	6.72 cu m	6.72 cu m	0
	222.88 cu m	**239.71 cu m**	**16.84 (7.55%)**

This increase mirrors, of course, the success of the field units in their ability and capacity to recover archaeological data before the development of each respective site. Of course, this should be welcomed and it is in contrast to the situation that encouraged the establishment of RESCUE in the first place. However, the development of the argument to store and to make accessible the *ex situ* heritage resource in ways other than by exhibition or publication has not expanded at the same rate. True, those engaged in the curation, care and public access to this material would argue that they have greatly facilitated access, and the increase in numbers of museum professionals trained in the design and implementation of outreach and public-access initiatives since the mid-1990s is an important success story that demonstrates this. However, the *ex situ* resource as a whole still remains under-used and developed while it is scattered between museums and the units that deposit with it.

Why has there been a poor response to solving this archaeological archive crisis? The stock answer, of course, is that there is not enough money. However, other heritage and archaeological initiatives have been most successful in the last two decades. The Archaeological Data Service (ADS) has, since 1996, supported research, learning, and teaching with freely available, high quality, dependable digital resources. It does this by preserving digital data in the long-term, and by promoting and disseminating a broad range of data in archaeology. The ADS promotes good practice in the use of digital data in archaeology, it provides technical advice to the research community, and supports the deployment of digital technologies. Among many initiatives, the ADS has enabled archaeological grey-literature to be made accessible, as well as some collections of records that were under threat of loss, such as the Newham Archive (a digital archive of the Newham Museum Archaeological Service that closed down in 1998; the archive represents some 10 years of fieldwork and incorporates the work of other units that had previously been closed including those associated with the Passmore Edwards Museum and the Manor Valley Museum). Of course, the ADS focuses upon the digitised elements of an archive but, nevertheless since this has over the years formed an increased element of the archaeological archive it has greatly improved access and disseminated the results of fieldwork.

The Portable Antiquities Scheme (PAS) has also successfully demonstrated and argued its case for funding. This is not the place to discuss the efficacy of the PAS but, entirely without prejudice to that scheme, the fact that the Government regards as suitable the use of public funds for the recording of the more attractive, mainly metallic, provenanced examples of our past material-culture, exists in stark contrast to the absence of any similar funding for provenanced, stratified, contextualised material, in assemblages and with associations, which is primary evidence for the chronological development of particular communities. Of course, the generators of the two types of material are different. One has, as its core constituency, the public as finders, whereas the other has as its core constituency the archaeologist. In modern political parlance, the latter can now be regarded as the 'vested interest'.

However, this supposes that our politicians are even aware of the existence of an archaeological archive crisis. In 1997–8, there was a willingness on the part of the Government to discuss initiatives that gave access to museum collections. By then, the conditions for the use of Heritage Lottery Funding (HLF) had changed. Prior to March 1997, HLF funding was restricted to acquiring, maintaining or preserving tangible heritage assets. However, the National Heritage Act widened the scope and scale of projects that would be eligible for funding. In fact, it was a perfect combination of the new government in May 1997, the changes to the National Heritage Act by the previous government and, in the Museum of London itself, a change in senior management, with a clear decision on the future needs of London's *ex situ* archaeological resource, that led to the successful opening of the HLF, Government, MoL, and voluntary sector-funded LAARC. Additional funds, for the enhancement of the archive (The Minimum Standards Project) came from the Getty Grant Fund. In one fell swoop therefore, according to the totals published by Swain (1998), 20% of the nation's archaeological archive problem was solved.

One would have hoped that the momentum for a national solution would have continued, but sadly this was not to be. The Archaeological Archive Forum (AAF) was established in 2002 with a view to:

- Link together in partnership all major parties with an interest in archaeological archives in order that common policies and practice can be developed and applied

- Identify the courses of action necessary to further best practice in the field of archaeological archives and to effect the means to achieve this action

There is no doubt that both these objectives have been achieved, and a series of guidance papers and reviews have established well the qualitative issues related to archaeological archives. The Forum includes members from across the discipline, especially those in heritage management and museums. Although there was a place for a representative of managers of commercial units, the published minutes show that the place was seldom filled. Sadly, the Higher Education sector, arguably potentially one of the most important prospective users of archaeological archives for teaching and learning purposes, was not included until 2008, when a representative of the Higher Education Funding Council for England's (HEFCE) was co-opted onto the forum (Shepherd *et al* 2008).

However, if the second objective of the AAF, (*'identify the courses of action necessary to further best practice in the field of archaeological archives and to effect the means to achieve this action'*) includes the establishment of a successful dialogue with national policy-makers, arguably an essential to achieve best-practice which must, by definition, include proper deposition of archives in the public domain, then there may still be a very long way to go. It is remarkable that, as late as 2007, a question from the floor of the House of Commons from Robert Key (MP for Salisbury and Trustee of the Trust for Wessex Archaeology) to David Lammy, the Secretary of State for Culture, elicited a response that was telling in its content and also very distressing considering the ever growing archaeological archive crisis. It is worth repeating the question and answer in full. The Secretary of State has just announced extra funding for the Renaissance programme, a source of new funding for museum projects.

'5th March 2007

[Robert Key (Salisbury) (Con)]: The Renaissance programme is welcome, but of course the more people who go to our museums and the more television programmes that are made, the greater the profile of archaeology and the bigger the problem of storage, especially of archaeological finds. I would be grateful if the Minister assessed that problem in the coming months, as many museums and county archaeology services are completely at their wits' end about what to do with all the finds that have to be dug up because of planning permissions and so on. It is becoming a serious financial burden on local authorities and independent regional museums.

[Mr. Lammy]: It is right that the Hon. Gentleman acknowledges the huge success of the Portable Antiquities Scheme, which has meant that many local finds go to our local museums, but it is probably also right to say that for most museums only between 10 and 20 per cent of their collections are exhibited. A lot can never be exhibited because our museums play a key role in the academic study of artifacts and contribute to our knowledge base for those artifacts and their history. We are exploring with the Museums, Libraries and Archives Council (MLA) how we can increase touring, especially, in dialogue with our colleagues in Europe, to Eastern Europe. I hope that that, in particular, will increase people's access to all that wonderful treasure'.

It is evident that the Secretary of State was unaware of the substance of Key's question but answered with regards to what he was aware of, namely the PAS and its 'wonderful treasure'. This author contacted Robert Key to express concern at the lack of awareness the Minister had for the growing crisis and, with a former colleague from the Museum of London, met with him to discuss the matter. He drafted a written question which was answered in the following February again reproduced here in full:

'23rd April 2007

> *[Robert Key]: To ask the Secretary of State for Culture, Media and Sport what discussions she has had with English Heritage on the creation of regional depositories of archaeological archives and material from excavations.*

> *[Mr. Lammy]: My right hon. Friend the Secretary of State has not had any discussions with English Heritage on the creation of regional repositories of archaeological archives and material from excavations, although officials have had some discussion. The Museums, Libraries and Archives Council is the Government's lead advisory body on archives policy'.*

The outcome of this was that Key was invited, along with representatives of the AAF, to discuss issues with the new Secretary of State, James Purnell in the summer of 2007. The result of this meeting was that the Minister believed that English Heritage should work with the MLA on the issue. Subsequently, EH and the MLA were to produce a memorandum of understanding (MOU). By late 2009, the MLA reported to the AAF its and the government's position on archaeological archives (Archaeological Archive Forum 2009). Quite simply, they did not fit within the current government position and were simply not a priority (or even an acknowledged issue) in civil service or government thinking. It was considered primarily a local government/local authority issue, with the disjuncture between planning control and the culture/heritage departments within local authorities a significant problem. Part of this invisibility issue for archaeological archives, allegedly, was the result of DCMS/EH and other organisations using completely different language about archives. There was, it was noted with chilling foresight, the potential that both the DCMS and EH would be cut in the future, so it would be necessary to look elsewhere for any new funding. No alternative sources for funding were suggested. Since 2010, the expected cuts, or savings depending upon one's political point of view, have severely affected museum provision in the UK. The full impact upon curation, collecting and knowledge is still not clear as local authorities continue to seek further reductions in their annual spending. Even the full funding of national museums is under discussion, with the merger of the DCMS with Department of Business and Innovation being proposed. Such decisions are creating a major shift in the role of museums and their opportunity to develop large storage and archiving programmes is unlikely to meet with any interest, let alone success.

One interesting paradox that came from the MLA representative's presentation was that the MLA were downsizing and retracting from the regions. However, the regional option was the MLA's preferred solution. Such a solution required considerable engagement and awareness-raising in government organisations like the MLA (and now the Arts Council for England) by the archaeological community and that it was through

MLA regional officers that local authorities are connected to the larger system. However, by 2009 there had been only one instance where archaeological archives had been raised by a local authority. The MLA, he reported, could help with these problems, including potential resource centres, if contact was made with them but it was simply not happening at the time. This was, he noted, one of the issues. The problem was, it would appear, that it was not that the MLA was failing to support, prioritise or fund initiatives but that the archaeological community was not asking them for help. Considering the extent of knowledge about the issues relating to archaeological archives among senior officers in the MLA, including among their number those who had conducted detailed evaluations of the archaeological archive crisis in the 1990s, this comment was most disingenuous.

The next 40 years?

From an archaeological point of view, Benjamin Franklin's 1789 assertion that '...*in this world nothing can be said to be certain, except death and taxes*' can be revised to include: and the *ex situ* archaeological resource getting ever larger. While it will always be possible to create new initiatives to publish hard-copy or disseminate electronic texts and data for a site, the wizened and corrupted Dorian Gray-like portrait of the primary records and finds will still be lurking in the background; and it is all just going to get worse.

To suggest that there is a single solution to the current crisis would be churlish and patronising. There isn't. For over three decades museum curators and collection managers have been expending considerable time, effort and funds to solve the problem that is visited upon them in a process over which they have little control. The presence of a variety of guidelines and standards makes the deposition process easier for the curator, if space is available for the deposition, though not necessarily for the unit working in numerous museum collecting-areas and with multiple fine-tuned standards to consider. There are national guidelines, but a first step to any local, regional or national storage exercise would be to adopt a set of national standards; expected archive contents lists, packaging, labelling; all these routine archiving tasks should be standardised across the country so that, at anytime in the future, collections from the date of implementation of these standards could be merged under a single accessioning and access system.

As for the material already out of the ground and recorded on the context sheet, there are many suggestions about sampling, rationalisation or editing of finds assemblages, of weeding of paper and photographic records etc, but we must be clear what these exercises entail. If they are simply to create space, then to be effective they must be cost-effective. To edit, say, a collection of non-ferrous objects might be a rewarding intellectual exercise but the cost in staff and x-ray access-time plus materials might not be worth the paltry additional volume created. Rather it is better to focus on the larger volume collections such as pottery, animal-bone and building-material. Here especially, any sampling or editing exercise can only be carried out when there is a clear understanding of the collection in the curator's care and, if the collection is understood, with appropriate reference collections in place, especially fabric collections, so that quantified and discarded material can be collated. However, the academic questions that need to be asked for pottery assemblages are numerous and, once again, one falls foul of the paradox that the time and resource expended is not worth the gain.

As for animal bone? The author's experience of managing access to the LAARC between 1997–2004 demonstrates that one key question always asked by a researcher examining specific animal bone assemblages is '*What is the level of residual pottery in this context?*' To my recollection contexts with a lot of residual pottery were only examined when they were known to contain rare specimens or exemplars. The potential that assemblages could be contaminated by material from an earlier phase of activity negates any quantification exercise. I have been told though, by interested parties, that we should not tamper with the bone assemblages because 'one never knows what new technique might become available etc'. However, attempts should be made to identify those contexts with highly residual pottery.

The building-material specialist, however, is far more pragmatic and well aware that a fabric series plus exemplars, and a fully-quantified record is sufficient for preservation by record. Much of this work now takes place at the post-excavation stage, but there is considerable advantage to editing building-material collections already in store. This was successfully carried out at the LAARC between 2000 and 2002 and has recently been carried out by Winchester Museums on their large urban assemblages. New space is created, at a price of course, but it is cost effective.

Rationalisation and editing, however, go only part-way to making life easier for current use and development of the archives. As for the future, a very strong case, based upon a thorough awareness of the existing content of each collection, could be made for collecting less. A debate needs to be had about this, though I predict that there will be a smooth discussion regarding building materials, concerns about animal bones, and a tortuous debate about pottery. As for the records themselves, these will continue to be produced at the rate and quantity that is regarded as necessary. Digitisation might solve some issues and would certainly improve dissemination, though longevity of the digitised record is another issue.

However, all of these adjustments to how we collect in the future, and what we keep in our present stores, do not really address the main issues; what are we going to do about the national archaeological archive that exists in numerous stores throughout the country, and how do we arrest the crisis by making sure we do not exhaust finite space too soon? There has to be an increased engagement with national policy-makers, if only to increase their awareness and make them understand that there is an issue.

Perhaps the most important thing is that our discipline must begin to focus less upon what we are keeping: we now seem to have that largely covered. Units and their specialists are quite adept at sampling prior to deposition. Neither should we keep asking ourselves about why we are keeping it. We keep it because it is important, because it is the primary evidence for past occupation and activity. We should not apologise for its existence or be ashamed of its volume. The LAARC total volume is in the region of 3000 cubic metres. That is a very large volume in terms of a single collection, but in terms of it being the sole *ex situ* evidence for the sum of human habitation in the 1600 square miles that is Greater

London, this is not a large quantity at all. In fact, it is a very small sample of what the total could be and therefore is worthy of preservation for that reason alone. In fact, the sooner we start to think in terms of the national total being a small sample compared to the monumental archaeological collections of some Mediterranean countries, the easier it may be to gain political support. The size of a particular archaeological archive at present is seen in terms of the size of the rest of the museum storage facilities. It will always be too big. Questions will always be asked about whether all of it needs to be kept. This persistent trend needs to be bucked and to do this the profession must have a much bigger ambition for the archaeological archives for the country.

The main paradigm shift, therefore, is one of perception. The sum of all archaeological fieldwork throughout the country may be a large figure, whether in numbers of sites, context sheets, gigabytes, boxes, tonnes or cubic metres, but it is only a small sample of what there used to be. Of course it requires editing down and that can be done, if resources were made available, so that we do not clutter this collection with superfluous data that is preventing long-term storage of other material. But what does exist is unique. Along with *in situ* heritage resources and monuments, it makes up the sum of heritage assets for the country. We need, therefore, to champion it at a national scale; and we need, perhaps, to find a national solution rather than what exists at the moment, which tends to be at a more local scale. Regional solutions are proposed but, as has been shown above, where these have worked there has been a single parent-body responsible. Perhaps we need to re-examine the entire concept of deposition into the local authority museum-sector. Any alternative must not, of course, undermine existing tenuous provision of museums with an ever-dwindling cohort of museum staff and knowledge, but there is perhaps the need to open a debate about the establishment of a national mechanism for housing and making accessible, especially to local museums for their own exhibitions, outreach projects etc, material from their collecting areas. Perhaps it is time to start campaigning for a National Archive for Archaeology.

We can start, as already mentioned, by championing archaeological archives rather than regard them as a burden. In recent decades, as has been the trend since the 70s, policy regarding preservation *in situ* has dominated the agenda, led by a consortium of national heritage managers, local planning archaeologists and the commercial sector units. Preservation of archaeological remains *in situ* has even got its own natty acronym; PARIS. Preservation of Archaeological Remains *ex situ* has never been so dignified. (PARES perhaps?) However, considering that the archaeological record, is itself the sole remaining primary-record of what has been lost, it should surely be the *Primus inter Pares* of our discipline and profession.

References

Archaeological Archive Forum, 2009, meeting minutes May 2009, at http://www.britarch.ac.uk/archives/AAF%20Minutes%205%20May%202009.pdf (accessed Feb 2013)

Bird, J, and Kington, S (eds), 1976, *Time on our side? A survey of archaeological needs in Greater London,* MOLAS, London

Curwen, E C, 1937, *The archaeology of Sussex,* Methuen, London

Frere, S S, 1975, *Principles of publication in rescue archaeology,* Ancient Monuments Board for England, Committee for Rescue Archaeology, Dept of the Environment, London

Shepherd, J, Milne, G, Hicks, D, and Skeetes, R, 2009, *Excavating the archives: Archive archaeology and the higher education sector,* HEA Guidelines for Teaching and Learning **7,** Liverpool

Swain, H, 1998, *A survey of archaeological archives in England. A report prepared for English Heritage and the Museums and Galleries Commission,* English Heritage, London

Chapter 14

Rescue archaeology: the threat to maritime heritage

Joe Flatman

Introduction

In 1974 when Rahtz's *Rescue Archaeology* was published, the current system of maritime heritage management was in its infancy. At that time, the work of people like George Bass had already demonstrated the cultural significance of submerged remains, along with the possibility of undertaking high-quality archaeological fieldwork under water, fieldwork every bit as good as that undertaken on land (*see* Bass 1966). As a consequence of such advances, by 1974 avocational and professional groups alike were busy applying the lessons of Bass' work around the world, most notably in the UK on the wreck site of the Tudor warship *Mary Rose* from 1971 onwards (Marsden 2003), as well as through the early work of the proto-Nautical Archaeology Society (then known as the Council for Nautical Archaeology and later the Nautical Archaeology Trust). Similarly, clear excavation methodologies were being applied on sites within at least an implicit research framework, for example, on the series of Spanish Armada shipwrecks off Scotland and Ireland investigated in this period by Colin Martin and his colleagues (Martin 1975). Crucially, legal instruments like the 1973 Protection of Wrecks Act in the UK had also come into force by 1974, and would in turn do so in many other nations around the world within the next few years. Thus, at the time of publication of Rahtz's *Rescue Archaeology*, the stage was set for significant growth on all fronts in the marine zone. Nonetheless, the threat to maritime heritage in 1974 was still acute. The looting of wreck sites by individuals and organisations alike was rife in this period, due to a lack of public awareness of the significance of such sites combined with a lack of legal protection or government acceptance of responsibility. There was no coordinated management of marine historic sites in relation to either rescue or research (and so, no consistent rescue archaeology in advance of development comparable to the informal networks in place on land by this time). Crucially, nor was there very much understanding of, or records to indicate the extent and significance of, maritime heritage, and thus only a limited possibility of strategic investigation. Marine sites were discovered and then investigated in most cases by accident and analysed in isolation in this period, and to most people, bar a few far-sighted individuals (*see* Flemming 1972 for example), 'maritime heritage' meant only shipwrecks, not the wealth of different site-types above and below water that this term encompasses today.

Fast-forward to 2014 and what does the situation look like now? In many ways, vastly improved. The global marine archaeological resource is very much better understood, managed and protected, with both reactive rescue and proactive research archaeology by avocational and professional archaeologists alike. Laws are in place in many nations around the world to manage, protect and crucially to promote maritime heritage, and there is significant international collaboration. Public understanding of heritage is also high, and public involvement too, thanks to long-term training schemes such as that of the Nautical Archaeology Society (NAS), in use around the world since 1986. Above all, maritime cultural heritage is understood in a holistic framework, the significance of a diverse range of sites above, across and below the waterline, appreciated in complex relation to one-another, and also in relation to natural heritage. 'Maritime' heritage is increasingly simply just 'heritage' in this context, as should be the case, echoing Bass' call of 1966 that 'archaeology under water, of course, should be called simply *archaeology*' (Bass 1966, 15, emphasis in the original). Crucially, marine planning regimes are also in place in many locations around the world (including in the UK), giving broadly commensurate protection to heritage to that seen on land through terrestrial planning policy. Sadly, in other ways the situation in 2014 is certainly no better than in 1974 and in some regards very much worse. Our understanding of the extent and relative significance of the transnational maritime heritage 'resource' remains limited in 2014, especially in many industrialising nations but even in fully-industrialised states like the UK, US and Australia. Similarly, legal instruments for the protection and promotion of maritime heritage remain thin on the ground, frequently unsuited to the task, under-enforced and regulated, and crucially, do not often overlap effectively with commensurate terrestrial heritage or planning laws or regulations. Meanwhile, despite all of the advances in public archaeology in the last 40 years, the threat of looting remains a concern around the world. To this can be added new environmental threats to maritime heritage, as the seas and oceans become more intensively industrialised. In 2014 there is everything still to play for as regards maritime heritage in the early-mid 21st century, and the stakes have never been higher. As the author outlines elsewhere (*see* Flatman 2012), this century is likely to be one of intensive exploitation of the marine-zone by a wealth of different communities and industries, and one thus of equally intense geopolitical wrangling. It is imperative that the well-established process of prioritising, protecting and promoting maritime heritage accelerates in the light of this expanding industrial regime. The challenge is formidable and not to be under-estimated: it will take every ounce of strength in every regard to achieve even modest results, and the biggest lesson of all must be how to garner public support for, and commitment to, the maritime cultural heritage, and then how to translate this support into genuine, long-lasting political influence at both the domestic and international level.

The legal and management situation

The legal and management situation of maritime heritage remains confused at both a domestic and international level in 2014. This is true around the world and without exception. No nation can claim to have a comprehensive, integrated and effective management regime for maritime heritage. As noted above, legal instruments for the protection and promotion of maritime heritage remain thin on the ground, frequently unsuited to the task (especially the nuanced protection of submerged landscapes rather than 'spot' finds of wreck sites), under-enforced and regulated, and crucially, do not often overlap effectively with commensurate terrestrial heritage laws and development control regimes; to this can be added a lack of co-ordination with related natural heritage management and legislation, and a similar lack of co-ordination with wider planning/ development control laws and regulations. There also remains a lack of international co-ordination and collaboration as regards marine heritage. Although the 2001 UNESCO Convention on the Protection of the Underwater Cultural Heritage has been in force in ratifying nations since 2009, many nations continue to refuse to ratify the convention for a variety of different reasons (*see* JNAPC 2006; British Academy/Honor Frost Foundation 2014). Even were more nations to ratify the convention, this would still only apply in the 0–12 nautical mile off-shore territorial sea-zone that is agreed under the 1982 UN Convention on the Law of the Sea. In the still disputed 12–200 nautical mile off-shore exclusive economic zone (EEZ) the application of the convention is ambiguous at best and open to legal challenge at worst. Meanwhile, in the vast swathe of deep ocean beyond this 200 nautical mile off-shore limit we have yet to fully understand how the convention could or would apply. At present, the only laws that apply here to maritime heritage are those of Sovereign Immunity as regards specific vessels lost under particular circumstances and even vaguer (and more disputed) international salvage laws (*see* Roach 1997; Dromgoole 1999). Such protection of historic sites as these principles afford are on a case-by-case basis, and Sovereign Immunity in particular could not be used to protect non-wreck materials such as submerged cultural landscapes. Nor are such principles designed with heritage in mind, but rather in the case of Sovereign Immunity to protect national rights over war graves (offering at best the accidental chance of protection of heritage through their broader principles of sovereign rights), and in the case of salvage law to assist the return of goods to the market by encouraging entrepreneurial activity in the salvage of wrecks. The expansion of the UNESCO convention, or at least its core concepts, in the deep sea, remains an interesting area of potential future development.

Leaving aside the legal protection of sites, examples of international collaboration in the analysis, management, and protection of maritime heritage remain few and far between. There is no reason why nations that have bordering (in some cases overlapping or disputed) territorial sea or EEZ boundaries could not work more closely together to manage maritime heritage; such management would not require legal instruments, just working agreements in the forms of 'memoranda of understanding' or suchlike. Steps have been made in precisely this way towards the international management of the submerged maritime heritage of the southern North Sea zone by the bordering nations of the Netherlands, Belgium and the UK under the aegis of the North Sea Prehistory Research and Management Framework (English Heritage 2009), and such models of international collaboration surely represent the logical way forward, if nothing else on the purely economic basis of shared financial as well as shared management responsibility.

Moving to the domestic sphere in the UK, there are other specific management concerns. The example of England is an instructive one as regards both some of the problems and also some of the solutions of nation-state marine-heritage management. It should be noted that at the time of writing, in the summer of 2014, England, as part of the larger political entity of the UK, has not ratified the 2001 UNESCO convention. However, the UK government has publicly indicated its belief in the principles of Annex A of the convention (in a series of statements in Parliament by successive Culture Ministers), as well as being a signatory of various key European heritage protection conventions that it can be tacitly assumed, apply in the marine zone. For example, the 1992 European Convention on the Protection of the Archaeological Heritage (Revised) and the 1970 Convention on the Means of Prohibiting and Preventing the Illicit Import, Export and Transfer of Ownership of Cultural Property to name but two examples. There has also recently been a comprehensive analysis of all aspects of the convention and its relevance to the UK (British Academy/Honor Frost Foundation 2014; UK UNESCO 2001 Convention Review Group 2014).

The basic structure of marine heritage management in the UK comes, in principle if not always in practice, through the marine [planning] consent regime. This regime is broadly equivalent in impact if not structure to the planning-consent regime on land, enforced as of April 2012,through the new National Planning Policy Framework. In a minority of cases, specific heritage protection is afforded through the use of statutory instruments, particularly the 1973 Protection of Wrecks Act and the 1979 Ancient Monuments and Archaeological Areas Act, and in rare occasions, through the 1983 Protection of Military Remains Act. This management regime is effectively a 'broad brush' commercial management system in which the majority of sites are not protected except via the development management regime, and where no historic site is automatically protected on the basis of its cultural significance. The Crown Estate is also a massive player in this process, raising an interesting question of the potential dichotomy between being both steward and landlord of large swathes of the seabed, in which overlapping demands of management and development often have to be juggled.

Given this management regime, the intermeshed issues of site-extent and significance on the one hand, and holistic management on the other hand, continue to prove vexatious in England. English Heritage[1] has been formally responsible for explicitly 'maritime'

---

[1] At the time of writing, the Department for Culture Media and Sport was consulting on its proposal for the *New Model for English Heritage* (see https://www.gov.uk/government/news/new-model-for-english-heritage-moves-a-step-closer-following-consultation [accessed 1 December 2014]). Following a public consultation, and after this book had entered the production phase, the then Minister of State for Culture and the Digital Economy announced that the Government had approved the proposal to separate English Heritage into two organisations from 1 April 2015. English Heritage has now become a new body, envisaged to be a self-funding charity by 2023, to manage and promote the more than 400 properties and sites in the National Heritage Collection (*see* http://www.english-heritage.org.uk/).The other functions are now managed by Historic England which provides expert advice and acts as a champion for the sector. Some English Heritage roles referred to in this chapter are therefore now the responsibility of Historic England (*see* http://www.historicengland.org.uk/).

cultural heritage from the high-water-mark out to the 12nm extent of the territorial sea since its remit was expanded in this respect under the 2002 National Heritage Act; a responsibility that has been clarified through the introduction of the National Heritage Protection Plan (NHPP) since 2011 and its replacement from April 2015, the Historic England Action Plan (HEAP). Outside of the Territorial Limit, including within other administrative boundaries (ie UK Controlled Waters), either off England or elsewhere, management responsibility remains a significant challenge for the government. English Heritage has implemented an impressive array of, in particular, Historic Seascape Charactersation (HSC) and Rapid Coastal Zone Assessment Surveys (RCZAS) (*see* English Heritage 2012a, 2012b; Murphy 2014) to help quantify the marine cultural-resource and thus prioritise its analysis and protection. Such analysis provides crucial data-overlap with comparable Historic Landscape Characterisation (HLC) and core national and county historic environment data held on terrestrial archaeological sites. The HEAP is crucial to this process, being an informed (and publicly consulted) way forward, holistic and comprehensive, covering all environments and responsibilities within the legal boundaries of English Heritage's remit. Such data overlap is essential if anything approaching the holistic management of sites above, across, and below water is to be achieved. However, although these programmes have done much to bring marine data-sets up to a comparable standard with terrestrial data, there remain problems as regards the effective holistic management of heritage. This problematic management situation is not, it should be noted, the fault of English Heritage, nor of its related government department, the Department for Media, Culture and Sport (DCMS). Rather, the situation is to do with the nature of English property management, land ownership, and crucially, planning law and regulation, which maintains a marked difference between 'land' and 'sea' that has become more, not less complicated over the previous 40 years, most recently as a consequence of the Marine and Coastal Access Act (2009), the Localism Act (2011), the National Planning Policy Framework (2012) and other ongoing modifications to the terrestrial and marine planning consent regimes. Further confusing this management regime, in England there is also the issue of the inconsistent application of specific deliberate or *de facto* heritage management regimes. In particular, the Portable Antiquities Scheme (PAS) on land has an accidental comparison at sea in the 1995 Merchant Shipping Act. However, the Portable Antiquities Scheme on land is voluntary and only rewards finders of specific discoveries of materials deemed 'treasure' under the 1996 Treasure Act, whereas at sea the Merchant Shipping Act is compulsory but rewards, in principle, all finders of all materials, of historic significance or not. There is a strong case to be made for the English 'small finds' reporting regime to be more effectively intermeshed through the blended application of these two systems.

Despite such concerns, England, and indeed the broader UK, remains a positive example in many ways. Three facts bear this statement out. Firstly, in English Heritage there is an organisation dedicated to, and with the legal responsibility for, holistically managing heritage above, across and below mean low water, comprising highly trained staff that understand the need for and are dedicated to such holistic management. Secondly, there has been in the past a model of innovative heritage management, the Aggregates Levy Sustainability fund (ALSF), that the country ought to attempt to return to, an example of the types of progressive management regime that can be developed when people put their minds to it (*see* discussion below and Flatman and Doeser 2010). Thirdly, England has an unparalleled array of lobby and advisory groups on the one hand (especially the Joint Nautical Archaeology Policy Committee (JNAPC) and RESCUE) and community-based organisations on the other hand (especially the Nautical Archaeology Society (NAS) and its training scheme and the Council for British Archaeology (CBA)) that comprise an extraordinary pool of talent, knowledge and enthusiasm.

Threats and challenges

There remain a distressingly large number of ongoing threats and challenges regarding maritime heritage. For the purposes of this discussion these can be grouped into two distinct but interrelated areas: firstly, site management and secondly, legal developments.

Site management

Site management issues comprise the largest area of present concern. The term covers a multitude of inter-related problems, natural and cultural, individual and communal. At the basic level, there is the general problem of managing sites that are physically hard to reach (and crucially, to monitor) in a dynamic, corrosive environment. Although wreck sites in particular usually achieve an equilibrium of stability, a host of factors, both natural and cultural, can destabilise them. This is the key to the lie that looters perpetrate, that their actions 'save' wrecks that would otherwise inevitably be lost to the oceans, a lie disproved by archaeologists such as Muckelroy as long ago as the 1970s (Muckelroy 1978) but still regularly repeated.

The reality is that most sites, particularly most sites investigated by people seeking materials for re-sale, are stable until human interference destabilises them, initiating a new cycle of erosion. That being said, there are a smaller number of sites that do require intensive management in response to entirely natural processes of erosion. This issue is particularly true on the coastal fringe and foreshore where ongoing erosion, exacerbated by anthropogenic global change, is now recognised as having a marked impact on coastal archaeology (*see* Flatman 2009; Murphy 2014). In turn, larger coastal-management projects, by responding to increased incidences of coastal instability, increasingly threaten heritage too. 'Managed retreat' of coastlines to 'equilibrium' environments of foreshore salt marshes, as well as more formal coastal-management such as sea-defences, all potentially threaten coastal historic resources, and this is likely to become a growing concern over the next 40 years.

A very different management concern arises from a specific class of wreck-sites: that of modern sites as environmental risks. A number of WW1, WW2 and cold-war wreck-sites, many of them war graves, have been identified as environmental hazards due to the toxic materials housed or leaking out of them, including fuel oils, heavy metals and armaments, incorporating toxic, corrosive and poisonous materials. As such vessels (generally large and steel-hulled) degrade, this environmental hazard is growing. Perhaps an even worse threat than this are the large number of marine locations used either as military testing or dumping grounds for munitions, including toxic and radioactive materials, that pose an escalating threat to the cultural and natural marine environment alike (*see* Murphy 2010). The ultimate example of such sites are the dozens of wrecks of nuclear powered and/or armed submarines that litter the global ocean floor, a threat for thousands of years to come (*see* Delgado 2011). Meanwhile, moving away from such site-specific management issues, there is the issue of the management of entire submerged landscapes, especially prehistoric submerged landscapes. The global extent of such landscapes is now clear to professionals, politicians and the public alike (*see* Flatman 2012), and the UK is leading the way in mapping the extent and significance of such environments, for example, in the North Sea (*see* Gaffney, Fitch and Smith 2009; Evans et al 2014). The challenge for the mid-21st century, however, is how to meaningfully *manage* such sites, to reconcile the many different stakeholders claims to the sea, seabed surface and sub-surface components of such landscapes; environments that cover hundreds of thousands of square miles and tens of thousands of archaeological sites. There is no comparable terrestrial management challenge to this situation anywhere in the world, nowhere that combines so many different overlapping environments, communities and environmental and cultural pressures. In this, the marine heritage community perhaps for the first time ever faces an entirely new challenge.

Returning to the threat of looting of historic wreck sites, there has been a marked shift in attitudes to this issue over the past 40 years, and the situation has both improved and worsened. On the one hand, the type of low-level, individual looting of material from shallow-water wreck sites by sport divers that was common the 1950s, 1960s and 1970s has very much reduced. A mixture of training and outreach by organisations like the Nautical Archaeology Society together with a rise in awareness that wreck sites are best enjoyed through repeated visits rather than being stripped of materials, has seen this threat if not stop then markedly decline. In addition, the recent success of the Heritage Crime initiative in England has led to increased joint-working by enforcement agencies and a number of ongoing investigations. Such proactive enforcement based on intelligence-sharing has seen a dramatic reduction in unlicensed activity. How this process of popular awareness has occurred makes an interesting companion study to Pete Wilson's discussion of metal detecting and community outreach on land in Chapter 15. However, marine technologies have also advanced across this period, opening up access to deep-water sites at depths beyond those accessible to divers. The particular threat in such instances comes not from individuals but rather from professional salvage organisations that actively search out high value wrecks for systematic recovery of bulk materials for re-sale either on the international antiquities or metal markets.

The issue of *in situ* preservation is another area of site-management that rarely gets discussed but which is, in its own way, crucially important to debates surrounding the past, present and future of rescue archaeology (*see* Broadwater and Nutley 2009; Staniforth and Shefi 2011). The principle of the *in situ* preservation of marine historic sites as the first, preferred option is made clear in rule 1 of the annex of the 2001 UNESCO Convention on the Protection of the Underwater Cultural Heritage. The application of this principle as the *preferred*, initial option is not in question, and is in line with best practice (as well as law and treaty obligations) on terrestrial historic sites. On land, at least in the UK, a pragmatic approach is regularly taken, where historic sites are regularly invasively excavated both because of reactive 'rescue' development-led pressures and also proactive research demands. However, in the marine zone the invasive investigation of archaeological sites by *archaeologists* (not looters) remains uncommon. Partly, this lack of excavation is a response to fear of the costs, not just of investigation, but also of recovery of materials (especially large, articulated sections of hull) and crucially the costs of long-term conservation and display of marine materials. The generations-long expense of projects to recover, analyse and display vessels like the *Vasa* in Sweden (1956 onwards), the Skuldelev Viking ships in Denmark (1962 onwards) and the *Mary Rose* in the UK (1971 onwards) have created an understandable culture of risk avoidance in this respect. As a consequence, it has proven harder and harder to learn 'in practice' how to excavate a marine historic site, especially a wreck site (although innovative projects such as that of the Bournemouth University Swash Channel Wreck excavations have demonstrated one way forward in this regard). As a general rule, the last generation of practitioners to know in *practical detail* how to excavate a marine historic site are now in their 40s, 50s or older, and are less and less able to actively enter the marine zone to teach others. The next generation of active practitioners are in their 30s and 40s and have rarely had any such experience (ie the author and his contemporaries), and the next generation after that, of present students, have had even less experience. As a result there is something of both a training and skills gap. Were a significant historic wreck site to be identified in UK waters, and subjected to intensive, invasive exploration, it can be questioned whether or not there are sufficiently skilled individuals among the current professional archaeological community to ensure that investigation could take place to a comparable level to an on-land site of equal significance. Such a skills gap has additional negative consequences. 'Avocational' as much as 'professional' opportunities are denied, and boredom with the limited fieldwork-opportunities on offer can easily lead to 'rogue' fieldwork (ie illicit archaeological excavations), undoing the years of progress made by organisations like the Nautical Archaeology Society promoting a popular understanding of and support for regulated site management and training. The gap also means a lack of strong stories to keep popular and media interest alive in marine archaeology, missing in turn opportunities to promote advances in this field, and the chance to garner public and crucially political support. The gap also means an increasing not a lessening gap between archaeological practice on land and at sea, when the desire is for these management regimes to fully intermesh. Finally, the gap also means that it is harder to refute the accusations of looters that they are the only individuals doing something active about historic sites that are under threat, be this threat real or imagined.

This lack of ability to show the world what genuinely excellent marine archaeological excavation looks like and entails makes it harder to reject the spurious claims of such looters to be 'protecting' sites through their work. There is a strong argument to be made that more extensive (but still informed) invasive marine archaeological fieldwork opportunities need to be identified and implemented on a series of key sites around the world, sites worthy of research attention, with a clear research agenda and methodology in place. Such projects could focus on training, research and funding opportunities in an international collaborative spirit. Such projects would also have the added benefit of acting as a focus of popular and thus media enthusiasm for maritime heritage. The success of training and public management schemes like that of the Nautical Archaeology Society demonstrates that there is a significant and enthusiastic sector of society that is willing to be become actively *involved* in site analysis and management, often at considerable personal cost. Focused projects of the type proposed above would thus provide perfect outlets for this popular enthusiasm, garnering additional support (both financial and in-kind), from individuals and organisations alike. One need only consider the number of commercial sponsors of the Mary Rose Trust in its 1982 heyday to recognise the potential of such support. Such popular support could also conceivably translate into political attention and possibly even reform (for example, persuading specific governments to ratify the 2001 UNESCO convention). There is, inevitably, a concern that such projects would exacerbate existing problems of museum and conservation management facilities (ie the costs of, and specialist facilities needed for, dealing with marine zone finds) as well as other problems with site archives and public accessibility of materials (*see* Shepherd, Chapter 13 on museums and archives for discussion of such considerations). But such concerns, if planned for in advance, and with responsibility shared among a series of partner institutions over an anticipated project timeline and project budget *planned* to last decades from the outset, are not necessarily insurmountable and crucially, are not sufficient justification by themselves to avoid at least discussion of the possibility of undertaking such work.

Legal developments

Advances in the legal protection of maritime heritage fall more under the title of 'opportunities' than 'threats and challenges'. With the 2001 UNESCO convention ratified by the first key 20 nations in 2009, and with 48 nations having ratified at the time of writing (the summer of 2014), the hope has to be that more nations will choose in time to ratify the convention, especially key industrialised or industrialising nations. Many of these nations already abide by both domestic and international laws and heritage treaty conventions on land that are broadly comparable to the 2001 convention, and thus the formal step of ratification is not as great as these nations might fear, or opponents of the convention might scaremonger. But ratification is only the starting point of the 2001 convention. Much more work needs to be done, once ratified, to make the convention genuinely useful, a tool for international collaboration and advancement of best practice, building on the work of UNESCO-led training and capacity building initiatives already taking place under the aegis of the convention's Scientific and Technical Advisory Board.

Stepping beyond the consideration of existing legal frameworks, there is one other 'legal' issue that is tentatively starting to emerge in some locations around the world: the issue of Indigenous Communities' ancestral claims on submerged lands and resources. Indigenous Communities in the Americas and Australasia in particular have fought, and continue to fight, for such rights on land over the past 40 years (*see* Sillar and Fforde 2005; Gilbert 2006). The now submerged landscapes of the continental shelves are the next part of this battle for such communities' control. If it is recognised that the presence of cultural remains are a starting point for such claims on land, then the presence of similar materials under water arguably has just as strong a claim. Such a process, if challenged and won successfully in court, would have a profound impact on both industrial and archaeological activity alike in the territorial seas and exclusive economic zones of many nations. This is particularly so given the likely growth in industrial activity on the continental shelves of the world over the next 40 years, where a vast array of activities are either already underway or being planned, from traditional activities like fishing, mineral and hydrocarbon energy extraction, to 'new' industries like wind, wave and solar energy collection/production (*see* Flatman 2012 for a discussion of these possibilities). As new industries develop, new forms of management may arise, requiring in some cases new legal instruments, but also new opportunities for innovative site management, both cultural and natural. The tremendous success of the Aggregates Levy Sustainability Fund (ALSF) in the marine zone between 2002 and 2011 is an example of this of issue (*see* Flatman and Doeser 2010). Here, a new joint approach was promoted to the mutual benefit of developers, professional archaeologists, and local communities alike to successfully manage aggregates extraction and at the same time to undertake world-class archaeological research. Because the ALSF was proactive, rather than reactive, different types of site management regime could be implemented than traditional (usually reactive) industrial planning systems normally allow. For example, many ALSF projects were concerned with site prioritisation and risk avoidance, developing better tools to identify and minimise the impact of aggregate extraction on heritage. In order to do this, archaeologists regularly worked in collaboration with marine industries in true partnership, developing and undertaking shared projects, using industry 'legacy' data and other strategic approaches to make projects both timely and cost-effective, and undertaking community-friendly outreach and PR to the benefit of all involved, culminating in holistic site-management, with data-integration across the high-water-mark.

The future

To conclude, what then is the possible status of maritime heritage in another 40 years, in or around the year 2050? Assuming that the worst threats of anthropogenic global climate-change and carbon dioxide management have been dealt with, in itself a very big assumption; it is clear that a vastly more commodified maritime zone will be in place in 2050. As explained in the introduction, the world is turning more and more to the marine zone for resources of all types, and this process shows the likelihood of accelerating within the general pattern of the existing free-market system. This marine zone will also be significantly larger. Processes of anthropogenic accelerated global climate-change, leading to coastal erosion and flooding, are now so well advanced that some significant loss of the current landmass of the world is inevitable, bringing with it a concurrent loss of coastal heritage. There is also likely to be alongside this very much more 'settlement' of one type or another at sea, be this on static or moveable platforms both above and below water. That will in turn lead to the discovery of many more maritime heritage sites, including some discoveries that have the potential to radically alter our understanding of prehistoric archaeology. For example, it is extremely likely that much older evidence of settlement, or more complicated prehistoric technologies will be discovered in submerged environments that necessitate a reconsideration of prehistoric global colonisation timelines and technologies (*see for example* the data for early seafaring activity in the southern Ionian Islands by Neanderthals some time between 110 and 35 ka BP in Ferentinos, Gkioni, Geraga and Papatheodorou 2012). Above all, the hope, as stated in the introduction, has to be that across the next 40 years the global archaeological community learns the lessons painfully gained from rescue archaeology on land over the past 40 years, so as to avoid the worst mistakes of site management, community engagement, and crucially of industrial and political involvement again. The type of unseemly free-for-all witnessed on land around the world since the 1970s, which did so much to irrevocably damage or destroy heritage there, must not be allowed to be repeated in the 'brave new world' of the developing marine zone.

Acknowledgements

I am indebted to my colleagues Roger Bowdler, Andy Brown, Mark Dunkley, Paul Jeffery, Ian Oxley, Chris Pater and Steve Trow for their comments on earlier versions of this chapter and for their wider thoughts on marine heritage. It must be emphasized that this chapter is the personal opinion of the author, and does not represent the official position of Historic England. All errors of fact or judgment remain the sole responsibility of the author.

References

Bass, G F, 1966, *Archaeology under water*, Thames and Hudson, London

British Academy/Honor Frost Foundation, 2014, *The 2001 UNESCO Convention on the Protection of the Underwater Cultural Heritage: The case for UK ratification*, at http://honorfrostfoundation.org/wp/wp-content/uploads/2014/03/BA-HFF-Case-for-UK-ratification.pdf (accessed October 2014)

Broadwater, J, and Nutley, D, 2009 The management of marine archaeological sites *in situ* and site sustainability, in Flatman, J, (ed), Conserving marine cultural heritage, *Conservation And Management Of Archaeological Sites* **11(1)**, 70–77

Delgado, J, 2011, *Silent Killers,* Osprey, London

Dromgoole, S, (ed), 1999, *Legal protection of the underwater cultural heritage: national and international perspectives*, Kluwer Law International, London

English Heritage, 2009, *North Sea prehistory research and management framework,* English Heritage, London, at http://www.english-heritage.org.uk/content/publications/docs/10278_North_Sea_Prehistory_web.pdf (accessed October 2014)

English Heritage, 2012a, *Historic seascape characterisation (HSC)*, at http://www.english-heritage.org.uk/professional/research/landscapes-and-areas/characterisation/historic-seascape-character/ (accessed October 2014)

English Heritage, 2012b, *Rapid coastal zone assessment surveys (RCZAS)*, at http://www.english-heritage.org.uk/professional/advice/advice-by-topic/marine-planning/shoreline-management-plans/rapid-coastal-zone-assessments/ (accessed October 2014)

Evans, A, Flatman, J, and Flemming, N, (eds) 2014, Prehistoric archaeology on the Continental Shelf: A global review, Springer, New York

Ferentinos, G, Gkioni, M, Geraga, M, and Papatheodorou, G, 2012, Early seafaring activity in the Southern Ionian Islands, Mediterranean Sea, *Journal of Archaeological Science* **20**, 1–10

Flatman, J, 2009, A climate of fear: recent British policy and management of coastal heritage, *Public Archaeology* **8(1)**, 6–22

Flatman, J, 2012, What the walrus and the carpenter didn't talk about: maritime archaeology and the near future of energy, in Rockman, M, and Flatman, J, (eds), *Archaeology in society: its relevance in the modern world*, New York, Springer, 167–92

Flatman, J, and Doeser, J, 2010, The international management of marine aggregates and its relation to maritime archaeology, *The Historic Environment* **1(2)**: 160–84

Flemming, N C, 1972, *Cities in the sea*, Doubleday, New York

Gaffney, V, Fitch, S, and Smith, D, 2009, *Europe's lost world, the rediscovery of Doggerland*, Council of British Archaeology, York

Gilbert, J, 2006, *Indigenous peoples' land rights under international Law*, Ardsley, Transnational

Joint Nautical Archaeology Policy Committee, 2006, *The UNESCO Convention for the Protection of the Underwater Cultural Heritage, Proceedings of the Burlington House Seminar October 2005*, the Nautical Archaeol Soc for the Joint Nautical Archaeol Policy Com, Portsmouth

Marsden, P, (ed), 2003, *Sealed by time: The loss and recovery of the Mary Rose (Archaeology of the Mary Rose* **1***)*, Oxbow, Oxford

Martin, C, 1975, *Full fathom five: wrecks of the Spanish Armada*, Viking, London

Muckelroy, K, 1978, *Maritime Archaeology*, Cambridge University Press, Cambridge

Murphy, L E, 2010, Balancing historic preservation, science and the environment in underwater cultural heritage site management. Long-term management strategies for the sunken battleship USS *Arizona, Conservation and Management Of Archaeological Sites* **12(1)**, 13–38

Murphy, P, 2014, *England's coastal heritage: a review of progress since 1997*, English Heritage, London

Rahtz, P A, (ed), 1974, *Rescue Archaeology*, Pelican, Harmondsworth

Roach, J A, 1997, Sovereign Immunity, in Delgado, J, *Encyclopedia of Underwater and Maritime Archaeology*, Yale University Press, New Haven, 398–99

Sillar, B, and Fforde, C, (eds), 2005, Conservation, identity and ownership in indigenous archaeology, *Special Issue: Public Archaeology* **4 (2–3)**, James and James, London

Staniforth, M, and Shefi, D, 2011, Protecting underwater cultural heritage: a review of *in situ* preservation approaches and some directions for the future, in *World Universities Congress, 20–24 October 2010, Proceedings 2*, Pozitif, Ankara, 1546–52

UK UNESCO 2001 Convention Review Group, 2014, *The UNESCO Convention on the Protection of the Underwater Cultural Heritage 2001: an impact review for the United* Kingdom, at http://www.unesco.org.uk/uploads/UNESCO%20Impact%20Review_2014-02-10.pdf (accessed October 2014)

Chapter 15

Metal detectors: friends or foes?

Pete Wilson

Preamble

What follows is very much a personal view of the issues that we as archaeologists grapple with when it comes to considering metal detecting. It is not a statement on behalf of English Heritage and has been written in my own time. At the most basic level the metal detector is a tool, no more no less; the use that it is put to and the treatment of material found through detecting, particularly hobby-detecting, provide the basis for the bulk of what follows.

Introduction

The history of metal detecting and archaeology in the UK has been covered many times, the most comprehensive recent treatment being a series of papers in *Metal Detecting and Archaeology* (Thomas and Stone 2009). Peter Addyman's paper in that volume (Addyman 2009) traces the difficult relationship between archaeologists and metal detectorists prior to the establishment of the Portable Antiquities Scheme (PAS) and demonstrates the key role that RESCUE had in raising concerns around the unrecorded removal of material, damage to sites and the impact of loss of context on our potential to understand the finds themselves and the sites from which they derive (eg Burchard *et al* 1975). The other organisation that has been at the forefront of the debate is the CBA, who have lobbied relentlessly to try and protect archaeological sites from the ravages of illicit metal detecting and other threats (for example by leading much of the public debate on the potential impact of the National Planning Policy Framework on archaeology). Given its inclusion in the 'Crisis Points' section of this volume it would be possible to devote the whole of this paper to a review of the past history of the problem, highlighting yet again low points such as:

- The looting of Wanborough Roman Temple in Surrey during the 1980s (*see for example* Thomas 2009 and references therein)

- The case of the Icklingham Bronzes (*see for example* Gill 2010) and John Browning's determined, laudable and ongoing 30-year plus battle to protect a key Roman-period site on his land that, on the face of it, should be protected by its status as a scheduled monument

- The bitterly fought STOP campaign of the 1980s and its consequences

However, such an approach would not serve the purposes of this volume which must be primarily about where we are now and, in this section, how we might move forward for the benefit of our collective past.

The legal position

Under most circumstances in England metal detecting is legal if the detectorist has the permission of the landowner, this position being predicated on the legal ownership of non-Treasure finds by the landowner. Clearly there are exceptions, not least sites designated as Scheduled Monuments where it is a criminal offence under Section 42 of the Ancient Monuments and Archaeological Areas Act (1979) to use a metal detector without a licence from, in England, English Heritage, or to remove material without Scheduled Monument Consent from the Secretary of State at the DCMS. The situation in Wales is similar, it '*is an offence to use metal detectors on a scheduled ancient monument without prior consent from the [Welsh] Assembly to whom a written application will need to be made*' (Cadw 2002, 11). In Scotland, as in England and Wales, Section 42 of the Ancient Monuments and Archaeological Areas Act (1979) applies, but more widely '*under the* regalia minora *common law rights of the Crown, it is the prerogative of the Crown to receive all lost and abandoned property which is not otherwise owned*' (Treasure Trove Scotland 2013a), however and where ever it is found, although the Crown will normally disclaim items such as '*Victorian and modern coins, Victorian and modern horse-gear, brasses, buckles and fragments of machinery etc*' (Treasure Trove Scotland 2013b; Historic Scotland 2012). In Northern Ireland restrictions are more wide-ranging as the law does not distinguish between known and as yet undiscovered archaeological sites or monuments (Northern Ireland Environment Agency (NEIA) 2011). Under the Historic Monuments and Archaeological Objects (NI) Order 1995 it is an offence to search for archaeological objects without an archaeological excavation licence issued by the NEIA (NEIA 2013) and archaeological objects discovered by members of the public must be reported to NIEA Built Heritage Directorate, the Ulster Museum, or to the police, within 14 days of discovery (Northern Ireland Assembly 2013).

In England the Ancient Monuments and Archaeological Areas Act (1979) also precludes the use of metal detectors in five designated Areas of Archaeological Importance, which are the historic cities of Canterbury, Chester, Exeter, Hereford and York. Other restrictions on metal detecting can include:

- Areas designated as SSSIs where operations associated with detecting, such as ground disturbance, are deemed likely to damage the special interest of the site
- Environmental Stewardship provisions

- Local authority and Forestry Commission byelaws
- Requirements for licences or permit, such as for Crown Estate or National Trust land (*see* National Trust 2003)
- Prohibition of access under the Countryside and Rights of Way (CRoW) Act 2000 Schedule 2 if a person '*uses or has with him any metal detector*'

The Portable Antiquities Scheme

Launched as a pilot with six Finds Liaison Officers in 1997 the Portable Antiquities Scheme (PAS) now covers the whole of England and Wales, although at the time of writing the Scheme in Wales is being modified to reflect devolved status and the impact of the Comprehensive Spending Review. PAS exists to record finds made by members of the general public, predominantly, but not exclusively by metal detectorists, and represents a significant engagement between archaeologists and detectorists that would have been inconceivable at the time of the STOP campaign in the 1980s. The statistics are impressive as the headlines on the PAS website demonstrate: 539,470 records representing 836,351 objects recorded since the inception of the scheme (Portable Antiquities Scheme 2013a). Similarly the incorporation of PAS data into Historic Environment Records (HERs) has been possible since 2005 following the signing of a data transfer agreement between the PAS, the National Council for Metal Detecting, the Council for British Archaeology and the Association of Local Government Archaeological Officers. This agreement allows the data that the Scheme collects to be transferred to the relevant HER and used for Development Control and other activities. Roger Bland provides a comprehensive summary of the work of the PAS, highlighting what is its key objective, that of

> '*arrest[ing] the large level of archaeological information lost every year by actively recording this material on a systematic basis for public benefit*'

He goes on to state:

> '*we do not seek to encourage metal detecting but we recognise it exists ... We believe it is better to engage with [legal] detector users, to encourage them to behave responsibly and report their finds, than to ignore them .... They will go on detecting regardless and we will all be the losers if we fail to record their finds.*'
> (Bland 2009, 70)

The product of that recording is being used by a wide range of researchers with the PAS recording 43 undergraduate essays or dissertations either proposed or in progress utilising their data, or examining the work of the PAS, with a further 85 at Masters level along with 62 PhD theses. Additionally PAS data is noted as being used by over 100 researchers working on commercial, academic, and personal projects, as well as by small numbers of A-Level and Archaeological Society projects, all of which suggests that the data recorded by PAS is making a very real contribution to our understanding of the past. The publication in 2010 of the proceedings of a conference held in 2007 to demonstrate '*the research potential of archaeological objects made by members of the public'* (Bland 2010) provides a wide-ranging sample of research based on data recorded by the PAS (Worrell *et al* 2010). Perhaps the most persuasive arguments for the benefits of the approach to metal detecting that hinges on reporting of finds through the PAS are provided by Mike Heyworth (2012), often the object of vitriol in the detecting press, who contrasts the situation in England and Wales with that in Austria where detecting is effectively banned and has been forced underground.

Working through the Portable Antiquities Advisory Group, which advises the PAS, the PAS, CBA, English Heritage, Cadw and other Heritage organisations, along with bodies representing land-owning interests, the Country Land and Business Association (CLA) and the National Farmers Union (NFU), and the two national metal-detecting associations, the National Council for Metal Detecting (NCMD) and the Federation of Independent Detectorists (FID), a voluntary *Code of Practice for Responsible Metal Detecting in England and Wales* was agreed in 2006. The Code provides a broadly agreed set of minimum standards for hobby-detecting and compliments the Codes promulgated by the NCMD (2013a), amended in 2012, and FID (2013) established in 1996.

Working together

From the position in the 1980s when confrontation was the norm, archaeologists and metal detecting groups or individual detectorists now often work together in close cooperation, recognising that a metal detector is no more than a remote-sensing tool and one that is best operated by experienced users. Detectorists, either directly on site as at Groundwell Ridge villa, Swindon (Morley and Wilson *in prep* a and b) or through the incorporation of their finds as at Hayton, East Riding (Milett *et al* in prep), have contributed significantly to many archaeological projects. English Heritage has sponsored work, usually in response to illicit detecting and plough-damage, that incorporates metal-detecting as a fundamental element of the project design, for example at Owmby, Lincolnshire (English Heritage 1996–97) and Catterick, North Yorkshire (Brickstock *et al* 2007, 65–118) and generally increasing co-operation appears to be the norm.

Metal Detectorists' views on archaeology and archaeologists and detectorists relationship with the historic environment are widely covered in *Treasure Hunting* and *The Searcher*, two widely distributed detecting magazines. While it is perhaps inevitable that it is generally bad news and contentious views that receive greatest prominence, it seems clear that, despite the co-operation referred to above, there are many detectorists who remain convinced that the 'archaeological establishment' is intent on banning or restricting further metal-detecting. That position is illustrated by a report by Trevor Austin, General Secretary of NCMD, of a seminar hosted by English Heritage after the launch of '*The Nighthawking Survey*' (Oxford Archaeology 2009). The report quotes the then Acting Chair of English Heritage, Sir Barry Cunliffe as stating:

> '*Responsible metal detectorists are not being targeted and that neither EH, the CBA or any other body as far as they are aware had any intention of banning metal detecting.*'

Despite that Austin's report states:

'it became apparent from a number of speakers that there was intent to introduce restrictions and controls wherever possible' (Austin 2010).

That having been said the detecting magazines do carry letters, often in response to 'anti-archaeology' ones in preceding issues and on occasion longer articles, on positive experiences of working with archaeologists, for example Winter (2010). However an article by Del Cook (2010) provides evidence of some of the continuing issues. He starts by revisiting the mantra that archaeologists are not interested in finds from topsoil as 'they are out of context' despite the high profile use of surface-collected and metal-detected assemblages in major research projects such as those listed above.

Laws, rules and guidance

Trevor Austin (2009, 120–21) provides forceful support for the PAS and argues that;

'...detector users would like to see a broadening of horizons; they want involvement, discussion, information, debate, research and conservation, and more opportunities to work alongside archaeologists...'

Aspirations which few could argue with; however those positives are followed by an attack on English Heritage, other Government Agencies and ALGAO for:

'producing reams of documents, codes and guidelines ... [that have] ... *'been very counterproductive to the mission of the PAS and has at times served only as a threat to the success of the Scheme.'*

He goes on to state:

'I want to send a clear message to all these bureaucrats: 'get off our case', and leave the responsible hobby alone.'

A cry some might have some sympathy with if it truly reflected the situation. The NCMD is the first to argue that detectorists and other finders should only record their finds with the PAS if they have the landowners agreement, but when Government Agencies as land managers for the Crown, or bodies such as the National Trust seek to develop strategies to manage those areas in their ownership, or care for the common good, they become bureaucrats intent on curtailing what is almost presented as an inalienable right for detectorists to go where they please.

In 1996, English Heritage produced the document *'Our Portable Past'* which in its opening paragraph was defined as:

'a statement of policy and good practice [which] sets out the approaches and standards related to portable antiquities that English Heritage will apply to work on designated sites, projects that it funds, and work that it undertakes directly'.

Despite that clear remit and stating on page 2 that it '*is not intended to cover hobby metal-detecting*' and referring readers to the '*Code of Practice for Responsible Metal Detecting in England and Wales*', which the NCMD endorses, '*Our Portable Past*' was condemned as 'too archaeological' and presumably represents one of the 'counterproductive' documents referred to by Trevor Austin.

It is perhaps unnecessary in this publication to state that English Heritage, English Nature, Defra and other public agencies have statutory and other roles that mean they are charged with delivering to future citizens the Historic Environment, or those parts that their activities and responsibilities can impact on, in as good a state as possible. Given this, it is reasonable for the impact of metal detecting to be a consideration in framing policies for managing our landscape. In this context Environmental Stewardship, and the earlier Countryside Stewardship Scheme, have been the source of considerable friction due to the restrictions, and perceived restrictions, that they place on metal-detecting; difficulties that have been compounded by apparent variation in how the rules are interpreted in different parts of the country.

In this context NCMD have sought to provide clarification for their members, notably through two articles by Roger Mintey (2011, 2012) in their *Digging Deeper* newsletter and by producing summaries of Entry Level Stewardship and Higher Level Stewardship Handbooks, which they have made available to their members (Mintey 2012, 10). The NCMD promotes itself as 'The Voice of Responsible Metal detecting' in advertisements in the detecting press and elsewhere and as an organisation has a track-record of trying to assist detectorists in carrying out their hobby responsibly. In addition to Mintey's articles referred to above, Trevor Austin, General Secretary of NCMD, in a series of articles in *The Searcher* (2011 issues 309–14) has provided advice on detecting in various types of location and other issues. Clearly these articles are meant to be helpful to detectorists but they can also serve in part to exacerbate the issues between detectorists and archaeologists; one example being Austin's suggestion that City of York Council's policy on detecting amounts to a blanket ban on detecting on '*Council owned or managed site[s]*' and implies that it is contrary to Government policy (Austin 2011). However his discussion apparently ignores York's status as an Area of Archaeological Importance and the implications of that under the Ancient Monuments and Archaeological Areas Act (1979).

Crisis? What crisis?

While the above suggests that relationships and the state of trust between detectorists and archaeologists are perhaps less than ideal in some respects, archaeologists must acknowledge that metal detecting in the UK is legal under most circumstances, subject to landowner consent. It is also clear that responsibly detected and fully reported finds are contributing to our understanding of the past. What then are the issues?

It is an oft-repeated chorus that detectorists are '*rescuing our material heritage*' (Winter 2011), or similar. In general the claim is that they are rescuing artefacts from inevitable destruction by agri-chemicals, or disinterest in plough-soil horizons on the part of the wider archaeological community. While no archaeologist would claim that there is no issue with respect to artefact survival in the face of agricultural chemicals (*see for example* Pollard *et al* 2004) the case for stripping artefacts from sites to ensure their survival is far from proven. All too often we see pictures of badly corroded artefacts offered as proof of chemical and other threats, but just how representative are they? We also see large numbers of well-preserved artefacts offered for sale on eBay and elsewhere.

Given that, with the exception of potential Treasure finds, there is no legal requirement to report or record finds, and the fact that estimates suggest that less than 50 percent of detectorists are reporting their finds to the PAS, it is clear that we are seeing large-scale loss of data. Issues also surround finds recorded through a group or system such as the UK Detector Finds Database (UKDFD 2013) which lacks protocols for data transfer to Historic Environment Records and thus does not provide for long-term availability of data, or, necessarily, for records of a quality and detail that will aid future research and understanding. It is difficult to see how material can be regarded as having been 'rescued' when it disappears without a publicly accessible record into a private collection, or is sold without recording or a detailed provenance. It is therefore necessary to ask if it is justifiable, in terms of its impact on public and researcher understanding of the past, to have large numbers of finds disappear unrecorded? Before there are howls of anguish from the detecting community, the same question could be asked of material from surface collection/field-walking projects undertaken by archaeologists.

While few would question the importance of what the PAS has achieved since its inception in 1997, there are questions that are perhaps worth raising, and at least one myth that needs busting. To take the latter first, a key question is the suggestion that the PAS promotes or encourages metal detecting. This is not the case. While accepting that the bulk of finders are detectorists, the PAS exists to '*encourage the voluntary recording of archaeological objects found by members of the public in England and Wales*' (Portable Antiquities Scheme 2013b). However, even accepting that most finders who record with the PAS are honest, questions that may legitimately be asked include:

- Whatever the source of material recorded by PAS, to my knowledge there has never been any attempt to assess the validity of information on find-spots provided by either detectorists or other finders. To what extent is the PAS being used to legitimise stolen or falsely provenanced material?

- Is the range of material recorded with the PAS fully representative of at least the metallic elements of site assemblages?

- How do metal-dominated assemblages distort understanding of sites?

Finds recorded through the PAS and primarily derived from detecting have added significantly to archaeological knowledge, adding many new sites to HERs (*see for example* Winter 2010) and provide the basis for much new research and understanding. Why then don't all detectorists record their finds? It is easily understood that the PAS would have a capacity crisis if the 40-60% of detectorists who do not currently record started to offer material for recording. PAS would be faced with even greater problems if large numbers of collections accumulated, in some cases over decades, were made available. However if most detectorists are primarily motivated by an interest in the past it is difficult to understand why they do not record, although a letter from Isley Walton (2010) presents arguments against find-spot recording on the basis that finds may contribute to protection through scheduling or restrictions through Stewardship schemes; arguments that are effectively rebutted by Michael Cuddeford (2010). Despite detectorists concerns it is true to say that metal-detected finds alone have never by themselves led to a site being given statutory protection, and even where they form part of the data considered, the bar for scheduling remains set very high.

Detectorists' organisations are very keen to press the points that adherence to the *Code of Practice for Metal Detecting in England and Wales* is voluntary, and that finds should only be recorded with the landowners' agreement. As with detectorists, it is difficult to understand why landowners might want to withhold agreement, unless they are being persuaded that recording will inevitably lead to scheduling or other restrictions on their use of their land. My experience of landowners in general (both as an archaeologist of over 30-years-experience and as a member of a rural community) is that the bulk of landowners are either fascinated by and proud of, the past history of their farm or estate, or largely disinterested. Neither of those positions suggests a natural inclination to oppose recording. While accepting there will be some who are against recording, the 'landowner doesn't want anything recorded' argument seems likely to be being substantially overplayed.

Perhaps the most obviously contentious issue for archaeologists is that of Metal Detecting Rallies. Many of these events are organised as purely commercial ventures and others with the intention of at least some income going to a local worthy cause. It is difficult to get a clear picture of the number of rallies that are held each year as many are only advertised in closed forums. Some are small-scale and essentially only open to members of a particular detecting club while others are massive and can attract a thousand or more detectorists. The PAS (2006, 9) summarise the key issues around rallies very clearly:

> '*large metal-detecting rallies can be problematic, as often the organisers of such events make no provision for recording finds – indeed FLOs are not always invited or are even actively discouraged from attending! Also the numbers of detectorists involved – often several hundred – make it impossible to record all finds to the highest standards.*'

As the quote from PAS implies, some organisers do invite FLOs to attend to record finds, but the key word here is 'invite'. FLOs attend at the whim of the organiser. Their role is purely that of finds recorder and, contrary to the desires of some archaeological colleagues, they have no curatorial role and cannot police adherence to exclusion zones around scheduled monuments, or act in relation to other areas of concern, although they can and do pass on evidence of wrong-doing when presented with finds from protected places. As dedicated as the FLOs are, they would have little chance of recording everything found on a large-scale rally; particularly if it was being held on land under a post 1/10/2008 Entry Level Stewardship (ELS) Agreement whereby it is a requirement to record all finds, not only those pre-dating *circa* 1650 which is normal PAS practice. Organisers and detectorists often claim that finds are recorded post-event, which if true would presumably meet the requirements of ELS conditions, but there has to be a question-mark over the extent to which that really happens. That said, it is accepted that useful archaeological information can derive from rallies when recording is permitted (*see for example* Levick and Sumnall 2010). One wonders at the recording logistics of the two larger events discussed by Levick and Sumnall: a two-day rally which attracted 750 detectorists each day and one of the largest commercial rallies ever held, a three-day event at Letcombe Regis attracting 2,000 detectorists. Levick and Sutton (2008) discuss the three-day event and rightly praise the organiser for willing and enthusiastic support for recording. This was facilitated by the PAS deploying FLOs from surrounding counties. However in an editorial comment on the online version of the article Mike Pitts (2008) notes some key issues identified by the PAS with respect to the Letcombe rally; perhaps the most telling of which, given the number of detectorists present, is the number of objects offered for recording: '*700 objects were seen, of which about 550 were recorded, but still many more must have been found that were not recorded*'. In case anyone doubts that non-recording at rallies is an issue a post from an unnamed author on a detecting forum, quoted by Geoff Dannell (2008) should give us all cause for concern:

> '*I pay to go on rallies or weekend digs [sic], so anything found is mine and mine alone. From a single find to a hoard of gold, if ive [sic] paid to detect no one is informed of my findings, ill [sic] decide if they are to be recorded when I return home*'.

While we might hope that the detectorist concerned would at least declare any Treasure when s/he got home; a straight reading of the post suggests that would probably be wishful thinking.

In 2009 a consortium of archaeological organisations: CBA, English Heritage, Association of Local Government Archaeological Officers (ALGAO), PAS and the Society of Museum Archaeologists endorsed a document providing *Guidance on Metal-detecting Rallies in England and Wales*. This document covering curatorial issues in relation to rallies had been discussed in the Portable Antiquities Advisory Group (PAAG). NCMD and FID are both represented on PAAG and declined to endorse the *Guidance* indicating that they would prefer a document that extended to cover welfare facilities etc for those attending rallies and, in the case of NCMD at least, on the grounds that they do not organise rallies and the document was therefore irrelevant for them. While at a national level the NCMD may not organise rallies their website states that '*various social events, rallies, exhibitions etc are arranged by NCMD regions*' (NCMD 2013b). As organisations that wish to promote responsible metal-detecting, and therefore by definition good practice, it is unfortunate that NCMD and FID felt unable to provide support for a document that seeks to address one of the most divisive issues impacting on relationships between archaeologists and detectorists. They are uniquely placed to bring influence to bear on both those of their members who attend rallies and, perhaps more importantly, the rally organisers who all too often provide no, or inadequate recording cover for their events.

The *Code of Practice for Responsible Metal Detecting in England and Wales* advocates:

'*...wherever possible working on ground that has already been disturbed (such as ploughed land or that which has been formerly ploughed), and only within the depth of ploughing*'.

Although it does go on to recognise that some detectorists work on undisturbed pasture. It has been clear for some time that detectors are capable of penetrating below the depth of normal plough-soil as the discovery during a rally at Glemsford, Suffolk of a largely complete Roman lantern using '*an old [Minelab] Explorer XS*' detector which located a signal despite the lantern only becoming visible when the finder had dug down '*around 18 inches*' [0.45m] (Winter 2009). Heritage Action (2010) has highlighted a new generation of detectors that provide a new and troubling threat. The Suffolk Lantern appeared initially as a weak signal to its finder, detectorists themselves report that the Minelab GPX5000 can '*easily detect a Roman brooch at 24 inches*' in pasture (Metal Detecting Forum 2011) and other cheaper machines appear capable of doing the same (Heritage Action 2012). This is a potential game-changer in that all archaeological responses to 'responsible metal-detecting' have been predicated on the fact that detectorists largely operate within disturbed horizons overlying intact archaeology, deposits that for too long many archaeologists didn't value adequately. Even with the realisation that plough-zone material could contribute significantly to the understanding of sites by providing evidence of damaged or destroyed horizons, or even represent the totality of evidence for a completely destroyed site, it was generally accepted that detectors, responsibly used, with full recording of finds, could make significant and worthwhile contributions to understanding the past. Machines that reach below the plough zone as a matter of course have the potential to unleash an orgy of looting of intact archaeological deposits that it will be impossible for archaeologists to accept.

Following on from *Metal Detecting and Archaeology in England* (Dobinson and Dennison 1995) the *Nighthawking Survey* (Oxford Archaeology 2009) demonstrated, despite brickbats from the detecting community, that illicit detecting remained a problem, and in particular that it is not only confined to designated sites. Since the development of the Heritage Crime Initiative (now Heritage Crime Programme (English Heritage 2013a)) illicit metal-detecting has figured large in the cases on which advice has been sought. The Nighthawking Survey, for all the negativity from Paul Barford and some others (*see for example* Barford 2009), served to raise the profile of the problem and we are now seeing the results as high-profile cases begin to come to court. Nighthawking is theft, and thieves will always be with us, but archaeologists and those metal-detectorists who care about the image of their hobby, are having an impact in cooperation with Police Services and other Agencies. The opposition to the Nighthawking Survey and suspicion and criticism of the Heritage Crime Initiative/Programme from within the ranks of responsible detectorists, and on the part of some of their spokespeople, demonstrates a continuing gulf between archaeologists and some leading detectorists. Despite the condemning of the criminals who bring their hobby into disrepute, any initiative to enforce compliance with the law is often represented as an attack on detecting generally (*see for example*: Smith 2010; Deeks 2010). That said NCMD have joined the Alliance to Reduce Crime against Heritage (ARCH), a voluntary network developed in support of the Heritage Crime Programme '*to tackle heritage crime and galvanise local action*' (English Heritage 2013b) demonstrating a recognition that detectorists can work with the wider Heritage Sector for the common good.

Archaeologists will always have problems with detecting while so much emphasis is placed on the financial value of objects; *see for example* the regular 'Identification and Valuation Desk' in *The Searcher* and the many advertisements from dealers seeking to purchase artefacts in both *The Searcher* and *Treasure Hunting*. It is clear from the amount of material offered for sale that while archaeologists and detectorists both claim to be interested in the past, amongst the detecting community there are those who value the past in financial terms rather than as a foreign country that we differently seek to understand (with apologies to L P Hartley and *The Go-Between*).

Summary

This section aims to look to the future, therefore only a brief summary is offered here. Looking back to the 1980s STOP campaign, although it is clear that since then much has been achieved in terms of better understanding and cooperation between archaeologists and detectorists, there are still issues of concern:

- Non-recording of finds and the consequent information loss
- Illicit detecting and looting of sites
- A failure to get across the message that whatever the situation in the past, archaeologists now recognise the potential of plough-soil assemblages, our alleged lack of interest being the 'first strike' defence of many detectorists
- The threat posed by the newest generation of detectors that will, as a matter of course, put undisturbed deposits within range of those who choose not to comply with the *Code of Practice for Responsible Metal Detecting in England and Wales* and are willing to loot, vandalise and destroy intact archaeology

As a profession we cannot step back from these issues and leave all contact with detectorists and guidance on detecting to the PAS as Trevor Austin (2010) would have us do. However I would also argue that, as well as being robust in our dealings with the issues, we need at the same time to seek ever greater positive general engagement for the benefit of the historic environment. Metal detecting is not going to go away, but we have a duty to hand on the archaeological resource to future generations in as good a state as possible and, where preservation is not possible or appropriate, we should be seeking to ensure the maximum possible level of understanding of what is being lost including that derived from the responsible use of metal detectors.

Friends or Foes? Neither; a metal detector is just another tool. Any judgement depends on where and how it is being used and what is done with the material that is found using it.

References

Addyman, P V, 2009, Before the Portable Antiquities Scheme, in Thomas and Stone 2009, 51–62

Austin, T, 2009, Building bridges between metal detectorists and archaeologists, in Thomas, and Stone 2009, 119–23

Austin, T, 2010, Nighthawking seminar, *The Searcher* 293, 8

Austin, T, 2011, Detecting in parks and public walks, *The Searcher* 313, 60

Barford, P, 2009, *The Nighthawking Survey Summary Document*, at http://paul-barford.blogspot. co.uk/2009/02/nighthawking-survey-summary-document.html (accessed Feb 2013)

Bland, R, 2009, the development and future of The Treasure Act and the Portable Antiquities Scheme, in Thomas and Stone 2009, 63–85

Bland, R, 2010, Foreword, in Worrell *et al*, 2010, v

Brickstock, R J, Cardwell, P A, Busby, P A, Cool, H E M, Huntley, J P, Evans, J, Makey, P, Ronan, D, and Wilson, P R, 2007, The Catterick metal detecting project 1997–99, *Yorkshire Archaeol J* 79, 65–153

Burchard, A, Rance, A, Rudkin, D, and Schadla-Hall, T, 1975, The problem of treasure hunting, *Rescue News* 10, 2–3

Cadw, 2002, *What is Scheduling?* Cadw, Cardiff

Code of Practice for Responsible Metal Detecting in England and Wales, 1996

Cook, D, 2010 Detecting alongside archaeologists on rescue digs, *Treasure Hunting*, Jan 2010, 70–71

Cuddeford, M, 2010, Readers letters, *The Searcher* 311, 60

Dannell, G B, 2008, Detecting the past 3. Not for private gain, *British Archaeology* 98, 25

Deeks, J, 2010, Readers' letters, *Treasure Hunting*, Sept 2010, 20

Dobinson, C, and Dennison, S, 1995, *Metal detecting and archaeology in England*, Council for British Archaeology, York

English Heritage, 1996–97, Owmby-by-Spital, Lincolnshire, conservation and management of a plough damaged site, *English Heritage Archaeology Review 1996–97*, 4.13.3

English Heritage, 2013a, *Heritage Crime*, at http://www.english-heritage.org.uk/professional/ advice/advice-by-topic/heritage-crime/ (accessed Feb 2013)

English Heritage, 2013b, *Alliance to reduce crime against heritage (ARCH)*, at http://www.english-heritage.org.uk/professional/advice/advice-by-topic/heritage-crime/arch/) (accessed Feb 2013)

Federation of Independent Detectorists, 2013, *Code of Conduct*, at http://fid.newbury.net/html/ code.htm (accessed Feb 2013)

Gill, D J W, 2010, The Portable Antiquities Scheme and the Treasure Act. Protecting the archaeology of England and Wales? *Papers from the Institute of Archaeol, University College London* 20, http://www.pia-journal.co.uk/index.php/pia/article/view/pia.333/36 (accessed Feb 2013)

Heritage Action, 2010, Metal detecting. Minelab announces a major and disastrous technological advance! *The Heritage Journal,* at http://heritageaction.wordpress.com/2010/10/30/metal-detecting-minelab-announces-a-major-and-disastrous-technological-advance (accessed Feb 2013)

Heritage Action, 2012, A second (and third) open letter to the Heritage Forum. *The Heritage Journal,* at http://heritageaction.wordpress.com/2012/03/21/a-second-open-letter-to-the-heritage-forum/ (accessed Feb 2013)

Heyworth, M, 2012, Metal detecting, ban or befriend: The evidence, *British Archaeology,* Jan–Feb 2012, 66

Historic Scotland, 2012, *Metal detecting; yes or no?* Historic Scotland, Edinburgh

Levick, P, and Sumnall, K, 2010, Metal detecting rallies and landscape archaeology. Recreating lost landscapes on the Berkshire Downs, in Worrell *et al,* 2010, 39–46

Levick, P, and Sutton, K, 2008, Detecting the past 1: The landscape rally, *British Archaeology* 98, 20–23

Metal Detecting Forum, 2011, Minelab GPX5000, at http://www.metaldetectingforum.co.uk/viewtopic.php?f=26&t=8288 (accessed Feb 2013)

Millett, M, (ed), in prep, *Hayton, East Yorkshire: archaeological studies of the Iron Age and Roman landscapes*

Mintey, R, 2011, Detecting and rallies on land under Entry Level Stewardship Agreement, *Digging Deeper* 8, 6–7

Mintey, R, 2012, Detecting on land under Higher Level Stewardship, *Digging Deeper* 9, 9–10

Morley, G, and Wilson, P, in prep a, *Groundwell Ridge Roman Villa, Swindon, Wilts. Excavations in the bath suite and wider area, 1996–2005,* English Heritage Research Dept Report, London

Morley, G, and Wilson, P, in prep b, Groundwell Ridge Roman Villa, Swindon, Wilts. Excavation of the bath suite and associated structures, 1996–2005, *Wiltshire Archaeol and Natural History Mag*

National Council for Metal Detecting, 2013a, *Code of Conduct,* at http://www.ncmd.co.uk/code%20of%20conduct.htm (accessed Feb 2013)

National Council for Metal Detecting, 2013b, *About us,* at http://www.ncmd.co.uk/about%20us.htm (accessed Feb 2013)

National Trust, 2003, *Metal detecting on National Trust Land,* National Trust, Swindon

Northern Ireland Assembly, 2013, *Archaeology and Treasure,* at http://www.nidirect.gov.uk/index/information-and-services/leisure-home-and-community/history-heritage-and-museums/archaeology-and-treasure.htm (accessed Feb 2013)

Northern Ireland Environment Agency, 2011, *A guide to metal detecting, archaeology and the law,* Northern Ireland Environment Agency, Belfast

Northern Ireland Environment Agency, 2013, *Information for the finders of treasure in Northern Ireland,* at http://www.doeni.gov.uk/niea/built-home/information/treasure-2.htm(accessed Feb 2013)

Oxford Archaeology, 2009, *The Nighthawking Survey*, at http://www.helm.org.uk/server/show/ nav.00h01j/chooseLetter/N (accessed Feb 2013)

Pitts, M, 2008, *Editorial Note*, at http://www.britarch.ac.uk/ba/ba98/feat2.shtml (accessed Feb 2013)

Portable Antiquities Scheme, 2006, *Portable Antiquities Scheme Annual Report 2005–06*

Portable Antiquities Scheme, 2013a, *Finds database*, at http://finds.org.uk/database (accessed Feb 2013)

Portable Antiquities Scheme, 2013b, *Welcome to the Portable Antiquities Scheme website*, at http:// finds.org.uk (accessed Feb 2013)

Pollard, A M, Wilson, L, Wilson, A S, Hall, A J, and Shiel, R, 2004, Assessing the influence of agrichemicals on the rate of copper corrosion in the vadose zone of arable land, *Conservation and Management of Archaeological Sites* 6, 363–76

Smith, N, 2010, Readers' Letters, *Treasure Hunting*, Aug 2010, 9

Thomas, S, 2009, Wanborough revisited: the rights and wrongs of Treasure Trove Law in England and Wales, in Thomas and Stone 2009, 153–65

Thomas, S, and Stone, P G, (eds), 2009, *Metal detecting and archaeology*, Boydell, Woodbridge

Treasure Trove Scotland, 2013a, *The legal position*, at http://www.treasuretrovescotland.co.uk/ html/legal.asp (accessed Feb 2013)

Treasure Trove Scotland, 2013b, at http://www.treasuretrovescotland.co.uk/ (accessed Feb 2013)

UK Detector Finds Database, 2013, at http://www.ukdfd.co.uk/index.html (accessed Feb 2013)

Walton, I, 2010, Readers Letters, *The Searcher* 301, 60-61

Winter, J, 2009, Danny's find lights up rally, *The Searcher* 292, 30–31

Winter, J, 2010, Saving Somerset's heritage, *The Searcher* 295, 20–25

Winter, J. 2011 *Metal detecting: the hobby and its detractors*, at http://www.johnwinter.net/ jw/2011/11/metal-detecting-the-hobby-and-its-detractors-2/ (accessed Feb 2013)

Worrell, S, Egan, G, Naylor, J, Leahy, K, and Lewis, M, (eds), 2010, *A decade of discovery, Proceedings of the Portable Antiquities Scheme Conference 2007*, British Archaeol Rep, British Series 520, BAR, Oxford

SECTION FOUR: Rescuing the future

Introduction

Reuben Thorpe

If previous sections have highlighted fissures in contemporary practice, Section Four hopes to offer a modicum of unity. The principle on which the following chapters were elicited was specifically to present alternatives and give time to some blue skies thinking in the hope of encouraging discussion to ensure that archaeology is fit to face the next 40 years. The themes discussed relate very closely to the principal aims expressed at the foundation of RESCUE and concern funding, training, legislation, outreach/inclusion and communication. All the chapters in this section draw on the past (how can they not?) to draw out issues of sustainability in the world as it is but they also point to a world as it could be. Clearly better worlds are possible and are achievable but they require more than Panglossian optimism or Chamberlain like acquiesce.

In Chapter 18 Anthony Sinclair outlines threats to the future of teaching archaeology at university. Our challenge is to consider what students of archaeology want and what archaeology wants of those graduates who go into the profession. Archaeology at university has never been a vocational training ground and, as a broad based humanities degree, it has a wider social function to play as part of the education of citizens within a civil society. This begs the wider question then of whether it is the role of universities to provide vocational training or whether it is the role of employers to provide apprenticeships. Some grounding in technical practice has to be imparted at university for students to appreciate the centrality of method to the practice of archaeology, but it has never been the case that well-rounded technically proficient and methodologically informed archaeologists have sprung fully-formed from our universities like Athena from the head of Zeus. The wider issue then is about the provision of, and opportunities for, augmented, vocational training outside universities specifically tailored to the world of work, which augments the grounding in archaeology that universities give. This boils down to the issue of paid archaeological apprenticeships and longer-term career structures. As many MSC archaeologists of the 1980s demonstrated, it is not necessary to have a degree to be an excellent archaeologist, but it is necessary to have an enquiring mind and good training. Additionally we also need to ask ourselves whether the threats to the teaching of archaeology risk the wider impoverishment of the discipline's theoretical base. Will we be able to seek to generate new and original ideas from the data? If we fail to do so will this result in a consequent narrative impoverishment and the narrowing of the audiences that we can and seek to reach?

This matter of concern resonates with other chapters in this section. As a humanist and materialist profession we have a commensurate duty to encourage the engagement of all sections of society in that past beneath our collective soles. The by-product of archaeology as an investigative profession is, as one early 20th century writer put it, one of the 'benefits of civilisation'[1] and is empowering in its own right. However engagement occurs on multiple levels, differentially, for differing communities. There is an incumbent responsibility on us to build an inclusive, theoretically aware archaeology, which can be focussed toward the engagement of every community in Britain. Equally there is a responsibility to more widely encourage and support the engagement of people with diverse backgrounds in the practice of archaeology. Opening up our discipline as a profession and as professional practice to socially and ethnically diverse participation ought to be one of our key goals. Archaeology is a heterogeneous discipline and is made all the stronger for it with its broad church of practitioners, but this heterogeneity does not reflect the diversity of the wider communities in which it is situated either in terms of class, ethnicity or gender. Can the past and its interpretation be left to a narrow sector of society representing core constituencies and clients, or do we need to press for a pluralistic archaeology which embraces difference and co-existent multi-linear narratives which question traditional balances of power?

One of the ways we can engage with a wider audience, and recruit passionate engaged people to its practice, is by making the materiality of archaeology available in local, regional, and national museums and by ensuring that the knowledge products are available in our public libraries. Both are under considerable threat in our current economic climate, begging questions about institutional attitudes to the empowerment of a diverse society through access to knowledge and access for all to these benefits of civilisation. Paul Blinkhorn's contribution (Chapter 21) charts the popularity of archaeology as television programming over the last half-century. Recently programmes on archaeology have been as ubiquitous as those on property and renovation, though it would be too simplistic to marry these fluctuations to the charisma of dynamic individual presenters. Interest in history is sustained and sustainable, as demonstrated by public service television and the programming of BBC4. A focus on narrative rather than just process, the general as well as the particular is probably at the heart of the appeal. The ability to tell a good story was one of Sir Mortimer Wheeler's gifts but this is a gift also shared by contemporary archaeologists and historians. Format matters, content matters equally, but ultimately if the attraction of archaeology to the public is treasure, the neck-line of the TV presenter, as a modern iteration of bread and circuses, or if its function is traduced to land-clearance as part of the planning process then archaeology as meaningful social enquiry itself risks becoming increasingly meaningless.

[1] Robert Tressel. The Ragged Trousered Philanthropists

Chapter 16

Between Pangloss and Cassandra:
tendering, politics, risk, research and the conduct of
archaeology in England

Reuben Thorpe

Pangloss: '*Philosopher... Tutor of Candide, maintains that we live in the best of all possible worlds, where everything is connected and arranged for the best.*' (1947 introduction to Voltaire 1759, 8)

Cassandra : '*[...]Daughter of King Priam. Apollo ...conferred upon her the gift of foreseeing the future on her promising to yield herself to him. But Cassandra refused to fulfil her part of the bargain. Apollo then begged for a single kiss. In this way he breathed into her mouth and, though he left her with the power of foretelling the future, he took from her the power of persuasion so that from then onwards no one would believe what Cassandra predicted.*'(Graves 1959, 118)

This paper is an attempt to give air-time to issues around the procurement, funding and execution/practice of rescue archaeology in England, the conduct of which is situated within the sphere of land-planning and its practice within the world of commerce (Thorpe 2012a, 44). That there are significant issues, of deep concern, with current practice is not a view held by everyone. Indeed there are two narratives within our discipline, our craft. On the one hand one of the most vocal and prolific of the published narratives is that the market model, as adopted in the UK, provides us with the best of all *possible* worlds (Aitchison 2007; 2009a, 668–9; 2009b, 388; 2010a; 2010b; 2012) the argument being that in the current model we have an approximation of the best and we should be positive because under whatever circumstances more money is coming into, and we are doing more, archaeology than before.

In contrast a hefty literature of dissent (Aitchison 2000; All-Party Parliamentary Archaeology Group 2003; Blinkhorn 2014; Blinkhorn and Cumberpatch 1998; 1999; Carver 1996; 2006; 2011; Chadwick 2000a; Cumberpatch and Blinkhorn 2001; Cumberpatch and Roberts 2012; Cumberpatch 2000; Everill 2007, 2012; Graves-Brown 1997; Harward

2012; Heaton 2006a, 2008; Morris 1995; Schadla-Hall 1991; Tarlow and Pluciennik 2007) asserts that things should and indeed could be better and that improvement is either moot, too slow, or of limited scope. These counter narratives cover a wide range of inextricably related issues encompassing, but not limited to, effects on pay and conditions, provision for training, quality of excavation and the downgrading of the role of research. In this chapter I will examine the funding and procurement model of rescue archaeology in England, its execution in relation to the original mission, compare it with other models and then attempt to draw some wider conclusions and points for further reflection.

How archaeology in England is procured

At the time of writing (August 2012, revised autumn 2014) potential threats to the archaeological resource from development are identified via planning applications submitted to local planning authorities (LPAs) via a mechanism specified under the National Planning Policy Framework, the successor to PPS5 and PPG 16 (Department for Communities and Local Government 2010; 2012; DOE 1990). Archaeology *is* a material consideration in development and the LPA seek guidance from their planning archaeologist who determines potential archaeological considerations in consultation with a Sites and Monuments Record (SMR) or Historic Environment Record (HER). If an application is deemed to have possible archaeological implications then a condition might be attached to the planning consent which has to be fulfilled prior to development commencing. The land owner, or developer, will then seek to discharge the condition by commissioning an archaeological contractor to undertake the required work in compliance with an agreed Written Scheme of Investigation (WSI). This WSI is produced in response to a brief issued by, or on behalf of, the planning authority. The mechanism by which the developer identifies and secures an archaeological contractor is usually through competitive fee tender and the criteria for successful selection is usually based on cost, (Aitchison 2000, 21; 2012; Carver 2011, 77; Thorpe 2012a, 47, *contra* Thomas 2007; 40). A tender will usually be made and accepted *before* the commissioned contractor produces a research design and written scheme of investigation for approval by the LPA (*contra* Aitchison 2012, *see* Figure 1), as this minimises non-chargeable project time for the contractor. This is a state of affairs 40 years in the making. Its trajectory of development is congruent with the social and political context within which it has developed, but the emphasis in practice, as a result of the mechanism of procurement, has, I would argue, departed *de-facto* in spirit from the explicit aims and purposes of its establishment.

Procurement in context

The regeneration of British towns and cities in the 1960s and the wider provision of national infrastructure, roads, motorways, pipelines, brought to light a great deal of archaeology, of which there was often no prior-knowledge, and for the investigation and recording of which there was insufficient provision (Biddle 1968, 114–15; Jones 1984, 5–8; RCHME 1960; 1963; Walsh 1969, iii). The provision that did exist (*see* Rahtz 1974a; but particularly Alexander 1974, 16–27; Barker 1974a and b; Biddle 1974 a and b; Thomas 1974) lacked an adequate legal framework, institutional capacity, personnel and finances. A Parliamentary Committee of Enquiry (Walsh 1969), which considered the archaeology of the countryside ('field monuments'), recommended the creation of SMRs to be held by planning authorities (*ibid*, 26–7, 72), compiled by local authority archaeologists. These recommendations were given added force by The Council for British Archaeology (CBA) publication *The Erosion of History: Archaeology and Planning in Towns* (Heighway 1972). Thus the responsibility for the identification, quantification, and registering of archaeological sites was placed primarily with local authorities. This required the establishment of the means to identify threats to the archaeological resource from development within LPAs. The Historic Buildings and Monuments Commission (HBMC) and later English Heritage, encouraged local authorities to build this capacity, '*at a time of economic difficulty*' (Walsh 1969, iii), by providing 50% funding, over three years, for the establishment of archaeological officers within local authorities (Wainwright 2000, 918). In 1970 there were 12, by 1976 around 50 (Jones 1984, 6–7) by 1979 every county had a Sites and Monuments Record and by 1989 every county in England had an archaeological officer (Wainwright 2000: 918–19).

In terms of funding, the Walsh Report (1969, 49) looked hard at direct developer funding for rescue archaeology but surmised that, as the product of archaeological fieldwork (increased knowledge of the past) was to the public benefit, it should be publicly funded, adding that developer funding might be an incentive to concealment. The report also recommended that the national budget for rescue archaeology be increased. By December 1971 spending had gone up by nearly 50% to £310,000 (the equivalent of £4.2 million in 2014). However pressure exerted by RESCUE: The British Archaeological Trust (Wainwright 2000, 915) led to further increases up to £813,000 (£8.6 million) in 1973/74, and £2.1 million (£15.4 million) in 1976/77. These monies were disbursed towards supporting rescue archaeology, including paying core staff-costs to build capacity, and funding individual excavation and publication programmes. The CBA and RESCUE continued to advocate a State Archaeology Service (Rahtz 1974b, 2) but in 1973 the Department of the Environment (DOE) proposed the establishment of a system of regional archaeological units, each region encompassing more than one local authority area, each fully organised for all excavation and post-excavation work and accountable to a regional research committee (RESCUE and CBA 1974, appendix 1). This was to be paid for by DOE grants (ultimately sourced from general taxation), while local authorities picked up the costs of their local authority archaeological/SMR officers which were largely met by the DOE at that specific point in time. There was some resistance within archaeology to the regional organisation of rescue excavations, as a separate entity to the local-authority-based planning sector and confusion over how it would work, and (party and non-party) political point-scoring pitted local authorities against national government. A leak to the press about the proposed creation of regional units accompanied by a lack of clarity on what would be centrally funded and what would be local authority funded has been described as:

> '...*costly...ruined the only real chance England has had of a structured, resourced, and well-managed state archaeological service[...] an opportunity lost through lack of vision, mismanagement and corporate rivalries*' (Wainwright 2000; 917–18).

Those archaeological units which had been established within local authorities continued to be part funded, as they had been, out of the public purse. RESCUE and the CBA tried to resurrect the 1973 regionalisation plan via a National Archaeology Service operating through regional and county offices and in 1974 proposed:

> '...*the creation of an integrated structure for archaeology in Britain... a National Archaeological Service, operating through regional offices and staffed by professional archaeologists. This professional executive service will be paralleled by a series of advisory committees at national, regional, and county levels.*'
> (RESCUE and CBA 1974, 18)

This proposal was seen by some as contradictory and illogical, divorcing research from the excavation process, and it failed to get sanction from the Council of the CBA (Wainwright 2000, 917). However, regional advisory committees were established by the government and these advised the local authority units and the regional units that did exist. By 1979, following a change in government and in the absence of the regional infrastructure they were set up to advise, these advisory committees were wound up by the then Secretary of State for the Environment. In 1980 the DOE started to dispense grants to local authority and regional units on a project by project basis (Wainwright 2000; 919) and ceased to core-fund staff-costs outside project-funding. The publication of *Rescue archaeology funding: a policy statement* (English Heritage 1986) clarified that English Heritage would disburse monies for rescue archaeology only on projects where local-authority provision was unable to mount a suitable response unaided. This being said DOE funding to the units remained at the same levels, in real terms, as in the final quarter of the 1970s; £4.5 million in 1981/82 (£15.07 million in 2014) and £5.9 million in 1986/87 (£15.1 million) (Wainwright 1987, 117). However, an increase in local government provision for archaeology, the encouragement of developer funding, and an increasing emphasis on archaeological implications being addressed within the planning framework (English Heritage 1986, paragraph 4.4) allowed English Heritage to reposition itself and The State to withdraw further from underwriting the costs of undertaking rescue archaeology in the UK.

Developer funding of rescue archaeology, based on the polluter-pays principle became increasingly common from this point on (Chadwick 1991, footnote 3). It co-existed for a time, quite happily, within a framework of local authority units and regional trusts that negotiated their scopes of work and scales of cost with the developer, usually through the county archaeologist (Carver 2011; 77) (*see* Figure 1). The issuing of Planning Policy Guideline 16 (PPG 16, DoE 1990) in November 1990 broadly coincided with a general limitation on local authority budgets, imposed under the provisions of the Rates Act of 1984 and the imposition of the politically and socially incendiary Community Charge (Poll Tax). Thus, while PPG 16 advised local authority planning departments that archaeology was now to be a material consideration in the planning process, the removal of budget setting and revenue collection powers from local authorities (by rate capping and the introduction from the centre of the Universal Business Rate) meant that many local authorities had to make cuts in public services in the face of Westminster-controlled revenue-fall.

This was seized upon as an opportunity to promulgate de-regulation of local authority archaeological provision (an information gathering service on behalf of the public) in line with wider Government dogma on local authority service deregulation and to open it up to market forces. Local authority units were closed down and the resulting vacuum occupied by units who were either now allowed to tender outside their original local authority area, new start-ups, or regional units that had been initially established and core-funded by the DOE with taxpayers money. Thus the market, demand and supplier, was manufactured (Collis 2001, 166) within the political context of reining in local authority spending and moving what had been local taxation powers towards Westminster. In addition, it was argued at the time, the structure of development-led archaeology, as established, created a potential conflict of interest (Chadwick 1991, 9) where a county archaeologist might advise a planning authority, might advise the developer on mitigation, and might also be the head of the unit that would undertake the mitigation (*see* Jones 1984, 153–8). This created a fissure which allowed archaeological consultancies to provide advice to developers in the engineered niche between local authority county archaeologists (themselves expert independent advisors), and the local authority archaeological unit as contractor.

Archaeology as service, public service/private contractor

Irrespective of its application the polluter-pays principle, which underpins the financing of almost all rescue archaeology in England, seems un-contentious and the situation of archaeology within land-use planning appears pragmatic. The *habitus* of rescue archaeology in England, however, is not without controversy, which it might be useful to recap here.

The appropriateness of the polluter-pays principle is contested by some, on the grounds that its emphasis places value on the *removal* of the archaeological resource. Value is, primarily, conceived of in economic rather than cultural, social and informational terms (Tarlow and Pluciennik 2007, 124). In effect the polluter-pays principle has contrasting, although *not* irreconcilable, emphases dependent on the position and agenda of the interlocutor.

- On one hand the developer may be seen as being financially penalised for developing a piece of land (Aitchison 2007, 121). Coerced '*by the planning process to pay for archaeological intervention*' (Carver 2011, 77). In such a scheme of interpretation the developer, penalised for creating wealth, should at least have the choice of contractor they employ to do the work (Shepherd 2008) and how much they will pay for it. This is a view that foregrounds the developer in the role of client (Cumberpatch and Blinkhorn 2001, 40) from whom prosperity trickles down, rather than as polluter, for whom archaeologists balance the requirements of development against the archaeological resource as a facet of sustainable development (Aitchison 2012, 145).

Figure 1 Tendering and the procurement process of archaeological work from pre-1990 to present

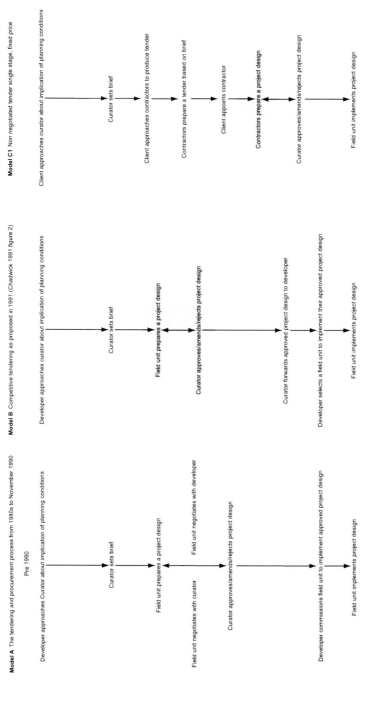

Model A The tendering and procurement process from 1980s to November 1990

Pre 1990

Developer approaches Curator about implication of planning conditions

Curator sets brief

Field unit prepares a project design

Field unit negotiates with curator

Curator approves/amends/rejects project design

Developer commissions field unit to implement approved project design

Field unit implements project design

Model B Competitive tendering as proposed in 1991 (Chadwick 1991 figure 2)

Developer approaches curator about implication of planning conditions

Curator sets brief

Field unit prepares a project design

Curator approves/amends/rejects project design

Curator forwards approved project design to developer

Developer selects a field unit to implement their approved project design

Field unit implements project design

Model C1 Non negotiated tender single stage, fixed price

Client approaches curator about implication of planning conditions

Curator sets brief

Client approaches contractors to produce tender

Contractors prepare a tender based on brief

Client appoints contractor

Contractors prepare a project design

Curator approves/amends/rejects project design

Field unit implements project design

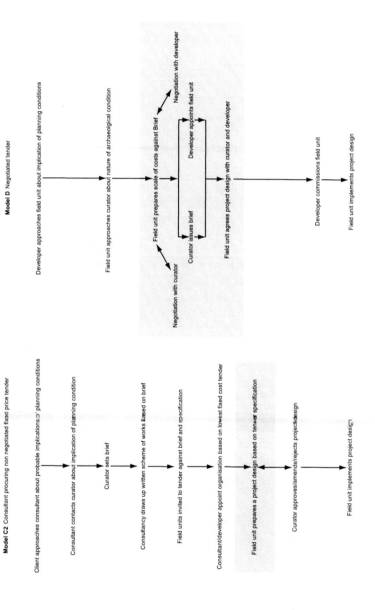

Figure 1 contd

Model C2 Consultant procuring non negotiated fixed price tender

Client approaches consultant about probable implications of planning conditions

Consultant contacts curator about implication of planning condition

Curator sets brief

Consultancy draws up written scheme of works based on brief

Field units invited to tender against brief and specification

Consultant/developer appoint organisation based on lowest fixed cost tender

Field unit prepares a project design based on tender specification

Curator approves/amends/rejects project design

Field unit implements project design

Model D Negotiated tender

Developer approaches field unit about implication of planning conditions

Field unit approaches curator about nature of archaeological condition

Field unit prepares scale of costs against Brief

Negotiation with developer

Curator issues brief

Developer appoints field unit

Negotiation with curator

Field unit agrees project design with curator and developer

Developer commissions field unit

Field unit implements project design

- On the other hand it can be argued that developers are fulfilling their moral and ethical responsibilities to society at large, in effect their part of a social contract, by addressing archaeological conditions on land they develop. The archaeological resource is part of our collective past, it is non-renewable, it is irreplaceable, though not necessarily priceless. Its value quintessentially derives therefore from its ability to cast light on the human story (Carver 2011, 65).

The first view implicitly sees the primary product of archaeology as being a cleared site. The other sees the primary purpose of archaeology to find things out about the past for the benefit of society (Biddle 1994, 17). The implementation of the polluter-pays principle is therefore problematic given the superficial intractability embodied by or created between a simplistic bottom line profit/loss culture versus one of social and ethical values.

As lived experience, this polarity of emphasis is thrown into sharp relief by the compromises required of archaeological project managers, those designing fieldwork, to balance what is known as the constraints triad of time:cost:quality (Figure 2). Explained in simplistic terms the better a piece of archaeological fieldwork the more likely it is to take more time and/or to cost more, the cheaper the archaeological fieldwork the more likely it is to win the tender. This triumvirate of tension is both real and apparent in archaeology in England and stems not from the polluter-pays principle as a principle but is a direct result of how archaeology has situated itself within the market place (Albarella 2006; Carver 2006, 2011; Heaton 2006a, 2006b, 2007, 2008, 2014; Hinton and Jennings 2007, 107; Thorpe 2012a; Wilkins 2012).

In 1991 HM Treasury advised the public sector that:
'Competition is the best guarantee of quality and value for money.[...] We will expand the frontiers of competition outwards,' (HM Treasury 1991, 1) and so while *'The majority of commissions for professional services in the construction and property industries[...]are let on a competitive fee tendered basis.'* (Hoxley 2000, 600; 2007, 189)

Figure 2 The cost constraints triad

Archaeology, in its role as a professional service within the construction industry, has not built-in the checks and balances in practice that others in the same industry have (Heaton 2006a, 2008, 2014) in order to offset the more Hobbesian (1651, 57) characteristics of unfettered competition. The imposition of Compulsory Competitive Tendering on the building professions in the 1980s was unpopular and contentious (Fulcher 2013). It came hot on the heels of the abolition of mandatory fee-scales for architects and chartered surveyors, (analogous to IfA minimum-pay scales), making it illegal for any chartered institute to have mandatory minima and was accompanied by a perceived decline in professional standards (Hoxley 1998, 4–5). A survey on value for money and competitive tendering in construction, undertaken on behalf of the Royal Institution of Chartered Surveyors, in 1996 found that clients wanted to be perceived as having quality of work at the heart of their received tenders, but dishonestly represented themselves on this (Pasquire and Collins 1996, 10). Indeed the report identified a simplistic assumption by clients and their consultants that cheapest equated to best and concluded that they:

'...*were deceiving themselves into believing they were adequately balancing the time:cost:quality triangle through the existing methods of tendering.*' (Pasquire and Collins 1996, 16)

It has been cogently argued (Heaton 2006a) that we as archaeologists have been immature in the way we have situated ourselves within the construction industry. In a race to drive prices down, which was the political intention behind deregulation and the prohibition on fee-scales, we have become largely self-chained within the market place to one central method of determining service provision, lowest cost, fixed price, competitive tender. This has huge ramifications on the way that projects are put together, designed and resourced and is a root cause of disquiet expressed about pay, conditions, disenfranchisement, research and training (Baker *et al* 2006; Carver 2011, 77; Everill 2007, 133–5; 2012, 202-6; Grenville 2006; Harward 2012; Lucas 2001, 9). Are there alternatives? Could there genuinely be another way?

From inside the bell jar looking out

Rescue archaeology is political (as is all archaeology); its practice is contingent on popular national and ideological perceptions of ownership. This idea of ownership is not about who physically owns the remains of the past, (though it can be) but is more centrally focussed on who the output of the investigation of the remains of the past is for. What is the point of doing archaeology? For what purpose or for whom is it being dug up? The answer to these questions has both conditioned policy on whether to provide for rescue archaeology at all within legislation, and determined how the procurement of archaeological expertise has been problematised (*see* Hunter and Ralston, 2006; Bozóki-Erney, 2007a; Willems and van den Dries, 2007; Schlanger 2010). In a recent paper Kristian Kristiansen synthesised the provision of rescue archaeology in Europe into an (admittedly) simplistic contrast of socialist opposing capitalist models (Kristiansen 2009, 642–43). More recently (*see* Table 1) Martin Carver has also conjured implied oppositional models of regulated, deregulated and unregulated provision, based on the '*type of state concerned*' (Carver 2009, 366; 2011, 66–7). All of these representations place the debate on archaeological provision within an arena circumscribed by parameters recognisable from the cold war or, more alarmingly, within spurious ethno-cultural boundaries and resulting traditions (*see* Demoule 2002a, 2002b, 2007, 2010; Thomas 2002). These contrasts fuel fruitless oppositional dogma where aspects of procurement and provision are rejected on spurious ideological grounds alone rather than on their *utility* or efficacy. Situating the argument about the procurement of rescue archaeology within the ideological constraints of socialism or capitalism, right or left, serves to mask the issue. This should be an entirely utilitarian one; what circumstances are the most conducive to the practice of research-enhanced technically-excellent archaeology, that fulfil in a realistic and added-value way, our responsibilities to, and the material needs of, contemporary society? A summary of the approaches of other countries to the procurement and funding of rescue archaeology is presented in Table 2 and may be illuminating (compare with Table 3 for a re-casting of Table 1 in this light). All the countries studied have at their core the polluter-pays principle; some have a mixed economy and exact project-funding through development taxation while retaining an element of core-funding, others have the developer pay for the cost of archaeological work directly.

Most systems of service provision are open to some form of competition, ranging from full-blown excavation by a private company in unregulated and de-regulated systems, to competing for sub-contract services to state bodies in regulated systems. As an aside, regulated systems of provision occur in some of the worlds most enlightened democracies. In Germany each federal state has its own laws and systems of provision, as does Belgium with its three regions, so they have not been included in this study. Most nations in the examples cited procure their archaeology through land-management systems, all nations with one exception, England, regard the material remains of the past to be part of the patrimony, if not the physical property, of the nation and thus *all* archaeological sites (both known and waiting to be discovered) are statutorily regarded as part of the cultural heritage of the nation.

Table 1 Archaeological procurement in three different organisational systems.

	Regime		
	Regulated	**Deregulated**	**Unregulated**
Source of Finance	State	Developer	Charities
Method of Procurement	State Programmes of Works. Response to Discovery	Planning System. County Archaeological Officers	Ad Hoc
Who does the fieldwork	Labourers directed by an Inspector	Archaeological Contractor. Professional excavators.	Volunteers, students directed by individual researcher
Research Output	Dependent on Government Priorities	Not part of Contract	Peer pressure. Depends on interests of director.
Quality Control	Inspectors. Licenses	Consultants	Peer-Group

Source: After Carver 2011 Table 3.1; 66

The Scandinavian countries are divided in the degree to which the market conditions the practice of rescue archaeology. Sweden has recently and rather cautiously de-regulated archaeological provision. As a nation it places great store in the social contract between its citizens and the state, and in an attempt to ameliorate the effects of the introduction of the market it has situated research, because it delivers social value to society, at the very heart of all archaeology (Lekberg 2007, 156–8). Private contractors and the excavation services of regional or city museums compete. Developers are bound to funding research. Quality is given primacy in the constraints triad (Kritz 2011) but this has not been without its own problems and professional (and public) dissent. There is popular concern among archaeologists that as a result of the market (either direct or indirect), the quality of excavations, research and reports is decreasing due to an overemphasis on reducing costs (Goldhahn 2010; Lönn, M, *pers com*, 20 June 2012). In contrast, in the rest of Scandinavia; in Denmark, Finland, and Norway rescue excavation is undertaken by teams from national and/or regional museums who negotiate cost with developers. Research quality is monitored by independent inspectors from within national or regional institutions (Ravn 2013, 647). While publication costs are paid by the developer in Sweden, Norway and Denmark, in Finland only the cost of post-excavation and analysis is paid for by developers, the state pays for publication and as such maintains control of the research product (Schauman-Lönnqvist 2007, 53).

France enacts the polluter-pays principal via a development tax (a form of unified business rate) levied equally on all development at 0.5% of development-costs in urban areas and 0.5% of retail value per square metre in rural areas. This tax is redistributed to regional archaeological bodies on the basis of need and is divided equally between costs for evaluations, a fund for needy developers, research and public outreach (Schlanger and Rossenbach 2010, 70). Full excavation and publication costs are negotiated directly between the developer and archaeological contractor, and the developer selects the organisation that will undertake mitigation through a mechanism of competition, with work based on defined and agreed research priorities established by the state. Archaeological provision is based on the principle that rescue archaeology is research in the public service, situated within the realm of development control. Links between universities and units are close and work is qualitatively overseen/monitored by archaeological agencies of the state at regional (Department) level.

Greece has highly regulated provision for rescue archaeology. All excavation is undertaken by regional branches of the state archaeology service, (The Greek Archaeological Service) which may tender-out and subcontract some elements of service-provision to private companies. Budgets are negotiated with developers but can range up to 10% of development cost (the highest in Europe) though these costs include analysis, conservation and publication. In cases where the social or economic benefit of development outweighs the archaeology and the developer cannot afford to pay then the state contributes to the costs.

Table 2 The past is a foreign country do they do things better there?: Procurement in parts of Europe and North America

Nation State	Source of Finance	Method of Procurement	Who does fieldwork	Market ?	Research	Quality Control
Denmark	Polluter pays directly	Planning/land management system	Professional archaeologists based in regional centres (Museums).	✗	Paid by developer.	Regional inspectors
Finland	Polluter pays project and analysis costs	Planning/land management system	National Board of Antiquities (Private companies specialise in Building recording and survey)	✗	Analysis paid by developer. Reporting paid by state	National Board of Antiquities
Norway	Polluter pays directly	Planning/land management system	Professional archaeologists based in regional centres (Museums) or university institutions	✗	Paid by developer	Riksantivaren Directorate of Culture Heritage
Sweden	Polluter pays	Planning/land management system	Private companies & Regional archaeological units based in regional museum	✓ Based on quality of research aims against scales of cost	Paid by Developer	Regional Museum authorities Quality Standards and evaluations document
Czech Republic	Polluter pays direct	Planning/land management system Permits to excavate issued only on conclusion of agreement on "scope and conditions of archaeological research" between developer, curator and contractor	National and regional Museums Not for profit organisations "95% of archaeologists employed by public organisations" Commercial companies cannot undertake excavations but can offer excavation services	✓ Restricted market	Paid by Developer	Archaeological Institute of Academy of Sciences monitors compliance with conditions of research
Hungary	Polluter pays agreed project cost up front to avoid defaulting. min of 0.09% development cost Mitigation in event of chance finds paid by state	Planning/land management system	Competent museums advertises a bill of prices. May subcontract to Research Centres, not for profit organisations	✓ Restricted market	Paid by Developer	National Office of Cultural Heritage
Poland	Polluter pays	Agreement for development sought from Regional Conservator	Private Companies Centre for Protection of Archaeological Heritage but will subcontract out projects	✓	Paid by developer	Centre for Protection of Archaeological Heritage

Table 2 (contd)

Nation State	Source of Finance	Method of Procurement	Who does fieldwork	Market ?	Research	Quality Control
Romania	Polluter pays	Application for development triggers pre-development assessment	Preventive Archaeology Dept of National History Museum. Regional and County museums appoint licensed archaeologist	✓	Paid by Developer	National Committee of Archaeology Certification of Archaeologists
Ireland	Polluter pays	Planning/land management system	Private companies with licensed archaeologists mandated to undertake excavations on behalf of state	✓	Not part of contract	Fieldwork: National Museum of Ireland Post-excavation: Unmonitored
Italy	Polluter pays	Regional Archaeological Superintendent monitors development. Set requirements for archaeological works	Private companies and co-operatives	✓	Not part of contract	Superintendents
Spain	Polluter pays	Planning/land management system	Private companies	✓	Not part of contract	Local Authorities
Greece	Polluter Pays on project by project basis up to threshold of 10% of total development costs.	Planning/land management system	Regional divisions (Ephorates) of Greek Archaeological Service (GAS). May tender out some elements	✓ limited to service provision to GAS	Paid by Developer	Self regulating
Netherlands	Polluter pays	Planning/land management system	Private companies and Municipal archaeology departments	✓	Paid by Developer supplemented by regional or/and state funding	State Inspectorate for Archaeology/College for Archaeology and state Archaeological Quality
France	Polluter pays development tax and full cost of mitigation	Planning/land management system	INRAP (National archaeological institute) undertake all (evaluations) diagnostics and set brief based on their findings. INRAP will tender to provide excavation services, however market is not closed to competent private contractors	Limited	Analysis and publication costs paid by developer	
Canada	Polluter pays	Planning/land management system	Private companies with Licensed archaeologists	✓	Research subject to seperate negotiation	Ministry of culture standards and guidelines
USA	Polluter pays	Planning/land management system	Private companies	✓	Research subject to seperate negotiatio	State Heritage Protection Offices
England	Polluter pays directly	Planning/land management system	Private companies	✓	Not part of contract. Subject to separate negotiation	County archaeological officers

The Czech Republic has a partially regulated system where competition ranges between state and regional agencies and not-for-profit organisations. Permits to excavate are issued only on the conclusion of an agreement on the scope and conditions of research between the developer, the excavating organisation, and the Academy of Sciences (Bureš 2007, 20) and this ensures quality.

Hungary identifies the need for rescue archaeology on archaeological sites which appear on its incomplete national register (SMR). Where development is authorised rescue archaeology is funded via a tax amounting to not less than 0.9% of the development budget, and is undertaken by county museums (Bánffy and Raczky 2010, 86) which have a public list of prices/quantities. On developments where hitherto unknown archaeological sites are discovered, excavation is paid for by the state (Bozóki-Erney 2007b, 108).

Poland, on the other hand, has recently embraced a deregulated sector. Formerly robust laws pertaining to the tutelage of archaeology and the conduct of rescue archaeology, including post-excavation, conservation and publication at developer expense (Gassowski 2007, 161) had ensured a *'high quality of archaeological works'* (Marciniak and Pawleta 2010, 89). These laws have, however, been largely circumvented by government reform which required the regulating authorities of state and regional institutions to withdraw from the role of quality management to be replaced by 'developer-appointed committees' (*ibid* 89) with the result that costs, time and quality have been driven down (*ibid* 96).

In Holland, which has a deregulated market place, there is an explicit underpinning principle that *'the acquisition of knowledge about the past is the government's responsibility'* (van den Dries and Willems 2007, 52). There is a tacit recognition that commercial and financial interests may prejudice the acquisition of that knowledge, and as a consequence commercial companies have to be licensed by law, which means that they operate under licence on behalf of the state archaeology service. This is not without problems however a tendency to:'*...perform projects...as a craft rather than as a scientific enterprise...academic output and relevant research results is not as high as the investment itself'* (*ibid* 61) is undermining the knowledge value being extracted archaeologically. In effect the proclaimed responsibility of the state, the acquisition of knowledge, is not being fulfilled by the mechanism of procurement, and as a consequence of the imbalance in the constraints triad:'*there is often hardly enough money and time to put a real effort in the knowledge products such as excavation reports'* (*ibid* 62).

Spain, Italy and Ireland have an open marketplace for archaeological services.

Ireland has a licensing system for archaeologists which in theory underpins quality control procedures for the conduct of excavations. Post-excavation analysis, reporting and publication quality is problematic however, due to lack of developer concern or institutional capacity to compel developers to pay for research (Gleeson 2007, 144; Gowan 2007, 30; Ciuchini 2010).

In Spain, where the majority of archaeologists are employed in the private sector, full analytical publication as a result of developer-funded archaeology is rare, with interim publications appearing yearly or twice yearly (Martínez Diaz and Castillo Mena 2007, 199–201).

In Italy private archaeological companies undertake most rescue archaeology in a market system, described diplomatically as '*not necessarily based on quality*' (Maggi 2007, 153), to specifications set out by the regional superintendent responsible. The developer has a free hand to select its contractor and the superintendent has no juridicial [sic] power '*to force contractors to hire universities rather than low-cost units*' (*ibid* 154). Implicitly there are qualitative problems of work undertaken where units:'*...may hire anybody willing to call himself an archaeologist. Hiring qualified archaeologists is the exception rather than the rule.*' (*ibid* 153).

In the USA and Canada archaeological organisations, 'consultants', tender for work from developers and archaeological issues are flagged via the land-management system. However, there are problems with levels of pay and conditions (Patterson 1999) and with quality in fieldwork and reporting (La Salle and Hutchings 2012, 14). Methodology practiced by rote, and methodologies applied in inappropriate circumstances, have been highlighted as reducing or erasing, the research value of the material collected or recorded '*utility is compromised when field methods are applied across the board by rote*' (Peacock and Rafferty 2007, 120). There is also a growing awareness that regulation has created static research-frameworks, typologies and chronologies which strait-jacket post excavation. Over-prescriptive standards have been implemented without thought about their applicability to the archaeology they are being used upon (*ibid*). One cannot help but wonder if the reflexivity absent in such practice is due to market-forces and the pressure to finish a site (Shanks and McGuire 1996).

It would seem then that in all the examples given above archaeology is tacitly accepted as a research- and inquiry-based discipline the purpose of which is simplistically to find things out about the past. This is axiomatic, *even* with rescue archaeology (Lambrick 1991, 24; Willems 1999, 2; Willems and van den Dries 2007b, 7). The purpose of archaeology is to enhance narratives of human existence and our past personal, sociological, societal, economic, spiritual and environmental interactions. Archaeology as a discipline is not a 'big science' like chemistry or physics but it does speak to humanity on issues every bit as important to our understanding of the world and our place in it as the *Origin of Species* or Einstein's general theory of relativity. The value of archaeology, over and above the financial cost that it takes to physically excavate it in advance of development, is in its research potential. Therefore the full cost of archaeological work is that which allows, qualitatively, the research potential of archaeological work to be achieved. Denmark,

Finland, France, Greece, Norway and Sweden attempt to assure that the research potential of an archaeological site is maximised by maintaining control over the means and agency of knowledge production. France and Sweden have opened up to competition in the provision of excavation services, but the agencies of its citizenry maintain a commanding position in the market place, and both countries place the generation of knowledge at the core of commercial archaeology. Importantly, in all of these nations, the state, as the authorised and mandated agency of its citizenry, maintains a commitment toward a level of archaeological service-provision to its citizens, to whom it is responsible and accountable.

Table 3 Archaeological procurement and its emphasis recast in three different organisational systems

	Regime		
	Regulated	**Deregulated**	**Unregulated**
Source of Finance	Developer and/or State	Developer	Charities
Method of Procurement	State Programmes of Works/ Response to Discovery/Planning System	Planning System. County Archaeological Officers	Ad Hoc
Who does the fieldwork	Qualified/Experienced archaeologists	Archaeological Contractor. Professional excavators.	Volunteers, students directed by individual researcher
Research Output	Dependent on Research Priorities (Local, Regional, National and international research frameworks)	Not part of Contract	Peer pressure. Depends on interests of director.
Quality Control	Inspectors. Licenses	Consultants	Peer-Group

On the other hand England, and the other nations in this synthesis, attempt to ensure quality of service-provision through quality management mechanisms which are divorced from the primary mechanism of service-procurement, market competition. In all examples where markets are given free reign, and where cost is the prime or major determinant, the quality of research product and/or information procurement is at best called into question, and at worst its utility, or information content, is compromised.

Fixed cost tender and bargaining the past

'There is scarcely anything in the world that some man cannot make a little worse, sell a little more cheaply...the common law of business balance prohibits paying a little and getting a lot – it cannot be done.' attributed to John Ruskin 1860

Fixed-cost competitive tendering is the dominant process in the selection of archaeological contractors within England. It operates primarily as a mechanism by which the financial risk of the unforeseen; the unforeseeable or third-party inadequacies (*see post 1990 models in Figure 1 above*) are passed from the land-owner or developer onto the archaeological contractor. As a result, the task of the archaeological project-manager, as it has evolved in response to the situation outlined above, is not so much to design fieldwork programmes which maximise the amount of information recovered, but to minimise the amount of risk the tendering organisation is exposed to in undertaking the fieldwork, and to win contracts by submitting a successful tender. In compiling tenders for this type of work the project manager usually produces a headline-cost based on excavating the minimum sample-size permissible for the type of features expected, calculated against the indicated minimum amount of expected archaeology using established formulas of volume and complexity. The time it takes for a project manager to produce a tender is non-billable time. This exacerbates a tendency to cost excavations on a formulaic basis, rather than on a detailed excavation design which would increase organisational overheads (Chinyeo 2011). This industrialisation of archaeology (Shanks and McGuire 1996) with fixed costs based on calculations of units of production is entirely understandable, after-all one can only manage what one can quantify, but it has taken rescue archaeology away from on-site inquiry and tailored response (Carver 2011, 77; Thomas 2010) toward the bland conformity of lowest-common-denominator archaeology, with standards in the field the worst they have been for half a century (Carver 2006, 8). Archaeologists design their strategies to suit the ground conditions and the archaeology that they can see, but this may not be the same archaeology on which the site was originally costed or even the archaeology that is there. As Carver notes '*how hard you look pre-determines how carefully you record*' (Carver 2011) and what you expect to record dictates the price you submit.

Fixed-cost tendering is a mechanism promoted by a number of consultancies whose position within the archaeological process is growing in power, prominence, and influence through a close alignment with the business interests of development companies (Carver 2009, 372). The rationale for their evolution is that consultancies can offer developer/ client-centred advice on the necessity, scope, and range of costs of archaeological works. They sit within the contractual sphere of archaeological provision as partisan mediators between those who do archaeology, and those who are legally required to pay for it, and often act as a counter-voice to the research and methodological requirements stipulated by local-planning-authority archaeologists. As one well-placed commentator notes:

'*the input of consultants into this process [project design] appears to be a largely negative one; seeking to cut costs by limiting work on specific aspects of a project[...] is hardly a positive contribution to the production of an adequate site report, yet it is the raison d'etre of the consultancy industry.*" (Cumberpatch and Roberts 2012, 30).

Often the mission statement of archaeological consultancy firms is to secure minimum archaeological work for the lowest price and, it has been implied, their position within the process of procurement between experienced archaeological contractors, developers and curators is potentially divisive, a factor driving both the quality of archaeological works and its cost down, as well as undermining the purpose of archaeological enquiry (Carver 2011, 77–8; Thorpe 2012b).

In contrast, my own experience with negotiated tenders or two-stage tenders directly between developer and archaeological contractor is that it is possible (and more honest) to produce a guide-price or estimate based on stated quantities. This then allows for the building-in of contingencies and scales of cost which can be invoked in stated situations following consultation. The difference is that fixed-price tendering is a dogmatic, 'one size fits all', approach designed primarily to move risk away from the developer (which if the risk is 'too much' archaeology, converts to over-spend paid for by the contractor) and maximise developer profit. Negotiated tendering on the other hand cannot offer such certainties on paper, but does present a bill of quantities and a scale of costs with overtly stated, discovery-dependent, and thus research-led circumstances where contingency costs would, on consultation, be invoked. It shares risk while accepting the needs of an archaeological contractor to generate a surplus to allow for investment in training, methodological research and development, and improving salaries. To put it in simplistic terms, in the former the power arrow lies with costs and profits and land-clearance, with the latter there is enhanced potential for maximising both the knowledge to be gained from the archaeology, and to reasonably estimate and quantify project surplus via negotiation by balancing, through design, cost, time, and quality in an ongoing process.

Some commentators have been enthusiastic, if inadvertently Panglossian, in their assessment that the current manner of the procurement of archaeology represents the better of all *possible* worlds (Aitchison 2009b, 383; Aitchison 2010a; Thomas 2002, 238). There is slightly more than a touch of Panglossian optimism when business opportunities can be forged from dilemma (Aitchison 2010b, 29) in our times of economic crisis.

'...*what we find evil will, if rightly considered, be found conducive to the good of some other creature, and therefore necessary to the general design: We must put up with it as best we can, for the sake of the general good*' (Voltaire 1759, 9)

However in the interests of fairness Cassandra-like commentaries have also been offered on the appropriateness of the market as a mechanism to deliver archaeology (Chadwick 2000b; Graves-Brown 1997; Morris 1995). Indeed it appears that archaeology as a craft and profession has fragmented in the face of the market, no longer is there the over-whelming sense of quiet confidence in the future expressed by Mytum (1987b, 3). While Pangloss may reflect optimistic complacency and almost certainly unwarranted faith in a guiding hand, Casandra equally certainly (and probably with as little warrant) professes doom to unhearing ears in her '*considering whether we have the balance right*' (Shepherd 2008). We are not *yet* in national crisis, nor have we *yet* stepped over the precipice of doom, but nor are we in a safe place, or approaching, on current course, the best of all possible worlds.

Since 1990 we have replaced one set of imperfect circumstances with an improved, yet still inadequate, set of circumstances. We have established along the way, at least for now (but for how long?), the principle *de jure* that archaeology is a valuable non-renewable resource; but we have *failed* to put into place the mechanisms which maximise the value extracted from that resource in the process of archaeological fieldwork, and are as yet, still, to realise the potential of our practice to fulfil its purpose.

Funding rescue, favouring quality

'*At no time in our history,[...] has a collective sense of responsibility in regard to our antiquities been more acutely necessary. The surface of our land is changing and changing rapidly...Progress in itself is a good and necessary thing, and it is, indeed, to progress in the past that we owe many of our most valuable historical monuments. But in a small and crowded country like ours, the utmost care and consideration are necessary on the part of every one of us, if we are to prevent ourselves from converting reasoned progress into a blind or hasty devastation of the great fabric which our forefathers so well and truly wrought, and on which our own creative efforts are based...the history of our country and our civilisation is built up not merely in our documents, nor even in the bricks and mortar of our ancient buildings, but that it is enshrined also in the soil which may, on its surface bear no visible vestige of antiquity. The responsibility of safe-guarding this historic soil lies, in the first instance, not with a few harassed officials in Whitehall but with the great public as a whole.'* (Wheeler 1927, 830–31)

The funding and procurement model for rescue archaeology in England is a struggling, sometime failing, work in progress, aimed at striking a balance between the conduct of archaeology as research, and the *Progress* spoken of in the quote above. The model as implemented lacks adequacy and needs to be re-cast because it does not achieve that balance. It places price over product, cost over quality and short-term profit over the past. It lacks adequacy because of the unequal stresses in emphasis in the cost/constraints triad, where the needs of business and developer are those most forcefully articulated, and it is inadequate because debate within the profession about funding and procurement suffers a mire of dogma and didactic statement. The issue is not whether one conforms to rigid models of service-delivery dictated by political dogma, the issue is not even about polluter pays, the issue is precisely one of whether the funding and procurement model meets its primary purpose. That purpose is to produce high-quality archaeological research which has the potential to educate, enthral and enrich lives through the narratives that it tells. Achieving the research dividend, this benefit of civilisation, is the *raison d'être* of our profession which if mature, reflexive and self-confident, necessitates its constituent parts to be well-trained, methodologically, technically, and theoretically informed, and appropriately valued and re-numerated. The contemporary social and political context of the practice of rescue archaeology is one which favours the use of the market and cost-based competition to determine archaeological provision. It imposes constraints in advance of full resource-quantification, and prioritises cost as the bottom-line with everything that that entails, while failing to support the central role of the County Archaeologist as arbiter and adjudicator of quality. The mechanisms of site-evaluation, as practiced, are a less than adequate means of quantifying resource (*see* Powlesland, Chapter 15) and identifying research potential. Thus many budgets, built on such resource quantification, without suitable contingency in-built, are probably inadequate.

To achieve the latent potential of any archaeological site one needs adaptive strategies and flexible approaches. This is the sort of flexibility that cannot be built into a fixed-cost tender, a flexibility which needs to be negotiated as contingent:

'...*commercial considerations put great pressure on archaeologists who also have a professional and ethical duty to deliver high quality academic research and public benefit*' (Shepherd 2008).

If we continue to attempt to excavate sites based on budgets submitted on minimum expectations, costed to give rock bottom rates, then all we can get is the minimum. When the unexpected happens (as it does) in order to maintain the cost and time requirements, qualitative elements, how much knowledge we can generate, have to be trimmed (Heaton 2008). This, I would argue, defeats the whole purpose of rescue archaeology, and goes against the core principles enshrined in both the European Convention on the Protection of the Archaeological Heritage (Revised) (Valetta convention 1992) and the Council of Europe Framework Convention on the Value of Cultural Heritage for Society (Faro convention 2005). There are notable and high-profile examples of work done to high technical and academic standards, but the system of fixed price, lowest bid, tendering is not innately conducive to it. This a fact once recognised in public service procurement (DOE 1997) and increasingly within the construction industry (Scot III *et al* 2006) and by an all Party Parliamentary Archaeology Group (APPAG 2003).

However, moving toward negotiated tendering, as is happening in the world of property management (Hoxley 2007, 189), requires engagement in the market-place in a different, more mature, reflexive and self-confident way; using mechanisms such as indicative pricing, scales of costs based on stated quantities, built-in margins of surplus, review processes (as with design-and-build contracts) and negotiations based on fuller appreciations of the resource potential. This will of course make archaeology more expensive, but should reduce budgetary and time-based uncertainty, a sticking point for business highlighted in the Barker Review on planning (Barker 2006; CBI 2006; CgMs 2006). The biggest reduction in uncertainly however would be knowing the ceiling of costs, based on an agreed formulaic percentage of development cost or development value, and putting aside a sum for archaeology, as a legal requirement, at the beginning of development planning. However, this does not provide a procurement and funding model which allows developers engagement with archaeology, or the engagement of archaeology with development, to continue in the way it has. France finances rescue archaeology via development taxation, creating known-costs early in the planning stage. While such taxation in England might be a hotly contested issue, would this be more or less contested than the introduction of the minimum wage in 1999, or standard business rates in 1990? Might the levying of locally-set and adjusted development taxation not be more in keeping with a localisation agenda? The appropriate resourcing of the bulk of rescue archaeology, associated post-excavation, artefact conservation and publication has been identified in England as a duty incumbent on the developer, but the current model of procurement, judged on utilitarian criteria, in the world as we find it some 40 years after the foundation of RESCUE, still struggles to keep its head above the waves as it treads water.

References

Aitchison, K, 2000, The funding of professional archaeological practice in England, *Cultural Trends* **10.39**, 1–32

Aitchison, K, 2007, Ethical issues in European professional archaeology, *Public Archaeology* **6.2**, 116–23

Aitchison, K, 2009a, After the gold rush: global archaeology in 2009, *World Archaeology* **41.4**, 259–71

Aitchison, K, 2009b, Book review of, *Archaeology and Capitalism: from ethics to politics*, in *Conservation and Management of Archaeological Sites,* November 2008, **10.4**, 386–88

Aitchison, K, 2010a, Grey literature, academic engagement, and preservation by understanding, *Archaeologies: J of the World Archaeol Congress* **6.2**, 289–300

Aitchison, K, 2010b, United Kingdom archaeology in economic crisis, in Schlanger, N, and Aitchison, K, (eds), 25–30,

Aitchison, K, 2012, *Breaking new ground: how archaeology works*, Kindle edn, Landward Research Ltd, Sheffield

Albarella, U, 2006, The ragged trousered corporatists, *Assemblage* **9**, at http://www.assemblage. group.shef.ac.uk/issue9/albarella.html (accessed 7 May, 2012)

Alexander, J, 1974, The world situation, in, Rahtz, P A, (ed), 16–27

All-Party Parliamentary Archaeology Group, 2003 *Current State of Archaeology in the United Kingdom,* at http://www.appag.org.uk/report/report.html (accessed 28 November,2013)

Baker, D, Smith, K, and Shepherd, I, 2006, Local Authority opportunities, in Hunter, J, and Ralston, I, (eds), *Archaeological resource management in the uk: an introduction*, Stroud, 131–46

Bánffy, E, and Raczky, P, 2010, The crisis and changes in cultural heritage legislation in Hungary: cul-de-sac or solution? in Schlanger, N, and Aitchison, K, (eds), 81–6

Barker, K, 2006, *Barker review of land-use planning*

Barker, P, 1974a, The scale of the problem, in Rahtz, P A, (ed), 28–34

Barker, P, 1974b, The origins and development of RESCUE, in Rahtz, P A, (ed), 280–86

Biddle, M, 1968, Archaeology and the history of British towns, *Antiquity* **42.166**, 109–16

Biddle, M, 1974a, Foreward of the Chairman of RESCUE, in Rahtz, P A, (ed), ix–x

Biddle, M, 1974b, The future of the urban past, in Rahtz, P A, (ed), 95–112

Biddle, M, 1994, *What future for British archaeololgy?* The opening address of the eighth annual conference of the Institute for Field Archaeologists Bradford, 13–15 April 1994, Oxford

Blinkhorn, P, 2014, Not so much a pot, more an expensive luxury: Commercial archaeology and the slow death of pottery analysis, in Blinkhorn, P, and Cumberpatch, C G, (eds), *The chiming of crack'd bells: recent approaches to the study of artefacts in archaeology*, BAR Internat Ser **2677**, Archaeopress, Oxford, 99–104

Blinkhorn, P, and Cumberpatch, C G, 1998, The analysis of artefacts and the tyranny of the field archaeologist, *Assemblage* **4**, *at* http://www.assemblage.group.shef.ac.uk/4/ (accessed 21/6/2012)

Blinkhorn, P, and Cumberpatch, C G, 1999, Archaeology in England 1999, *World Archaeology Bulletin* **9**, 45–55

Bozóki-Erney, K (ed), 2007a, *European preventive archaeology: Papers of the EPAC meeting 2004,* Vilnius, Budapest, National Office of Cultural heritage, Hungary: Council of Europe

Bozóki-Erney, K, 2007b, Preventive archaeology in Hungary: One step behind, in Bozóki-Erney, K, (ed), *European preventive archaeology,* 105–21

Bureš, M, 2007, From planning application to the final report in the Czech Republic, in Bozóki-Erney K, (ed), 19–32

Carver, M O H, 1996, On archaeological value, *Antiquity* **70.1**, 45–56

Carver, M O H, 2006, Thinking allowed, *Rescue News* **100**, 6–8

Carver, M O H, 2009, *Archaeological Investigation,*Oxford

Carver, M O H, 2011, *Making archaeology happen: design versus dogma,* Walnut Creek, CA

CgMs, 2006, *Barker review of land use planning call for evidence submitted by CgMs Ltd,* at http://www.cgms.co.uk/bulletin/barker_review.pdf (accessed 12 July, 2012)

Chadwick, A, 2000a, How green is our valley? The state of contemporary archaeological practice in Britain, *Rescue News,* **82,** 4–5

Chadwick, A, 2000b, Taking English archaeology into the next millennium: A personal review of the state of the art, *Assemblage* **5**, at http://www.assemblage.group.shef.ac.uk/5/chad.html (accessed 12 July, 2012)

Chadwick, P, 1991, Competitive Tendering in archaeology: The Curator's role, in Swain, H, (ed), 7–14

Chinyeo, E, 2011, The cost of tendering, *Working Paper Series, Proc of the Engineering Project Organization Conference,* Colorado, USA, August 9–12, 2011

Ciuchini, P, 2010, Developer pays...or does he? *Archaeology Ireland,* **24.4**, 12–13

Cobb, H, Harris, O J T, Jones, C, Richardson, P, (eds), *Reconsidering archaeological fieldwork: exploring on-site relationships between theory and practice,* Springer, New York

Collis, J, 2001, *Digging up the past,* Sutton Publishing, Stroud

Council of Europe, 'Valetta', 1992, European Convention on the Protection of Archaeological Heritage (revised 1992), at http://conventions.coe.int/Treaty/en/Treaties/Html/143.htm (accessed 12 July, 2012)

Council of Europe 'Florence', 2000, European Landscape Convention, at http://conventions.coe. int/Treaty/en/Treaties/Html/176.htm (accessed 12/7/2012)

Confederation of British Industry (CBI), 2006, CBI submission to the Barker Review of Planning, at http://www.cbi.org.uk/ndbs/positiondoc.nsf/81e68789766d775d8025672a005601aa/CD783 E43D3A6A0B9802576D2004F65ED/$file/CBI%20response%20-%20Barker%20review%20 of%20planning%20mar2006.pdf (accessed 12 August, 2010)

Cumberpatch, C G, 2000, Some problems in contemporary English archaeology, *Archeologia Polona* **38**, 225–328

Cumberpatch, C G, and Blinkhorn, P, 2001, Clients, contractors, curators and archaeology: who owns the past? in Pluciennik, M, (ed), *The responsibilities of archaeologists: archaeology and ethics,* British Archaeol Rep Internat Ser **981,** Oxford,39–46

Cumberpatch, C G, and Roberts, H M, 2012, Life in the archaeological marketplace, in Rockman, M, and Flatman, J, (eds), *Archaeology in society: Its relevance in the modern world,* Springer, New York, 23–43

Demoule, J-P, 2002a, Rescue archaeology: the French way, *Public Archaeology* **2**, 170–77

Demoule, J-P, 2002b, Reply to Roger Thomas, *Public Archaeology* **2**, 239–40

Demoule, J-P, 2007, Preventive archaeology in France, in Bozóki-Erney, K, (ed), 57–64

Demoule, J-P, 2010, The crisis-economic, ideological, and archaeological, in Schlanger, N, and Aitcheson, K, (eds), 12–17

Department for Communities and Local Government (DCLG), 2010, *Planning Policy Statement 5: Planning for the Historic Environment*, The Stationery Office, London

Department of the Environment (DoE), 1990, *Planning Policy Guidance 16: Archaeology and Planning (PPG 16)*, HMSO, London

Department of the Environment (DOE), 1997, Better value for Local Authority services, News Release 2nd June

English Heritage, 1986, *Rescue archaeology funding: a policy statement, English Heritage, London*

Everill, P, 2007, British commercial archaeology: antiquarians and labourers; developers and diggers, in Hamilakis, Y, and Duke, P, (eds), *Archaeology and capitalism: from ethics to politics*, Walnut Creek, CA, 158–87

Everill, P, 2012, *The Invisible Diggers. A Study of British Commercial Archaeology* (2nd edn eBook), Oxford

Fulcher, M, 2013, The Thatcher years: architects on the legacy of the Iron Lady, *Architects' Journal*, **237.13**, 12–13

Gassowski, J, 2007, Rescue archaeology in Poland, in Bozóki-Erney, K, (ed), 161–66

Gleeson, P, 2007, Rescue excavations in Ireland, roads and codes, in Bozóki-Erney, K, (ed), 137–45

Goldhahn, J, 2010, The key chain of archaeology is not stronger than its weakest link, *Current Swedish Archaeol* **18**, 35–40

Gowan, M, 2007, Quality management and Irish commercial sector archaeology, in Willems, W, and, Van den Dries, M, (eds), 22–34

Graves, R, 1959, *New Larousse encyclopedia of mythology*, (1968 Trans by Richard Aldington and Delano Ames with an introduction by Robert Graves)

Graves-Brown, P, 1997, S/He who pays the piper: archaeology and the polluter-pays principle, *Assemblage 2*, at http://www.assemblage.group.shef.ac.uk/2/2gb2.html (accessed 12 July, 2012)

Grenville, J, 2006, The curators egg: a new overview, in Hunter, J, and Ralston, I, (eds), Stroud, 158–76

Harward, C, 2012, Reskilling the diggers: handing over the means of interpretation, *The Archaeologist* **83**, 26–29

Heaton, M J, 2006a, Costing the earth…and the finds and the soil samples: alternatives to the 'Fixed Price', *The Archaeologist* **59**, 13

Heaton, M J, 2006b, Show me yours: cost comparison in archaeology, *The Archaeologist* **61**, 11

Heaton, M J, 2007, Whither the profession, *The Archaeologist* **66**, 14–15

Heaton, M J, 2008, W(h)ither the profession II: The economic, legal and organisational structure of successful commercial archaeology, (Paper given at the annual conference of the Institute of Field Archaeologists, Swansea University, 18–20 March 2008)

Heaton, M J, 2014, Constructing archaeology: the application of construction management practices to commercial archaeology in Britain, *The Historic Environment Policy and Practice* **5.3**, 245–57

Heighway, C M, (ed), 1972, *The erosion of history: archaeology and planning in towns,* Council for British Archaeology, London

Hinton, P, and Jennings, D, 2007, Quality management of archaeology in Great Britain: present practice and future challenges, in, Willems, W, and van den Dries, M, (ed), Oxford, 100–112

HM Treasury, 1991, *Competing for quality: Buying better public service,* HMSO, London

Hobbes, T, 1651, *Leviathan,* (1969 reprint with introduction by Macpherson, C B), Pelican, Harmondsworth

Hoxley, M, 1998, *COBRA 98: the impact of competitive fee tendering on construction professional service quality,* Loughborough

Hoxley, M, 2000, Are competitive fee tendering and construction professional service quality mutually exclusive? *Construction Management and Economics* **18.5**, 599–605

Hoxley, M, 2007, The fee tendering and service quality issue revisited, *Property Management* **25.2**, 180–92

Hunter, J, and Ralston, I, (eds), 2006, *Archaeological resource management in the UK: an Introduction,* (2nd edn), Stroud

Jones, B, 1984, *Past imperfect: the story of rescue archaeology,* Heinemann, London

Kristiansen, K, 2009, Contract archaeology in Europe: an experiment in diversity, *World Archaeology: Debates in Archaeology* **4**, 641–48

Kritz, A, 2011, *Kriterier för bedömning av kvalitet i uppdragsarkeologin,* Stockholm

La Salle, M, and Hutchings, R, 2012, Commercial archaeology in British Columbia, *The Midden* **44.2**, 8–16

Lambrick, G, 1991, Competitive tendering and archaeological research: the development of a CBA view, in Swain, H, (ed), 21–30

Lekberg, P, 2007, Making it matter, towards a Swedish contract archaeology for social sustainability, in Willems, W, and van den Dries, M, (eds), 148–58

Lucas, G, 2001, *Critical approaches to fieldwork : contemporary and historical archaeological practice,* Routledge, London

Maggi, R, 2007, The approach to preventive archaeology in Italy, in Bozóki-Erney, K, (ed), 147–54

Marciniak, A, and Pawleta, P, 2010, Archaeology in crisis: the case in Poland, in Schlanger, N, and Aitchison, K, (eds), 87–96

Martínez Diaz, B, and Castillo Mena, A, 2007, Preventive archaeology in Spain, in Bozóki-Erney, K, (ed), 187–208

Morris, R, 1995, What is this thing called archaeology? *British Archaeology* **11**

Mytum, H, and Waugh K, (eds) 1987a, *Rescue archaeology: what's next: Proceedings of a Rescue conference held at the University of York, December 1986,* Dept of Archaeol, University of York Monograph **6,** York and Hertford

Mytum, H, 1987b, Introduction, in, Mytum, H, and Waugh K, (eds) 1987a, 3

Pasquire, C, and Collins, S, 1996, *The effect of competitive tendering on value in construction,* Loughborough

Patterson, T, 1999, the political economy of archaeology in The United States, *Annual Review of Anthropology* **28,** 155–74

Peacock, E, and Rafferty, J, 2007, Cultural resource management, guidelines and practice in the United States, in, Willems, W, and van den Dries, M, (eds), 113–34

Pluciennik, M, (ed), *The responsibilities of archaeologists: archaeology and ethics*, British Archaeol Rep Internat Ser **981**, Oxford

Rahtz, P A, (ed), 1974a, *Rescue Archaeology, Pelican*, Harmondsworth

Rahtz, P A, 1974b, What kind of Regional Units do we need?, *Rescue News* **4**, 2–5

Ravn, M, 2013, It's about knowledge not systems: a contribution to a complex discussion of good, bad and ugly production of archaeological knowledge in Europe, *World Archaeology* **454**, 642–52

RESCUE: The British Archaeological Trust and CBA, 1974, *Archaeology and Government: A plan for archaeology in Britain*, Hertford and London

Royal Commission on the Historic Monuments of England (RCHME), 1960, *A matter of time: An archaeological survey of the river gravels of England*, HMSO, London

Royal Commission on Historic Monuments (England) (RCHME), 1963, *Monuments threatened or destroyed. A select list: 1956–6*, HMSO, London

Schadla-Hall, T, 1991, Competitive tendering in archaeology, in Swain, H, (ed), 41–50

Schauman-Lönnqvist, M, 2007, Rescue archaeology in Finland: goals and practices, in Bozóki-Erney, K, (ed), 51–56

Schlanger, N, and Aitchison, K, (eds), 2010, *Archaeology and the global economic crisis: multiple impacts, possible solutions*, Culture Lab Éditions, Tervuren

Schlanger, N, 2010, Postscript: on dead canaries, guinea-pigs and other Trojan Horses, in Schlanger, N, and Aitchison, K, (eds), 107–16

Schlanger, N, and Rossenbach, K S, 2010, One crisis too many? French archaeology between reform and re-launch, in Schlanger, N, and Aitchison, K, (eds), 69-81

Scot III, S, Molenaar, K R, Gransberg, D D, and Smith, N C, 2006, *Best-value procurement methods for highway construction projects*, Washington DC

Shanks, M, and McGuire, R H, 1996, The craft of archaeology, *American Antiquity* **16.1**, 75–88

Shepherd, N, 2008, Presentation to the Sub-Committee on Cultural Heritage, Council of Europe Conference on rescue archaeology, Paris 8th December 2008

Swain, H, (ed), 1991, *Competitive tendering in archaeology: Papers presented at a one day conference in June 1990, 51–3*, RESCUE: The British Archaeological Trust, and Standing Conference of Archaeological Unit Managers, Hertford

Tarlow, S, and Pluciennik, M, 2007, Making trouble for business ethics, *Public Archaeology* **6.2**, 124–25

Thomas, C, 1974, Archaeology in Britain 1973, in Rahtz 1974a, 3–15

Thomas, R, 2002, Comment: Rescue archaeology, the French way, by Jean-Paul Demoule, *Public Archaeology* **2**, 236–38

Thomas, R, 2007, Development-led archaeology in England, in Bozóki-Erney, K, (ed), 33–42

Thomas, R, 2010, *Rethinking development-led archaeology.* Lecture given at 2020 vision a new era for British archaeology session at the Federation of Archaeological Managers and Employers Conference, York, June 2010

Thorpe, R, 2006, RESCUE: relevant today (and tomorrow), *Rescue News* **100**, 9

Thorpe, R, 2012a, Often fun, usually messy: fieldwork, recording and higher orders of things, in, Cobb, H, *et al* (eds), 31–52

Thorpe, R, 2012b, *Book Review of Making archaeology happen: design versus dogma,* in *RESCUE News* **116,** 7

van den Dries, M and Willems, W, 2007, Quality assurance in archaeology, the Dutch perspective, in Willems, W, and van den Dries, M, (eds), 50–65

Voltaire 1759, *Candide or Optimism,* (1947 with introduction by John Butt), West Drayton

Wainwright, G, 1987, Preservation by record: retrospect and prospect, in Mytum, H, and Waugh, K, (eds), 1987a, 115–22

Wainwright, G, 2000, Time Please, *Antiquity* **74.4,** 909–43

Walsh, D, 1969, *Report of the Committee of Enquiry into the arrangements for the protection of Field Monuments 1966–68*

Wheeler, R E M, 1927, History by excavation, *J of the Royal Society of Arts,* **85,** 812–35

Wilkins, B, 2012, Where the rubber hits the road: a critical analysis of archaeological decision making on highways projects in Ireland, in Cobb, H, *et al* (eds), 53–66

Willems, W, 1999, *The future of European archaeology,* (Oxbow Lecture 3), Oxford

Willems, W, and van den Dries, M (eds), 2007a, *Quality management in archaeology,* Oxford

Willems, W, and van den Dries, M, 2007b, The origins and development of quality assurance in archaeology, in Willems, W, and, van den Dries, M, (eds), 1–12

Chapter 17

'What force or guile?'[1]
A light from the past on our present. Tactical methods, strategic objectives and cultural motivation in British archaeology

John Walker

'*Airy generalizations about cultural change are the most superficial form of social comment. Take a few casual impressions, add some personal hunches, sprinkle with some statistics, and a plausible case can be made for almost any thesis about how the values of the British have changed*' (Kavanagh and Sheldon 1989, 240)

So cautioned Ivor Crewe in 1989: Although this piece contains all the elements that Crewe disparages, it has at least the virtue of reflecting some of the unpublished experience of working at Board level in archaeology over 35 critical years, and over a longer period having been both a national representative of employees and of the employers.

The present

As I sit in York, within a short distance of my office, The York Archaeological Trust, are excavating the largest site ever explored in the city. At the same time at the Jorvik Viking Centre are close to welcoming their 17 millionth visitor. This is all a startlingly different picture to the dire situation in York in 1972, recorded by Addyman (1974, 153–62). The last 40 years have seen a huge growth in archaeological provision in England, as a result, at least in part, of the arguments advanced by RESCUE in response to widespread destruction.

The early founders of the archaeological revolution saw some dangers in the growth and change they so eagerly sought. In the same volume (Rahtz 1974) in which York was described Chris Musson (1974, 81) noted the emergence of professional teams working in the fashion of consultant architects or engineers in private practice. These, he felt, should be closely considered to observe '*the light they throw on methods, objectives and personal motivation*'.

---

[1] '*What force or guile*' is a quote from a Robert Burns poem of c.1791 entitled '*Such a parcel of Rogues in a Nation*' the most popular version of which was released by the electric folk group Steeleye Span in 1973 as the Rahtz volume was being written.

Here I am attempting to look at these issues, to assess whether changes in these areas have been as beneficial as we might expect. Such an assessment is difficult because of the rarity of histories based upon the intimate knowledge of those working closely in more than one sector of archaeology. Jones's *Past Imperfect* (1984) stands out as one of the few written, from such a viewpoint, about the development of archaeology in England. Two newer volumes, one by Everill (2009) the other by Aitchison,(2012) have appeared which mark a step forward in this kind of historiography being based upon interviews, surveys or wide ranging case studies.

Musson's concerns addressed these different levels of archaeology, the tactical (methods), the strategic (objectives) and the cultural (motivation).These are considered in turn by examining what has happened in certain areas at each level.

Method: Tactical concerns and the digger's lament

A principle methodology of archaeology is excavation, at the centre of which is the excavator or digger; the only person in direct day-to-day contact with the archaeology. The digger, therefore, is an integral part of the archaeological process whatever approach to excavation is taken (*see* Carver 2009).

Paul Everill's study (2009) illustrates how little has improved for the diggers in terms of working conditions and opportunities since the 1970s. More recently an article entitled *Reskilling the Diggers: handing over the means of interpretation* (Harward 2012) described a 'disengaged, disenfranchised and disillusioned workforce' which prompted a response from the Federation of Archaeological Managers and Employers (FAME) (Tindall 2012). Harward is critical of the support, training and opportunities available to all archaeologists in the field in rescue archaeology, in what has now become a multi-million pound activity. The resulting dialogue within FAME raised a series of controversial points about the historical development of archaeology. There are, of course, those who dismiss this problem as simply the mutterings of a disgruntled, and relatively insignificant, few. Amongst those in seniority who do engage with the issues the answers offered, as to why problems persist, usually run along the following lines; over supply or uncertain demand. In the case of the Heathrow Terminal 5 project its organisers saw a different cause, and made strenuous and novel efforts to engage their diggers in all aspects of the process of investigation. It might be, however, that this continued problem itself is a symptom of aspects of deeper change that have occurred since the early days, which affect a core methodology (Thorpe 2012).

In the 1970's Musson's group were well known for hard digging and a deep commitment to archaeology, at a time when many field archaeologists were sovereign, organising, funding and leading excavations. As late as 1990, as can be shown by SCAUM papers, Unit Directors, still saw themselves as capable of over-riding government plans and policies.

The emergence of a competitive market (in which over 70% of archaeologists now operate) brought about significant changes (*see* Thorpe, Chapter 16; Powlesland, Chapter 11; Everill, Chapter 12). Archaeologists could apparently, more easily, become sovereign by setting up their own business, but many found that these new 'petty states' were fragile and dominated by forces outside of their control. Such forces included fierce untrammelled competition which weakened their voice in dealing with the state, and they became, in the words of one English Heritage staffer, no more than 'jobbing builders'. Over the same period, as the average value of fieldwork projects declined, heads of organisations were seen less as actively leading fieldworkers and more as 'suits' and disparaged as 'managers'; quasi-business people controlling many more, but smaller, projects.

The rise of the curatorial role in local government, fostered by Planning Policy Guidance 16, (PPG 16, DOE 1990) saw the emergence of a new level of detailed external command and control of fieldwork, further weakening the status of its practitioners (Walker 2001, 142). No longer were fieldworkers expert in their field; instead they were there to fulfil a task shaped by others. Ultimately, however, the controlling forces within local Government saw a continuing decline in the status of County Archaeologists within their own organisations, from major figures, to relatively minor members of staff within larger teams. These teams themselves are now being cut and closed.

From the Ministry of Public Buildings and Works of the early 1970s the quango English Heritage emerged in 1982 with the role of administering state funding for fieldwork, preserving sites, and advising on legislation. In time this agency came and to establish further command and control mechanisms over fieldwork practice (Wainwright 2000, 918) and to be merged with the RCHME (Royal Commission on the Historic Monuments of England). In terms of preservation, they failed to deliver a new Heritage Act and have cut their technical staff and, perhaps more significantly, their Inspectorate of Ancient Monuments.[2]

At national-level new bodies emerged, such as the Institute of Field Archaeologists (IFA, from 2008 the Institute *for* Archaeologists (IfA) and from 2015 the Chartered Institute for Archaeologists) with its role to develop and shape the profession. However, despite the increasing number of archaeological standards and guidelines fostered by the IfA, anyone can call themselves a professional archaeologist without necessarily holding formal IfA membership.

In parallel to these developments in local government provision and regulation, most Universities have seen a steady decline in the power and influence of professors and heads of department, as larger schools and faculties have been created. Various rounds of research and teaching assessments dominate academic activity and we have now reached the point where many universities, such as Birmingham, Manchester, Sheffield and Nottingham have ousted their fieldwork units. Today most Archaeology Departments

---

[2] At the time of writing, the Department for Culture Media and Sport was consulting on its proposal for the *New Model for English Heritage* (see https://www.gov.uk/government/news/new-model-for-english-heritage-moves-a-step-closer-following-consultation [accessed 1 December 2014]). Following a public consultation, and after this book had entered the production phase, the then Minister of State for Culture and the Digital Economy announced that the Government had approved the proposal to separate English Heritage into two organisations from 1 April 2015. English Heritage has now become a new body, envisaged to be a self-funding charity by 2023, to manage and promote the more than 400 properties and sites in the National Heritage Collection (*see* http://www.english-heritage.org.uk/). The other functions are now managed by Historic England which provides expert advice and acts as a champion for the sector. Some English Heritage roles referred to in this chapter are therefore now the responsibility of Historic England (*see* http://www.historicengland.org.uk/).

quietly dread the effects of a new fees regime and are now strenuously attempting to meet the latest assessment criteria (*see also* Everill, Chapter 10; Sinclair, Chapter 17)

As these new institutions have grown, so has the tendency for them to seek additional powers within archaeology for their own purposes, even though, like heads of department, council officers or state agents, their position within their own host-body may well be trivial. Naturally along with this has come, as the works of Max Weber (Anter 2014) argue, a series of controls and social norms based upon rational-legal authority seeking both to justify the superiority of each group's members, and of their group. The resulting debates about archaeological significance and values often touch on the absurd, but sadly they affect real lives, public good, and the potential of the discipline.

The successful field archaeologist of the 1970s had a host of alternative but related career opportunities, being able to move into museums, academia, agencies or local government. Today's sad result, reflecting the declining prestige of fieldwork and the rise of quasi-legal professional codes has been that such mobility is very rare as each subsector consolidates its own position and pursues its own agenda.

What has marked these 40 years is growth; but growth in which the sovereign power of the dynamic individual in the field, and their role as site or project director, has declined, and with it the prestige and importance of the fieldworker. In tandem unit directors, county archaeologists, professors, and even the representatives of national bodies have seen their real power decline and they struggle to shape the discipline, especially when it comes to the practice of fieldwork. Given what has happened at the top it is no surprise that some diggers should feel themselves 'a disengaged, disenfranchised and disillusioned workforce' (Harward 2012) because in practice there is no-one who is willing or able to solve their problems.

Objectives: Strategic confusion?

The majority of the early progenitors of change had as their objective the creation of a state service (*see* Thorpe, Chapter 16) whereas what has emerged is a mixed economy in which the state-led heritage cycle has a major role. Carver (2009, 370–75) has outlined how in modern archaeology the 'heritage cycle' in archaeology has a very strong emphasis on conservation objectives and management. These emphases mirror one of the key demands of the Rescue movement (Rahtz, 1974), but a fixation with them can mask another critical, early, objective to explore the remains of the past.

This concern with the objective of preservation has led, in planning circles, to many seeing archaeological remains as part of what has become known as the historic environment (HE). In terms of exploring the past the concept of the historic environment fosters an appreciation of the interrelationships between different aspects of the past, such as archaeology and history. Although this concept echoes the work of such pioneers as Grinsell (1958) and Hoskins (1955) it goes much further. *Historic Environment,* the refereed journal of the Australian branch of ICOMOS, for example, to quote its preface '*brings together dynamic, critical, interdisciplinary research in the field of cultural heritage and heritage conservation*' (Australia ICOMOS 2013). In England Historic Environment is something that The Department of Culture, Media and Sport (DCMS) defines as '*the physical legacy of thousands of years of human activity in this country, in the form of buildings, monuments, sites and landscapes*' (DCMS 2012)

Clearly the physical legacy (in all its forms, including artefacts) of thousands of years of human activity is the domain of archaeology. But what of other related subjects, and the interdisciplinary approach that, to some, is the hallmark, or even rationale, of historic environment work? For history, the Blue Plaque Scheme, run by English Heritage, celebrates famous former residents of buildings (although not Dame Thora Hird according to a recent decision, BBC 2012). Clearly, both history and archaeology have their own sets of values about what is worthy of preservation. The problems arising from this relationship between historical events and the historic environment is illustrated by the difficulties in dealing with battlefield sites. The historical significance of Historic Battlefields seems clear and dramatic. They are seen to be worthy of preservation, yet physically they are not only difficult to locate precisely, and often leave few tangible remains. In practice, as soon as questions of value, especially academic value, arise, even between two relatively close disciplines such as archaeology and history, an interdisciplinary approach to the preservation of a historic environment becomes fraught with difficulties about establishing what constitutes common value.

To address this kind of dilemma, particularly within the defined neo-liberal economic context of the United States, there is a renewed interest in attempting to quantify the monetary value of heritage assets. Like so many things originating in the US this approach began to be adopted in Europe under various guises; non-use value, bequest-value, option-value or contingent-value method (CVM). To some extent this export of liberal market economics has been less successful on this side of the Atlantic. Gibson and Pendlebury's (2009) recent book, for example, highlights how the value of historic assets lies not in simple economic criteria but in the complex interplay of cultural, economic, political and social factors at any given time or state of knowledge.

The current Government Green Economy Council sponsored by DEFRA is the spearhead of a movement to commodify the landscape, and to it are submitted the findings of the Ecosystems Markets Task Force. Together the 33 members of these bodies, of whom 32 are drawn from major commercial, industrial or financial bodies, seek to revolutionise the British approach to the environment from a market prospective.[3] Perhaps this overall approach to the environment, historic and otherwise, is best summed up by Professor Bateman's address in May 2012 to the Task Force (Bateman 2012). In his view Her Majesties Government uses three broad approaches to achieve its ends; voluntary agreements, regulation and/or market mechanisms. He argues that the first two approaches have severe limitations and implies that a market-based approach must be best. It follows

---

[3] The report of the Ecosystems Markets Task Force was, submitted to the Department of the Environment and rural affairs in March 2013 and published in September 2013. It makes 22 recommendations, including their top 5 priorities: biodiversity offsetting; bio-energy and anaerobic digestion; sustainable local wood-fuel; nature based certification and labelling; and water cycle catchment management. DEFRA, (Department for Environment, Food & Rural Affairs, 2013, *Realising nature's value: The final report of the Ecosystem Markets Task Force: Government response*, at https://www.gov.uk/government/publications/government-response-to-the-final-report-of-the-ecosystem-markets-task-force (accessed 1 December 2014)

logically that to create a market in what were public goods requires that they be charted and mapped and private rights established. He admits it will not all be easy and illustrates the point by considering the case of tigers. He states *'people hold values for tigers even if (they have) no plans to visit, but just for their existence; however measuring these values is extremely problematic'* and recommends a cost-effectiveness approach requiring *'information on costs (mainly foregone profit) and effectiveness...to identify a minimum conservation area...that delivers an efficient win-win'*. The Task Force have now reported to the Green Economy Council to the DTI and Defra who have fostered this development.

There are many who have lived through the growth of liberal market economics and the continuing collapse from 2007 who would find such views either naïve or, suspiciously, the start of another wave of privatisation of public goods for personal gain. Certainly the wave of historic landscape characterisation and similar Historic Environment initiatives will aid this process (*see* DCMS 2013, 35).

There is, of course, an alternative view; for centuries a fundamental of English law is that common goods were vested in the Crown. Surprisingly even freeholds were effectively not a right but held by permission of the Crown. Whilst in Scotland all antiquities are still the property of the Crown under the law of *Bona Vacantia*, and aspects of the same right are still exercised in England by the Duchy of Lancaster, in England during the recent debacle over selling public forests (DEFRA 2011) it was scarcely noticed that all the antiquities they contained, save those covered by the limited Treasure Act, would pass from public ownership to private hands.

In the world of planning-archaeology commercial objectives and values came to be even more important, through competition within archaeology and in the world of development, in framing archaeological responses to destruction. Such competition, together with the advance of state agencies and professional bodies encouraged the growth in regulation or oversight (Walker 2001).

The justification of such rules, often of dubious legality, relied in most cases on arguments about fairness, standards, quality and, in the case of public-agency grants, ensuring value for money. As objectives they are all laudable, but raise two issues: are they achievable and if so at what cost?

The costs are twofold. Firstly, there has been an enormous rise in the cost of preparing designs and monitoring work since the 1970s, and it has been suggested that overall this has led to a rise in costs of 15% (Walker 2001). Another hidden cost which significant numbers of fieldworkers in the profession, both in academe and in the commercial sector, complain of a laboriously enforced uniformity of approach being imposed upon them, often by officials divorced from the realities of fieldwork, and the existence of so-called 'cowboy' enterprises.

Whatever else has happened, the current form of competition and commodification in archaeology sets new objectives for organisations. The formal logic of survival, for organisations in such a market, is to have low overheads, minimum fixed-costs, minimum capital-investment, and to possess long pockets gained through an ability to reap abnormal profits (Walker 2001 142). Immediate survival, to many, appears to depend on achieving objectives at the minimum cost and maximum price, not as before delivering the maximum public benefit from the available resources.

Culture: Personal motivations

The success of regulatory aims depends not merely upon enforcement or realism but also upon the moral motivations of those involved. Mussons' third point (1974, 87–9) was to wonder about what kind of new personal motivations of archaeologists might emerge. It is, of course, enormously difficult to chart such motivations but some attempt can be made to describe the dominant cultural motifs of the period of growth.

The 1970s were a period in archaeology of political and cultural dynamism. The picture until recently in England has been more staid. The conception of neo-liberal market economics has perhaps been the dominant economic motif in England since the election of Margaret Thatcher in 1979. In practice this concept re-shaped the conduct of archaeology both directly through changes to the funding-regime, and by applying the idea of open competition to institutions as diverse as universities and local charities.

To many this concept was welcome as it went hand-in-hand with the creation of Planning Policy Guidance 16 (DOE 1990). The rise of the associated market has allowed archaeology to grow since 1974. As this growth has, to some, been beneficial (*see* Aitchison 2012) the virtues of applying this market model to archaeological provision are obvious and, as such, deserve support.

In fact what limited evidence there is suggests that supporters of the market may have confused cause with mechanism. Aitchison's (2012) survey of the numbers of archaeologists in England and Europe shows that the number of archaeologist in each nation are proportional to its GDP at the time. What these archaeologist do, however, depends (as first suggested by Daniel 1976) upon their national culture. One could equally well argue that the current system for funding archaeology in England is simply the easiest mechanism to adopt given the country's political fixations in recent decades.

In addition to the new commercial objectives besetting each sector of archaeology there is a growing body of evidence that the market imposes deeper moral values. Most recently for example the work of Professor Michael Sandel (2012) of Harvard suggests markets have adverse consequences for morals because the processes are often unfair and degrade what is being marketed. The reality in archaeology now is that we have probably moved from a phase of accommodating a new commercial reality to one, in many cases, of seeing it as a new truth containing within it a deeper moral virtue. Yet at the same time archaeology is failing to confront the abundant evidence that markets fail to deal adequately with public goods such as preserving or recording our past.

Conclusion

In the past I (in Walker 2001), and others, have argued that the present system is seriously under-performing. Looking back at the worries expressed in 1974, we can add some further concerns at a tactical, operational and cultural level. If we cannot solve the concerns of those who excavate our past, are not clear about the fundamental objectives of archaeology, and accept that there are inappropriate market effects in dealing with public goods, then we must accept that despite the positive growth experienced, we are far from perfection.

The early founders of RESCUE looked to Government to provide answers, but if Prof Bateman is right that the state has a prejudice against voluntary agreements and further regulation, then the only answer does appear to be the market. This is scarcely credible at a time when the effect of the deregulated banking-market has created so many unseen problems. As faith in politicians, the market, and the state has reached a new low, so the search for new approaches to common problems, goods, and needs is growing (Taylor 2012).

Those early RESCUE founders, in seeking the support of Government, effectively sought an answer based upon creating institutions. The intervening years have seen the growth of a view that institutions, be they companies, trusts, universities, agencies, or voluntary societies are disposable assets to be shaped and formed by market conditions or political imperatives.

More recently there has come a belated recognition from such unlikely sources as the International Monetary Fund (Abed and Gupta, 2002) and Cameron's Big Society agenda that institutions are crucial to the delivery of any progress. They represent delivery mechanisms greater than the sum of their parts, and effectively shape actions and possibility.

Perhaps for those whose hopes of an enlightened state have proved disappointing there is a small glimmer of hope? In terms of British archaeology perhaps the most significant long term change has been in allowing Scotland and Wales, through devolution, true legal autonomy in dealing with their heritage. In practice, as some studies have shown (Aitchison 2012, Walker 2001), many of the real innovations and advances in archaeology over the last 40 years have not occurred at state-level but locally. These changes reflect the reality that cultural needs and archaeological remains vary wildly across the country.

Here, perhaps, is a key to the future at a time of great uncertainty. Should we not turn away from the rigidity of Research Assessments, briefs and specifications and regulations, and encourage local and regional creativity in the hope that in such diversity new opportunities and possibilities may emerge?

The nature of British archaeology is a product of its culture. Archaeology, however, is at its most exciting when its actions and discoveries shine a light from the past on our present cultural problems and potential. To do this it requires its own institutions and approaches. The tension between these two factors is at its height at a time when our archaeological culture is both more controlling and under greater financial pressure than 40 years ago and yet the benefits of so much past human activity and experiment have yet to be studied or reaped.

References

Abed, G T, and Gupta, S, (eds), 2002, Governance, corruption and economic performance, International Monetary Fund

Addyman, P, 1974, York: The anatomy of a crisis in urban archaeology, 153–62 in Rahtz, 1974

Aitchison, K, 2012, *Breaking new ground: how professional archaeology work,* Kindle edn, Landward Research, Ltd, Sheffield

Anter, A, 2014, *Max Weber's theory of the modern state: origins, structure and significance* (trans Keith Tribe)

Basingstoke Australia ICOMOS, 2013, Historic Environment: about the journal, at http://australia. icomos.org/publications/historic-environment (accessed 29 January, 2013)

Bateman, I, 2012, Address in May 2012 to the Ecosystems Market Task Force, at http://www.defra. gov.uk/ecosystem-markets/files/Briefing-Paper-for-the-EMTF-Professor-Ian-Bateman-final. pdf (accessed 20 July, 2012)

BBC, 2012, English Heritage defends Thora Hird blue plaque decision, at http://www.bbc.co.uk/ news/entertainment-arts-17895094 (accessed 20 July, 2012)

Carver, M, 2009, *Archaeological Investigation*

Daniel, G, 1976, *One hundred and fifty years of archaeology* (2nd edn), Harvard

Department of Culture Media and Sport (DCMS), 2012, *What we do; Historic Environment,* at http://www.culture.gov.uk/what_we_do/historic_environment/default.aspx (accessed 20 July, 2012)

Department of Culture Media and Sport (DCMS), 2013, *English Heritage New Model. Consultation,* at http://www.gov.uk/government/uploads/system/uploads/attachment_data/ file/263943/121_B_English_heritage_Accessible_1_.pdf (accessed 24 Nov 2014)

Department for Environment, Food and Rural Affairs (DEFRA), 2011, *Consultation document on the ownership and management of the 18% of England's woodland currently run by the Forestry Commission,* 27 January 2011, at https://www.gov.uk/government/news/new-direction-for-england-s-public-forest-estate (accessed 6 Nov 2014)

Department of the Environment (DOE), 1990, *Planning Policy Guidance 16: archaeology and planning (PPG 16)* HMSO, London

Everill, P, 2009, *The Invisible Diggers: A study of British commercial archaeology,* Heritage Research Series 1, Oxbow Books, Oxford

Gibson, L, and Pendlebury, J (eds), 2009, *Valuing Historic Assets*

Grinsell, L, 1958, *Archaeology of Wessex,* Methuen London

Harward, C, 2012, Reskilling the diggers: handing over the means of interpretation, *The Archaeologist* **83,** 26–29

Hoskins, W G, 1955, The making of the English landscape (Pelican edn 1970) Harmondsworth

Jones, B, 1984, *Past imperfect: the story of rescue archaeology,* Heinemann, London

Kavanagh, D, and Sheldon, A, (eds), 1989, *The Thatcher effect: a decade of change,* Oxford

Musson, C, 1974, Rescue digging all the time, in Rahtz 1974, 79–89

Rahtz, P A, (ed), 1974, *Rescue Archaeology,* Pelican, Harmondsworth

Sandel, M, 2012, *What money can't buy: the moral limits of markets,* Farrar, Straus and Giroux, New York Taylor, M, 2012, *Power failure,* RSA Journal Autumn 2012, 10–15

Thorpe, R, 2012, Often fun, usually messy: fieldwork, recording and higher orders of things, in Cobb, H, *et al* (eds), *Reconsidering archaeological fieldwork. Exploring the on-site relationship between theory and practice,* Springer, New York, 31–52

Tindall, A, 2012, Response to Harward, *The Archaeologist* **83**, 31

Wainwright, G, 2000, Time Please, *Antiquity* **74.4**, 909–43

Walker, J, 2001, Some Myths of Public Service, in Higham, N J, (ed), *Archaeology of the Roman Empire: a memorial to Professor G D B, Jones, British Archaeol Rep Internat Ser* **940**, 141–6

Chapter 18

Teaching the next generation

Anthony Sinclair

Introduction

For a number of years, archaeological employers have stated that the next generation of archaeologists is poorly prepared for entering the profession. In surveys of the professional labour market in the UK, employers have identified a large number of essential skills lacking in the next generation (Aitchison and Edwards 2008, 109). They have also noted that new entrants require considerable training to make them effective archaeological professionals (Aitchison and Edwards 2003, 57). A similar view has been expressed by a majority of commercial archaeologists (Everill 2012). Yet this impression contrasts dramatically with the perceptions of archaeology students themselves. In the National Student Survey, taken in the final year of study, students state overwhelmingly that they are satisfied with their university education (Sinclair and Taktak 2012). Furthermore, archaeology students express higher levels of satisfaction than students of engineering, medicine, law, and accountancy, all degree courses that are designed with employment needs clearly in mind, and often professionally accredited (HEFCE 2011, 25–6; HEPI 2012, table 5). The last external review of the teaching of archaeology in the UK, judged teaching in departments as 'good', and mostly 'excellent' (QAA 2003). Evidently something is both right and wrong in the teaching of archaeology today.

Archaeologists working in universities are seen to argue that the present demands of higher education: for internationally excellent research outputs, an active research environment, research-led teaching, the attraction of a sufficient number of students, and the teaching of a broad range of skills so that graduates might be employed across a range of graduate employment sectors, do not allow them to dedicate their degrees to the purpose of training professional field-archaeologists. '*This is rightly the task of employers*', they might say. Archaeological employers, competing for contract work or curating the archaeological resource, are exasperated that the principal group currently responsible for teaching archaeological skills, the universities, do not produce graduates with the right skills needed to enter the profession bearing their own name. '*That should be the first priority of a professional education*', they could reply.

If we hope to prepare the next generation better than the present one, however, we need first to understand how, to whom, and in what circumstances archaeology is taught.

We can then place this understanding firmly in the context of archaeology's changing nature, as both a developing investigation into the human species and human societies, and as an evolving educational and professional practice in a contemporary market economy. Here I shall concentrate on education rather than professional practice, and I shall take as my focus the nature of teaching in the 'average department of archaeology in a UK university'. Of course there is tremendous variation in what is taught in terms of chronological period, geographical area, practical skills both in the field and laboratory, and in the manner of teaching between departments and within. This reflects their different staff specialisms on the one hand and the absence of a strict curriculum for the subject on the other (QAA 2007, Sinclair and Beck 2012). I recognise that there are also now a suite of vocational qualifications for archaeology, the National Vocational Qualifications in Archaeological Practice, but these qualifications are taken by individuals who already hold a prior degree, almost always in archaeology, as part of a program of continuing professional development.

I shall also not argue for a particular form of teaching and learning, such as has been the case for enquiry-based learning, or blended-learning in a number of disciplines. The diversity of things that need to be learned as an archaeologist makes a single approach inappropriate. Through the years I have met graduates from most universities who are well-able to meet the needs of the professional archaeological sector; I have even heard reports of them from colleagues in the professional sector. The problem as perceived, though, relates to the 'average level' of archaeological skills of the 'average graduate' from the 'average department'. The issues I address below focus on why this average is where it is. Surveys also suggest that archaeology is not the only profession where employers are concerned at graduate skills: it is one of many (Adecco 2012, CBI 2011).

I believe that the difficulties we currently face cannot be resolved without significant structural changes to the broader systems in which we work. Unfortunately, these structural changes go against the primary driving forces that give shape to Archaeology in the UK today and are likely to do so for the next few years. In the spirit of 'blue-skies thinking', however, I shall identify what some of these structural changes must be and what we might do about them in an ideal world. In brief, I shall argue firstly that students need to get an understanding of archaeology as a specific subject before they start in higher education, so that the learning which takes place on degree courses can enhance this basic learning rather than starting from a hypothetical blank slate. This is essential because of the expansion of archaeology in terms of knowledge and practice. Secondly, we need to ensure that archaeology in higher education can be studied widely beyond the confines of the self-called 'research-intensive universities' in which it is predominantly studied at present in order to ensure that professional and vocational skills are as valuable to teachers of archaeology as is research reputation. Thirdly, students who aspire to become the next generation of professional archaeologists must be able to get an authentic experience of professional practice during their education so that they can develop the expertise required by employers. This will require educational institutions and employers to work more closely together as partners in a common enterprise and not as producers and consumers respectively of a human product. Finally, professional archaeology must be able to offer long-term career prospects to new entrants to the profession to persuade students (and their parents) to invest in the educational training necessary for archaeological practice.

Archaeology as a problematic

Problem 1: the availability of archaeology as a subject of study

A curious combination of qualities makes the teaching and learning of archaeology immensely difficult to get right.

- Archaeology overlaps significantly in its interests with a number of other well-established disciplines (history, geography, biology, physics and chemistry). For most students, these subjects are present from an early stage in the curriculum, allowing the inherent knowledge and skills required to be developed cumulatively and progressively. Archaeology, however, never comes together as a single subject until almost the last moment. Following the demise of the GCSE archaeology in 2006 (Henson 2008), archaeology as a single subject can be studied only from the age of 16 in the form of an A-level.

- Archaeology graduates are not accepted on all teacher-training courses in the UK, resulting in a limited availability of staff to teach A-level archaeology in schools. A-level archaeology courses are taught in just a few schools and predominantly in further education colleges.

- Many fewer students take the A-level in archaeology than is the estimated potential demand for the subject (CBA 2009).

- Restricted availability of the A-level means that, for most students with an interest in the subject, the first available formal teaching in archaeology takes the form of a degree in higher education.

The impact of these factors is that students must make an active and often exceptional choice to study archaeology; it is not a subject they just drift into. Students must seek out the opportunity to do the A-level at an institution often different to that in which they have completed their GCSEs, or in which they may be doing the rest of their A-levels. Or they must choose it as a degree subject without any previous experience of what it is like or how interesting they might find it, or indeed how good they might be at it. In turn, curriculum-designers of undergraduate degree programmes must assume that most students will bring no prior knowledge or experience of archaeology to their course, creating a very short window of time (usually 3 years) in which to progress from novice to 'expert'. This becomes ever more difficult as archaeology develops as a discipline and a practice. This time-stress is further compounded for students studying in England and Northern Ireland (and non-Welsh or non-Scottish students studying in Wales or Scotland respectively) by the loss of university maintenance grants available to all and the advent of tuition fees in 1998. Most students now combine some form of part-time work alongside their largely full-time degree studies. The reality is that students taking degrees in archaeology are usually studying, on average, for approximately 27 hours per week (HEPI 2012, fig 5).

Within UK education, the curriculum narrows sharply in range, especially after 16 years of age. In Scotland, many students will take just 5 subjects after 16 years of age. In England the situation is more extreme still. Students will usually specialise in 3, sometimes 4, subjects prior to university. The advantage of this specialisation is that it can work well in preparing individuals for a specialist higher education, assuming that they have made the right choice of subjects at A-level (Sutton Trust 2010), and that they can follow and develop a subject strand through their educational career. The (usual) absence of archaeology from the curriculum prior to higher education, however, means that archaeology degree-programmes have a student cohort with a huge range of variation in prior knowledge, and with no necessary and common core of knowledge on which to build. Attempts to broaden the 16–19 curriculum, which might help archaeology in higher education, such as the recommendation for the introduction of a 5-subject system like the European baccalaureates (DfES 1988) have had little real impact, because of the perceived quality of existing academic qualifications, principally the A-level.

Problem 2: the diverse mix of knowledge and skills

The second significant difficulty in the educational system for archaeology is that it requires the acquisition of a specific suite of specialist knowledge and cognitive skills as well as specialist practical techniques.

- Archaeology requires a considerable knowledge of evidence that must be gained through extensive reading of published sources and practical sessions in laboratories, as well as a technical practice requiring considerable individual experience to develop a mastery of its skills most usually acquired through participation on fieldwork training projects (QAA 2007, 1–4).

- Archaeology, rarely amongst the arts and humanities, is a discipline with a substantial and independent existence beyond the academic, and a significant number of students take archaeology as a degree with this aim in mind (Jackson and Sinclair 2009). Students, therefore, also require a specific knowledge of legislation and professional practice (QAA 2007: 12) not needed for other humanities subjects.

- Archaeology as a discipline has expanded enormously in its range of interpretive tools (appropriated from across the arts and social sciences) and in its methods (appropriated from an expanding range of sciences), its time-depth of study, and its geographic scope. The conceptual knowledge of the archaeologist has therefore increased considerably decade upon decade (for an example of this in relation to Palaeolithic archaeology *see* Sinclair 2009, 2012). The investigative methods available to address current questions have also increased considerably.

Archaeology straddles two major fault-lines in the educational system of the UK. The first divides subjects into arts and humanities on the one hand, and sciences on the other; the second divides subjects that can be classified as academic on the one hand and practical/vocational on the other. In the UK this fault-line has structured the educational system from secondary education upwards with, at its most extreme, the development of separate schools, colleges and higher education institutions for the two groupings, along with separate qualification systems (GCSEs, GCEs and degrees for academic subjects; national diplomas, technical qualifications and NVQs for the vocational). Students are selected for entry into the academic side of the system from an early age. Progression within the academic system depends on the level of achievement reached in academic qualifications that primarily test linguistic and logical skills. Academic qualifications are, therefore, graded according to levels of achievement most of which are defined above the level of a 'pass'. Vocational qualifications, however, are designed to recognise the attainment of competence in a skill, and may address a wide diversity of skills. An effective archaeologist requires a broad range of skills, and students taking degrees in the subject bring with them skills from across this range.

Reviews of the UK educational system have consistently identified the separation between academic and vocational as problematic; vocational education is persistently undervalued in comparison with academic education. As students have been required to remain in full-time education for longer, and as systems of apprenticeship into crafts and industries became less available, the quality of vocational education has suffered (DfE 2011). Attempts to recombine academic and vocational qualifications into a single system, such as those proposed in the Tomlinson Report (DfES 2004), or via the aborted Diploma qualifications designed to replace GCSEs and A-levels for 14 to 19 year olds (Gillard 2011) have made no headway because of the continued perceived quality of existing academic qualifications; the 'gold standard of the A-level'.

Whilst archaeology straddles this fault-line as a discipline, in the real world of education it is firmly placed within the academic grouping. The principal qualification needed to become an archaeologist is a first degree. Almost all professional UK archaeologists younger than 30 years of age possess a first degree as their lowest educational qualification (Aitchison and Edwards 2008, table 39; Everill 2012); many possess higher degrees. Archaeological degrees are offered at approximately 40 higher education institutions out of 145 within the UK. Almost all of these institutions are traditional universities (recognised by charter prior to 1992), and most would consider themselves to be 'research-intensive' universities (Sinclair 2010). These universities pride themselves on their increasingly global reputation, gained largely through the size of the research grants received, the number, quality and citations of research outputs produced by their staff, and their attractiveness to foreign students. Entry to these universities is made ever more difficult by a steady increase in the required level of prior academic attainment (the required tariff score on the UCAS entry form), but this only serves to increase competition amongst students for places.

Students actively seek entry to these universities because they (and their parents) believe that they possess a reputation that enables their graduates to move into good employment or on to further academic study. An arts and humanities degree is seen as a route into a broad range of potential graduate-level forms of employment. Major employers across a broad range of employment sectors seem to actively target these universities for their new intake of graduate recruits on account of the reputation of the university. The specific nature of the degree taken is often less important than the possession of a range of graduate-level skills.

Whilst there have been repeated attempts to widen participation into universities, and especially the traditional universities, by raising aspirations through schools outreach programmes, or providing incentives in the form of means-tested bursaries, the majority of students at these universities come from a social/parental background that is still overwhelmingly professional, well-educated, with a higher percentage of students coming from a private education (currently 18% for archaeology), and with a low proportion coming from families whose parents engage in manual labour (Sutton Trust 2010). Archaeology is also poor in terms of its ethnic mix with no more than 3% from a non-white-British background (Benjamin 2003, 2006).

Problem 3: archaeology as competitive professional practice

Finally, significant developments in the nature of professional archaeological practice in the UK over the last 20 years have changed both the suite of graduate skills required by archaeological employers, and their ability to offer continuing professional development to their staff. These developments have also widened the gulf in shared experience between professional archaeologists who are practitioners and those who are 'researcher/lecturers'.

- The advent of Planning Policy Guidance note 16: 'Archaeology and Planning' (PPG 16), which was the logical response to the practical and financial problems of Rescue Archaeology cemented a change in archaeological practice in which archaeological fieldwork went from a desired but occasional activity (rescue and research archaeology) to a requirement within the planning process in which the costs were no longer met by local or national government but by developers (English Heritage 1995; Darvill and Russell 2002, Thorpe, Chapter 16).

- Commercial archaeology is highly competitive, professional archaeological contractors compete with each other regionally and often nationally for contracts.

- The employment of archaeologists with a high level of practical skill and experience can help complete a contract more quickly than the employment of those with lower levels of skill.

- Competition between archaeological contractors means that employers cannot easily afford to fund the training of new recruits in the way that other graduate recruiters do.

- Competition between archaeological contractors for work, allied to the cost of labour as a proportion of the overall cost, serves to ensure that professional contractors keep wages low in order to remain competitive with one another. Many archaeological contractors employ the site staff they need for the duration of the contract alone.

This particular and peculiar set of characteristics and developments in archaeology helps explain the contradictory views on archaeological education set out in the introductory paragraph. The majority of students of archaeology have followed a largely academic track in their education from their early teens. They have actively chosen a degree at a traditional university with a high academic reputation that is taught with a research performance in mind in a subject in which they may have little if any prior experience. They progress fast and well in higher education since they already have a high academic record of achievement and they are taught from a low expected base-knowledge. Archaeology graduates then enter a broad range of careers much like their contemporary arts graduates who follow degree courses with no obvious vocational direction (Jackson and Sinclair 2009). The nature of teaching on archaeological degree programmes within research-intensive universities addresses this cohort very well and the high level of student satisfaction in the National Student Survey records this.

Archaeological employers, on the other hand, seek individuals with a level of practical/ vocational skills ('professional competence') high enough to enable them to compete effectively for developer-funded contracts initiated through the planning process. They believe that a university education in archaeology should be able to produce individuals with such skills. Unfortunately, the academic rather than the vocational education-system in which archaeology exists is not designed, or expected, to produce individuals with this level of practical skill. Students, themselves, are rarely aware of this aspect of archaeological practice prior to making their decision to study archaeology. Professional archaeologists in universities often have little depth of experience of professional field-archaeology: they are usually employed on the basis of a proven record that will contribute to a university's research reputation and income, and not for their knowledge or experience of professional practice.

There are notable exceptions amongst both universities and employers in terms of training offered to staff, and preparation for professional archaeological employment, but the overall picture is as described above; it should not surprise any professional archaeologists, whether they happen to be researchers, teachers, field archaeologists, local-government curators or staff in national agencies. Missing, however, has been an appreciation of the complexities of the situation. Professional archaeology and archaeology in higher education both exist within much larger systems beyond their own immediate control. Only changes to the broader systems will impact lower down.

Changes on the horizon

Some large-scale changes are coming, some already beginning to come into effect.

- The replacement of PPG 16 by Planning Policy Statement 5 *'Planning for the Historic Environment'* (DCLG 2010), and now a combined National Planning Policy Framework (DCLG 2012 *see below*) has directed the nature of professional practice away from one focussed on the mitigation of damage to the archaeological remains, and directs it more towards the interpretation of the archaeological record for the benefit of the general public. The recent report of the Southport Group has argued that this may change the nature of professional archaeological work, favouring contractors that offer a quality of interpretation (Southport Group 2011).

- Revisions to the research assessment system for universities now require departments also to demonstrate the impact of their research beyond academia (Research Enhancement Framework 2012). Impact or 'knowledge transfer', as this is also sometimes called, will ideally encourage interaction with professional archaeological contractors, making the work undertaken by both universities and contractors of relevance to the other.

- Since 2012 students are required to take out loans to pay much higher tuition-fees for their degrees (up to a maximum of £9000 *per annum*). The intention of these funding changes is that students should take a degree because of the employment advantages that arise from becoming a graduate, and they should pay directly for this optional benefit (Bekhradnia 2011). The publication of Key Information Sets on university costs, teaching contact hours, National Student Survey results, and graduate employability rates for degree courses will be used to inform their choice of university and degree course.

The longer-term impact of the first two changes remains as yet difficult to estimate. In July 2012, all planning policy statements were superseded by a combined, and significantly more compact, National Planning Policy Framework (DCLG 2012), and whilst it is believed that the aims of PPS 5 remain intact (English Heritage 2012) we have yet to see its potential changes to archaeological practice since the economic crisis critically affecting the professional archaeological sector in the UK (Aitchison 2010) has yet to lift. The revised research assessment system for universities will make its first assessment in 2014. Experience of the previous system suggests that it is likely to take a decade before the introduction of 'research impact' restructures university practices. This leaves the changes to university funding as the fundamental change that will first affect the system described above.

Universities are considerably exercised by the possible consequences of the new funding system. As independent businesses, they must predict income and expenditure in circumstances unlike any in the recent past. Specifically whilst the expenditure for any academic year is largely determined a year in advance, a third of the income from students is not certain until a month or so before the start of the academic year. Current policy (BIS 2011) will lead to a major reduction in the financial support offered for the teaching of the hard sciences and the medical sciences, and a complete removal of this support for the arts, humanities and social sciences. University managers recognise that they need to attract sufficient students to come to their university, meet the expectations of these students in terms of value for fees, and, finally, make a profit on each transaction. Other sources of income beyond tuition fees for UK students will be an essential part of any financial plan. It cannot be stated loudly enough that since 2012 higher education for students taking degrees in the arts, humanities and social sciences (including archaeology) in England and Northern Ireland have effectively become a form of private education and a considerable personal investment.

Archaeology departments will certainly be affected by funding changes, but it is unlikely that they will lead to a more vocational form of archaeological teaching. In the last 15 years university-based archaeology has enjoyed an almost golden age (Sinclair 2010). Most departments have increased their staff numbers, improved their evaluations of research quality, and increased the number of postgraduate students, especially doctoral students completing their theses. A number of new departments were created at the Universities of Aberdeen, Central Lancashire, the Highlands and Islands, and Worcester.

This story of growth and success is now problematic. Archaeology in higher education has managed to develop in the way that it has, whilst retaining a steady undergraduate student population, despite falling application numbers. Staff increases have led to many departments now having a high staff: to student ratio with fewer than 20 students to 1 member of staff (*The Guardian* 2012). The costs of teaching archaeology are considerably higher than other subjects in the arts and humanities because they are increased by fieldwork and laboratory-based teaching. Funding council data indicates that the cost of teaching archaeology is £8,567 per annum (HEFCE 2012, Annex C), leaving a very small margin of profit against a full £9000 annual fee for each student. Archaeology will not be the first teaching-area considered for expansion by university managers. Indeed the recent review of the Institute of Archaeology and Antiquity at the University of Birmingham with a proposal to cease teaching a single honours degree in Archaeology (University of Birmingham 2012), emphasises the fragility of the financial model for teaching archaeology in higher education as currently perceived by university managers.

Even so, many departments will still need to increase their student numbers and/or reduce their staffing costs to break even. Staff retirement without replacement will lead inevitably to gaps in skills-teaching in some departments. Increases in student numbers will be more difficult to achieve. It is not clear that there is any cohort of well-qualified students who did not get a place to study archaeology as a single-honours degree, despite wanting to do so, who might now be admitted. Current university applications already indicate that any increase comes from students taking archaeology in addition to a subject with which they are familiar from A-level. Universities, therefore, must target joint degrees and combine archaeology with subjects in other formats (Major and Minor subjects for example), so as to spread some of the teaching load across the campuses by attracting new students into archaeology. In this circumstance the problems of practical teaching and a compact curriculum and prior experience will be exacerbated still further. There are real fears that the teaching of archaeology in universities will contract in the new funding regime.

A new structure for archaeology?

The discussion above presents a depressing picture for teaching the next generation. There may be fewer students on full-time courses, with those present taking just a part of an archaeology degree, whilst there are still too many archaeology graduates to find employment in professional archaeology (Aitchison 2004). There is every likelihood that students, and their parents, who must fund a degree in a research-intensive university are not likely to consider lowly-paid employment in professional field-archaeology attractive. This is especially so when accompanied by a high-level of student debt. Evidence for this can be seen in the fact that application numbers for single-honours archaeology degrees starting in 2012 have fallen below the sector average in these universities. Professional archaeology may need to search for its new recruits from abroad: individuals trained in cheaper higher-education systems. It could also recruit direct from the A-level cohort, but this would not address the skills deficit of new entrants. There would still be real issues about the level of skills and the suitability of such students to progress in the profession beyond basic excavation (Aitchison 2008). This would be a great loss, since archaeology still offers a great education for students and a great benefit to the nation. What might really change the system?

In the immediate and medium term the profession as a whole must seek to make archaeology more available and prominent in the education system below higher education. We should focus on the A-level: it already exists and the current syllabus (AQA 2007) is a good introduction to its methods, practices and key interpretive themes. Archaeology's status, as a mix of arts, maths, and science, and as an applied subject with commercial application in the contemporary world, has much to offer students at 16–19 years of age. I would hope that teacher-training institutions could be persuaded to accept more readily graduates with joint degrees with archaeology as trainee teachers for both their subject areas. Subjects such as geography, history, and classics, that are included in the most common joint degrees with archaeology, already make reference to Archaeological remains and archaeological skills of interpretation and evaluation of evidence in their GCSE syllabi. Secondary education teachers of these subject areas could draw students straightforwardly into an A-level in archaeology without expecting them to make a leap of faith. The A-level in archaeology could be made considerably more geographically available and accessible. Certainly more people with an experience and appreciation of archaeology would flow into the population at large. There are approximately 1500 students taking archaeology A-level, but according to research by the Council for British Archaeology many thousands (perhaps more than 30,000) would take the qualification if there were more centres in which was taught (CBA 2009).

With an expanded A-level cohort, more students might follow into archaeology in higher education. Indeed, it might become the norm for an archaeology degree student to have an A-level in the subject. This would allow university degrees to build on this learning at A-level and include learning that would support a broader and deeper knowledge of the subject. Indeed, the recent consultation on A-level reform instituted by the Office of Qualifications and Examinations Regulation (Ofqual 2012) has indicated a government desire to see universities and learned societies get more engaged in A-level curriculum design. Such engagement would further facilitate the creation of a progressive and cumulative curriculum in archaeology that is so needed. If all students had an A-level in archaeology (as current students in history, geography, english, and modern languages do) I estimate that universities would have the equivalent of another half to two-thirds of a year of full-time study within each degree program to use. This would provide a real opportunity to address a skills deficit for students who knew they wanted a career in professional archaeology.

In the medium term, we need to grow archaeology beyond the research-intensive universities in the UK. The situation in higher education, described in detail above, refers largely to degrees taught in these select institutions. These universities see their future success, and sometimes survival, as dependent on their standing in the international university league tables. Competition between these institutions for research reputation and the best national and international students, especially postgraduates, using the university reputation as a selling point has squeezed vocational training except in classic professions such as medicine, law and business studies. The activities of staff in these institutions are tightly constrained by the need to secure and advance the university's reputation, and the aspirations of students from professional social backgrounds that dominate their student cohorts. Archaeology departments are located in research-intensive universities because of its association with the classics, history, and to some extent, the sciences. Universities outside this grouping are more focussed on teaching and the needs of employers including, for example, the accreditation of workplace learning and the existence of employers' panels that advise on curricular developments. For current professional archaeologists this will mean reaching out to institutions without established departments, and ones from which they are not alumni.

The increasing attention to the explicit development of employability skills in the student cohort is encouraging all universities to think about introducing placements or workplace learning into their degrees. This is particularly noticeable in arts and humanities degrees and in the traditional universities. Whilst many students will take placements in a diverse range of employers, there is a real opportunity here for professional archaeological contractors, curators and national agencies to build closer links with these institutions by offering placements to students. These relationships could provide the authentic experience of professional archaeological employment that professional archaeological employers value and that is so hard to provide within a university. Such placements would also offer a diverse range of useful employment skills to students who might eventually find employment outside archaeology. Once again individuals with a knowledge and experience of archaeology beyond the profession might appreciate its value when acting as decision-makers elsewhere. For professional archaeology, the issue here would be about balancing voluntary-work with paid-work and ensuring that such placements do more than offer basic excavation-experience. If professional developer-funded archaeological work in the UK is to be enhanced and enlarged through the new planning policy, placements might be an effective way of undertaking some of this work.

Finally, the structural change that would have the greatest possible impact on teaching the next generation would come through the transformation of the conditions of archaeological employment, from their current state into one where there were clear long-term career-prospects. It is hard to sell a profession where pay is low, but when employment is fragmentary and without clear advancement it is very difficult indeed. Most current students of archaeology come from a professional social background. Their aspirations for their own future lives have been framed in such a background, and their expectations of a future lifestyle are mostly nurtured by what a professional background can afford. I have spoken to a number of former students who are planning to leave professional archaeology because they believe their expectations of a future life will not be met by working as professional field-archaeologists. These same individuals have not fallen out of love with archaeology; indeed they are often keen to undertake postgraduate study in archaeology in the hope that it will lead to a better career. The considerable increase in students graduating with PhDs in recent years is also an indicator of the desirability of a career in academic archaeology for many students.

Some aspects of professional archaeology, such as excavation, might not require a degree as preparation, as opposed to a practical training or apprenticeship offered to school leavers (Aitchison 2006). Indeed archaeological excavators in a number of countries such as Japan and Korea are not educated as professional archaeologists. The full range of skills, however, in all forms of professional archaeology, as outlined in the National Occupational Standards in Archaeological Practice are unquestionably professional in nature. These skills necessitate management of people and resources, competitive applications, negotiation with professionals in other sectors of employment, presentation to the public and so on. The challenge to the sector is to bring this change about. Wages need to rise and employment structures need to change. If as many students actively sought a long-term career in field archaeology as they do in journalism, the media, the law, the student demand as consumers of education would provide a clear driving force for change in the education of the next generation.

References

Adecco, 2012, *Unlocking Britain's potential,* at www.unlockingbritainspotential.co.uk/download/ index.php (accessed 28 May, 2012)

Aitchison, K, 2004, Supply, demand and a failure of understanding: addressing the culture clash between archaeologists' expectations for training and employment in 'academia' versus 'practice', *World Archaeology* **36.2**, 203–19

Aitchison, K, 2006, What is the value of an archaeology degree? *Papers from the Institute of Archaeology* **17**, 4–12

Aitchison, K, 2010, United Kingdom archaeology in economic crisis, in Schlanger, N, and Aitchison, K, (eds), *Archaeology and the global crisis: multiple impacts, possible solutions,* Culture Lab Éditions, *Tervuren* 25–30

Aitchison, K, and Edwards, R, 2003, *Archaeological labour market intelligence: profiling the profession 2002–03,* Cultural Heritage National Training Organisation, Bradford

Aitchison, K, and Edwards, R, 2008, *Archaeological Labour Market Intelligence: Profiling the Profession 2007–08*, Institute of Field Archaeologists, Reading

AQA, 2007, *Archaeology: GCE AS and A Level Specification*, at http://store.aqa.org.uk/qual/gce/pdf/AQA-2010-W-SP-10.PD (accessed 28 May, 2012)

Bekhradnia, B, 2011, Keynote address: delivered to the Guardian Higher Education Summit, March 2011, at www.hepi.ac.uk/files/Guardian%20summit.pdf (accessed 28 May, 2012)

Benjamin, R P, 2003, Black and Asian representation in UK archaeology, *The Archaeologist* **48**, 7–8

Benjamin, R P, 2006, *Engaging the past to develop black identity and social inclusion*, Unpub PhD Thesis, University of Liverpool

University of Birmingham, 2012. *Review of the Institute of Archaeology and Antiquity (IAA*, at http://www.birmingham.ac.uk/schools/iaa/news/2012/review-iaa.aspx (accessed 6 September, 2012)

BIS, 2011, *Higher Education White Paper: Students at the heart of the system*, at www.bis.gov.uk/Consultations/he-white-paper-students-at-the-heart (accessed 28 May, 2012)

Confederation of British Industry (CBI), 2011, *Building for growth: business priorities for education and skills, Education and Skills Survey 2011*, at www.cbi.org.uk/media/1051530/cbi__edi_education___skills_survey_2011.pdf (accessed 28 May, 2012)

Council for British Archaeology (CBA), 2009, *Engaging with the historic environment: a report into the appeal of archaeology as an AS/A level qualification*, Unpublished research report prepared for English Heritage

Darvill, T, and Russell, B, 2002 *Archaeology after PPG16: archaeological investigations in England 1990–99*, Bournemouth University School of Conservation Sciences Res Rep **10**, published in association with English Heritage

Department for Communities and Local Government (DCLG), 2010, *Planning Policy Statement 5: Planning for the Historic Environment*, The Stationery Office, London

Department for Communities and Local Government (DCLG), 2012, *National Planning Policy Framework*, at www.communities.gov.uk/publications/planningandbuilding/nppf (accessed 28 May, 2012)

Department for Education and Sciences (DfES), 1988, *Advancing A-levels: the Higginson Committee Report*

Department for Education and Sciences (DfES), 2004, *14–19 Curriculum and Qualifications Reform*, at http://news.bbc.co.uk/1/shared/bsp/hi/pdfs/15_02_05_tomlinson.pdf (accessed 28 May, 2012)

Department for Education and Sciences (DfES), 2011, *Review of vocational education: the Wolf Report*, at www.education.gov.uk/publications/standard/Post16Learning/Page1/DFE-00031-2011 (accessed 28 May, 2012)

English Heritage, 1995, *Planning for the Past: a review of assessment procedures in England 1982–91*, (3 vols)

English Heritage, 2012, *Comparison of PPS 5 Policies to NPPF. Part 1 and 2*, at www.english-heritage.org.uk/professional/advice/government-planning-policy/national-planning-policy-framework/ (accessed 28 May, 2012

Everill, P, 2012, *The Invisible Diggers: A study of commercial archaeology in the UK (2nd edn eBook)*, Oxbow Books, Oxford

Gillard, D, 2011, *Education in England: a brief history*, at www.educationengland.org.uk/history (accessed 6 September 2012)

The Guardian, 2012, *University Guide 2013: league table for archaeology and forensics*, at www.guardian.co.uk/education/table/2012/may/22/university-guide-archaeology-forensics (accessed 28 May, 2012)

Higher Education Funding Council for England (HEFCE), 2011, *National Student Survey: findings and trends 2006–10*, Issues Paper, at www.hefce.ac.uk/media/hefce/content/pubs/2011/.../11_11.docx *(*accessed 28 May, 2012)

Higher Education Funding Council for England (HEFCE), *Students number controls and teaching funding*. Policy Development Consultation Document February 2012/04, Higher Education Funding Council for England, at www.hefce.ac.uk/news/newsarchive/2012/name,72760,en.html (accessed 28 May, 2012)

Henson, D, 2008, History and archaeology at 14–19 in the United Kingdom, *Research in Archaeological Education* **1(1)**, 60–65, at www.heacademy.ac.uk/assets/hca/documents/archaeology/RAEjournal/issue1/1_1_Henson.pdf (accessed 28 May, 2012)

Higher Education Policy Institute (HEPI), 2012, *The academic experience of students in English Universities*, at www.hepi.ac.uk/466-2060/The-Academic-Experience-of-Students-in-English-Universities.html (accessed 28 May, 2012)

Jackson, V, and Sinclair, A, 2009, *Archaeology graduates of the millennium: a survey of the career histories of graduates 2000–2007*, The Higher Education Academy, London

Ofqual, 2012, A-Level Reform Consultation; June 2012, at http://www.ukipg.org.uk/meetings/further_and_higher_education_working_party/2012-06-18-a-level-reform-consultation.pdf (accessed 6 September, 2012)

QAA (Quality Assurance Agency for Higher Education), 2003, *Learning from subject review 1993–2001: sharing good practice*

QAA (Quality Assurance Agency for Higher Education),, 2007, *Archaeology benchmark*, at www.qaa.ac.uk/academicinfrastructure/benchmark/honours/default.asp (accessed 28 May, 2012)

Research Enhancement Framework, 2012, REF2014: Assessment criteria and level definitions, at www.ref.ac.uk/panels/assessmentcriteriaandleveldefinitions/ (accessed 28 May, 2012)

Sinclair, A, 2009, To stones and bones, add genes and isotopes, life histories and landscapes: accumulating issues in the teaching of palaeolithic archaeology, *Research in Archaeological Education* **1.2**, at www.heacademy.ac.uk/assets/hca/documents/archaeology/RAEjournal/issue2/rae_issue2_sinclair.pdf

Sinclair, A, 2010, The end of a golden age? The impending effects of the economic collapse on archaeology in higher education in the United Kingdom, in Schlanger, N, and Aitchison, K (eds), *Archaeology and the global economic crisis: multiple impacts, possible solutions*, Culture Lab Éditions, Tervuren, 31–44

Sinclair A, 2012, Getting a conceptual grip for the teaching and learning of palaeolithic archaeology, in Freeman, P, and Trigg, J, (eds) *Of things gone but not forgotten: essays in honour of Joan J Taylor*

Sinclair, A, and Beck, W, 2012, A future for benchmarking degrees in archaeology? Comparing the development and nature of learning standards in the United Kingdom and Australia, *Research in Archaeological Education* **2.1**, at www.heacademy.ac.uk/assets/hca/documents/archaeology/ RAEjournal/issue3/rae_issue3_sinclair_Beck.pdf

Sinclair, A. and Taktak, D, 2012, *The national student survey and archaeology teaching in the United Kingdom,* Higher Education Academy, Subject Centre for History, Classics and Archaeology

Southport Group, 2011, *Realising the benefits of planning-led investigation in the historic environment: a framework for delivery,* at www.archaeologists.net/sites/default/files/node-files/SouthportreportA4.pdf (accessed 28 May, 2012Sutton Trust, 2010,

Sutton Trust, 2010, Sutton Trust submission to Sir Martin Harris: widening access to selective universities. January 2010, at www.suttontrust.com/research/sutton-trust-submission-to-sir-martin-harris/ (accessed 28 May, 2012)

Chapter 19

A diverse profession?
Challenging inequalities and diversifying involvement in British archaeology

Hannah Cobb

Introduction 1: a personal prologue

The broader context of this chapter arises from my own personal experiences. As a result I choose to start with my own back-story, to help contextualise the critique presented here; it is important to note that it is not a remarkable or new back-story that I have to tell. Rather, it is a tale that I suspect will resonate with the experiences of many people working in archaeology, or also in other careers.

In summer 2008 I completed my doctoral research, and although the financial climate was worsening and the archaeological sector contracting dramatically, I applied for every job and post-doctoral scheme that I could find. Initially I worked in a number of temporary posts as a teaching assistant, a lab-manager and in a temporary lectureship. Then, in autumn 2009, I got my first permanent job, as Technician and Instructor in Applied Archaeological Techniques at the University of Manchester. The post was newly created and as a result it was challenging and exciting, balancing technical support with lecturing in archaeological methods. The first year of my post was unsurprisingly busy; I provided technical support and training in various techniques. I wrote and delivered two new courses, integrating departmental field-training with assessment for the first time. I attended various excavations and directed two of my own. I wrote papers, attended conferences and participated in an international research project; and I got pregnant.

In 2010 I took six months maternity leave, and towards the end of this period of leave I began to reflect on my job and my career trajectory. I loved my job and was looking forward to returning to work, but I recalled that initially I had taken the technician role with the thought that it would be a stepping stone, and that I would be applying onwards and upwards, for lectureships and post-docs, whenever and where-ever they arose. But as I reflected, I realised that for the first time I was not going to be able to apply, on a whim, for further roles across the UK and Europe. For now, with the introduction of childcare responsibilities, my partner and I both needed to be in permanent posts to meet the costs of having a child. The involvement of extended family in our care arrangements also meant that any application elsewhere would need to be thought through carefully, with questions of where my partner would work, and how childcare would be arranged if we were both working. Of course, as I note above, this is not a remarkable story; archaeologists the world over, irrespective of gender, have to weigh up these sort of factors every day.

But as I reflected I recalled Joan Gero's 1985 paper '*Socio-Politics and the Woman-at-Home Ideology*'. In one of the first analyses of its kind, Gero identified that the division of gender roles in archaeological practice reflected the traditional definition of gender roles that had been much critiqued in broader socio-political discourse (Gero 1985). Here she illustrated how male archaeologists predominantly adopted the role of primary data collectors, working in the field and the public realm:

'*...visible, physically active, exploratory, dominant, and rugged, the stereotypic hunter – and the practicing field archaeologist who himself conquers the landscape, brings home the goodies, and takes the raw data!*' (Gero 1985; 344).

Women, on the other hand, were almost always women-at-home, relegated to the intellectual equivalent of the domestic realm, in which they were regarded as simply doing the archaeological housework:

'*...secluded in the base-camp laboratory or museum, sorting and preparing archaeological materials, private, protected, passively receptive, ordering and systematizing, but without recognised contribution to the productive process*' (*Ibid*).

And so, in 2010, as I reflected on my job and my life I realised that, 25 years after this cutting-edge paper was published, 25 years after an extensive feminist critique had significantly affected archaeological *theory*, in *practice*, as a woman, as a mother with childcare responsibilities, and as an archaeological technician, I was a perfect example of Gero's critique, with a job akin in many ways to 'archaeological housekeeping' shaped by my own life choices outside of the profession.

Introduction 2: A diverse profession?

As I returned to work after maternity leave a series of chance encounters with colleagues and students led me to reflect on disciplinary diversity beyond my own situation. On the one hand I was teaching students about the rise of ground-breaking studies that attempted to explore professional inequalities and encourage the multi-vocality of archaeological practice (eg Croucher and Romer 2007; Edgeworth 2003; Everill 2009; Hodder 1997; Lucas 2001; Phillips *et al* 2007; Spector 1993). Yet in practice I was encountering students who felt their disabilities would prevent them having a career in archaeology, and students from ethnically diverse backgrounds who had to battle with their families to justify their degree choice in archaeology.

It is clear that the disjunction between theory and practice that I was experiencing personally is also reflected, in the UK at least, in the findings of the Institute of Field

Archaeology's *Profiling the Profession* exercise (Aitchison and Edwards 2008). This detailed study of the archaeological profession in the UK demonstrated that whilst there were slightly more women than men in the profession under the age of 30, after 30 the numbers of women fell rapidly, to the extent that most UK archaeologists over the age of 30 were male (*Ibid*; 49). Moreover the study found that 98.99% of all archaeologists were white and 98.36% were not disabled (*Ibid*).

The implications of these statistics are troubling on a number of levels. In simple terms there remain significant professional inequalities; the prevalence of men over 30 suggests that men are likely to retain most of the senior and managerial positions. This in turn means that both decision-making, report-writing, and ultimately, the developing of final interpretations, remain dominated by a very specific white, male, able-bodied, and predominantly heterosexual, world view. Many recent accounts have pointed to the way in which the narratives that we create about the past are used to legitimise and reinforce modern, Western, andro- and Euro-centric and hetero-normative ideals (eg Croucher and Romer 2007; Dowson 2000, 2006; Gatens 1992; Gero and Conkey 1991; Joyce 2006; Tringham 2000). In the light of such work, it is clear that the perpetuation of specific (white, male, straight) voices in the writing and decision making processes of archaeology in turn perpetuate such legitimising, normative narratives.

This perpetuation of such a specific perspective is further troubling because the *Profiling the Profession* statistics do not mirror national trends, with the 2001 census showing that almost equal numbers of men and women over 30 were in employment (ONS 2004a), that 92.1% were white (ONS 2004b), whilst one in six people reported a limiting long-term illness (ONS 2006). These differences reinforce the extent to which our disciplinary make-up leads to both bias in the interpretations of the past that we write, and the way that we practice in the present. Moreover they also point to the potential for the discipline itself, and the narratives that we create, to be alienated from wider society more generally.

Moving beyond simple, personal anecdote, and considering the existing statistics, it seems that Gero's rallying call in 1985 has achieved little in terms of gender, and subsequent narratives about multivocality and disciplinary diversity, remain little more than pipe-dreams only put into practice through well-funded and often non-commercial archaeology (Members of the Ardnamurchan Transitions Project 2012). Some excellent guides for diversifying archaeology do exist of course (eg Phillips *et al* 2007, Croucher and Romer 2007) but these remain in the minority, and largely focus on academic practice rather than the profession more broadly. So what next?

So what next?

It is clear that we need to act upon these issues and develop decisive strategies to enhance disciplinary diversity. However, I suggest that the picture painted above is not sufficient as a basis for action. That is because the *Profiling the Profession* study (Aitchison and Edwards 2008), whilst an excellent and fundamental piece of labour-market data, is primarily aimed at just that, collecting labour-market data. It was not designed to examine diversity in the profession, and as a result the data on this subject are necessarily limited. For instance, the categories of gender, ethnicity and disability are all broad and homogenising. Gender is limited to 'male' and 'female', ethnicity to 'white', 'mixed', 'black or black-British', 'Asian or Asian-British', 'Chinese' and 'other', and disability status is limited to 'not disabled', 'work limiting disabled only', 'DDA disabled only' and 'work limiting and DDA disabled'. The latter is understandably problematic as it was guided by the existing legislation of the time *The Disability Discrimination Act* (1995/2005), which has subsequently been replaced by the more inclusive Equality Act (2010). However if we accept that our understandings of gender and ethnicity are culturally constructed, this means that both are much more extensive than those given in *Profiling the Profession* in 2008. In addition, because diversity was not a focus of the study, on the publication of the results it was not possible to relate aspects of diversity to other areas in the survey. Thus whilst age and gender were related, it was not possible to review the relationship between, for example, ethnicity and job-role, or disability and salary. Understanding these relationships will be fundamental for any concerted approach towards diversifying the profession.

Things have changed dramatically in the profession in recent years. The *Profiling the Profession* exercise from which the above statistics are drawn took place in August 2007. At this point the impacts of the economic crisis were yet to be felt and the profession was at its peak, employing just over 6800 people in the UK (Aitchison and Edwards 2008: 11). Subsequently the profession has significantly contracted, and by January 2011 employment figures were 21% below their 2007 peak (Institute for Archaeologists 2011). This, and the continued contraction of archaeology in the UK, has the potential to have significantly affected the demographic make up of the profession, and it is likely that minority groups will have suffered considerably. As a result a renewed survey is needed to examine these elements specifically.

Finally, and most crucially, the snapshot we have represents the profession only; that is, all those who are *paid* to work in archaeology. Yet archaeology is now a graduate profession, with all professional archaeologists under 30 holding a degree in the subject (Aitchison and Edwards 2008: 13). Thus to challenge and increase disciplinary diversity we need to explore these issues amongst not only professionals, but the student-body too.

In summary then, if we are to truly overcome the issues facing us with regards to the lack of disciplinary diversity, we must first come to a more nuanced understanding of this broad and important area. This means that we need to collate an up-to-date, post-recession, understanding of diversity from across the profession, as well as from the body of students who will one day also be employed as archaeologists. By exploring both of these groups and comparing trends between them, issues that may preclude greater diversity are likely to be highlighted. This in turn provides a concerted basis for developing strategies for the profession to move beyond its current limited make-up. With these critiques in mind, in 2011 the Digging Diversity project was formed to do exactly this.

Digging Diversity: Phase One, methodology

The Digging Diversity project aims to examine the existing picture of disciplinary diversity in the profession and the student-body. In addition, it also aims to explore examples of best practice in enhancing diversity in archaeology and beyond the discipline. The project then aims to disseminate the results of the study to provide the basis for devising practical solutions for challenging current issues with disciplinary diversity. To meet these aims, the project is envisaged to take place in three phases; Phase One comprised an initial pilot study, Phase Two will see the development of a further survey, detailed research into disciplinary diversity and best practice examples, and Phase Three will be focussed upon dissemination of the findings.

Phase One was undertaken in the autumn of 2011. An initial survey was designed which asked a wide range of questions about diversity. To make the categories as wide-reaching and inclusive as possible, participants were given both a set of prescribed responses for all questions (from which more than one option could always be selected), but also the opportunity to enter another explanation or category. However, for the question of disability it was decided to take a non-prescriptive approach and as a result the wording from the Equality Act 2010 was employed. Thus participants were simply asked:

> *'The Equality Act 2010 defines a disability as "A physical or mental impairment which has a substantial and long-term effect on the person's ability to carry out normal day-to-day activities". Does this apply to you?'*

Participants were then given a space to specify the nature of their disability if they felt it was applicable. For comparative purposes the categories of the 2011 census were employed for ethnicity. Similarly, to enable comparison and analysis, the types of archaeological job-role listed in the *Profiling the Profession* 2007 exercise were presented in this study.

Because Phase One was conducted as an unfunded pilot study it was created as an online survey and disseminated through social-media and discussion-lists. These included the BAJR message board, the World Archaeology Congress email list, and the Britarch and Arctheory JISC based discussion lists. Facebook was also used, with the survey being advertised on Facebook pages such as those for the Council for British Archaeology and British Women Archaeologists, and users being asked to re-post the link in their status to help further disseminate the study. There are, of course, a number of limitations to the study, and the means of dissemination is undoubtedly one of the most limiting factors. Ultimately, because only a limited and self-selecting range of people were reached through this study, the results are clearly not representative of the profession and the student body as a whole.

None-the-less, a total of 510 people responded, of which 42% were in professional archaeological employment (Figure 1). This constitutes responses from just under 5% of the archaeological profession (based on January 2011 Institute for Archaeologists (IfA) figures suggesting that around 5800 are employed in the profession). 58% of respondents were students (ranging from undergraduate to doctoral students).

Figure 1 Employment status of all respondents to the Digging Diversity pilot study

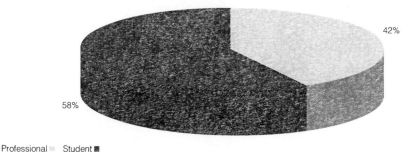

Professional ▦   Student ■

Figure 2 Gender of all respondents

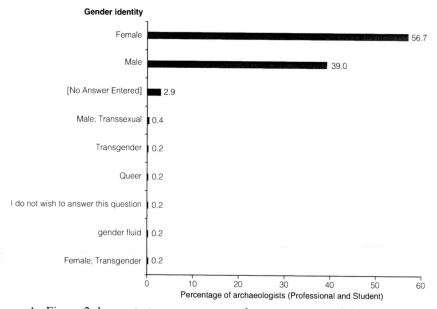

As Figure 2 demonstrates, more women than men answered the survey. This result should be approached with some caution. Given the subject matter it is unsurprising that people who may have felt that the agenda of the study had more relevance to them were more likely to respond. However, beyond these obvious caveats there are still some important points to note. Most crucially for this study, 'Male' and 'Female' were not the only applicable gender categories in the study. Several respondents were transsexual or transgender whilst, as noted above, one respondent defined their gender as 'Queer', and another defined their gender as 'Gender Fluid'. The fact that this variety of gender identity is represented already indicates how valuable a study of this kind is for understanding diversity within the discipline and, as I will go on to discuss in the next section, the further results of the study corroborate this.

Digging Diversity: Phase One, results

Although a variety of results were obtained from this study, it is only possible to present a select few here. In particular it seems pertinent to compare the results from this pilot study with those obtained from the 2007 *Profiling the Profession* study, given that this provides the closest existing assessment, and thus point of comparison, for disciplinary diversity.

Turning first to the question of age and gender in the profession, as noted above (*and see* Figure 3 *below*), *Profiling the Profession* demonstrated that whilst there were slightly more women than men in the profession under the age of 30, after 30 the numbers of women fell rapidly, to the extent that most UK archaeologists over the age of 30 were male (Aitchison and Edwards 2008; 49). If we compare the data from the professional (ie non-

Figure 3 Correlation of age and gender amongst all professional respondents in the 2007 Profiling the Profession study

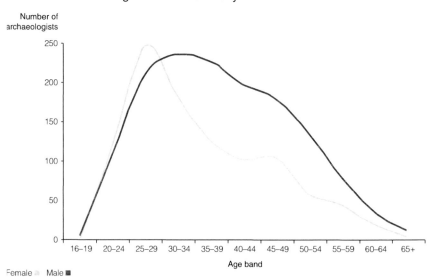

Number of archaeologists

Age band

Female   Male ■

Source: After Aitchison and Edwards 2008; 49

student) respondents only in the Digging Diversity pilot-study we may have expected to have seen some challenge to this trend given the notable increase in female respondents compared to any other gender. Yet it seems that the same pattern is evident, albeit with a slightly older age profile; As Figure 4 demonstrates, whilst more women than men are noted in this study up to the age of 39, from 40–59, there are still notably more men in the profession. Thus even in this study, with the evident caveats and problems with the dissemination of the study and the potential bias in the self-selection of respondents that are noted above, none the less the prevalence of men over 40 still suggests that men are likely to retain most of the senior and managerial positions. Indeed the study correlated gender identity with job role to confirm that this is indeed the case (Figure 5).

Figure 4 Correlation of age and gender amongst all professional respondents in the
pilot study

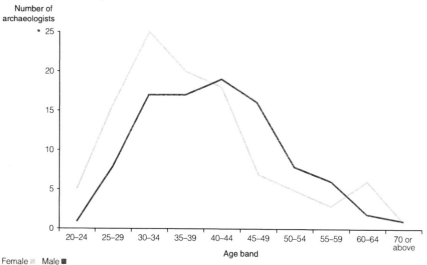

Female ▒   Male ■

Figure 5 Correlation of gender and senior/managerial job roles amongst all
professional respondents

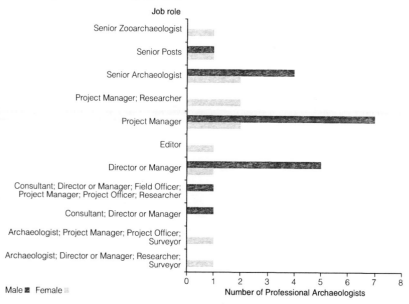

Male ■   Female ▒

Figure 5 shows all senior and managerial or equivalent job-roles that were selected by
professional (that is non-student) respondents in the Digging Diversity study. As noted above,
job titles used here are those also used in *Profiling the Profession* and respondents were able

to select more than one applicable role. Although women did hold some of these roles, twice as many men than women were senior archaeologists, over two-thirds more men than women were project managers and four times more men than women classified themselves as directors or managers. In this respect then, not only does the Digging Diversity pilot study corroborate the *Profiling the Profession* data on age and gender, but it confirms the implications of that data; that men remain dominant in many of the senior parts of the profession. If we return to Gero's hypothesis regarding the pervasiveness of the 'woman at home ideology' within the profession, the detail in Figure 5 seems to confirm this. Indeed, in examining some of the key roles that Gero identifies as secondary, 'base camp' activities undertaken by women (Gero 1985; 344), there is still some clear bias towards women fulfilling these roles (Figure 6).

None-the-less, it is worth noting that the situation is not as extreme or as bleak as Gero portrayed it in the 1980s, and things certainly have changed to some extent. In Figures 5 and 6, it is clear that there is some balance, with women and men occupying both senior/managerial roles and specialist positions. This is further challenged when reviewing data from two key areas within the discipline; field archaeology and academia. Figures 7 and 8 demonstrate that in both of these cases the gender balance is exactly this, well balanced. Under the role of 'archaeologist', for example, twice as many archaeologists were female than male.

Once again it is important to refer to some of the key caveats of this study (namely dissemination methods, the size of the population studied, and the self-selection of respondents) to emphasise that this does not present the most accurate reflection of the profession to date.

Figure 6 Correlation of gender with Gero's (1985) *'base camp'* job roles amongst all professional respondents

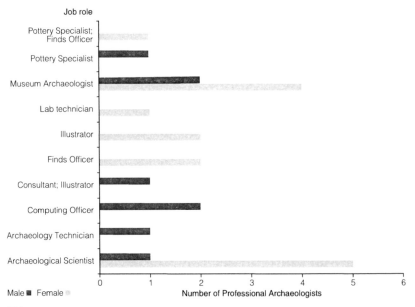

Figure 7 Correlation of gender and field archaeologist job roles amongst all professional respondents

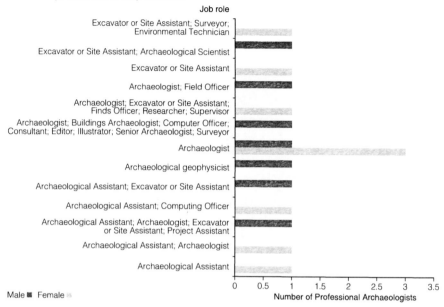

Job role

Excavator or Site Assistant; Surveyor; Environmental Technician

Excavator or Site Assistant; Archaeological Scientist

Excavator or Site Assistant

Archaeologist; Field Officer

Archaeologist; Excavator or Site Assistant; Finds Officer; Researcher; Supervisor

Archaeologist; Buildings Archaeologist; Computer Officer; Consultant; Editor; Illustrator; Senior Archaeologist; Surveyor

Archaeologist

Archaeological geophysicist

Archaeological Assistant; Excavator or Site Assistant

Archaeological Assistant; Computing Officer

Archaeological Assistant; Archaeologist; Excavator or Site Assistant; Project Assistant

Archaeological Assistant; Archaeologist

Archaeological Assistant

Male ■ Female ▨

Number of Professional Archaeologists

Figure 8 Correlation of gender and academic job roles amongst all professional respondents

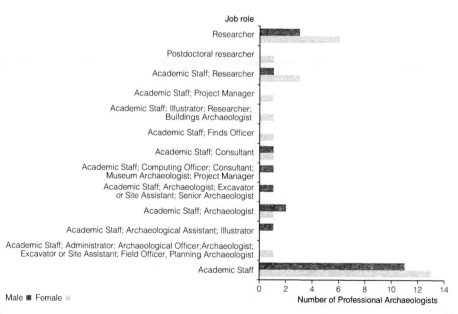

Job role

Researcher

Postdoctoral researcher

Academic Staff; Researcher

Academic Staff; Project Manager

Academic Staff; Illustrator; Researcher; Buildings Archaeologist

Academic Staff; Finds Officer

Academic Staff; Consultant

Academic Staff; Computing Officer; Consultant; Museum Archaeologist; Project Manager

Academic Staff; Archaeologist; Excavator or Site Assistant; Senior Archaeologist

Academic Staff; Archaeologist

Academic Staff; Archaeological Assistant; Illustrator

Academic Staff; Administrator; Archaeological Officer; Archaeologist; Excavator or Site Assistant; Field Officer, Planning Archaeologist

Academic Staff

Male ■ Female ▨

Number of Professional Archaeologists

235

Table 1 Distribution of ethnicity in the profession in 2007

	Archaeologists		All Staff	
	Number	%	Number	%
White	2539	98.99	2650	98.88
Mixed	4	0.16	4	0.15
Black or Black British	1	0.04	4	0.15
Asian or Asian British	10	0.39	11	0.41
Chinese	1	0.04	1	0.04
Other ethnic group	10	0.39	10	0.37
Total	**2565**	**100.01**	**2680**	**100.00**

Source: After Aitchison and Edwards 2008; 52

Table 2 List of ethnicities provided in the pilot study, after the 2011 Census categories

White: English/Welsh/Scottish/Northern Irish/British
White: Irish
White: Gypsy or Irish Traveller
White: Any other White background, please specify below
Mixed/multiple ethnic groups: White and Black Caribbean
Mixed/multiple ethnic groups: White and Black African
Mixed/multiple ethnic groups: White and Asian
Mixed/multiple ethnic groups: Any other Mixed/multiple ethnic background, please specify
Asian/Asian British: Indian
Asian/Asian British: Pakistani
Asian/Asian British: Bangladeshi
Asian/Asian British: Chinese
Asian/Asian British: Any other Asian background, please specify
Black/African/Caribbean/Black British: African
Black/African/Caribbean/Black British: Caribbean
Black/African/Caribbean/Black British: Any other Black/African/Caribbean background, please specify
Other ethnic group: Arab
Other ethnic group: Any other ethnic group, please specify
Other, please specify

However there are clear, and positive, trends in job-roles which demonstrate that, at least as compared to Gero's assessment of professional make up in the United States in 1985, there is a good balance in the number of men and women employed as both field archaeologists and academics.

Turning now to ethnicity, the pilot study demonstrates that, as with questions of gender, the picture is not quite as straightforward, nor as bleak, as in *Profiling the Profession*. As noted above, the criteria that were used in *Profiling the Profession* for ethnicity were relatively limited (Table 1) and instead the full list given in the 2011 census was the starting point for the Digging Diversity pilot (Table 2). Once again the same caveats as repeated above are important to note here, but none the less this study showed a number of interesting factors by examining ethnicity in more detail. Most importantly, overall it seems there is to some extent a greater ethnic-diversity emerging in the professional sector since the 2007 *Profiling the Profession* study, with a fall from 98.99% of archaeologists being white to 96.1% of all professional archaeologist respondents in the Digging Diversity pilot being white (Figure 9).

Figure 9 Ethnicity amongst all professional respondents in the pilot study

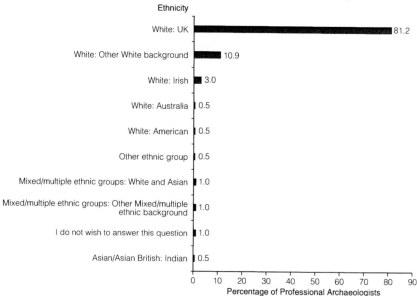

Figure 10 Ethnicity amongst all student respondents in the pilot study

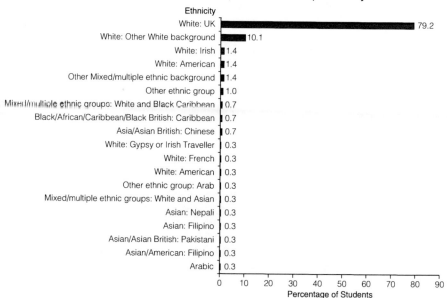

Moreover, amongst the student-body, the Digging Diversity pilot showed that there is even more ethnic diversity, with 93% being white (Figure 10). This figure is much closer to the national average (National Statistics 2004b). The study also demonstrates the need

to move beyond simply classifying 'white' as one homogenous group, and recognising and that in this category ethnic diversity also exists which also has the potential to enrich the discipline.

Whilst the figures here are an encouraging development, compared to the 2007 *Profiling the Profession* results, they none the less raise an important question; Given that UK archaeology is now essentially a graduate profession, and the balance in student ethnicity comes close to the national average in the UK, what are the barriers that exist to preclude that diversity extending into professional practice? Moreover what can we do to overcome such barriers? Furthermore, it is clear that other barriers exist within the profession that need addressing. For instance, as demonstrated in Figure 11, all of the respondents in the Digging Diversity pilot study who occupied senior roles were white.

Figure 11 The ethnicity of those in senior roles within the Digging Diversity pilot study

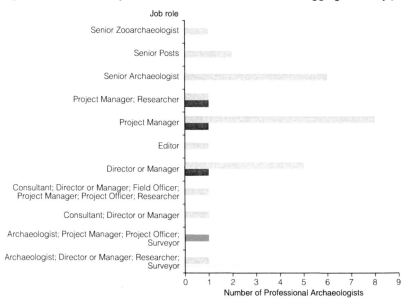

Finally let us turn to the question of disability in the discipline. *Profiling the Profession* found that 98.36% of all archaeologists were not disabled (Aitchison and Edwards 2008; 52), and the full breakdown of their findings on disability is outlined in Table 3. Unfortunately this area is the least comparable with the Digging Diversity pilot study as markedly different criteria were used following a change in the legislation (*as discussed above*). Thus, whilst 91% of professionals and 91% of students both equally reported themselves as not disabled in the Digging Diversity pilot, it is unclear if this is a reflection that things have changed in the discipline since 2007, if it is simply a reflection of different criteria being used, an effect of the problems with a smaller study-population, reflects

Table 3 The distribution of disabilities in the profession in 2007

Disability Status	Number	%
Not disabled	2285	98.36
Work limiting disabled only	28	1.21
DDA disabled only	5	0.22
Work limiting and DDA disabled	5	0.22
Total	**2323**	**100.01**

Source: Aitchison and Edwards 2008; 52

limited dissemination and self-selecting respondents, or is a combination of all of these factors. As a result, rather than directly comparing this to the *Profiling the Profession* results, it seems more productive to examine some of the most significant trends in the data yielded by the pilot study. In particular, whilst the same number of student and professional respondents classified themselves as disabled, and there are similarities in some disabilities (equal numbers of professionals and students had dyslexia and dyspraxia, and these were the most common disabilities noted) the range of disabilities noted in students was much higher than in professionals (Table 4). Moreover it seems that there are some disabilities that were common amongst students, such as epilepsy, that are not noted in the professional body at all. In the case of epilepsy, the practical demands of a professional role in archaeology, such as driving, may be a reason that this is not noted in the professional body. However, for other disabilities, such as those related to mental health, there seems little logical reason why this may be so highly prevalent in students but not in the broader profession. Of course issues of self-definition may have an effect on this element of the study.

Digging Diversity: Phase One, discussion

The results of the Digging Diversity Phase One pilot study raise some important points. Critically they demonstrate that issues of diversity within the discipline are more complicated than prior studies have shown, ranging from how current archaeologists categorise their own gender identities; the relationships between gender and job-role; and the ways in which disability and ethnicity differ between student and professional demographics. This complicated picture means that things are not as bleak as the simple statistics from earlier studies such as the 2007 *Profiling the Profession* initially indicated. The gender balance in key areas of the profession such as academic- and field-archaeology, is more positive than initially thought. When the student body is taken into consideration other positive dimensions in the diversity of this group are clear. Amongst student archaeologists, for instance, there is greater ethnic diversity, diversity in sexuality and a greater range of diversity in disabilities than amongst the professional sector.

Yet at the same time the results from this small and simple study also reveal some key problems. The comparative inequalities in diversity between students and professionals, given that archaeology is a graduate profession, indicate that barriers must exist in

Table 4 The different disabilities listed by professional archaeologists and students in the Digging Diversity pilot study

Disability	Number of Professional Archaeologists	Number of Students
A chronic health condition	–	1
Anxiety	–	2
Asthma	–	2
Autistic Spectrum Disorder (PDD)	1	–
Back injury	1	–
Chronic fatigue syndrome	1	1
Cognitive impairment	–	1
Crohn's Disease	1	–
Degenerative disc disease	–	1
Depression	–	2
Diabetes	1	1
Dyscalculia	–	1
Dysgraphics	–	1
Dyslexia	6	6
Dyspraxia	3	3
Epilepsy	–	3
Golfer's Elbow	–	1
Hearing impairment/loss	1	1
Hyperacusis	–	1
Ischemic Heart Disease	1	–
Meniere's Disease	1	–
Mental illness	–	3
Missing left leg	–	1
Mobility problems	–	2
Moderate Cardiac Heart Failure	1	–
Multiple Sclerosis	–	1
Myotonic Dystrophy	–	1
Myre Irlens Syndrome	–	1
Osteo-arthritis	–	1
Peripheral Neuropathy	–	1
Prefer not to specify	1	–
Reduced mobility from scoliosis and injury	1	–
Sleep disorder	1	–
Stress	–	1
Tetraplegic (C6) wheelchair user	–	1
Tinnitus	–	1
Unstable Angina	1	–
Vestibular disorder	–	1

the progression from student to professional. It is time for some critical self-reflection in the discipline if we are to identify why careers in archaeology appear to preclude diversity in ethnicity and certain types of disability. We also need to critically consider how people progress through the profession. As the results here have shown, barriers do exist within the profession surrounding age, gender, and ethnicity, with most senior roles occupied by white, and predominantly male, employees. Admittedly archaeology is a difficult profession in which to have a family. Field-archaeology particularly, involving travelling and working away for extended periods of time, does not fit well with childcare responsibilities. This may explain the significant drop in the number of women in the profession from their thirties onwards. However childcare does not simply affect women, and the lack of correlation with national statistics means that the prevalence of white men in senior roles is not simply representative of societal trends either. Once again some serious critical analysis of these trends is required, and some productive strategies are needed to challenge them.

Better understanding of the issues surrounding disciplinary diversity, I suggest, is one of the first key steps to overcoming them. Clearly, the Digging Diversity pilot study remains a basic and small study, and now a more detailed and wide reaching study is required. This will overcome some of the limitations to the existing results presented here, such as the small survey population, limited means of dissemination and self-selecting respondents, which are all likely to have limited and skewed the data presented here to some extent. Moreover future study needs to consider a range of other issues. For instance, a more focussed/narrow question on disability would have been useful, as well as questions about socio-economic background, and salary, which were not included in the pilot study. In addition, a qualitative study with key participants, beyond the straightforward quantitative survey presented so far, would be an important supporting-element to explore in more depth anecdotal evidence for aspects such as the potential barriers between being a student of archaeology and a professional archaeologist.

It is envisaged that Phase Two of Digging Diversity will examine these aspects, but Phase Two must also be accompanied by an explicit attempt to highlight best practice and positive strategies from within and outside the discipline, to challenge issues in diversity. There are, of course, already some key examples from Higher Education that are worth pointing to here. In particular Croucher and Romer's 2007 Higher Education Academy Guide to Teaching and Learning, *Inclusivity in Teaching Practice and the Curriculum*, is a useful document which deals broadly with diversity in archaeology in Higher Education. Croucher and Romer argue for an inclusive approach to teaching and learning, which must move beyond the box ticking exercises of recruitment schemes. Instead they suggest a number of methods to develop inclusivity in teaching archaeology. In particular, they argue that integrating diversity into the Higher Education curriculum is a fundamental measure. This should not be as an 'add on' which would act to ghettoise or marginalise issues of diversity further, but in an integrated manner (for example exploring past disability in a session on human osteology, or non-normative identities in a lecture about death and burial) (Croucher and Romer 2007; 8). Such changes to the curriculum should be accompanied by an awareness of how teaching style can be modified to assist disabled students in particular (*Ibid,* 11). Finally, they note that field training is often traditionally presented in a culturally exclusionary manner, where accommodation may be mixed, and a focus is often placed on the drinking culture of fieldwork. In contrast, they argue, cultural sensitivities should be maintained; single sex accommodation should be offered and the realities (not everyone drinks all the time!) should be emphasised to students *(Ibid,*12).

Whilst Croucher and Romer's guide provides a range of approaches to increasing diversity in Higher Education more generally, another more specific example of best practice, also aimed at Higher Education, is worth noting here; Phillips *et al* (2007) examines the challenges for making archaeological field-training inclusive and accessible to all, providing good practice guidelines and an online tool kit for evaluating field abilities (the ASSET self-evaluation tool kit http://www.britarch.ac.uk/accessible/abouttoolkit. php). One of the fundamental outcomes of the *Inclusive, Accessible, Archaeology* project is the argument for a culture of acceptance. Acknowledging that not everyone can do everything in the field immediately opens archaeology up to a more inclusive stance that contrasts markedly with an attitude of 'having to fit disabled students in'. Phillips *et al* (2007; 37) argue that such an approach means that the provisions made to include disabled students can be of benefit to all students participating in fieldwork training.

Beyond these best practice examples from Higher Education, there seems to be less in the way of comparative initiatives in the profession more broadly, and perhaps this is one reason for the lower levels of diversity discussed above. Of course the IfA does have an explicit Equal Opportunities Policy (Institute for Archaeologists 2008), and organisations such as the Council for British Archaeology and Archaeology Scotland play an important role in making archaeology accessible to the wider public. The British Women Archaeologists group also exists, although at the time of writing this largely operates as a professional discussion network represented by a Facebook group. In addition there are a number of schemes beyond the limits of the profession which archaeology could engage with. WISE (Women in Science and Engineering) and the UK Research Council (UKRC) are joint schemes whose mission statement outlines a commitment to '*advancing gender equality and diversity from classroom to boardroom in science, engineering and technology*' (The UKRC and WISE 2012), with a focus on providing accreditation, awards, mentoring and training. At the time of writing, however, there are no explicit connections to note between the profession and with these organisations.

Conclusion: A diverse profession?

I began this paper with my own personal back-story, and particularly the realisation that prompted the research presented here, that despite several decades of broad theoretical critique, I remain, in practice, a prime example of Gero's 'woman-at-home' ideology, in a technician role, undertaking the archaeological housekeeping. Yet, with hindsight I realise that this presents an overly-simplistic view. First and foremost, the past few decades have seen epistemological questions about the process of gathering and interpreting archaeological data explore the manner in which interpretation is present throughout the archaeological process (Lucas 2001; and *see* Cobb *et al* 2012 for a summary). In this sense there can and should be no prioritising of the 'public' realm of primary data collection. But beyond this, I realise that my own job is a diverse experience. With the support of colleagues and family alike, I am a working mother in a job that challenges Gero's simplistic division of public and private. In the 18 months since returning from maternity leave I have directed two excavations, taught core courses, edited a book, written several papers, organised a conference session, provided technical support and training, managed labs, overseen post-excavation analysis and more. In short, I do not fit into the simple division that Gero identified, and in archaeology in the UK today, I suspect that few people do.

As I noted at the start of this paper, mine is not a remarkable story. As the results from the pilot study demonstrate, whilst there are still gendered divisions in professional roles, the division of the profession into men's and women's public and private roles can no longer be regarded as as straightforward as that presented by Gero in 1985. Indeed, according to the pilot study results, the picture is not even as simple as that presented in the most recent comprehensive study of the profession in the UK, the IfA's *Profiling the Profession* study. There is more diversity in the student body than in the profession, for instance. None the less there is still much to do. Developing a more cogent understanding of the nuances in the diversity of both the student body and the profession alike, along with exploring best practice examples from archaeology and beyond, are important steps. In turn these should help us to explore and overcome the comparative inequalities in diversity between students and professionals and to critically consider how people can progress through the profession without the existing barriers surrounding age, gender and ethnicity that have been outlined in this paper.

In the original *Rescue Archaeology* publication (Rahtz 1974) key areas of disciplinary crisis were identified, and I argue that 40 years on, the lack of disciplinary diversity is perhaps one of the biggest crises that we face today. Developing greater diversity and inclusivity in the discipline makes us better archaeologists. As Croucher and Romer argue:

'[by] having a less homogeneous workforce and student group, more opportunities for awareness and questioning of many assumptions and habitual concepts in relation to a subject are likely. This helps to drive academic enquiry and development forward, ensuring that in a changing world, the subject of archaeology does not become stagnant and led by dogma.' (Croucher and Romer 2007; 7)

In short, developing disciplinary diversity is as much about our survival as it is about equality and fairness. Without it, ultimately, our interpretations of the past are destined to remain simply a reflection of, and a means to reinforce, the modern socio-political inequalities that are mirrored in the current disciplinary make-up.

References

Aitchison, K, 2011, *State of the Archaeological Market, October 2011,* Report for the Institute of Field Archaeologists and Federation of Archaeological Managers and Employers, Landward Research Ltd, Sheffield, at http://www.archaeologists.net/sites/default/files/node-files/JoblossesOctober2011.pdf (accessed 31 May, 2012)

Aitchison, K, and Edwards, R, 2008, *Archaeology labour market intelligence: profiling the profession 2007–08,* Institute of Field Archaeologists, Reading

ASSET self-evaluation tool kit, at http://www.britarch.ac.uk/accessible/abouttoolkit.php (accessed 31 May, 2012)

Cobb, H, Harris, O J T, Jones, C, and Richardson, P, (eds), (Cobb *et al*) 2012, *Reconsidering fieldwork: Exploring on site relationships between theory and practice*, Springer New York,

Cobb, H L, Harris, O, Jones, C, and Richardson, P, 2012, Reconsidering fieldwork, an introduction: Confronting tensions in fieldwork and theory, in Cobb *et al*, 1–14

Croucher, K, and Romer, W, 2007, Inclusivity in teaching practice and the curriculum, *Guides for Teaching and Learning in Archaeology* 6, at http://www.heacademy.ac.uk/assets/documents/subjects/hca/Number6_Teaching_and_Learning_Guide_Inclusivity.pdf (accessed June 8, 2012)

The Disability Discrimination Act 1995, HMSO, London

Dowson, T A, 2000, Homosexuality, queer theory and archaeology, in Thomas, J, (ed), *Interpretive Archaeology*, Leicester, 283–9

Dowson, T A, 2006, Archaeologists, feminists, and queers: sexual politics in the construction of the past, in Geller, P L, and Stockett, M K, *Feminist Anthropology*, Philadelphia, 89–102

Edgeworth, M, 2003, *Acts of discovery: an ethnography of archaeological practice*, BAR Internat Ser 1131, Oxford

Equality Act, 2010, HMSO, London

Everill, P, 2009, *The Invisible Diggers: A study of British commercial archaeology*, Heritage Research Series 1, Oxbow Books, Oxford

Gatens, M, 1992, Power, bodies and difference, in Barrett, M, and Phillips, A, (ed), *Destabilizing Theory: Contemporary Feminist Debates*, Cambridge, 123–32

Gero, J, 1985, Socio-Politics and the Woman-at-Home Ideology. *American Antiquity* 50 (2), 342–50

Gero, J, and Conkey, M W (ed), 1991, *Engendering archaeology: women and prehistory*, Oxford

Hodder, I, 1997, Always momentary, fluid and flexible: towards a reflexive excavation methodology, *Antiquity* 71, 691–700

Institute for Archaeologists, 2008, *Institute for Archaeologists policy statements*, at http://www.archaeologists.net/sites/default/files/node-files/ifa_policy_statements.pdf (accessed June 8, 2012)

Institute for Archaeologists, 2011, *New job losses figures published,* at http://www.archaeologists.net/news/110216-new-job-losses-figures-published (accessed May 31, 2012)

Joyce, R, 2006, Feminist theories of embodiment and anthropological imagination: making bodies matter, in Geller, P L, and Stockett, M K, *Feminist Anthropology*, Philadelphia, 43–54

Lucas, G, 2001, *Critical approaches to fieldwork: contemporary and historical archaeological practice*, Routledge, London

Members of the Ardnamurchan Transitions Project, 2012, The struggle within: challenging the subject/object divide on a shoestring, in Cobb, H L, *et al*, 13–130

Office of National Statistics (ONS), 2004a, *Focus on gender*

Office of National Statistics (ONS), 2004b, *Focus on ethnicity and identity*

Office of National Statistics (ONS), 2006, *Focus on health*

Phillips, T R, Gilchrist, I, Hewitt, S, Le Scouiller, D Booy, and Cook, G, 2007, *Inclusive, accessible, archaeology: good practice guidelines for including disabled students and self-evaluation in archaeological fieldwork training,* Guides for Teaching and Learning in Archaeology 5, in http:// www.heacademy.ac.uk/assets/hca/documents/guides/Archaeology_teaching_and_learning_ guides/Number5_Teaching_and_Learning_Guide_Inclusive_Accessible_Archaeology.pdf (accessed June 8, 2012)

Spector, J, 1993, *What this awl means: feminist archaeology at a Wahpeton Dakota Village,* St Paul, Minnesota Historical Society Press

Tringham, R, 2000, Engendered places in prehistory, in Thomas, J (ed) *Interpretive Archaeology: a reader,* Continuum, London 329–50

UK Research Council (UKRC), and WISE (Women in Science and Engineering), 2012, *About us: The UKRC,* in http://www.theukrc.org/about-us (accessed June 8, 2012)

Chapter 20

Communicating archaeology: the message, not the medium

Mike Pitts

On my desk are two sources in which professional archaeologists spoke to a wide public. One is a fading press cutting over 40 years old. The other is a radio programme broadcast in Australia during the week in which I am writing, available as audio on demand and as a downloadable transcript.

On August 22 1971 (seven months after the launch of RESCUE) the *Observer* published a full-page article written by two archaeologists (Barker and Fowler 1971). It is confident, strident and packed with information. We are told, for example, that:

'Between AD 1500 and 1950 about 300 [deserted medieval villages] were destroyed... between 1950 and 1970, 300 more were destroyed, and they are now disappearing at the rate of 20 to 30 a year.'

The piece ended with what was effectively an advert to attract new paying members of RESCUE.

Archaeology in Britain was a smaller world 40 years ago than it is today, and the distinction between professional and public less complex. Barker and Fowler were younger, and angry, archaeologists taking an unusual approach (a polemic in an upmarket Sunday newspaper), but they had grown up with the idea that leading archaeologists made it their job to tell the public about what they were doing.

The BBC were soon to broadcast two films featuring Mortimer Wheeler looking back on his life (Hawkes 1982, 366), accompanied by a double-spread feature in the *Radio Times* (Campbell 1973). Wheeler remains one of the greatest communicators archaeology has ever seen, but other key 20th century archaeologists who had written popular books, given radio talks and appeared in television programmes were alive and active in 1971.

Stuart Piggott, described by Richard Bradley as one of British archaeology's 'three wise men', who *'more than anyone else... laid the foundations for the study of British prehistory and... taught most of the senior figures in the discipline today'* (Bradley 1996), was 61. As well as his distinguished academic publications, Piggott had written several trade-books. Importantly, he expected these books to be read by both archaeologists and '*the general non-specialist reader*' (Piggott 1965, vii). In the preface to *Prehistoric India*, a Penguin paperback priced at 3 shillings, around £5 in today's terms he noted that: '*Much of the material presented in this book is either new and hitherto unpublished or is a synthesis made for the first time... But despite [the inevitable technical detail] it is hoped that a coherent story... has been presented to the non-specialist reader*' (Piggott 1950, 9).

Grahame Clark was 64 in August 1971. He wrote *Prehistoric Societies* with Piggott, a book favourably reviewed in the *Economist* and the *Sunday Times* (Clark and Piggott 1965). The *Manchester Guardian* described his *Prehistoric England* (Clark 1940, reissued in several editions) as '*an excellent and detailed introduction to a fascinating subject for the non-expert reader*'; for the *Illustrated London News* Clark treated '*an essentially learned subject in a... readable and attractive manner*'. Like Piggott, Clark valued public knowledge: '*If we are ever to recover the story of a common past, it can only be through the pressure of an informed public opinion*' (Clark 1939, vii).

Glyn Daniel, author of *The Megalith Builders of Western Europe* ('*Unusually clear and sensible*', *Observer*) and the travel guide *The Hungry Archaeologist in France* (Daniel 1958 and 1963), as well as detective novels (eg Daniel 1954), was 57. In *A Picture Book of Ancient British Art* (Piggott and Daniel 1951, vii) we see a familiar refrain: '*Our aim has been twofold*', that is, to appeal to both '*the serious student*' and '*the general reader*'.

Perhaps the greatest writer of popular but learned archaeology-books was Gordon Childe. Had he not killed himself in 1957, he might still have been alive in 1971. He would have been 79, a year younger than Wheeler. He wrote few books exclusively for archaeologists, but his many trade books (eg Childe 1936, 1942) were influential within the profession as much as at the railway-station bookshop, as Miles Burkitt said in his *Nature* review of *What Happened in History*, Childe wrote to '*stimulate thought*' (quoted on the 1957 Penguin edition). His little *Story of Tools* (1944) was one of very few archaeological publications that Childe might not have expected archaeologists to bother with.

These men were some of the great thinkers in British archaeology, excavators of internationally significant sites (Maiden Castle, Stonehenge, Star Carr, Skara Brae) and responsible for texts that defined the profession and its subject matter (eg Wheeler 1954, Piggott 1954, Clark 1952, Daniel 1950, Childe 1957). And they appeared on TV: Wheeler and Daniel were the key figures on *Animal, Vegetable, Mineral?*, the BBC's most successful game and chat show in the mid 50s, which also featured Piggott, and even Childe (Hawkes 1982, 298–301; Lavell 1981, 119).

We are given a very different picture today by Rachael Kohn in conversation with Karin Sowada in a programme made by the Australian Broadcasting Corporation's Radio National (Kohn 2012). Sowada is, an Egyptologist and specialist in Biblical archaeology, but the insights are universal.

Sowada notes that the proliferation of TV broadcasters; she names the Discovery Channel, the History Channel, and the National Geographic Channel, has created an unprecedented demand for media content. '*They need to fill their airtime*', she says, leading to '*manufactured discoveries*'. These might be fabricated stories, or finds that were: '*made some years ago but are being reinterpreted through new eyes by non-scholars who see an opportunity to make a name for themselves, sell a book, generate an exhibition, whatever*'.

Such discoveries need to be told at a pace, and if university archaeologists are involved, they will be encouraged '*to get media attention, ... to bring in money [and] perhaps partnerships with TV stations*'. But scholarship takes time, proceeding through slow research and peer-reviewed publication. 'Academics', says Sowada: '*are under enormous pressure with teaching loads, research loads, their university key performance indicators are based on research output in scholarly journals and books. ... The TV documentary is ... an additional burden on the already overworked academics ... they find it very challenging.*'

Despite this, Sowada wants archaeologists to be seen more: '*The one-hour television documentary is the gold standard for how people receive their information. So whether an academic likes it or not, they need to ... engage much more vigorously with the media with their own discoveries ... taxpayers absolutely have a right to know where their money is going and to hear the results of those expenditures.*'

In 1971 the media offered a limited range of opportunities for archaeologists to tell the world what they wanted it to think about what they were doing. In 2012 the ever-changing and ballooning mix of print, video and audio, and online blogs and gossip, intimidates archaeologists. If they had some control over presentation in 1971, in 2012, it would seem, they have almost none (*though see* Blinkhorn Chapter 21).

So should archaeologists try harder? Should they seek a return to values of the gentler media world of the 1970s and before? Or should they be doing something altogether different? And regardless of what they aim for, how can they improve the hope of achieving it?

The art of writing

Words lie behind any communications designed to inform, whether they are written, spoken or hidden in the equivalent of stage-directions that steer and shape a presentation. How words are used is important. Here are a few points that have struck me as a part-time journalist, broadcaster and Editor of *British Archaeology*.

1. Bad writing distracts

Bad grammar, bad spelling and misplaced style hinder communication. It has become common online to flaunt lazy writing. But an archaeological blog replete with typos, unfinished sentences and grammatical errors fails. It fails because if it has something to say, that message will be obscured; and it fails because the sort of educated, busy reader the archaeologist might seek to reach will not read past the first sentence.

The same principles apply to print. Here are some real archaeological examples, from published and unpublished texts, starting with spelling; the message here is read your text and do not rely on your spell checker.

'A decisive navel battle was fought near Actium.'

'A line of post-medieval tits was recorded during the excavation.'

'Rabbis have been a feature of the English countryside since Norman times.'

And finally, an old favourite:

'Developers must put the evaluation in the pubic domain.'

There has been much said about the issue of unattached participles or gerunds, often to the effect that we should no longer worry about it. Only those who do not care to be understood should take that line. The alert reader will be distracted; the lazy will not be following you anyway.

'Walking through the picturesque graveyard of Llandadarn Fawr, the urn carved on an 1843 gravestone would make any archaeologist stop and look twice.' (It would indeed, though it was probably the archaeologist, not the urn, that walked.)

'Proposed for demolition twice, the casework panel felt that the building contributed to the conservation area.' (At least at that point, the panel was still standing.)

'Before making the 105 mile journey back to the fort, English Heritage appointed a team of skilled experts ... to conserve the 1,800 year old stonework.' (Despite their logo, English Heritage has never lived in a Roman fort.)

'Very delicate, rather beautiful and clearly out of place on an austere medieval monastic site, our excavation team was stumped.'

Academics like florid metaphors. The Sun likes it straight. There is perhaps a happy medium, but if you must use metaphors, read what you have written carefully, or you will end up with this:

'It is now established that the framework of the medieval countryside crystallised over the final centuries of the first millennium AD when a united England was forged from a patchwork of Anglo-Saxon kingdoms.'

In the real world, 'frameworks' do not 'crystallise', and a 'patchwork' is sewn, not forged. Rather than a vivid image of early medieval England, this sentence raises confused memories of school chemistry. Or again, an example that is just weird:

'*... drama-led formats, in which the goalposts shift towards entertainment.*'

Careful reading can reveal more subtle problems. These two examples are grammatically correct, but both give the reader an unintended, and distracting image:

'*As I left to make my way to the airport my colleagues asked if I had my sick bag ready...* [followed shortly by] *... It's amazing what you see from the air. Sites you think you know well throw up new surprises.*'

''*Chronological and imaginative leaps' become possible without, as *** puts it, a need for 'a plethora of crappy reconstruction'. 'With radio', *** continues, 'you can float ideas'.*'

2. If people cannot understand what you are saying they will stop listening

Most of us are aware that when we address people who have no special archaeological knowledge, we need to say what we mean when we use terms like liquid scintillation counting, Protruding Foot Beaker, or *terminus post quem*. Nonetheless, it is worth saying that such terms really do need to be explained; and if we can omit the term and go straight to the explanation, so much the better.

What is harder to appreciate is that archaeologists habitually use many words they do not think of as jargon, many of them related to excavation, that a wider public would not understand correctly. Thanks to *Time Team*, 'trench' and 'geofizz' often need no introduction (though it is worth bearing in mind that for many, these words have specific *Time Team*-related connotations). But others such as 'section', 'rob' (as in robber trench), 'concentration' (a tight cluster of finds), 'cut', 'parallel' (used to compare one artefact to another) and many more, may not feel like jargon, but in fact have very specific technical meanings, which are different from their everyday uses. So, for example, if you are on video describing a trench section, you can get away with saying 'this section' and a sweep of the arm. But without the picture, you should say what you mean by 'section', and as always with jargon, that very thought should encourage you to ask yourself if you need to use the word at all.

3. Clarity is power

Academics like long, convoluted sentences and obscure words. Much of the time this fondness for confusion hides confused thinking. This may be useful for the ambitious but less gifted archaeologist, but it repels the general reader seeking enlightenment. Obscurity can also result from unnecessary use of jargon. If you want people to read and understand your message, read it through and make it clear, or you will end up with sentences like these:

'It is often the material spreads themselves on such sites that provide snapshots for the temporality of the deposits.' (Spreads of debris can represent snapshots in time.)

'His burial post-dated the abandonment of the building.' (He was buried after the building was abandoned.)

'The new country that emerged was driven by a past master of repossessing lost pasts through a selective narratives process.' (The new country that emerged was driven by a master of historical reinvention.)

On the other hand, repetition of simple words and phrases can deaden the brain. More importantly, it may suggest to the careful writer that their text can be shortened by the removal of redundant passages; a better strategy than reaching for the thesaurus for alternative words. This was the case with an otherwise excellent text I edited (a feature on an urban excavation, of less than 2,000 words) in which the phrase *'a series of'* (as in *'a series of large brick drains'*) occurred 6 times, the word 'room' 15 times, and 'building' 40 times, including two appearances of the phrase *'the building was rebuilt'*.

4. The past was populated by real people

It is easy to get too close to your work, and to forget that the object of your research is not the excavation trench or the artefact in your lab, but the stories these can tell us about real people's lives. The oversight can show:

'At least eight individuals, presumed to have been men, were buried with swords, spears and shield bosses.' (And presumably the real warriors had whole shields.)

'...evidence of flint working and the processing of animal remains.' (Next season we hope to find the site where they processed the animals.)

'The axehead has mineralised remains of the wooden shaft still attached to it.' (It would be 'still' only if the shaft had survived.)

'The post-excavation analyses revealed... a group of post-holes... which had been intentionally burnt down probably not long after construction.'

5. The world of archaeology is very small

What matters within the world of professional archaeology does not necessarily matter as much outside. Much of the criticism levelled by archaeologists at media coverage is of the form we might label the wrong offside-law. In January 2012 a set of coins was launched to commemorate the London 2012 Olympic and Paralympic Games. One of 29 sports commemorated was football, with a 50p piece that illustrated the offside law. Except, complained football referees, it got the law wrong; apparently a technicality introduced in 1995 had been misrepresented (Hills 2012). In similar fashion, the Central

Council of Church Bell Ringers objected to artist Martin Creed's 2012 Olympics project, Work No 1197: All the Bells in a Country Rung As Quickly and As Loudly As Possible for Three Minutes. '*We think 8am is not the right time for ringing in very many towers*', said the council's blog (Higgins 2011).

In these cases, projects designed to entertain also had the clear capacity to draw in new interest that could have been encouraged by specialists. Yet they were dismissed by those with most to gain, for reasons that seem petty to the outside world. Some of the criticism aimed publicly by archaeologists at *Time Team*'s Big Dig or the Portable Antiquities Scheme, for example, is of this type (Kennedy 2003, Moshenska 2010).

6. Journalists are human beings

It is too easy, and often wrong, for archaeologists to blame what they do not like in the media on editors, journalists and presenters. If the latter are reporting an archaeological story, they are reliant on archaeologists to tell them what is important, right and wrong, and to not confuse them with minor irrelevances; they work under intense pressure. Clear use of words is never more critical than when you have a leading broadcaster on the phone for 30 seconds seeking help. These comments are taken from *JournAlert*, an online daily newsletter for journalists:

'*Well structured articles within 100 words of the word count and inside the deadline.*' '*A clear approach, decent grammar and honesty.*' '*Copy in on time and written to a professional standard.*' (Answers to the question, '*Name the most important attributes that make a freelance journalist stand out for you*'. Note that these are not preferences; they are essentials.)

'*If I can trust a contributor to deliver the goods and do so on time, I value them highly. If they don't, I kill them.*' (A warning from the editor of *Tattoo Master*.)

'*I don't like 'time suckers' on the phone. I don't take many calls when I'm working, as this industry is all about deadlines and 15-hour days.*' (In answer to, '*Do you like freelance journalists to get in touch with you directly to pitch ideas?*')

It may seem that an archaeologist, seeking a wide audience for their excavation, faces a dilemma: if editors are so busy, how do you reach them? The answer, simple to write, less so to execute, is to get to know the industry, and show it an archaeologist who can help. This takes commitment, and hard work. Somewhere along the line (it could be months, it could be years) if you get it right you will make the transformation from an archaeologist struggling to interest a news-desk in a discovery, to a valued writer that editors will phone for help when they want to follow up a press release.

Quality media do not print press releases: they want to put their own spin on a story, and to be seen to be contributing. And if they have the resources to do so, they might do their own research and find another story altogether (most journalists are repelled by press offices' attempts to spin a story to the benefit, say, of a university department). Editors have contact lists. If the list includes archaeologists who can write or speak intelligently, entertainingly and informatively when an archaeological story needs to be covered; to length and on time, often within hours, everyone benefits. And if it does not, the absence is as much an archaeological failure as an editorial one.

As with any form of communication, writing and talking are not specifically archaeological skills. There are many publications that can help (to take but two that helped me, in earlier editions, Dick (2003) and Horstmann (1997)). The books I repeatedly use when writing are Ernest Gowers' *Complete Plain Words* (Gowers 1973), Robert Dutch's edition of *Roget's Thesaurus* (in the abridged Penguin version, Dutch 1966) and the Economist's style guide (*The Economist* 2010). All are a pleasure to read, as well as to refer to.

Thinking big

The common thread, in the selective comments above, that I would like to draw attention to, is the fault of being too close to your material. If an archaeologist writes or speaks about an invasion of pots, or a woman buried with a belt buckle, uses language that obscures rather than explains, or appears obsessively concerned with issues that matter only to a few colleagues, they are unlikely to arouse interest in what they are saying. Importantly, they reveal a limited horizon, a particular danger in archaeology. The field attracts because of the grand, romantic and mysterious, but it deals mostly with the small, broken and tedious, and as Karin Sowada says, archaeology moves '*at a glacial pace ... it can take years to actually reach a conclusion*' (Kohn 2012). Wheeler was right when he wrote, '*Dead archaeology is the driest dust that blows*' (1954, v).

The media are in flux. New technologies and attitudes to information are shredding the simple and distinct trio of trusted brands in print, radio, and television that we all remember. In such a world it can be easy to think the key to better dissemination and communication is to understand new media. When behemoths like the BBC beseech us to use Twitter to tell them what we think, or when Facebook announces the acquisition of another 100 million users, it might seem that social networking is the essential route to spreading archaeological news.

There are undoubtedly important digital opportunities that archaeologists can take greater advantage of. If the time and effort put into lecturing and writing about archaeology and media as a topic, instead went into creating pages on *Wikipedia*, a much enlarged, new, public resource would exist. The entry for '*Excavation (archaeology)*' has since 2007 been marked with the editorial comment, '*This article needs additional citations for verification. Please help improve [it] ...*' It remains a wordy, worthy and arcane treatise with only one direct reference (an article by Lewis Binford published in 1978, that is not about excavation). Many organisations, the Council for British Archaeology, English Heritage and the Institute for Archaeologists among them, have useful entries, as do finds such as the Staffordshire Hoard or famous sites like Stonehenge (despite its length, there remain significant omissions in this entry, and it will be interesting to see how it copes with the coming full publication of complex revisions to the monument's phasing).

Many obvious candidates for Wikipedia entries, however, are substantially incomplete or missing. 'Long barrow', for example, has 650 words under the subheading *'Long barrows in the United Kingdom'*, followed by a short sentence under the other subheading, *'Long barrows in Russia'*. There is one cross-reference, to a single barrow in Denmark. There is no mention of the internationally significant radiocarbon dating work by Alex Bayliss, Alasdair Whittle and colleagues (eg Bayliss and Whittle 2007), of any excavations, or of the substantial evidence and research across the rest of Europe. There is a separate list of UK long barrows, which, as a Wikipedia editor has helpfully noted, is *'incomplete'*; only one barrow each in Wales and Scotland is described more fully, the entry for the latter giving no more than its length; the entry for 'Round barrow' is significantly less informative and contains no references.

Given that many such entries are written by enthusiasts offering their time freely, the record for professional archaeologists is poor. Yet the opportunity to reach an enormous international audience (and, for university teachers, their students), with no distribution costs, to hand the public the tools with which to write and enjoy history is unparalleled. British archaeology is blessed with an uncountable number of organisations, from national to parochial, in one way or another concerned with fostering archaeological knowledge. It is time some of them got together, developed a strategy to exploit and add value to Wikipedia, and implemented it.

Other essential digital tools are the website and the blog. Blogs can be valuable as a running commentary on excavation or research (a good example being one that describes the conservation of two Roman altar stones from East Lothian: AOC 2012). Properly curated, a good blog is also an important and unprecedented type of historical record. Yet surprisingly few archaeological projects or archaeologists are represented by good blogs. For the professional archaeologist, a blog or website can be approached in the same spirit as an academic publication; care taken with grammar, style, facts, and illustrations will repay itself. The chief difference between a journal article and a blog need be no more than reach, between a readership of a hundred or so and millions. As with Wikipedia, compared to traditional forms of publishing, blogs and websites are relatively cheap to produce, have an almost limitless audience, and are ripe for well-thought-out strategies developed at a high level within the profession. All such digital communications can also be controlled, or largely so, by archaeologists: while they might look televisual on a screen, they are a world apart from traditional television.

Important digital opportunities are available then. At a more superficial level tools like Twitter and Facebook can help promote projects, draw in readers and highlight campaigns. But the significant point here is that while these opportunities occur on the internet, what matters most is not the medium but the message. In an unpredictable and fast changing media world one of the few true constants is the value of content. An article about long barrows on Wikipedia may reach a wide audience: but what makes it valuable, to the public and to the archaeological profession, is the quality of the writing and information.

We might, then, think back to a world before 1971, when leading archaeologists were able to write well and entertainingly and, apparently, commercially successfully, about broad issues, such as the nature of archaeology, or the sweep of ancient cultures across the world. It would be a mistake, however, to assume that most archaeologists then had the communication skills of Wheeler or Piggott, or sought to emulate them. Wheeler famously had many detractors (Lavell 1981, 118); Barry Cunliffe has told how his arrival at Oxford University in 1972 was greeted with the news that some senior university members did not consider archaeology a '*serious subject*', because '*some archaeologists had appeared on television*' (Cunliffe 1982, 61).

Antiquity, touted in 1927 by its founder-editor O G S Crawford as a popular journal, found only a small circulation, partly, in Kenneth Hudson's words (1981, 103), because its editors have been '*more anxious to gain the good opinion of scholars than of the general public*'. Attempting to capitalise on the interest generated by *Animal, Vegetable, Mineral?* in the 1950s, the Council for British Archaeology failed to find '*the writers who might have done it*' (Lavell 1981, 120). The favourable book reviews in newspapers and literary journals, such as those quoted earlier, look less impressive when it is noted that reviewers were often other archaeologists; even *A Picture Book of Ancient British Art* was published by a university press.

The rapid growth in the profession from the late 1960s did not bring a proportionate rise in great communicators. When Jacquetta Hawkes defended the 'humanistic values' of archaeology in 1968, she appeared reactionary to many, perhaps most, younger colleagues. Now, when we read of her horror of texts:

> '*so overburdened with unhelpful jargon, so grossly inflated in relation to the significance of the matters involved, that they might emanate from ... an introverted group of specialists ... [contributing] nothing that is enjoyable, generally interesting or of historical importance*', she looks far-sighted (Hawkes 1968, 256).

The profession was turning inward and media coverage becoming more 'highbrow' (Kulik 2007, 118–20); a decade later, '*the professional archaeologist [was] moving in one direction, his public in the other*' (Cunliffe 1982, 61). Today, archaeologists deem 'popular writing' 'simplistic', and '*resent*' '*good story-telling by non-archaeologists, and the former are rarely taught literary skills*' (Clack and Brittain 2007, 28–9).

The ultimate way to engage a new and wider public, however, is not to seek to turn specialist academics, scientists, excavators, and bureaucrats into prize-winning novelists. It is to recognise the need for a different form of writing and thinking that rises above the excavation, the artefact, or the narrow theoretical debate, to develop big ideas and big stories about people in the past. It is to understand that extending archaeology's reach does not only mean watering down what is important to archaeologists until it is consumable by the less knowledgeable, and castigating broadcasters as irresponsible if they fail to participate (Lavell 1981, 120).

This does not mean popularising archaeology, if that implies the presence of something more important that most people will have little interest in. It means doing it properly; encouraging and valuing in its own right what Childe, in particular, sought and achieved: the stimulation of thought.

References

AOC, 2012, Lewisvale Park Roman remains, at http://www.aocarchaeology.com/lewisvale-roman-altars (accessed June 5, 2012)

Barker, P and Fowler, F, 1971, Rescuing our past, *Observer*, August 22, 1971

Bayliss, A and Whittle, A, (eds), 2007, Histories of the dead: building chronologies of five southern British long barrows, *Cambridge Archaeol J*, **17.1** (supplement)

Bradley, R, 1996, Stuart Piggott, *British Archaeology*, **19**, 23

Campbell, J, 1973, Sir Mortimer Wheeler, still digging at 82, *Radio Times*, March 22, 1973, 8–9

Childe, V G, 1936, *Man makes himself*

Childe, V G, 1942, *What happened in history*

Childe, V G, 1944, *The story of tools*

Childe, V G, 1957, *The dawn of European civilization*

Clack, T, and Brittain, M, (eds), 2007, *Archaeology and the media*, California

Clack, T, and Brittain, M, 2007, A short history of archaeological communication, in Clack, T, and Brittain, M, (eds), 11–65

Clark, G, 1939, *Archaeology and society*

Clark, G, 1940, *Prehistoric England*

Clark, G, 1952, *Prehistoric Europe: the economic basis*, Cambridge

Clark, G, and Piggott, S, 1965, *Prehistoric societies*

Cunliffe, B, 1982, Archaeology and its public, *CBA Annual Report* **32**, 59–64

Daniel, G, 1950, *A hundred years of archaeology*

Daniel, G, 1954, *Welcome death*

Daniel, G, 1958, *The Megalith builders of Western Europe*

Daniel, G, 1963, *The hungry archaeologist in France*

Dick, J, 2003, *Freelance writing for newspapers*

Dutch, R A, 1966, *Roget's Thesaurus*, Pelican, Harmondsworth

The Economist, 2010, *Style Guide*

Gowers, E, (revised B Fraser), 1973, *The complete plain word*, Pelican, Harmondsworth

Hawkes, J, 1968, The proper study of mankind, *Antiquity* **42**, 255–62

Hawkes, J, 1982, *Mortimer Wheeler: Adventurer in archaeology*

Higgins, C, 2011, This week's arts diary, *Guardian*, November 16, 2011

Hills, D, 2012, New 50p coin aimed at explaining offside law 'gets offside law wrong', *Guardian*, January 6, 2012

Horstmann, R, 1997, *Writing for radio*

Kennedy, M, 2003, Time Team digs up row over DIY excavation, *Guardian*, June 21, 2003

Kohn, R, 2012, Archaeology and the media, at www.abc.net.au/radionational/programs/spiritofthings/archaeology-and-media/4017372 (accessed June 5, 2012)

Kulik, K, 2007, A short history of archaeological communication, in Clack, T, and Brittain, M, (eds), 112–34

Lavell, C, 1981, Publication: an obligation, Archaeological documentation in Britain today, *Bull of the Institute of Archaeology* **18**, 91–125

Moshenska, G, 2010, Portable antiquities, pragmatism and the `precious things`, *Papers from the Institute of Archaeology* **20**, 24–27

Piggott, S, 1950, *Prehistoric India to 1000 BC*, Pelican, Harmondsworth

Piggott, S, 1954, *The neolithic cultures of the British Isles*, Cambridge

Piggott, S, 1965, *Ancient Europe*, Edinburgh

Piggott, S, and Daniel, G E, 1951, *A picture book of ancient British art*, Cambridge

Wheeler, M, 1954, *Archaeology from the earth*, Oxford

Chapter 21

Archaeology and the media: from Wheeler to *Time Team*

Paul Blinkhorn

Introduction

In the second decade of the 21st century, archaeology now appears to be a staple of the media, be it television, newspapers, radio, film or the internet. Given this author's personal experience of working in television since 1998, it is that medium, and its relationship with archaeology, which will be the most closely scrutinized here, and it could also be said that it is the one which gives most people their closest contact with archaeology and archaeologists.

The last 20 years have been something of a boom time in terms of the number of television series which look at archaeology. Indeed, in the future, we may even look back and see the end of the 20th and the beginning of the 21st century as something of a 'golden age' of television archaeology.

Terrestrial television led this boom, and in the last 10 years or so, the widespread take-up by viewers of digital and satellite channels has stimulated an almost bewildering range of TV archaeology programmes to choose from, and there are some channels whose output consists of virtually nothing but archaeology and history programming. This has resulted not only in a much greater public awareness of the discipline, it has also led to some archaeologists achieving near-celebrity status, although this is not the first time this has happened (*see also* Pitts, Chapter 20). The growing popularity of cable television, not to mention the internet, has had an effect which means that the glory days of terrestrial television, the last quarter of the 20th century, are gone; it is now entirely possible for the viewer to watch programmes with archaeological or historical content on cable TV for 24 hours a day without having to reach for the remote control. In 1992, in the early days of satellite television, the four terrestrial channels, BBC1, BBC2, ITV and Channel four were watched by around 95% of television viewers, but by 2011, even after the introduction of Channel 5, in 1997, just 55% of the viewing public were, on average, watching a terrestrial channel, with the rest watching one of the numerous cable channels now available (source: www.barb.co.uk). For terrestrial television, there has been a near 2% per annum rate of audience loss since 2006. Clearly, audiences are becoming more scattered, with the most likely cause being the rise of the specialist channel.

The headline-grabbers

While there has been media interest in archaeological activities since the 19th century, if not earlier, the first archaeological excavation which seems to have grabbed the attention of the media and the public on a global scale was the opening of Tutankhamun's tomb in 1922.

Certainly, the event made front-page news around the world, with major newspapers in the UK, the USA, Europe and beyond giving major coverage to the story, but perhaps the most significant coverage came from a medium, cinema, and, specifically, newsreels which, like television in the latter part of the century, was then in its golden age. In the USA, cinema attendances had virtually doubled from 50 million to 90 million during the course of the 1920s, and a similar pattern was seen in the UK. It was this which brought mass-audiences into contact with archaeology for the first time, with film of the discovery, excavation and dazzling finds of Tutankhamun's tomb seen around the world within days of the events happening. The effect of this discovery on society has probably rarely been seen since. It lead to a craze for all things Ancient Egyptian, encapsulated by the Art Deco movement, which incorporated scarabs, hieroglyphs, pyramids, lotus-flowers and other motifs into the design of everything from biscuit-tins to cinema-frontages. The apparently-early deaths of some of the participants in the excavation in the following years also gave the film industry the inspiration to make *The Mummy* starring Boris Karloff in 1932. The core of the tale, of foolhardy archaeologists bringing back to life an ancient evil, has since give the film industry a standard MacGuffin, or plot device; whenever an ancient-evil needs awakening to get the plot underway, one can virtually guarantee an archaeologist will turn up an do it (eg *The Exorcist*). Occasionally, the celluloid archaeologist provides another MacGuffin, in the form of the discovery of ancient artefacts which allows the hero, usually not an archaeologist, to stop an ancient evil once it is abroad (eg 'The Daggers of Meggido' in *The Omen*). The only other role of the archaeologist in film appears to be that of the heroic treasure-hunter, such as Indiana Jones or Lara Croft.

Having said this, there was, in the 1970s, perhaps the most accurate contemporary picture of an archaeological excavation committed to celluloid: Rank Studio's *Carry On Behind*. This 1975 slapstick farce, starring Kenneth Williams as archaeologist Professor Roland Crump, included a digging team which were portrayed as having something of an over-fondness for large quantities of beer, and site-accommodation consisting of tents and dilapidated caravans. When Professor Crump and company begin their fieldwork, an augur survey is carried out before excavation (this was back in the day before geophysics), a mosaic floor discovered during excavation is (correctly) referred to as a 'tessellated pavement', and Dumpy levels, planning frames, sieves, trowels, mattocks, wheelbarrows, scaffolding-plank barrow-runs, pumps and the like, are all seen, correctly deployed, at various points in the film. As someone who started digging in 1974, I can confirm that this is an entirely accurate picture of field archaeology at that time.

Since Tutankhamun, no single excavation has perhaps grabbed the attention of the world in the same way, but in the UK, each following decade seems to have thrown up at least one find or excavation which has made major national headlines, and some on a global scale, such as Basil Brown's excavation of Sutton Hoo in 1938–9 or the finding of the Staffordshire Hoard in 2009. Many of these received such prominent attention simply because they contained 'treasure', usually gold, and in large quantities, but this is not always the case. The raising of Henry VIII's flagship, the Mary Rose, in the Solent in 1982, received live covering on national TV, despite the fact that the 'treasure' in this case was largely waterlogged wood, and not precious metals.

A brief history of television archaeology

The first regular television broadcasts in the UK were started in 1932, only to be halted by the outbreak of war in 1939. They recommenced in 1946 and by 1947 there were around 50,000 licensed TV receivers in Britain; in the early 1950s, there were over a million, and it was in that decade that television archaeology began.

In late 1952, the TV panel game *Animal, Vegetable, Mineral?* created the first *bona fide* celebrity archaeologist in Sir Mortimer Wheeler, a regular on the show along with Professor Glyn Daniel. Other legendary names such as V Gordon Childe and Jacquetta Hawkes also occasionally appeared. The series ran until 1960, in parallel with another archaeology series called *Buried Treasure*, in which Wheeler also made regular appearances. *Animal, Vegetable, Mineral?* had such a high profile that Wheeler was voted Television Personality of the Year in 1954, and Daniel received the same award in 1955. The 1950's were, of course, in TV terms, a different world; Daniel, in the 1960's, recalled that Ian Jacob, the then head of the BBC, stated that in the late 1950s, the two most popular things on television were archaeology and show-jumping. Wheeler was a man who quickly grasped what was required to make good television, and it could be said that, 60 years on, little has changed, at least where archaeology is concerned. As Jacquetta Hawkes so succinctly put it:

'he soon learned to embellish (his performances) with artful devices of timing: the delayed recognition, the double-take, the appearance of being at a loss followed by the sudden kill... his enthusiasm and vitality, his popular humour and flashes of wit all radiated from the screen' (Hawkes 1982, 299–300).

He quickly became a household name and acquired a level of fame and respect which nowadays would doubtless have seen him referred to as a 'national treasure', with a concomitant fan-base. To again cite Hawkes,

'one lady, having heard that Sir Mortimer liked sherry, always stood a glass of it on her television set when he was present in the box below' (*ibid* 300)

In the 1960's and 1970's, the highest profile archaeology programme on TV was undoubtedly *Chronicle*, a BBC series with a wide-ranging brief. It particularly concentrated on important excavations, such as the Biddles' work at Repton, and live coverage of Richard Atkinson's reopening of the Merriweather tunnel through Silbury

Hill. Footage of this was later-used by English Heritage as they attempted to formulate a plan for the conservation of the monument, because the archaeologists involved in the original project had failed to make a useable record of their findings. *Chronicle* was also the vehicle for one of Wheeler's last major television-appearances, a two-part programme in which the great man reminisced about his life and work in conversation with Magnus Magnusson, broadcast in March and April of 1973.

The 1980's was something of a desert in terms of TV archaeology. The exception was Catherine Hills *The Blood of the British* in 1984, a series of eight 30-minute programmes looking at of the archaeology of Britain from the Ice Age to the early-medieval period, but there was not a great deal else, perhaps reflecting the entertainment priorities of that decade.

Wheeler aside, most of the television coverage of archaeology in the period from the 1960s to the end of the 1980s concentrated largely on individual sites and the associated finds, with the cult of personality rarely intruding. Certainly, no single individual archaeologist with Wheeler's fame and charisma appears to have impinged on the public's consciousness during that time, and in hindsight, the 1950's does appear to have been the first 'Golden Age' of television archaeology.

If the 1950s was the first Golden Age, then the period from 1990 to the present day can perhaps be regarded as the second. It started quietly enough, with Channel 4 broadcasting between 1990 and 1992 three series of *Down To Earth*, an archaeology magazine programme, again presented by Catherine Hills. The format of the series was a little different from the somewhat slower-paced, 'single-issue' programmes of the past. It was:

> *'faster and 'zappier'...Sites and subjects were included because of their news-value, each item having only a few minutes air-time during which only one or two points were presented to the public'* (Hoppitt, 1991, intro).

It was a series which is, perhaps, now largely forgotten, but it was also the first attempt to make an archaeological series which presented the discipline to the public in a similar manner to the news media, and the forerunner of some modern programmes, such as BBC Television's more recent offering, *Digging For Britain*.

In the summer of 1991, Channel 4 broadcast a 4-part archaeology series called *Time Signs*, in which archaeologists Mick Aston and Phil Harding spent 30 minutes each week exploring the archaeology of the Wolf Valley in Devon. The programme lasted only one series, but prepared the way for what has been without doubt the most influential and successful archaeological TV series of the modern era: Channel 4's *Time Team*.

The *Time Team* effect

Time Team first appeared as a series of four programmes in 1994, was increased to five programmes in 1995, and by 1999 was running in the 13 programme format which became the standard until 2012, when it was reduced to 11 new programmes per series, plus two compilations. On terrestrial TV, other archaeological series have come and gone in the same period, ranging from the respectable, such as *Two Men in a Trench* and *Meet the Ancestors*, to the best-forgotten, such as *Extreme Archaeology* and *Hidden Treasure* but *Time Team* trundled on, although finally, after 20 years, the last series was aired in 2013.

Time Team had a fairly straight-forward format; the archaeologists investigate a site using both intrusive and non-intrusive methods, but have only three days in which to do so: The programme, which airs for 47 minutes, starts with the presenter, Tony Robinson, setting out the aims of the excavation. It then works pretty much like a normal excavation in that geophysics are carried out, then a team of archaeologists open a series of trenches and excavate and record features. Finds are identified and dated, and then, with the aid of drawings and computer graphics, the site director arrives at an interpretation. Some aspects of the dig are very different to the conditions experienced by modern archaeologists; A helicopter is available to enable a fly-over of the site; the on-site facilities include flush toilets and a field-kitchen where a very good two-course lunch with a choice of three main dishes is freshly cooked; the participants are transported around in new Land-Rovers and housed in agreeable hotels; Teams of production 'runners' are on-hand to go into town to get anything required by the field-team. Other aspects of the show also differ from reality: a full team of artefact and ecofact specialists are usually on-site to offer instant identification and dating of the pottery, bone, and small finds, and whenever co-operation or information is required from English Heritage, it is usually received within 24 hours, including at week-ends and on Bank Holidays.

Often, in the middle of it all, is a 'cameo', in which aspects of ancient life are recreated, be it making an Anglo-Saxon shield or cooking a Roman banquet, and at the end of a day's digging, the team are often filmed in a nearby pub, enjoying a well-earned pint and mulling over the day's events. There have also been a number of digs which were covered live, with programmes throughout the day updating the progress of the excavations, and a summary and highlights programme in the evening. In addition, there are also the so-called 'specials', where various regulars from the programme pay visits to long-term, usually large-scale excavations which are being carried out by other archaeological organisations.

At its peak, the series commanded what were, for Channel 4, large audiences. The 2003 series had an average audience of 3.4 million viewers per programme, which is between 15-20% of market share (the number of people watching TV at the time the programme was broadcast). To put this in perspective, it is more or less the same average number of people and market share as Channel 4's reality series *Big Brother* attracted in 2004. In terms of visitors to cultural centres, any one *Time Team* programme is seen by nearly as many people as visited the British Museum in 2004, and is greater than the total number who visited every branch of the Imperial War Museum in that same year. It is a total which is seven times higher than the number of people who visited the Museum of London during the whole of 2004. More recently, the programme settled to a regular audience of 2–2.5 million, meaning it is still one of Channel 4's most popular programmes, although audiences for the latest series appear to have fallen to around 1.5 million per programme.

Perhaps the ultimate accolade for the series is that it is now regularly referenced in popular culture. The programme has been lampooned in the adult comic *Viz* and the archaeologist regulars from the programme, particularly Mick Aston and Phil Harding, have been impersonated on the TV version of the comedy impressionist series *Dead Ringers*.

Comedians such as Chris Addison and Eddie Izzard have constructed routines around aspects of the programme, and it is often the subject of sketches and skits in the highly popular ITV television series *Harry Hill's TV Burp*. Occasionally, there are references to it in cartoon strips in the tabloid newspapers. Mr Izzard, along with other well-known faces from TV such as Sandi Toksvig, Liza Tarbuck, Hugh Fearnley-Whittingstall, Bill Oddie and Al Murray, from the world of music, the ex-Rolling Stones bass player Bill Wyman, and the venerable punk band The Stranglers have all appeared on the programme, as have the (at the time) prime minister Tony Blair and senior members of the royal family.

A side-project to *Time Team* was the so-called *Big Digs*, a week of programmes, including two live shoots, in which members of the public were encouraged to excavate 1m-square test-pits in their back gardens, and then, after filling in recording sheets downloaded from the internet, report the findings to their local SMR. The idea for this originally came from Professor Mick Aston's ground-breaking landscape project at Shapwick in Somerset, and, since 2005, Carenza Lewis of the University of Cambridge has been utilizing a similar methodology in the Higher Education Field Academies, a project funded mainly by Aim Higher, designed to encourage children from non-academic backgrounds to think about going into higher education. The children spend two days digging test-pits in 'living' villages with medieval origins, and a third day at the University of Cambridge, analysing finds and getting a taste of university life. It is a project which has had unprecedentedly high levels of positive feedback from the participants, and resulted in many children, who had not considered high education before taking part in the project, applying for a university place.

Sadly, 2011 was the last year for the project, as the funding body, Aim Higher, with an annual budget of £76m, was scrapped by the education secretary, Michael Gove, in the so-called 'Bonfire of the Quangos', an action which seems somewhat at odds with his stated commitment to encourage social mobility. The project, simply by plotting finds of pottery from the test-pits, has also revolutionized our picture of the growth and development of medieval villages in the east of England. Recently, test-pitting by local communities of their places of residence has become common-place, with either local archaeology societies or professional archaeologists (or sometimes both) lending a hand.

This is partially because grants for such work are now available through the Heritage Lottery Fund and the like, but it seems unlikely to be coincidence that this has all happened since the *Time Team Big Digs* took place.

Ironically, when *Time Team* first began to publicise the *Big Dig* in 2003, a number of professional archaeologists were horrified. As Maev Kennedy reported in *The Guardian* newspaper on 21st March 2003, some described the project as 'ludicrous', 'a grotesque parody' and 'entertainment, not archaeology'. The report states that the IFA was amongst those that condemned the project, however according to their own *Community*

Archaeology leaflet, by 2010, the HLF had a budget of £180 million per-year to invest into community heritage projects. In 2011, IfA founded a 'voluntary and community archaeology group'. While there have been local archaeology groups for many years, the number has increased dramatically in the last 25 years. According to an article in issue 113 of *British Archaeology*, in 1987 there were 480 local societies in the UK, with a combined total of about 100,000 members; in 2010, there were over 2,000 groups, with the aggregate membership being around 215,000. I would argue that this surge in interest in archaeology was not only due to the public's interest in *Time Team*, but also that the *Big Dig* stripped some of the mystique away from archaeology, and made the wider public realise that it was possible to do it themselves.

I would argue therefore, that the long-running archaeology series enabled archaeology to achieve a level of public consciousness which the discipline has not managed since the days of *Animal, Vegetable, Mineral?*, and given the miniscule audience size and restricted social reach of television at that time, it is perhaps true to say that *Time Team* has raised public consciousness of archaeology to a level never seen before.

The discipline has now reached such a level of visibility that in 1998, the most popular regularly-scheduled programme on television, *Coronation Street*, had a sub-plot which involved environmental protestors stopping the development of a local recreation ground as it contained the remains of a Roman villa. In 2002, the reality show *Celebrity Big Brother* had an archaeologist sifting through the rubbish bags of the cast and discussing what it revealed about their lifestyles, and the housemates in the 2008 series of *Big Brother* had to carry out an archaeological excavation in a 'sandpit' and construct a 'time-line' of the finds as a task which, if correctly carried out, enabled them to win food and luxuries.

An, admittedly subjective, profile of the *Time Team* audience suggests that it has a fairly universal appeal. Fairly large numbers of people usually turn-up to watch the programmes being made, with the range of people present suggesting that its audience is mainly the over-50's, but most programmes are shot during the week when many people are at work, and youngsters are at school. Week-end and Bank-Holiday shoots usually attract a much wider demographic, particularly a family audience, and especially the under-16's. I don't have any hard data on the audience profile, but a TV producer did tell me a couple of years ago that the core audience for the history and archaeology programmes which are shown on cable TV are '*men between the ages of 25 and 55 who own sheds*', and advertising shots from cable television companies making archaeology and history programmes are mainly targeted at the ABC social groups.

So, although *Time Team* has achieved a level of penetration into the public's consciousness of archaeology that has not been seen for 50 years, it begs the question '*is it any good?*' In the world of TV, high audiences are no guarantee of quality, and, indeed, often the reverse. As the American showman PT Barnum once memorably said '*Nobody ever lost money by underestimating the public's intelligence*'. *Time Team* is certainly a programme which seems to provoke strong reactions amongst some sectors of the archaeological community, with some roundly loathing it. Henry Cleere, in 2000, presented one of the more polite critiques when he stated that:

Time Team 'presents a somewhat distorted and over-simplified picture of what archaeology is really about.' (cited in Holtorf 2006, 126)

which is perhaps true, but depends on what you define as an accurate picture of archaeology. Cleere went on to say that:

'The time has now surely come to have enough confidence in the appeal of the subject...to modify the format slightly so as to present a more balanced and honest picture' (ibid).

Part of the problem here is that archaeology, even excavation, takes on many different forms. The long-term excavations at sites such as Wroxeter or Silchester are very different to the majority of excavations carried out in the commercial sector, most of which are very small-scale and find very little, and these are both different again to amateurs digging test-pits in their gardens or on the village green. Certainly, writing as someone who spent a good number of years working in commercial archaeology but also appearing in archaeological television programmes, there is a yawning chasm between the two.

One only has to sit in any site-hut (if there is one) at tea-break (if there is one) on a commercial archaeological excavation to hear stories of the soul-destroying grind of under-funded, under-resourced excavations, poor pay, diabolical accommodation, awful working conditions, and the fact that there is rarely enough time to carry out an excavation properly.

This rarely, if ever, comes over on television, although a *Time Team* special on the Canterbury *Big Dig* in 2002 did touch on some of these issues, and gave a glimpse into the every-day lives of the diggers. Having said all this, a 'regular' *Time Team* episode, from Tottisford Reservoir, won the British Archaeology Awards prize in 2012 for 'The Best Representation of Archaeology in the Media', and Dr Phil Harding, one of the main members of the team since the programme started, won *Current Archaeology magazine's* Archaeologist of the Year award in 2013, so it seems at least some archaeologists think it is an accurate representation of archaeology, or that other programmes on the subject are very wide of the mark indeed.

One does occasionally hear mutterings amongst professional archaeologists that *Time Team* do not 'do the job properly'. I would dispute this, and, furthermore, personal experience suggests that at least some commercial archaeologists are in no position to criticise their TV counterparts, many of whom actually work in the commercial-sector when not appearing in TV programmes, myself included. I have, on occasions, been sent, by commercial units, boxes of 'medieval' pottery which turn out to be entirely Romano-British. One does have to wonder if a state of affairs where an excavation can be carried out by a team who have no clue as to the date of the site on which they are working, is entirely satisfactory.

Personally, if I owned a pet, I would prefer to have an operation on it carried out by a vet who could tell a cat from a dog. I recently test-pitted a site with schoolchildren which had been previously trial-trenched by a commercial organisation; the commercial report said there were no finds or features of archaeological significance. Our test-pit, dug right next to one of their trial-trenches, revealed a 30cm thick medieval occupation horizon containing large quantities of pottery and animal bone. Having a pottery expert on-site, as *Time Team* do, would eliminate some of these problems, but, of course, in the commercial sector, this does not happen as it is 'an unnecessary expense'.

The time constraints of the excavations on *Time Team* are artificial, but also practical. Archaeology is an expensive business, and the budgets for TV programmes, although perhaps generous when compared to those of the average commercial excavation, could not stretch to a dig lasting much longer than three days. On the plus side, *Time Team*, unlike commercial archaeologists, rarely excavated sites which were threatened with imminent destruction, so, once the cameras have been packed away, the trenches back-filled and the circus moved on to another town, the unexcavated portions of the site remain *in situ*, and safe for the immediate future, rather than being bulldozed away in advance of a housing development. In most cases, *Time Team* carried out research excavations.

It is this fact, I think, as well as popularising archaeology, which makes the programme valuable. As an eminent archaeologist recently said to me during the making of another TV series, '*nowadays, in Britain, one only ever sees research archaeology being carried out when there are TV cameras around*', and while not perhaps totally accurate, this certainly has more than a grain of truth in it. English Heritage, who it could be said were perhaps a little suspicious of *Time Team* in the early years, now are happy to have them look at sites in their guardianship. In many cases, the sites have never been examined below ground, and as a result of the programme carrying out small-scale excavations, a much clearer understanding of the site is achieved. This enhances EH's ability to manage the site in question, particularly, as often happens, if a large-scale geophysical survey is carried out during the making of the programme, all at no cost to the tax-payer. In these days of savage cuts to the heritage sector, this work would simply not have been otherwise carried out.

Other examples spring to mind. A TV series in which I recently took part, *Rory McGrath's Pub Dig*, managed to confirm, amongst other things, that there were intact Tudor deposits related to Britain's first royal dockyard at the potential World Heritage Site at Chatham, and that the planned medieval town of Banbury was far larger than previously thought, enabling the district archaeologist to attach archaeological conditions to any future developments in the area for the first time.

Part of the problem is a lot of the archaeologists who criticize *Time Team* and other archaeological programmes seem to forget that TV archaeology is, first and foremost, entertainment. The reportage of a project meant to interest and inform, not merely report the findings of the excavation. The archaeologists on the programme are often criticised by their peers for 'over-interpreting the evidence', but, the rigors of the medium demand that some sort of interpretation is made as the excavation is being carried out, not six months later when all the artefact and ecofact reports are in, and the site matrix has been thoroughly examined and any kinks ironed out, although recent experience suggests that, in commercial archaeology, matrices are also becoming another 'unnecessary expense'.

The final form of the programme is dictated by a television producer, not an archaeologist, and it is structured in a way that he or she thinks will entertain the public while still getting the archaeological findings across in an easily-digestible manner. Also, in the case of *Time Team*, 3-days-worth of excavation, or 15 to 20 hours of video footage, has to be distilled into 47 minutes. There simply is no time for, eg, a detailed break-down of the faunal data, the statistical analysis of the height and diameter ratios of post-holes, or most of the other arcana which make up an archaeological site-report.

When site reports command the same sort of audience as TV programmes, then perhaps we will be able to make TV programmes in the same format. Similarly, if a way can be found to make an entertaining programme out of the sort of excavation which makes up a large part of 'real' archaeology these days, such as a watching brief during the excavation of house-footings, which produces no finds or features of archaeological significance whatsoever, then I'm sure a television production company would be happy to pick it up and pitch it to a broadcaster. Making TV programmes about 'real' archaeological excavations would require a vast financial investment; having even just a single camera crew and director on site every day for, say, three months of an large-scale dig would be effectively impossible due to cost, not to mention the days, if not weeks, spent in an editing suite turning the vast amount of footage into something watchable.

The resulting audiences would simply not be large enough to make the operation financially viable. *Time Team* has, to a degree, tackled this with their 'Specials'. This way of filming a dig, in the manner of *Down to Earth,* of course, misses much of the immediacy and excitement of finds being made 'live' on camera, but seems a sensible, indeed the only compromise. The recent BBC offering *Digging For Britain* has a very similar format, with Dr Alice Roberts visiting in-progress excavations and discussing the finds with members of the excavation teams. This seems to be an appropriate way of filming large archaeological excavations in the modern TV world, and with end of *Time Team*, it would appear that this is the only way in which archaeology will appear on TV in the future. The reality is that, in the 21st century, the multi-platform world of the digital era has led to a fragmentation in the way people receive information and entertainment. TV audiences are falling, and in the world of commercial TV, low audiences mean low advertising revenues, and archaeology is an expensive business. By series 20, *Time Team*'s audience had fallen to around one million, which is simply not enough to support the cost of making it, although this fall was almost certainly due to Channel 4 insisting on changes being made to the programme's format, rather than any loss of interest in archaeology by the general public; a documentary on Channel 4 about the excavation of the skeleton of Richard III in Leicester which was broadcast in February 2013 attracted nearly 5 million viewers.

Perhaps even more worrying is the direction which some TV companies are taking with regards to archaeology and heritage. The recent ITV series *Britain's Secret Treasure* concentrated almost entirely on finds from metal-detecting, with emphasis placed on the amount of money the finder received for their artefacts, and virtually no mention of the Portable Antiquities Scheme or Finds Liaison Officers at any point in the series. Perhaps In an attempt to head off criticism, a Palaeolithic stone axe, one of the few non-metal finds featured, was deemed the most important artefact ever found by a member of the public, but the programme had far more in common with *Antiques Roadshow* than *Time Team*. Even more disturbingly, a series called *American Digger* was screened in America last year. This comprised the exploits of a team of treasure-hunters, led by ex-professional wrestler Rick Savage, who, having persuaded land-owners to give them permission, strip archaeological sites of artefacts using metal detectors and heavy digging machinery, then sell them at auction 'to get rich'. It was condemned by, amongst others, the American Anthropological Association. The editors of *American Digger* magazine, a publication aimed at artefact-hunters, were so appalled by the programme that they cancelled Mr Savage's column in their magazine and sued the programme for infringing their trademark. Despite this, a second series, renamed *Savage Family Diggers*, has been commissioned.

Given that such programmes are considerably cheaper to make than those which directly fund archaeological excavations, and also misleadingly suggest that archaeological artefacts are a viable source of wealth, it is to be hoped that this is not to be the future of the past on television.

Love it or loathe, it is difficult to deny that television archaeology, and particularly *Time Team,* led to a general raising of public consciousness of archaeology; 20 years ago, it is doubtful that many people outside the archaeological community would have been even aware of the existence of geophysical survey; now, there are millions of people who know that before you dig, you have to do the 'geofizz'. Catherine Hills has gone into print stating that *Time Team* is the main thing that first attracted many students to archaeology (*see* also Clarke, Chapter 8), and the CADW Annual Report for 2002 stated that:

> *'Public demand for information on the archaeological heritage has rapidly grown over the past few years, due no doubt to the greater coverage of archaeology on television and radio'*.

Stimulating the public's interest in archaeology can, in the long term, only be beneficial to the discipline. This is perhaps illustrated by an incident in 2011, when the leader of Fenland District Council's announcement that he was to scrap archaeological planning controls in the region led to such a public outcry that he was forced to hastily back-track, and it could be said that the incident also influenced the government during their overhaul of national planning regulations, and led to there being less watering-down of archaeological intervention

At a time when, because of an electoral system which offers little hope of disturbing the *status quo*, we have successive governments which appear obsessed with deregulation, and savage cuts are being made to the heritage sector as a result of the venality of globalised, free-market economics, and the money-pit which was the London Olympic games, archaeologists need all the help they can get, and I would argue that television programmes such as *Time Team* were probably our best hope of maintaining public support for archaeology. It may not have been perfect, but without the public's interest, it is likely that archaeology, other than as a university-based academic discipline (although even this is under threat as I write) or amateur hobby, would probably cease to exist.

References

Hawkes, J, 1982, *Mortimer Wheeler, Adventurer in archaeology*

Holtorf, C J, 2006, *Archaeology is a brand! The meaning of archaeology in contemporary popular culture*

Hoppitt, R, (ed) 1991, *Saxon, the Newsletter of the Sutton Hoo Society,* **14**

Chapter 22

In conclusion ...

Chris Cumberpatch

'*In summing up ... I wish I had some kind of affirmative message to leave you with ... I don't ... will you take two negative messages?*' (Woody Allen 1999 [1964])

Writing a concluding article to sum up and reflect upon the contents of a diverse volume such as this is no easy task. Not only have the individual papers dealt in detail with their particular areas of concern but the section editors have contributed their own introductory comments which themselves serve to bring out the salient features of the papers comprising the individual sections. I find myself in an ambiguous position somewhat similar to my experience when acting as the discussant at a conference session; the papers have been presented and the audience is ready for some debate and the clarification of a few side issues before retiring to the bar for the kind of detailed but informal discussion mentioned (with a detectable sense of nostalgia perhaps) by several authors in the context of field archaeology in the 1970s and 1980s. Who really wants to listen to (or read) a supplementary paper rehashing what they have just heard (or read) with the additional, somewhat dubious benefit of someone's personal interpretation? But that is the task I was offered and accepted ... so here we go.

The intention of this book was always to stimulate debate both about RESCUE, its past and its future and also to raise wider questions about the state of British archaeology in the early years of the 21st century. Whether this debate happens is largely the responsibility of our readers and reviewers but if British archaeology thrives on anything it is heated, often polemical and frequently partisan, debate within the profession (or discipline). It is unfortunate that the rise of militant managerialism in archaeology has acted to weaken this culture of debate and discussion; note for example the disclaimers included by Flatman and Wilson in their papers disassociating English Heritage from the views offered in both papers. This lack of institutional self-confidence combined with an unthinking recourse to authoritarianism seems to be a characteristic of modern management culture generally and is not something unique to archaeology.

Perhaps the best that can be offered in a contribution such as this is a reflection on some of the themes that unite the papers, some observations on the fault-lines within archaeology and idiosyncratic comments on what seems to have been omitted and why this might be.

Themes and fault-lines

The papers comprising this book were written, largely independently from one another, over a period of several years and it is perhaps unsurprising that a number of common themes emerge from them. How far these themes represent general concerns is unclear but their re-occurrence throughout the book and amongst the wealth of supporting data referenced in support of them suggests that they are widely shared within the discipline. In many cases, these common themes are also characterised by what might be termed 'fault-lines'; issues which divide archaeologists into two or more camps, distinguished by their apparently mutual incompatibility. Such fault-lines can be profound and seemingly irreconcilable, such as the divisions over the role of the Portable Antiquities Scheme but others may offer scope for useful debate. The latter might include Holbrook's suggestion of something akin to the university REF system (Chapter 6) to raise standards of publication in commercial archaeology as opposed to Walker's suggestion (Chapter 18) that it may be time to turn away from 'the rigidity of Research Assessments, briefs and specifications and regulations, and encourage local and regional creativity in the hope that in such diversity new opportunities and possibilities may emerge'. Academics familiar with the REF system might be sceptical of its role in raising standards, but that having been said, Blinkhorn's recent analysis of pottery reports (2014) suggests a disturbing trend in the reporting of artefact assemblages which needs to be tackled as a matter of urgency. Similarly the question of the retention of archaeological archives, the critical but largely undebated issue of the appropriateness of commonly adopted 'on-site' sampling strategies for artefact assemblages, and the marginalisation of artefact and other specialists within the fieldwork process, are all matters that require open debate. It is to be hoped that this book will provoke positive debate within the profession and, most importantly, across the internal boundaries that are such a marked but unwelcome feature of archaeology in the early 21st century.

Education and training; the future of the profession

In the course of the individual papers several issues arise around the themes of education and training. The most fundamental of these questions concerns the extent to which an undergraduate degree in archaeology should be tailored towards producing graduates who are 'trench-ready' at the conclusion of their studies (*see* Everill, Chapter 10) and how far a degree should be more general in nature, providing a broad archaeological education (*see* Sinclair, Chapter 17). More recently, this debate has been further complicated by the requirement to orientate courses towards students who simply want a generally applicable humanities degree and have no real intention of entering archaeology as a career (Sinclair, Chapter 17). This is not, it should be noted, an issue within archaeology alone as recent articles in *de zeen magazine* (2014, 2015) serve to illustrate.

This debate has been running for many years and on the evidence of the papers presented here, seems to be a long way from any resolution. In practice it seems likely that the lack of interest (and even hostility) manifested by university administrators and managers towards archaeology as a subject (as witnessed by the recent closures of university-based archaeological units and the move in some departments to downgrade archaeology into a series of modules suitable for servicing joint or triple honours courses) seems to suggest that there will be little interest, at least in the foreseeable future, in restructuring curricula to reflect the needs of commercial archaeology. In terms of change within the commercial archaeology sector itself, it has long been acknowledged that, from its inception in the late 1980s and early 1990s, commercial archaeology established and, (in part through the IfA, now the CIfA), actively espoused a model based on the contract-tender system in which price was the dominant factor (Cooper-Reade, Chapter 2; Holbrook, Chapter 6; Clarke, Chapter 8; Thorpe, Chapter 16; *see also* Schadla-Hall 1991; Cumberpatch and Blinkhorn 2001; Cumberpatch and Roberts 2012). The adoption of this 'cut-price' model effectively killed off any chance of establishing a structure of practice in which the costs of staff training and professional development could be incorporated into overall costs through the levying of fees at levels which would include an element designed to ensure the long-term stability of archaeology as a profession operating within the commercial sphere. This may have suited the interests of our commercial clients, but it neglected practices that have proved effective elsewhere, notably in the legal profession. Here it is deemed normal for commercial firms to take graduates with a basic degree and to provide them with the opportunity to enhance their range of skills through part-time courses, on-the-job mentoring and training. It is understood that the fees levied for professional services should be adequate not only to pay for the job-in-hand but must also to contribute to the long-term replacement of skilled practitioners, and so ensure the continuation of the profession in the long-term. Under such a model the education and training of new entrants becomes a shared responsibility between the universities which provide the essential, broadly-based education, and the commercial firms which recognise their role in honing the skills of graduates so that they can deal with the realities of a career in a field that is both internally diverse and requires a wide range of skills and, crucially, experience. One cannot but think that this would be preferable to the current situation in archaeology. It would foster far more productive relationships between the academic and commercial fields than those we have at present, while at the same time providing for the reproduction of the discipline in a way that is clearly not happening at the present time. We might, with some justification, ask those senior members of the profession who led the charge into commercialism in the early 1990s whether they ever considered that prioritising competition above all else was really the right way to go, and why they valued archaeology so little that they were prepared to lead a 'race to the bottom' in terms of price (Walker, Chapter 17). I well remember the look of astonishment on the face of an engineer who I met in the context of the Enterprise Allowance Scheme (with the assistance of which I established my own business in 1992) when I told him my hourly rate and my qualifications (a BA and a PhD). His response; *'I wouldn't get out of bed for that'*, left me questioning much about the, then novel, notion of commercial archaeology: Of course, now that archaeology is firmly established as amongst the cheapest of the specialist contractual-services required as part of the development process, it is hard to see how our position in the hierarchy can be changed for the better. The recent chartership granted to the Institute for Archaeologists notwithstanding. Generations entering the profession in recent years and those who will join it in the future might be forgiven in resenting the lack of forethought that has led directly to the lamentable pay and working conditions so well described by Clarke (Chapter 8; *see also* Cooper-Reade, Chapter 2; Everill, Chapter 12).

In terms of the scope and context of training, I am somewhat sceptical about the apparent inclination towards the prioritisation of training in excavation technique above other aspects of archaeology (Everill, Chapter 10). Clearly it is desirable that anyone working in archaeology should have an adequate first-hand knowledge of the practicalities and theory of fieldwork (which should also include various types of survey and not just excavation) but archaeology has always been about more than excavation and this is more true today than it ever has been, given for example, the critical curatorial roles undertaken by archaeologists within the planning system, and the ever-expanding areas of specialisation required within the discipline. As Howe outlines (Chapter 5) the archaeological curator must be conversant with a range of planning laws and non-statutory instruments as well as being an able and effective negotiator, a drafter of briefs for complex schemes of investigation and, not least, able to hold his or her own in the nightmarish world of local government bureaucracy with its continual internal 'reviews' and politico-managerial infighting. The skills needed to deal with the latter are particularly important at a time when philistinism and ignorance are powerful weapons wielded by those who are actively engaged in reducing our towns and cities to shabby clone towns characterised by low quality architecture and dismal sub-modernist city-scapes which seem to represent 'sophistication' for local politicians, and large financial rewards for architects and the development industry (Everill's anecdote regarding the 'fifteen windows' (Chapter 12) is instructive in this context).

Even in terms of a career spent solely in field archaeology (and this is physically impossible for some, Howe, Chapter 5; *see also* Cobb, Chapter 20), some broader knowledge beyond the confines of excavation and recording technique is highly desirable. Early in my career I was told by a very experienced archaeologist that excavation constituted only 5% of any project with post-ex and publication absorbing the rest of the archaeologist's time. Admittedly he was in the process of publishing, with the most minimal logistical and financial support, the results of many years of excavation of an extensive Iron Age site in north-west Bohemia which had produced extremely large artefactual assemblages and a huge quantity of documentation. He may have exaggerated the proportions involved but the point stands. As a pottery specialist who spends, at best, only a few weeks a year in the field (and those in the context of university training and HLF-funded research excavations) I have to dissent, at least in part, from the prioritisation of training for fieldwork. When presented, as I was some years ago, with several archive boxes full of late-Roman Dales ware from a site in South Yorkshire (an area well-known to be aceramic throughout later prehistory) and asked to write a report on 'the assemblage of Iron Age pottery', one has to be somewhat sceptical, not only about the skills-deficit amongst the field-staff and finds-managers but also about the adequacy of the research that preceded the start of the excavation, a matter touched on by Thorpe (Chapter 16). Such an experience is far from unique as Paul Blinkhorn's comments on the same subject (Chapter 19; *see also* Blinkhorn 2014) make clear. In spite of this it is rare to hear calls for knowledge of pottery, or other artefact types to be improved amongst project managers, project officers or field staff. A small number of workshops have been organised by a number of institutions (including the Society for Museum Archaeology, the Study Group for Romano-British pottery, the Medieval Pottery Research Group and English Heritage) but these are normally one or two day events and can do little more than provide the most basic guide to the pottery of any period. In this regard, one must look back to MAP II (English Heritage 1991) with considerable nostalgia, for its now largely abandoned definition of what constitutes an adequate project team. If we are to have a spatial and institutional separation between 'diggers' and 'specialists', with the latter routinely excluded from sites during excavation, then field staff must be adequately trained in basic finds-recognition, not to mention the application of 'first aid' conservation for finds during excavation and post-excavation cleaning, bagging, and transport, a subject not tackled in this volume. Are all of these skills, as well as excavation, recording and the vital tasks of post-excavation administration to be taught within three years of what is now, effectively, part-time higher education (Sinclair, Chapter 17)? Archaeology is too small and too fragile a profession for this issue to remain unaddressed, particularly given the fact that it is not a mere debating point and, as the anecdotes above make clear, significantly diminishes the quality and value of what we do. No simple routinisation of procedure will make up for the fact that, in some cases, field archaeologists are excavating sites without knowing even the approximate date of the site, or what types of material they are likely to recover during excavation, and may be quite unaware of the wider importance of what they are excavating. This is a particular problem in historical archaeology where the often inaccurate use of the stigmatising term 'Victorian' can be deployed to cut post-excavation costs by excluding finds assemblages from full analysis. As one colleague phrased it recently *'if I take my ferret to the vet, I want to be sure that the vet knows that it's not a horse'*.

A high proportion of artefact specialists are, under the current system, self-employed. If a return to the principles of MAP II is impossible (which I do not concede), would it not be possible for individual contractors to buy in, not only expertise after a site is completed, but also prior to the commencement of excavation, to ensure that the field staff had some idea of what they might be encountering, its potential significance and how to deal with it? This would not only provide cumulative training to field teams but might also encourage those looking to move away from excavation to consider post-excavation analysis and reporting as a career option and so help to alleviate the imminent crisis in the supply of artefact specialists.

Archaeological archives and the failure of the neo-liberal state

The question of the archiving and the curation of archaeological archives is mentioned in several papers (Cooper-Reade, Chapter 2; Cumberpatch, Chapter 7) and is the subject of one (Shepherd, Chapter 13). This issue has been of concern to RESCUE for a number of years and has been raised with government ministers on several occasions (*see, for example*, RESCUE 2004, 2005). Unfortunately, as discussed by Shepherd, few practical measures have been taken to address the issue in spite of its centrality to archaeology as conceived under PPG16 and its successors. If the principle of preservation by record is to be taken seriously (as its place in the planning system implies; see the papers in Section 1), then there can be no place for the destruction of archives. In this matter I have to dissent from the opinion expressed by one of the authors (Cooper-Reade) when she asserts that we cannot keep everything that we dig up (Chapter 2). Once we start destroying the subject matter of our discipline to save money or to create space in archive stores (to be filled by what exactly?) then archaeology is on its way to the slaughterhouse as both an academic discipline and as a professional practice (Howe, Chapter 4; Cumberpatch, Chapter 7; Shepherd, Chapter 13).

Unlikely as it may seem, it is here that a central issue in British politics and archaeological practice come together. This issue is the relationship between the state and the private sector in public life and in the provision of public services. Fortunately I am not required to meditate on this in the context of the National Health Service, the civil and criminal justice systems or the provision of assistance to the unemployed and can restrict myself to archaeology and, critically, to the funding of archive provision.

The responsibility for funding the excavation and some degree of publication has effectively been passed to the private sector under the provisions of PPG16, PPS5 and the NPPF, as discussed by the contributors to Section 1 (Cooper and Ralston, Cooper-Reade, Stubbs, Howe). Unfortunately no effective, properly funded provision has ever been made for the care and curation of archives, despite the central place of the archive in the principle of preservation by record in the various planning policy documents from PPG16 onwards. By default this has been left to local and regional museums whose funding arrangements take little account of this responsibility which is, in archaeological terms, one of their most important roles.

This is not to criticise the staff of these museums who have done, and are doing, an exceptional and often thankless job under adverse circumstances and who work under the constant threat of unemployment at the whim of politicians whose understanding of the wider issues is minimal at best and actively hostile at worst. Given the importance of preservation by record, the adequate funding of local and regional museums and regional archaeological stores or some combination of the two should be recognised as the responsibility of the state either through a central agency such as English Heritage (or its successor, Historic England), Cadw or Historic Scotland, or through explicit, ring-fenced, financial support for local and regional museums from central government. This responsibility should represent a form of public-private partnership which would demonstrate to the private sector that the state takes seriously its side of the 'bargain' enshrined in the planning regulations. It should indicate a degree of respect for the investment made by the private sector in the investigation of archaeological sites and landscapes through the planning system. When the prospect of throwing away unique archaeological data to 'save space' is seriously considered, should we be surprised that some private firms will be reluctant to spend money on the recovery of that same data? As Shepherd points out, the time for questioning why we keep archives is over; we keep such material because it is rare and important (Chapter 13). Moreover we keep it because archaeology is a dynamic discipline; it is not about creating a static model of the past, or of finding out 'what went on' but of providing interpretative accounts of aspects of the past which draw not only on new data, but also on revised and novel interpretations of existing data which exploit different aspects of the datasets and present new accounts of the experiences of different groups of people in the past (*see, for example,* Cumberpatch 1997, Jervis 2014). Our interests and concerns are not necessarily those which concerned our predecessors. Nor will they be those of future generations. Today, in a society which is not yet comfortable with multi-vocality but which has, pragmatically, to acknowledge its existence, we can ask a wide range of questions which will not take the experience of the adult heterosexual male as the only one which is of significance or interest, as might have been the case until very recently (*cf* Cobb, Chapter 20). If we are to write an archaeology that is relevant and engages new audiences (as opposed to one which remains rooted in the social and political attitudes of past generations) then we must have access to complete archives, stored in conditions where they can be examined and re-examined by researchers keen to exploit new angles and new techniques. Moreover, returning briefly to the discussion of training, access to such archives should be facilitated for students and trainees-in-employment (if the latter existed) who will gain skills and experience through contact with the materiality of such archives. Much has been written about the adequacy or otherwise of the contract-tender system and the planning policy notes that underlie it, but the fact that the state has never fully accepted its side of the implicit deal represented by these policies has yet to be widely acknowledged. It is to be hoped that the wealth and importance of archaeological archives will remain a theme of RESCUE's campaigning activities until the matter is satisfactorily resolved and we hear no more of the faux-macho voices counselling the destruction of our past in order to save valuable empty space.

Regulation: the roles of the state and the private sector

A related argument to that proposed above can be made in the case of Sites and Monuments Record (SMR) or Historic Environment Record (HER) provision. A commercialised system will inevitably spawn a class of consultants dedicated to acting in the interests of their clients and, *de facto*, against the interests of archaeology (Thorpe, Chapter 16; Strickland 1993; Cumberpatch and Blinkhorn 2001; Fenton-Thomas 2006). In such a situation, there must be a statutory responsibility on the planning authorities to maintain a wholly independent and publicly-funded system of regulation and control designed to mitigate the impact of development on archaeological and heritage assets, as outlined by Howe (Chapter 4). The present system can be characterised as one in which a non-statutory policy-document (the NPPF) is overseen by an under-funded and under-staffed body of curators whose positions are at constant risk, as local authorities are forced to cut ever more deeply into core functions as a result of central government policies, while the economic and moral power of the market grows ever stronger. This is not a system that can be sustained or defended. However many policy documents are formulated and however the advice contained within them is simplified, codified or made 'accessible', they are utterly meaningless unless they are backed by a robust and formidable system of monitoring and regulation based upon an equally robust statutory framework, on the lines of the unfairly maligned provisions of health and safety law. Archaeological sites and significant buildings, whether designated or undesignated, should have the protection, not only of paper planning-policies, but also of a dedicated and secure system of inspection and monitoring. As the system is presently constituted, this has to mean SMR/HER provision that is rooted in statute. If RESCUE campaigns for one thing in the next few years, it must be this principle. If we fail to secure statutory provision of curatorial functions and the system is allowed to continue on its way to the 'death of a thousand cuts' then we shall have failed to carry the intentions of the founders of RESCUE to their logical conclusion. More seriously, we shall have failed the country as a whole. This still leaves major areas of concern, notably the position of the rural landscape as highlighted by Powlesland (Chapter 11, *see also* Howe, Chapter 4; Sheldon, Introduction), but a statutory framework underpinning the NPPF and its successors, would at least ensure a framework of protection within which solutions to specific issues (in the case of the rural landscape, perhaps on the lines suggested by Powlesland), can be investigated and put into operation.

Public and popular archaeology

Three of the papers in this collection deal with the question of archaeology and its relationship to the wider population (Pringle, Chapter 9; Blinkhorn, Chapter 19; and Pitts, Chapter 21) while Wilson (Chapter 15) tackles the perennial problem of metal-detecting, something I have discussed recently elsewhere (Cumberpatch 2013) and which lies at the heart of one of the most pernicious and profound conflicts within British archaeology.

'Archaeology and the public', the invariable title or subtitle to dozens of conference sessions held in the last 30 years or more, is today an even more high-profile issue than it was in 1974. Even at the annual Theoretical Archaeology Group (TAG) conference, reviled by some for its focus on theoretical issues, 'Public Archaeology has featured ... almost from the very beginning and has remained as a low-level but constant presence' (Gaydarska 2009, 1157). This trend continues and at the 2014 Manchester TAG conference the session on the subject ran for a full day, was very well-attended and included some useful and politically aware papers (eg Hedge 2014). RESCUE has always been aware that without public support, archaeology as a practice has little hope of survival in any useful form. From papers in the 1974 RESCUE Archaeology volume (Thomas and Arnold 1974, Kiln 1974, Rahtz 1974) though regular articles in

RESCUE News (eg Redhead 2005), the publication of manuals and textbooks and, most recently, to the establishment of the RESCUE website and Facebook page, the Trust has always sought to forge connections with the wider world outside the profession. Indeed, education and outreach form part of the Trust's remit as a charity. On one hand this is essential to a subscription-based organisation that receives no state aid, and only limited, project-specific funding (normally to facilitate the production of books, including the present volume as well as technical manuals such as *First Aid for Finds, The Manual of Field Drawing,*) but at the wider level it is vital to maintain archaeology as a democratic practice in which there is a primary role for the amateur and the enthusiast alongside the professional. In this, modern archaeology owes a considerable debt to the archaeological and natural history societies of the late 18th, 19th, and early 20th centuries which did so much to establish archaeology as a coherent discipline with a strong local and regional focus as well as a global one.

As Pringle notes (Chapter 9) there is a potential conflict between voluntary involvement in archaeology and the move to 'professionalise' archaeology. This was certainly true in the 1990s although in my own experience, the arrival of the Heritage Lottery Fund (HLF) and the funding of local heritage initiatives, has opened up new avenues for collaboration between volunteers and professionals which have been, and remain, a considerable success. The focus on the teaching of archaeological methods and the framing of research questions around the concerns and interests of local communities indicates that this, rather than the model represented by the Portable Antiquities Scheme with its focus on the rogue individual amassing collections of context-free metalwork items for private contemplation or private profit, should be the way for archaeology to connect with the various constituencies which represent that nebulous concept 'the public'.

The significance of HLF-funded projects is, regrettably, under-represented in the papers in this volume and it may be that this is due in part to the lack of connectedness between different projects and the lack of any broad overview of the results obtained from many disparate projects. As with the accumulation of data arising from commercial archaeology which has only recently been tackled through the work of the Archaeology Data Service and the syntheses undertaken by Richard Bradley, David Yates and others, it seems that the volume of data being generated is outstripping the capability of archaeology to analyse and interpret the results at the local and regional scale. Perhaps more significantly, we have yet to see the establishment of a structure that will use the data from such community projects to establish second- and third-generation projects which will tackle the wide range of detailed questions raised by the first generation. This issue notwithstanding, the regular close co-operation between professional archaeologists and enthusiasts, volunteers, school children and others, gives the lie to the frequent claim made by artefact hunters and their allies, that archaeology is in some way an elitist practice designed to exclude the wider population from participation in the investigation of its own past. It is profoundly unfortunate that this engagement with archaeology and the materiality of the past runs counter to the interests of the mainstream media industry which is still seemingly incapable of distinguishing treasure hunting from archaeology. Thus the grotesque parody of archaeological method seen in the excavation of the Lenborough Hoard of Saxon coins received wide coverage in newspapers and television, while the efforts of many thousands of people across the country to uncover the history and archaeology of their local communities is covered only by local newspapers and on dedicated websites. The decline in the vitality of the local press is particularly unfortunate in this regard. Pitts is right (Chapter 21) to remind us that good quality writing is essential in communicating archaeology to a wider audience, but we can also be forgiven for feeling that we are being short-changed by journalists, particularly those working to a 'news' agenda, who seem incapable of coming to terms with reality when it conflicts with their presuppositions about the scope of archaeology and the potential it has to engage and inform a range of constituencies within the wider population. This contrasts, of course, with the more feature-led agenda of the television programmes discussed by Blinkhorn (Chapter 19) which give a more rounded view of archaeology that goes beyond the meretricious glitter of 'buried treasure' and which have been instrumental in encouraging amateurs to initiate and engage with HLF funded investigations. Given that rising costs and constraints on budgets make the appearance of a new *'Time Team'* style programme unlikely (Blinkhorn, *pers comm*), one must wonder whether the easy availability of hardware and software capable of producing sound and video content of near-professional quality, combined with the advent of local digital television channels, will not lead to the production of segments or even complete programmes based on HLF-funded projects. These might usefully supplement the established output of such projects which currently includes audio-guides, guided walks, websites, pamphlets, articles in local journals and temporary and longer-term exhibitions.

Conclusion

At the start of this paper I quoted the comedian and film maker, Woody Allen, who offered his audience two negative messages as a substitute for a positive conclusion to his set. Are negative messages the best that can be offered at the conclusion to this volume?

Clearly archaeology faces many serious challenges from both government, its allies and many of its financial sponsors (or paymasters) in the development industry, and from the ongoing effects of attrition, particularly in the countryside where industrial agriculture, mining, and quarrying look set to continue to have a catastrophic impact on individual sites and landscapes. The planning system looks set to be reorganised yet again after the 2015 election and considerable effort will have to be made by heritage organisations, including RESCUE, to ensure that the gains of the early 1990s are not lost in the face of politically manufactured panic regarding the need for housing and industrial development. It is to be expected that archaeology (along with ecology and natural history) will be cast, wholly unjustifiably, as an impediment to such development, rather than as a social, educational, and economic asset to the country as a whole. At the same time it looks likely that the rump of English Heritage represented by Historic England will decline in both size and influence as further cuts whittle away its tangible and intellectual assets. Nor does there seem any immediate sign of HERs being made a statutory responsibility on local authorities, although it is to be hoped that other heritage organisations besides RESCUE will continue to campaign for this most basic and vital of reforms to local government. Negative messages are all too easy to find. But are there any positive messages? I believe, perhaps over-optimistically, that there are, although considerable effort will have to be made in order for them to have any real impact.

The legacy of *'Time Team'* and the practical engagement of local communities in a wide range of heritage projects, facilitated in large part by the Heritage Lottery Fund, have given us an informed and active constituency amongst a wide range of people who have discovered the very real pleasure and fulfilment to be derived from archaeology and related historical enquiries and research. At the same time, local activist initiatives, such as the campaign to prevent inappropriate and destructive housing development close to Old Oswestry hillfort, are attracting both local and international support. It is true that we still have to forge better links with environmental and ecological campaigners (regarding, for example, threats to ancient woodland which are as much archaeological assets as ecological ones) and this should perhaps be a priority for campaigning heritage organisations in the next few years; the basis for co-operation is there in both shared goals and shared methods.

The consequences of the 2008 credit and banking crisis were as bad for individuals employed in archaeology as they were for those in other sectors of the economy, and as a direct result of individual and corporate greed, combined with culpable managerial incompetence, we have lost a significant number of experienced and skilled individuals. Nevertheless, it is the case that both the publicly-funded and commercial archaeological sectors have survived, albeit battered and with a significantly reduced capacity. Moreover, the public sector will certainly face more savage cuts in the years to come. In the past, I have been highly critical of many aspects of the commercialisation of archaeology (Blinkhorn and Cumberpatch 1999; Cumberpatch and Blinkhorn 2001; Cumberpatch 2000) and I stand by those criticisms, but a robust case can now be made in favour of the commercial sector on the grounds that it has an existence that is at least partially independent from the ill-informed whims of government policy. So long as a planning policy on the lines of PPG16 exists in which heritage and archaeological concerns are recognised in practical terms, then archaeology has an income stream that is independent of government, whether local or national. The seemingly inevitable fate of Historic England and the savage cuts already made to the budgets of the Arts Council for England and the Council for British Archaeology render arguments for purely state-level provision of archaeological expertise and capacity difficult, perhaps impossible, to sustain. We should now be arguing, I would suggest, not over the relative merits of state *versus* commercial provision, but for a hybrid system in which an active commercial sector is closely regulated by a properly funded, legally established and aggressively independent system of monitoring and control, based on the local planning system.

There remains a central role for a state archaeology service (such as Historic England) to provide, not only guidance notes and advice on 'best practice' but also an actual capacity to undertake excavation and to provide central conservation, scientific and analytical resources, particularly given the current ambiguous role of the managerially- and financially-driven university sector. In addition to the roles already envisaged for Historic England, such a body (if expanded and properly funded) might also play a role in either running (or commissioning from others), training schemes suitable for both professionals and committed amateurs through the organisation of large scale combined training and research excavations, perhaps on the model of the recent Stonehenge Riverside project. Such flagship projects, although traditionally located in southern England, could run almost anywhere and might, with advantage, focus on agriculturally threatened landscapes such as those of South and East Yorkshire, or other areas under threat of large scale mining and quarrying. The scale of such projects and the range of techniques and approaches that could be employed would also make them attractive prospects for media companies looking to reclaim the millions of viewers who continue to regret the loss of 'Time Team' and similar programmes. This vision depends, of course, on the maintenance of adequate state support and, as we have seen, this can neither be assumed nor expected.

Is this the naïve utopian vision of an angry (or at least mildly irritable) middle-aged archaeologist seeking to turn back the seemingly unstoppable decline of his profession? Quite possibly. But archaeology has an informed and enthusiastic nucleus of popular support and an array of tangible assets that continue to fascinate and to compel a wide cross-section of the population as well as the foreign visitors who make a substantial contribution not only to local and regional economies, as well as the overall GDP (as evidenced by the annual Heritage Counts and Visit Britain survey, for example). The question is, how do we translate this level of interest and support into a movement that will take on politicians and the development industry (and its powerful lobbying tentacles) to achieve a more than barely adequate provision for archaeology and the historic environment within a vibrant economy? We need to oppose those moves which threaten archaeology (notably the weakening of the planning system and the scandalous neglect of the museum sector) but also to argue vociferously for the prospects and opportunities which offer tangible benefits to society more widely. The clear educational benefits of archaeology in schools and colleges, the undoubted therapeutic benefits of doing archaeology in cases of both mental and physical damage (cf Operation Nightingale see http://www.dmasuk.org/) and the integrative effects of community and cross-community projects have been repeatedly demonstrated in practical terms. The task in hand is now to challenge the closed and often deeply prejudiced minds of local and national politicians with solid evidence of the contribution that archaeology and its related disciplines can make to a wider, inclusive society.

Acknowledgements

I have been writing articles on this theme since the mid-1990s and have accumulated considerable debts to many archaeologists who have discussed the issues with me at length. For all the usual reasons some must remain anonymous but I would like to thank in particular Paul Blinkhorn,

Duncan Brown, Adrian Chadwick, Tim Cockrell, Rob Hedge, Tony Howe, Jon Humble, Colin Merrony, Reuben Thorpe and Helen Wickstead for their contributions and Shaun Rylands for insights into the structure of the legal profession. All the opinions expressed are mine as are the inevitable errors and omissions.

References

Allen, W, 1999, Summing up, [1964], *Woody Allen standup comic*, (Audio CD) Rhino Entertainment Company

Blinkhorn, P, 2014, Not so much a pot, more an expensive luxury: Commercial archaeology and the slow death of pottery analysis, in Blinkhorn, P, and Cumberpatch, C G, (eds), *The chiming of crack'd bells: recent approaches to the study of artefacts in archaeology*, BAR Internat Ser **2677**, Archaeopress, Oxford, 99–104

Blinkhorn, P, and Cumberpatch, C G, 1999, Archaeology in England 1999, *World Archaeology Bulletin* **9**, 45–55

Cumberpatch, C G, 1997, Towards a phenomenological approach to the study of medieval pottery, in Cumberpatch, C G, and Blinkhorn P W, (eds), *Not so much a pot, more a way of life*, Oxbow Mono **83**, Oxbow Books, Oxford, pp

Cumberpatch, C G, 2000, Some problems in contemporary English archaeology, *Archeologia Polona* **38**, 225–38

Cumberpatch, C G, 2013, Metal detecting and archaeology: A tale of two methodologies, *The Crucible: Historical Metallurgy Society News,* Spring 2013, 8–9

Cumberpatch, C, and Blinkhorn, P, 2001, Clients, Curators, contractors and archaeology: who owns the past?, in Pluciennik, M, (ed), *The responsibilities of archaeologists: archaeology and ethics,* BAR Internat Ser **981**, Archaeopress, Oxford, 125–51

Cumberpatch, C G, and Roberts, H M, 2012, Life in the archaeological marketplace, in Rockman, M, and Flatman, J, (eds), *Archaeology in society: Its relevance in the modern world,* Springer, New York, 23–43

dezeen magazine, 2014, *Design education is 'tragic' says Jonathan Ive*, at http://www.dezeen.com/2014/11/13/design-education-tragic-says-jonathan-ive-apple/ (accessed 25 March 2015)

dezeen magazine, 2015, *UK architecture schools fail to equip students with skills needed for practice*, at http://www.dezeen.com/2015/02/02/uk-architecture-schools-fail-equip-students-skills-riba-appointments/ (accessed 25 March 2015)

English Heritage, 1991, *Management of archaeological projects,* English Heritage, London

Fenton Thomas, C, 2006, Consultants in archaeology: some observations from the field, *RESCUE News* **99**, 7

Gaydarska, B, 2009, *A brief history of TAG, Antiquity* **83**, 1152–62

Hedge, R, 2014, *There is no archaeology without instrumentalised archaeology,* Unpublished paper presented at the 2014 Theoretical Archaeology Conference (Manchester University)

Jervis, B, 2014, *Pottery and social life in medieval England*, Oxbow Books, Oxford

Kiln, R, 1974, *Archaeology as a hobby and how to start,* in Rahtz 1974, 256–73

Rahtz, P A, (ed), 1974, *Rescue archaeology,* Penguin Books, Harmonsworth

Rahtz, P, 1974, Volunteers, in Rahtz, 1974, 241–55

Redhead, N, 2005, Community archaeology: The Greater Manchester experience, *RESCUE News* **97**, 4–5

RESCUE: The British Archaeological Trust, 2004, *Museums in crisis: an outline of the RESCUE position*, at http://rescue-archaeology.org.uk/2004/06/16/museums-in-crisis/ (accessed 25 March 2015)

RESCUE: The British Archaeological Trust, 2005, *Understanding the future: museums and 21st century life: A RESCUE response*, at http://rescue-archaeology.org.uk/2005/06/28/understanding-the-future-museums-and-21-st-century-life/ (accessed 25 March 2015)

Schadla-Hall, T, 1991, Competitive tendering in archaeology, in Swain, H, (ed), *Competitive tendering in archaeology: Papers presented at a one day conference in June 1990*, RESCUE: The British Archaeological Trust, and Standing Conference of Archaeological Unit Managers, Hertford, 51–3,

Strickland, T, 1993, The consultant's perspective, in Carrington, P, (ed), *Evaluations in rescue archaeology; PPG16 three years on*, Chester Archaeol Service Occ Pap **1**, Chester Archaeol Service 18–20

Thomas, G, and Arnold, G, 1974, Rescue archaeology and the public, in Rahtz 1974, 241–55

RESCUE: the next 40 years

Diana Friendship-Taylor and Reuben Thorpe

Mission Statement

40 years ago, RESCUE provided a focus for and articulated the groundswell of concern among academics, archaeologists and members of the public, at the destruction of parts of our historic towns, disappearing with neither respect for their integrity, nor adequate record. RESCUE was instrumental in the establishment of archaeological units and provision for the preservation and recording of archaeology.

From these beginnings, RESCUE has expanded its rôle to meet new challenges, campaigning to influence legislation with the aim to ensure archaeology is widely regarded as a vital part of Britain's contemporary cultural, social, intellectual and economic life. One of RESCUE's great strengths is its unalloyed independence. While we are a partisan organisation, partisan in favour of our history and archaeology, our independence gives us the freedom to express unbiased and critical views and offer a radical programme for archaeology.

The 21st century is witnessing the dismantling of much of the infrastructure of archaeology set up during the last third of the 20th century, largely through withdrawal of funding, exposing the fragility of safeguards for heritage assets and the vulnerability of the process of investigation and preservation. Campaign achievements are only successful for as long as they remain intact and are not eroded by unintended consequences. In short, Britain's heritage is ill-equipped to withstand increasing pressures and RESCUE recognises that it will remain so for a lengthy foreseeable future. While we understand the reality of the present we do not agree that the consequences for archaeology and the historic environment are either inevitable or acceptable.

The funding and structure of archaeology will continue to feature prominently on RESCUE's agenda. Archaeological provision, in all its forms, needs statutory provision and robust protective legislation. Each new government initiative brings new hopes and new challenges for the historic environment. With all the advantages for archaeology that *Planning Policy Guidance Note 16: Archaeology and Planning* (PPG 16, DoE 1990) and *Planning Policy Guidance note 15: Planning and the Historic Environment* (PPG 15, DoE 1994) brought, at the end of the day, it was just 'guidance'. While RESCUE supports the 'polluter pays' principle, PPG 16 had the unfortunate consequence of an emphasis on price as the principal factor in determining which body won a specific contract, as determined by the developer. It has also inevitably left a legacy of an imbalance between a 'managerial ethos', which evolved in the practice and conduct of professional archaeology under PPG16 and the 'research ethos', with its investigative and research orientated approach of academic archaeology and in the independent/voluntary sector.

The *National Planning Policy Framework* of 2012, into which PPS5 (which replaced PPG15/16) was subsumed, immediately rang alarm bells for the safety of the historic environment, with its keynote statement that:

'development that is sustainable should go ahead, without delay – a presumption in favour of sustainable development that is the basis for every plan, and every decision'.

While the historic environment is considered alongside the social and economic elements of sustainability, the emphasis of the Framework is still on 'guidance'. RESCUE will, therefore, continue to campaign for a more robust legal framework, to strengthen the hand of local development control archaeologists and archaeological curators, to put them on a more equal footing with planners. RESCUE strongly advocates the statutory provision and maintenance of Historic Environment Records and their accessibility.

RESCUE sees the network of regional and local museums as lying at the heart of any national system for the care of archaeological archives. Yet these institutions and their staff have no centralised protection from both the effects of budget cuts and of corporate agendas devised by local authorities, which do not accommodate the ethos of museums. Without properly funded and staffed archive and conservation facilities, there is little prospect that projects carried out by local archaeological and heritage groups, universities and under the aegis of the planning system, will contribute effectively to future archaeological research, because of their inaccessibility and declining quality.

Besides the emaciation of staff and services in museums through budget cuts, some museums, whose agenda has been set by a funding body, or because they deem it necessary to survive in a commercial world, have 'popularised' themselves, as 'fun' venues for their visitors, resulting in a dilution of their expertise base, to the extent that they can no longer be viewed seriously as educational institutions, leaving them more widely open to cuts. There is a common misconception that anything 'academic' or 'educational' precludes creating an experience that is accessible, enjoyable or fulfilling for a wide range of visitors.

Closer co-operation between archaeologists and museum professionals will only become possible if the crisis of budget cuts to museums, to the detriment of storage, conservation and curation of archaeological archives, can be resolved, and if a reversal of the 'dumbing down' of specialist staff can be achieved. RESCUE seeks to campaign alongside national archaeological and museum bodies to highlight and resolve this dilemma. Appropriate resources are urgently needed to create opportunities for co-operation between archaeological units, universities and museums.

RESCUE is concerned that, in the early 21st century, there is increasing dissonance between policy, practice, and approaches to the past. This is manifest in the paradox of the increasing interest in the past and in our common heritage (as seen in the growing popularity of participation in archaeological research, in high profile television programmes, in museum displays and exhibitions) and the fact of increasingly inadequate protection given to buildings, sites and monuments, unprecedented reductions in funding for heritage organisations and museums and a growth in threats to the historic environment from development, climate change, criminality and armed conflict. The vulnerability of archaeology also arises from a common lack of understanding of the cohesiveness and relevance of the processes, involving a number of diverse disciplines which constitute an archaeological project. This diversity is both its strength and an inherent weakness in archaeology. To many, 'archaeology' is the 'glamour' of finding objects. Understanding does not always extend to the processes of recording, research, conservation, publication and display.

RESCUE: The British Archaeological Trust seeks to maintain the position of archaeology and our historic environment as a vital part of the nation's cultural life. RESCUE is a Registered Charity which exists to support, promote and highlight the interests of archaeology, archaeologists and the historic environment within the United Kingdom and elsewhere by participating in professional debate, lobbying MPs and local councillors, by supporting pressure groups and by other appropriate means. We are not affiliated to any political party or other organisations but we are members of The Archaeology Forum and The Heritage Alliance. We receive no state aid and our work is entirely dependent on the subscriptions and donations of our members who are drawn from the archaeological profession and the wider public. Members of the RESCUE Committee receive no remuneration in respect of their efforts on RESCUE's behalf and we employ one part-time member of staff.

RESCUE continues to campaign at the heart of concerns for the future of British archaeology, bringing a wide range of skills and experience,– with a role to play in the next 40 years, which will be every bit as vital and challenging as in 1971.

The views expressed by the contributors to this book suggest that over the next 40 years there will be a continuing need for strong advocacy and public pressure so that the gains of the past 40 years can be built on to ensure that the past has a meaningful future as a vital part of the nation's unique identity and cultural life. RESCUE needs vocal supporters, subscribers, donors and activists to ensure the work begun in 1971 will continue into the next century. If you care about the future of British archaeology join us now. Full details of our activities can be found on our website www.rescue-archaeology. org.uk

List of contributors

Paul Blinkhorn *has been a professional archaeologist for nearly 35 years, and has been specialising in the study of post-Roman pottery for the last 30 years. He is a visiting lecturer at the University of Cambridge, and a visiting fellow at the University of Bristol, where he is also involved with the Berkeley Castle Project. He has worked on numerous projects in Britain and abroad, and is currently involved in projects in Cyprus and elsewhere run by* Operation Nightingale, *organised by the Defence Archaeology Group with the aim of helping injured military veterans. He was a regular contributor to Channel 4 Television's* Time Team *from 1998 onwards, and has appeared on a number of other archaeology-themed television series, including* Pub Dig *for Channel 5, and* Michael Wood's Story of England *for the BBC.*

Chris Clarke BSc, MA, ACIfA: Senior Archaeological Consultant, CgMs Consulting, Floor 7, 140 London Wall, London, EC2Y 5DN, **chris.clarke600@hotmail.co.uk** *Chris started digging at the age of 17. After graduation from Bournemouth University in 2000 his work with AOC Archaeology took him across the country from Orkney to Cornwall. In 2003–04 he studied for an MA in Ceramics and Lithics Analysis at Southampton University. Chris left AOC In 2013 to join CgMs as an Archaeological Consultant. He has been involved with both the Institute for Archaeologists and Prospect, the Trade Union representing professional archaeologists, and is currently involved with the Thames Discovery Programme and other volunteer archaeological projects.*

Dr Hannah Cobb FSA Scot, MCIfA: Lecturer in Archaeology, Department of Archaeology, School of Arts, Languages and Cultures, University of Manchester, Oxford Road, Manchester, M13 9PL, **Hannah.Cobb@Manchester.ac.uk** *Hannah's research focuses on two areas: interpretive approaches to contemporary archaeological practice, and the Mesolithic and Neolithic of western Scotland. In the former, questions of pedagogy, training, equality and diversity are a central concern, in the latter Hannah's research examines the intersection between material culture, landscape and identity. Hannah's research interests are further developed through the field projects that she co-directs; the multi-period Ardnamurchan Transitions Project, and the Whitworth Park Community Archaeology and History Project, and she is one* *of the editors of* Reconsidering Archaeological Fieldwork *(Springer, 2012). Hannah has also worked for the Higher Education Academy's Subject Centre for History, Classics and Archaeology, where she researched the role of fieldwork in the undergraduate degree and graduate employability.*

Malcolm A Cooper FSA, FSA Scot, MCIfA, IHBC, MCIM, Hon FRIAS: Chief Executive Officer of the Federation of Archaeological Managers and Employers (FAME) and Director of Malcolm A Cooper Consulting, The Croft, Irthington, Carlisle, Cumbria, CA6 4NJ, **malcolmacooper@outlook.com**
Malcolm practiced as a field archaeologist before joining English Heritage where he held a number of senior posts over a 13 year period. He was then Historic Scotland's Chief Inspector for five years before setting up his own consultancy and joining FAME as their CEO.

Hester Cooper-Reade: Business Manager, Albion Archaeology, St Mary's Church, St Mary's Street Bedford, MK42 0AS, **h.cooper-reade@albion-arch.com**
Hester has worked in contract archaeology since the mid-1980s. After a number of years spent in the field, initially as a supervisor on a number of the large urban excavations in Ipswich and then as a Project Officer with the Hertfordshire Archaeological Trust, Hester moved into a management role with the former Essex County Council Field Unit before taking up her existing role with Albion Archaeology just over 11 years ago. Throughout her career Hester has been actively involved with a number of archaeological bodies including RESCUE, the now Chartered Institute for Archaeology and most recently the Federation for Archaeological Managers and Employers where she holds the role of Hon Treasurer.

Dr Chris Cumberpatch: 22 Tennyson Road, Sheffield, S6 2WE, **cgc@ccumberpatch. freeserve.co.uk**
Chris studied archaeology at Sheffield University between 1979 and 1981 and, after gaining several research scholarships to investigate late-Iron-Age slip-decorated pottery in central Europe, returned to complete a PhD between 1986 and 1991. Since 1991 he has worked as a freelance archaeologist specialising in the medieval and later pottery of Yorkshire and north-east England. He has also worked in Lebanon, Syria and Turkey. In recent years he has returned to the study of late prehistoric pottery with several major reports on assemblages from pipelines in eastern Yorkshire. He is the author of numerous papers on pottery, the relationship between archaeology and politics and the ongoing crisis in British archaeology. He has co-edited Different Iron Ages *(with J D Hill),* Excavations at 16–20 Church Street, Bawtry, South Yorkshire *(with J Dunkley),* Not so much a pot, more a way of life *and* The chiming of crack'd bells *(both with P W Blinkhorn).*

George Dennis BSc, MCIfA, (retired): **george.dennis@ntlworld.com**
George began employment in urban archaeology when full-time field units were first established in the early 1970s, was one of the first members of IFA, and has direct

experience in the campaigning issues led by RESCUE that characterised a profession struggling to emerge. He spent 30 years working for the Museum of London, particularly in managing multi-site infrastructure projects such as HS1, Crossrail, M2 and Thames Tunnel; and most recently as senior project manager in the Planning Team which specialises in risk studies and environmental impact assessment.

Robin Densem BA (Hons), MCIfA: **robindensem@btinternet.com**
Robin has worked in archaeology since 1973 and taught archaeology adult education classes from 1977–2013. His successive employers have included the Southwark and Lambeth unit, The Museum of London Department of Greater London Archaeology, The Museum of London Archaeology Service, Compass Archaeology, Birkbeck College, and, currently, The Heritage Network as well as becoming RESCUE Hon Treasurer in 2012.

Dr Paul Everill FSA, MCIfA, FHEA: Senior Lecturer in Applied Archaeological Techniques and Programme Leader for Undergraduate Archaeology, Department of Archaeology, University of Winchester, Winchester, Hampshire, SO22 4NR, **Paul.Everill@winchester.ac.uk**
Paul first gained experience of archaeology as a 16 year old trainee at Wroxeter, before graduating with a BA from SDUC Lampeter (1994); and an MA (1999) and PhD (2006) from the University of Southampton. He worked for 11 commercial fieldwork organisations between 2000 and 2008 before taking up a teaching post at the University of Winchester. Paul has co-directed a research and training excavation at the multi-period site of Nokalakevi in Mingrelia, western Georgia, since 2004. Publications include two editions of The Invisible Diggers *(2009; 2012) and the edited volume* Nokalakevi Tsikhegoji Archaeopolis: Archaeological excavations 2001–10 *(2014).*

Dr Joe Flatman FSA, MCIfA: Head of Central Casework and Programmes, Designation Department, Historic England
Joe studied at the University of Southampton between 1994 and 2003, followed by teaching positions at the universities of Cardiff (2003–04), Flinders (Adelaide) (2004–05) and London (2005–12). Between 2006–12 Joe was also Surrey County Archaeologist. In the autumn of 2012 he joined English Heritage. Publications include Archaeology: A Beginner's Guide *(2015);* Prehistoric Archaeology of the Continental Shelf *(2014);* Archaeology in Society: Its Relevance in the Modern World *(2012);* Becoming an Archaeologist: A Guide to Professional Pathways *(2011) and* Ships and Shipping in Medieval Manuscripts *(2009).*

Diana Friendship-Taylor BA: former Conservator at Northampton Museums; Trustee of the Upper Nene Archaeological Society and Piddington Roman Villa Museum, Northamptonshire; Co-Director of Piddington Roman Villa excavations, 1979-present; founder member, currently Meetings Co-ordinator, Archaeological Leather Group; RESCUE Chair 2009–14.

A combined honours graduate in History and Archaeology, of University of Exeter in 1970, Diana's early practical experience of archaeology was in Wiltshire and Somerset. Diana worked with the Exeter Archaeological Field Unit, then at Exeter Museums, before taking up a career in archaeological conservation. She is a specialist in archaeological leather, with particular interests in the period 1200–1700 and her native West Country.

Neil Holbrook FSA, MCIfA: Chief Executive, Cotswold Archaeology, Building 11, Kemble Enterprise Park, Cirencester, Glos. GL7 6BQ, **neil.holbrook@ cotswoldarchaeology.co.uk**
Neil has been Chief Executive at Cotswold Archaeology, one of the largest archaeological contracting organisations working in the UK, for over 20 years. For the last six years he has been working with Prof Michael Fulford at the University of Reading on a major project funded by the Leverhulme Trust and English Heritage to examine the contribution of commercial archaeology to our understanding of Roman Britain.

Tony Howe BA, MCIfA: County Archaeologist and Heritage Conservation Team Manager, Surrey County Council, County Hall, Penryhn Road, Kingston-Upon-Thames, Surrey, KT1 2DN, **tony.howe@surreycc.gov.uk**
Tony graduated in history and archaeology from the then King Alfred's College, Winchester in 1993. Following a short stint digging in the UK, including working on the now infamous Elms Farm site in Heybridge, Essex, he spent the period 1995–7 working in Beirut. Returning to the British archaeological field, he worked on a number of commercial projects principally in the south and south-east of England before taking up a County archaeological monitoring role at Surrey in 1999, and became manager of the Heritage Conservation Team in 2012.

Pamela V Irving BA, ALCM (retired): **pamvirving@gmail.com**
A combined honours graduate of Birmingham University, and some-time pottery specialist, employed between 1974 and 2000 by English Heritage (and predecessor bodies) initially as Roman Case Officer on the Pre-1972 Backlog Programme (once described by Richard Reece as a sort of archaeological social work). Subsequently Academic Editor, and latterly Manager of the EH programme of publication of its archaeological monograph series, and conservation publications, Editor of the Journal of Romano-British Pottery Studies 2003–07 and Editor of RESCUE News 2001–12.

Mike Pitts FSA, MCIfA: *archaeologist and award-winning journalist. Mike has published his own excavations and research in peer-reviewed journals, has written about his and other archaeologist's work in trade books, newspapers and magazines, and has written and presented programmes for radio. For the last 12 years he has edited Britain's leading archaeological magazine,* British Archaeology. *See mikepitts.wordpress.com*

Prof Dominic Powlesland DUniv, FSA: **dp481@cam.ac.uk; d.powlesland@ btinternet.com**
Dominic first joined excavations in Colchester at the age of 11 and later become an excavation supervisor for the Winchester Excavation Unit when he was 16, in 1971. Although he has well established links with academic institutions he remains a dedicated field archaeologist. He is perhaps best known for the vast excavations and landscape-survey projects that he has directed in his capacity as Director of the Landscape Research Centre in the Vale of Pickering, North Yorkshire and for his work on computer applications in archaeology. He holds Visiting Chairs in Archaeology, Medieval Studies, Applied Science and Remote Sensing at the Universities of Leeds, York, Huddersfield and Vienna and is an Associate Researcher at the McDonald Institute of Archaeology, University of Cambridge following a spell as Field Archaeologist in Residence.

Virginia (Ginny) Pringle Mres: **ginny@aerialarchaeology.co.uk**
Ginny graduated with a BA (Hons) (2011) and an MRes (2014) in Archaeology from the University of Winchester and her research interests include landscape and aerial archaeology with a focus on prehistoric Britain. She chairs both the Council for British Archaeology Wessex Region and the Basingstoke Archaeological and Historical Society and is an advocate of the volunteer sector. Ginny is a past director of the Wessex Academy for Field Archaeology and now co-directs a community archaeology project in north Hampshire. In her spare time she is a businesswoman.

Ian Ralston OBE, MA, PhD, DLitt, FRSE, FSA, FSA Scot, MCIfA: Abercromby Professor of Prehistoric Archaeology and Head of the School of History, Classics and Archaeology, University of Edinburgh, William Robertson Wing, Old Medical School, Teviot Place, Edinburgh EH8 9AG, **ian.ralston@ed.ac.uk www.ianralston.co.uk**
Ian first dug as a schoolboy at the Anglian timber hall on Doon Hill, East Lothian in 1965. Throughout his career at Aberdeen and subsequently Edinburgh universities, he has maintained interests in Scottish archaeology alongside research and fieldwork on the European Iron Age and involvement in applied archaeology. He is presently Chair of CFA Archaeology Ltd.

Harvey Sheldon: h.sheldon@bbk.ac.uk
Harvey was the Southwark and Lambeth Archaeological Excavation Committee's Field Officer from 1972 to 1975 and Head of the Museum of London's Department of Greater London Archaeology from 1975 to 1991. He taught archaeology for the University of London's Department of Extra-Mural Studies, later integrated within Birkbeck College, from the early 1970s on-wards and is currently an Honorary Research Fellow in the School of Social Sciences, History and Philosophy at Birkbeck. Harvey served as Chairman of RESCUE between 1986–91 and again between 1999–2004 and is a Past President of the London and Middlesex Archaeological Society. He is currently Chair of the Archaeology Committee of LAMAS and of the Rose Theatre Trust. He is also President

of three of Greater London's most active local archaeological societies, Hendon and District Archaeological Society, Enfield Archaeological Society, and the West Essex Archaeological Group.

John Shepherd FSA BA MCIfA: **john.shepherd88@ntlworld.com**
John first started digging at the tender age of 9 with Bill Penn at Springhead in Kent. He graduated from the Institute of Archaeology, London, in 1978 and in 1982 set aside his PhD research to take up the opportunity of becoming Prof W F Grimes's research assistant. This led to a 20-year involvement with the Museum of London, working on backlog archaeology in its collections. In 1988 John helped Grimes to get his archive in order for transfer to the Museum of London and, after Grimes' death later that year, became curator of the Grimes London Archive. Final publications on the Fort at Cripplegate and the Temple of Mithras were just some of the results of this period. In 1997 John took over the management of London's archaeological archive and built on the work that Nina Crummy had begun, resulting in the opening of the London Archaeological Archive and Research Centre (LAARC) in February 2002. He is now a freelance archaeology and history consultant.

Anthony Sinclair MA, PhD, FSA: Department of Archaeology, Classics and EgyptologySchool of Histories, Languages and Cultures,12–14 Abercromby Square, University of Liverpool L69 7WZ, **A.G.M.Sinclair@liverpool.ac.uk**
Anthony has been at the University of Liverpool, School of Archaeology, Classics and Egyptology since 1994 and is now Reader in Archaeological Theory and Method, and previously taught at the University of Cambridge, and at Meiji University in Tokyo. He was instrumental in 2005 in bringing the Subject Centre for History, Classics and Archaeology to Liverpool, becoming the Centre's Director in 2008 until the closure of the Subject Centre Network in 2012. He launched, and edited Research in Archaeological Education *whilst Directing the Centre. He has published on aspects of Palaeolithic archaeology, the consequences of conceptual change for the teaching of archaeology, and the first long-term research into the career histories and employability-skills of archaeology graduates, and is currently developing the first visual discipline maps of archaeological sources, authors and terminology.*

Kathryn Stubbs BA MA, DipTP, MRTPI, IHBC: Assistant Director Historic Environment, Department of the Built Environment, City of London Corporation, PO Box 270, Guildhall, London, EC2P 2EJ, **Kathryn.stubbs@cityoflondon.gov.uk**
Kathryn is a Chartered Town Planner and archaeologist, specialising in urban archaeology and the historic environment as an integrated part of the planning and development process. She has negotiated and advised on many complex building development schemes to achieve the protection and preservation of archaeological remains and to conserve and enhance the archaeological and built heritage.

Reuben Thorpe BA (Hons) MCIfA: chairman@rescue-archaeology.co.uk
Reuben started digging in 1984 and running excavations and surveys in 1988 moving eventually to the Central Excavation Unit (later CAS) of English Heritage in 1991 and from there to directing the Anglo-Lebanese urban rescue excavations in Beirut between 1995 and 2001. Latterly he has worked in government and private sector as projects manager and archaeological consultant, is now Chairman of RESCUE: The British Archaeological Trust *and is currently trying to complete his PhD.*

John S F Walker FSA: Hon President, Federation of Archaeological Managers and Employers; RESCUE council member; Visiting Professor University of York.
John began as a digger in 1971 and spent 36 years at the Directorate level in archaeological units. He mostly led university field units but was latterly Chief Executive of York Archaeological Trust, now retired. John has written various award winning contributions on industrial and late archaeology. He has acted as a national representative of both archaeological workers and employers.

Dr Pete Wilson FSA, FSA Scot, MCIfA: Foresight Coordinator, Heritage Protection Department, Historic England
Pete graduated with a BA (Hons) from the University of Birmingham (1979) and obtained a PhD from the University Bradford (1995). His archaeological interests lie in the Roman period with a particular focus on Yorkshire and the North of England. For over a decade he has been involved in issues associated with archaeology and metal detecting, including combating illicit detecting, and is a member of the Portable Antiquities Advisory Group. In 2014 he became Honorary Secretary of the Royal Archaeological Institute. Pete has worked for Historic England and its predecessor bodies (Department of the Environment and English Heritage) since 1981.